OUR
PATCHWORK
NATION

■ ■ ■

OUR PATCHWORK NATION

THE SURPRISING TRUTH ABOUT
THE "REAL" AMERICA

■ ■ ■

DANTE CHINNI
AND
JAMES GIMPEL

GOTHAM
BOOKS

GOTHAM BOOKS
Published by Penguin Group (USA) Inc.
375 Hudson Street, New York, New York 10014, U.S.A.
Penguin Group (Canada), 90 Eglinton Avenue East, Suite 700, Toronto, Ontario M4P 2Y3, Canada (a division of
Pearson Penguin Canada Inc.); Penguin Books Ltd, 80 Strand, London WC2R 0RL, England; Penguin Ireland,
25 St Stephen's Green, Dublin 2, Ireland (a division of Penguin Books Ltd); Penguin Group (Australia),
250 Camberwell Road, Camberwell, Victoria 3124, Australia (a division of Pearson Australia Group Pty Ltd);
Penguin Books India Pvt Ltd, 11 Community Centre, Panchsheel Park, New Delhi–110 017, India; Penguin Group
(NZ), 67 Apollo Drive, Rosedale, North Shore 0632, New Zealand (a division of Pearson New Zealand Ltd);
Penguin Books (South Africa) (Pty) Ltd, 24 Sturdee Avenue, Rosebank, Johannesburg 2196, South Africa

Penguin Books Ltd, Registered Offices: 80 Strand, London WC2R 0RL, England

Published by Gotham Books, a member of Penguin Group (USA) Inc.

First printing, October 2010
10 9 8 7 6 5 4 3 2 1

Community type maps appearing in chapters 1-12 by Chris Amico and Vanessa Davis

Gotham Books and the skyscraper logo are trademarks of Penguin Group (USA) Inc.

LIBRARY OF CONGRESS CATALOGING-IN-PUBLICATION DATA
Chinni, Dante.
      Our patchwork nation : The surprising truth about the "real" America / Dante Chinni and James Gimpel.
          p.   cm.
      Includes bibliographical references and index.
      ISBN 978-1-592-40573-2 (hardcover)
    1. Political culture—United States.   2. Communities—United States.   3. Voting—United States.
I. Gimpel, James.   II. Title.   III. Title: The surprising truth about the "real" America.
      JK1726.C45 2010
      307.0973—dc22   2010015228

Printed in the United States of America
Set in Minion with display in Trade Gothic
Designed by BTDNYC

While the author has made every effort to provide accurate telephone numbers and Internet addresses at the time
of publication, neither the publisher nor the author assumes any responsibility for errors, or for changes that
occur after publication. Further, the publisher does not have any control over and does not assume any
responsibility for author or third-party Web sites or their content.

FOR MY FATHER,
DANTE V. CHINNI
—DC

AND FOR MY WIFE,
VERONICA
—JG

■ ■ ■

CONTENTS

■ ■ ■

ACKNOWLEDGMENTS

■ ■ ■

More than two years of work went into this book, and we would be remiss not to mention some of the people who made it all possible. No book or effort as complicated as this one could happen without the love and support of our spouses, Christina Ianzito and Veronica Gimpel. They have endured with grace and charm the inevitable foibles and stress-outs that have accompanied this project, and we are eternally indebted to them.

We have nothing but profound gratitude for Alberto Ibarguen, Eric Newton, Gary Kebbel, and all the people from the Knight Foundation who took a chance on a new idea and stuck by it. There'd be no book without them. The same might be said of the late Richard Bergenheim, former editor of the *Christian Science Monitor*, who gave this idea a home, and the staff there, including Richard's successor, John Yemma, and Cheryl Sullivan, Ari Pinkus, and Judy Douglass (our editors there).

Great thanks go to the good people of the *PBS NewsHour*, who helped us elevate this project to the next level, including Lee Banville, Anna Shoup, and Chris Amico, as well as Jim Lehrer, Linda Winslow, Simon Marks, Joanne Elgart, and Ray Suarez (our television traveling buddy). And Malcolm Brown, the cameraman who made it all look good.

Research assistance at the University of Maryland was always provided with skill and finesse by Anne Cizmar, Brittany Bramlett, and Marilyn Le.

Bill Kovach served as guide, confidant, and, as always, a mentor. Atiba Pertilla offered the advice that linked up the coauthors of this book. Keith Allen was an inspiration.

Leonard Roberge, our personal editor, sandpapered the rough spots, cut the fat, and served as the arched eyebrow of skepticism. Megan Newman, our editor at Gotham, steered the project through the process with aplomb.

Gail Ross and Howard Yoon, our agents, were the shepherds. Their knowledge and wise counsel were instrumental in making this book a reality.

We need to thank the local sources who offered their on-the-ground insights of our communities in blog and in e-mail. That's too long a list to enumerate here fully, but it includes Kip Ward, Kathy Heicher, John Schmalzbauer, Don King, Nick Lantinga, Cynthia Wilbanks, Jesse Bernstein, Ed Pratt, Kirby Goidel, Clay Handy, Jay Lenkersdorfer, Ray San Fratello, Ann Dupee, Arn Menconi, Rachel Gomez, Roy Delgado, Dan Kemp, Carter Hendricks, Jim Rickman, Bill Enloe, Ryan Bowling, Sharon Whitehill Gray, Sandy Shea, and Janet Ryder.

And, of course, special thanks to our parents, who instilled in us a powerful interest in the vast landscape that is the United States through dinner-table conversations and cross-country drives.

FOREWORD
by Ray Suarez, *PBS NewsHour,*
Senior Correspondent

■ ■ ■

The United States begins the second decade of the twenty-first century with some 308 million people living within its boundaries. Too many to interview. Too many to photograph. Too many to ask about the details of their daily lives. Americans could use a way to frame the stories they tell themselves about their own country. They need a way to wrap their arms, and their heads, around a continent-sized country with a dizzying array of ways of life, and need an organizing principle to do it.

Enter Patchwork Nation.

Dante Chinni and James Gimpel looked at the country, sifted the data, and confirmed what you might have already expected: The country really is a patchwork. After you read this book, you should shift in your seat and knit your brow the next time you hear some carefully coiffed analyst start a sentence with, "Americans believe . . . ," or "Americans want . . . ," or "Americans know . . ." The mix of things our countrymen believe and want and know varies a great deal from place to place.

That's where it gets interesting.

Regions are way too big to use as a way to look at the varieties of American experience. States are too big. Even SMSAs, Standard Metropolitan Statistical Areas, are too big. Yet those are the data sets we commonly use to analyze trends in American life, make political forecasts, and explain the country to itself. Down at the county level we're finally getting to the finer-grained understanding of economics, culture, work lives, industries, religion, and ethnic origin that make places what they are. Chinni and Gimpel know two adjacent counties in one state in one region may have far less in common than one of those jurisdictions and another county clear across the country.

The reaction to a political event, the desires for government intervention (or the lack thereof), the opposition to a new American history curriculum for high schoolers, or the support for posting religious texts in public places are commonly measured in gross blocs of public opinion that simply don't tell you much. At the risk of stating the obvious, Philadelphia is not Bucks County, Ann Arbor is a far cry from Detroit, and Lincoln City, Oregon, while economically tied to Portland, is different in fundamental ways.

In 2009, I was lucky enough to hit the road with Dante Chinni and watch how the ideas underpinning the Patchwork Nation project really told you about American diversity. Lincoln City and Eagle, Colorado, had faced terrible setbacks in the economic downturn. Sioux City, Iowa, and Philadelphia had weathered the bad times fairly well compared to other times in recent history. But the reasons why an Iowa corn county and a Pennsylvania metropolis held their own couldn't be more different.

It is a great gift to survey ripening corn from the top of a grain elevator while getting a tutorial in the operation of grain markets. It is a rare privilege to talk to a baker as she stretches a thin layer of pastry dough in preparation for a strudel. It is a joy to hear the pride in a small-town mayor's voice as he shows a visitor around a skating rink and swimming pool that was a roll of the dice, and is a success.

I found Patchwork an appealing, versatile, and rich analytical tool for taking the country's economic, political, and social temperature. So much has changed in recent decades. Gimpel and Chinni offer the student of modern America provocative ways to understand what divides and unites the country in 2010.

The appeal of Patchwork Nation is the creation of two symbiotic sets of propositions: from the social sciences and journalism. Dr. Gimpel's analytical rigor comparing and contrasting American counties is made richer and more compelling by the careful, smart, and sensitive reporting of Dante Chinni. A fat book full of charts and diagrams packed with data would have been a chore. Chapter after chapter of revealing anecdotes would have been missing something important and fallen short of closing the sale. The combination of microchip and shoe leather fills out a portrait neither one of the collaborators would have painted as successfully on his own.

As any good social scientist or journalist knows, you have to constantly self-police to avoid the tempting prospect of heading out to find people and their stories that prove what's already in your data. You have to be equally vigilant about not highlighting data that reflects what you found out on the road, and suppressing data that contradicts the reporting. Gimpel and Chinni are too smart and too honest about the complexity of the stories they're telling to make those old mistakes.

Whenever you ask a town to stand in for many other places like it, there are going to be variables that do not fit as neatly as you'd like. Every place is not exactly like every other place in its Patchwork cohort. Emptying Nest communities were not stamped out by a cookie cutter. Monied Burbs are not all alike. The *Patchwork Nation* definitions are a proposal from Gimpel and Chinni about how to use a different set of tools for understanding the country. Get ready to be bowled over by data sets that will force you to say "I never knew that!" and stories of individual communities that will take you to parts of the country and ways of life very different from your own.

You will be intrigued, perplexed, and hopefully pissed off from time to time. You will chafe against the definitions, compare them to your own experiences of people and places . . . and that's not only okay but bound to make the ride more interesting. The social science and storytelling will draw you in for the journey of a cover-to-cover read. But I will be really surprised if you don't find yourself picking up the book again from time to time to scan the index, check stats, and recall individual stories.

YOU'RE HOLDING AN EYE-OPENING COLLECTION of journalistic observation, and a reference work, a handbook for understanding your own country. Welcome to *Our Patchwork Nation*.

INTRODUCTION

■ ■ ■

RED AND BLUE IS BLACK AND WHITE

There's something so satisfying about election night. Whatever the outcome, whatever your beliefs, you sit on your couch and you see the country take shape before your very eyes. This state or region lights up in one color; that state or region lights up in another. Slowly, as the hours pass, the two-tone jigsaw puzzle fills itself in.

Finally, all the votes are tallied and you have a new understanding of the United States. The entirety of the country—coast to coast, mountains and plains and everything in between—is neatly mapped into two camps: one red and one blue.

We hate that map. In so many ways, it represents a lie.

It's not that the red and blue map is itself misleading. It's useful as a political scoreboard, especially on that one all-important evening every four years. The problem is what it has become. We have invested it with a power it doesn't deserve, as a quick identifier for places and people and what they think and do.

On election night the media devote hours to talking about whether this district or that state will be colored red or blue. In the weeks that follow, newspaper stories, op-eds, and blog posts try to explain why certain places wound up red or blue. And in the months and years that follow, the general public latches onto the same language to explain themselves and their homes. People talk about being from red or blue states—or worse, from Red or Blue America. I once had someone tell me, "I'm from Texas, but the blue part of Texas."

The words have become a code. When we say "red" and "blue" in the context of American culture, it conjures up a set of stereotypes. Typical Red America markers might include watching Glenn Beck, hating NPR, opposing gay marriage, getting coffee at the doughnut shop, drinking beer, eating hamburgers, living in the country, and standing up for tradition—most of the time. Typical Blue America markers might include watching Jon Stewart, hating FOX News, supporting gay marriage, getting coffee at the coffee shop, drinking wine, eating tofu burgers, living in the city, and standing up for change—most of the time.

When we do this, we do ourselves a disservice. How can a country of more than 300 million people and 3.5 million square miles be reduced to an understanding so basic that we don't even bother to use all three primary colors? Take a look at a map and look at some of those red and blue communities.

In Michigan, where I grew up, the "blue" areas include Wayne County, the home of Detroit, and its much wealthier neighbor Washtenaw County, the home of Ann Arbor and the University of Michigan. Those two places have dramatically different populations, education levels, and economies. You can also add into the blue mix Oceana County, on the west side of the state, a place with a growing Hispanic population, and Marquette County, far up north on Lake Superior, which is sprawling, rural, and mostly white. How much do those parts of Blue America, all located in the same state, really have in common?

The same overgeneralizations are present in political science research. Although scholars have been studying voting behavior for sixty years now, they have been slow to investigate how being a Republican in Massachusetts may mean something very different from what it means to be a Republican in Arizona. Voters of the same party, but in different places, are likely to have very different understandings of what they are doing when they cast a vote for the same candidate. Traditional approaches to studying voting and candidate choice have ignored these nuances for broader, but less helpful, generalizations.

For instance, Orange County, California, population 3 million, and Alfalfa County, Oklahoma, population 6,100, are both reliably parts of Red America. But if you stop by Lavicky Farm Equipment in Cherokee, Oklahoma, chances are you won't meet people who act much like those in wealthy, suburban Southern California, where people are much more likely to be leading a corporate rather than an agricultural lifestyle.

FINDING THE "REAL" AMERICA

In 2004, then Illinois senator Barack Obama received huge applause at the Democratic convention in Boston when he told the crowd, "There's not a liberal America and a conservative America—there's the United States of America."

Yes and no.

It's clearly wrong to break the country into a simple red/blue, right/left dichotomy. But you can't ignore the differences in a country as big as the United States and simply say, "We are all united." There are too many divergent sets of backgrounds, experiences, and interests at play.

On the other hand, we know that there are commonalities, too; they just don't look the way you think they do. The similarities are about a lot more than how you vote in an election or what state you live in.

Consider Washtenaw County. It's very different from next-door Wayne County, but it has a lot in common with places that aren't even in Michigan: Dane County, Wisconsin, say, or Boulder County, Colorado, both home to large state universities. All three counties represent a particular type of American community, scattered across the United States but with its own cohesive culture. College towns are a kind of place in America.

There are other kinds of American place, too, of course. There are industrial hulks like Detroit, and there are places where cows outnumber people. There are almost exclusively white communities, and places where minorities aren't so uncommon. People in those places may all live in the same country, but they see everything framed through the various ways in which they live. Their local economies have different engines. Their racial, ethnic, and religious makeups are different. So are their housing stock, their household incomes, and their means of transportation. In essence, they experience different realities.

That's why the red/blue understanding of the United States is so inadequate. It's also why, no matter what politicians or the media may say, there's no "real America." Life in a big city, with its velvet-roped nightclubs, is different from life in a small town, where the local high-school football game may be the big Friday-evening draw. But it is no more or less "real."

The truth is, there are many different Americas within the borders of the United States. You just have to know how to look for them. That's what this book is about.

DISCOVERING A NEW WAY

In the eighteen years I (Dante) have been a journalist on the East Coast, I've thought a lot about those different types of places. Growing up in Warren, Michigan, one of the bedroom communities that sits on Detroit's northern border, I was always struck by how driving a few blocks or miles could completely change where you were. Drive down to 7 Mile Road and Ryan, and you were already deep into the tough neighborhoods of the Motor City. Drive up to 12 Mile Road and Ryan, and you were in the middle of middle-class suburbia.

And as a reporter I would visit various cities and towns and see firsthand just how different they are. Eveleth, Minnesota, the mining community near where Senator Paul Wellstone died in a 2002 plane crash, may be in the same state as Minneapolis, but it feels like it's in a different country.

Understanding new places is never easy for reporters who parachute in to cover the events that take place in them. The media bubble of Washington, D.C., where I live now, is a legitimate phenomenon. For all the desire there is here to see "how things are playing in Peoria," there isn't any good way to find out. Sometimes journalists just follow their guts. Sometimes they talk to pollsters. Sometimes they literally look at a map to find a place that is far enough away to be different from D.C. but close enough to get back home easily. All these methods are inadequate—because "Peoria" doesn't exist, not in the famed test market of Peoria, Illinois, or anywhere else in the United States.

There's no one place that defines the nation entirely. Stories about government mandates for ethanol use have a different meaning in farm country than they do in the suburbs. So, of course, do stories about things like crime, war, and the economy. And those differences have a special meaning in early-twenty-first-century America.

The United States is entering a transformative period. We're witnessing the end of a thirty-year political cycle, a global economic restructuring around an increasingly powerful China, and a technological remaking of our culture. And people living in the many different types of American place are experiencing this period of epochal change differently. Some see the end of a way of life; others see a way of life renewed. What's needed is a systematic way to explore those different places that define the United States' many socioeconomic, political, and cultural positions.

In 2007, with what looked like a seminal presidential race approaching, I thought about just how that could be done.

I reflected on all of the places I had visited growing up and as a reporter—the suburbs, the big cities, the college towns, the small mining areas. I wondered how they would see the election in my hometown of Warren, or in Eveleth, or in East Liverpool, Ohio, or in any number of big cities and small towns across the country. *That should be the focus of a new kind of coverage*, I thought. There should be a way to identify and get inside of those different kinds of realities and frame election coverage around them.

ANYTHING THAT REALLY LOOKED AT the nation seriously would need to reach beyond the broad generalizations created out of past coverage—the soccer moms and the NASCAR dads and the rest of them. The goal was to develop a multifaceted approach that would capture those differences that travelers commonly notice, something that took into account all of the politically relevant data available: age, race, religion, income, education, occupation, population growth, unemployment, consumer spending. Most important, once the information was gathered, it would have to be mapped so it could be analyzed.

To get beyond simple number crunching, special "representative communities" could be used as bases from which to watch people make decisions about the election. I wanted to know more than just how people voted; I wanted to create something that would get at *why* people voted the way they did.

It all made perfect sense. But I had no idea whether it was possible. I'm a journalist, not a statistician. I'd had some experience in analyzing data, but I didn't have the ability to break it down to create statistically meaningful categories. What measures could I use to create such a breakdown? And what level of geographic observation would be relevant? Counties? Zip codes?

So I cast about for someone to help me—an expert who understood both numbers and what I had in mind. A friend told me about James G. Gimpel at the University of Maryland, a professor of government and an expert in political geography who had worked on Capitol Hill. He had a perfect mix of academic and practical experience and, like me, was interested in different kinds of places. Much of his work has explored that topic.

We met on a snowy February evening at Jim's office, where I ran through everything I had in mind: the number crunching, the mapping, the idea of finding "representative" places that could serve almost as sociocultural ant farms that we could watch. It was all possible, he said, and counties would be the ideal starting point. They're smaller than states and congressional districts, have their own governments in most cases, and are essentially independent, individual entities. Plus, there is a convenience element: They're the smallest level at which many useful data are gathered. We could have tried to break things down to census tracts— small subdivisions within counties—but that process would have taken much longer. And when it was done, the groupings created would have limited use unless we could get other important data elements broken down in the same way.

For Jim, the project had some special significance. He grew up in Chadron, a small town in western Nebraska. He said that media coverage often ignores places like his hometown, which, combined, constitute a wide swath of the country. This project would allow us to explore those places, he said, and that in itself would be valuable. He was right, of course. Consider that NBC News has only five bureaus around the country: Atlanta, Los Angeles, Chicago, Dallas, and Washington. That doesn't exactly reach into the hinterlands.

Once I knew it was possible to execute my idea, I faced the next significant hurdle: money to make it happen. One editor I spoke with suggested that I try the John S. and James L. Knight Foundation, which funds new ideas and strategies in journalism. Knight liked the idea very much and signed on but insisted that I find a media partner. *The Christian Science Monitor*, for which I had written as a staffer, columnist, and freelancer, agreed to join the experiment.

We began to gather the essential data and go hunting for our communities.

CREATING THE PATCHWORK NATION

There are 3,141 counties in the United States. No two are completely alike, but some share a median age or household income or education level. Some are more dense and urban and some more sparsely populated and rural. When you parse all the available data, you find other likenesses and linkages, too.

We identified several different Americas within the United States, defined neither by single demographic details such as age or income level nor by geographic regions such as the Rust Belt or the Sun Belt. Instead, we used our numbers to identify common experiences and shared realities. Using the nation's counties as dividing lines, we created a new understanding of types of American place.

The idea is fairly simple: On a map two counties may be hundreds or thousands of miles away from each other, but in terms of their shared experiences, they're like neighbors—or siblings.

Charlevoix County, Michigan, and Lincoln County, Oregon, for example, are more than 1,800 miles apart. One sits on a Great Lake and the other on the Pacific Ocean. But their economies, driven by tourism and small-town services, look very similar. Both saw double-digit unemployment during the recession that began in 2007. Both have a population of about 20 percent college graduates. Both have two gun stores, and towns are dotted with independent coffee shops.

Does that mean that Charlevoix and Lincoln are dead ringers for each other? No. But they do share many traits relevant to political and economic life. And by studying them—their likenesses and differences—and other places like them, we can get better grasp of that particular kind of American community. We can look at other types of place in a similar fashion. And when we put them all together on a map, we can begin to get a fuller understanding of the nation's multifaceted character.

When we sat down in the fall of 2007 with the intention of creating this new vision of the United States, we basically gathered every piece of relevant county data we could. We measured income level and local economic activity; racial and ethnic composition and immigration patterns; levels of adherence to such religions as evangelical and mainline Protestantism, Mormonism, Judaism, and Catholicism. We looked at housing-stock indicators and population density, and at whether the county is located within a major metropolitan area. We also examined the education level of the population, along with recent population growth and migration figures. And we sorted consumer expenditure estimates for a variety of specific spending categories, including alcohol, tobacco, housing, new vehicles, property taxes, and charitable contributions.

When we were done we had created the framework for the Patchwork Nation: Twelve different community types identified by county, with every county falling into a type category. We then found our "representative communities," places we could dig into to see how the differences we had identified played out in the real world. We wanted to talk to people who lived in each of the realities we had described with our data. Over the past couple of years I've visited those places, kept in regular contact with people in each, and tracked the changes in their communities.

Why twelve types? From the beginning this has been a journalistic enterprise—and it's grown in that respect, as the *PBS NewsHour* has come on board to work with the Knight Foundation and the *Monitor* (*Politico* and WNYC in New York joined the effort in 2010). Our goal was to create a usable, easily understandable tool for the media—something that is both similar to that red and blue election map and very different from it. We started with the thought that anything beyond fifteen types would get too complicated to display and understand and that anything under ten probably wouldn't allow for enough distinctions. So we aimed for a number in between. When the work was done, the clustering suggested twelve.

The twelve types were all chosen by comparing each to the average U.S. county, a place populated by about 95,000 people with a median household income of about $37,000. Those people are 87 percent white, 9 percent African American, and 7 percent Hispanic. (Note that Hispanics, as far as the U.S. Census Bureau is concerned, can be of any race.) In the average U.S. county 11 percent of the families live in poverty and 15 percent live in mobile homes. Roughly 30 percent of people are employed in trade and service-sector jobs, 17 percent work in education, 16 percent work for some form of government, 15 percent work in manufacturing, 10 percent are self-employed, 7 percent are employed in agriculture, 5 percent are employed as professionals or executives, and 1 percent work in the military. In the average county 16 percent are enrolled in college. Using counties as our measure inflates the influence of farm and rural places because there are more rural counties than urban counties. But counties are advantageous in a lot of other ways—they are real "places" with their own governments and often their own subcultures.

That's a snapshot of the baseline. How do our twelve types compare and what do they look like? Briefly, and in alphabetical order, here are the community types we identified and the places we went to study them.

BOOM TOWNS—384 counties, 59.3 million people. These relatively wealthy locales were, before the late-2000s economic crash, both growing rapidly and seeing their minority populations increase. In **Eagle, Colorado,** a small mountain town on the far side of Vail, I watched the real-estate market tumble and spent one morning visiting a lavish year-old clubhouse/spa/restaurant for a golf course with a membership of eleven.

CAMPUS AND CAREERS—71 counties, 13.1 million people. A younger population, lots of college students, and people just starting their postgraduate careers mark these places. I visited **Ann Arbor, Michigan,** and talked to the locals and students sitting in cafés lit by the glow of laptops.

EMPTYING NESTS—250 counties, 12.1 million people. These counties are older than average, with lots of boomers and retirees living on fixed incomes. They're also less diverse than the nation as a whole. I spent time in **Clermont, Florida,** where the orange groves have been replaced by rows and rows of houses and condos, including two seniors' communities that have the population and the votes to run the town.

EVANGELICAL EPICENTERS—468 counties, 14.1 million people. The median household income in these counties, full of young families and evangelical Christians, is below the national average, but people here aren't necessarily bothered by that. In **Nixa, Missouri,** in the southwest of that state, I experienced Christian theater and discovered what happens when a community is divided into religious tribes.

IMMIGRATION NATION—204 counties, 20.7 million people. Located primarily in the Southwest, these places have large Hispanic populations, lower than average incomes, and higher than average poverty. I visited **El Mirage, Arizona,** and learned of an informal phone tree Latinos there put into action whenever a Maricopa County sheriff's car was spotted in town.

INDUSTRIAL METROPOLIS—41 counties, 53.9 million people. Home to the nation's big industrial cities, these places are more densely packed, younger, and more diverse than the average county. I took the train to spend time in the overlooked middle sibling of East Coast cities, **Philadelphia, Pennsylvania,** and walked and drove through a "city of neighborhoods."

MILITARY BASTIONS—55 counties, 8.4 million people. Located near the nation's military bases, these middle-income locales are full of soldiers, vets, and their families. **Hopkinsville, Kentucky,** sits just north of the gigantic Fort Campbell. Over two years of visits I heard both unabashed respect for the soldiers down the road and stories of the economic woes that accompany repeated deployments in the new more-with-less military.

MINORITY CENTRAL—364 counties, 13.5 million people. Heavy populations of African Americans and Native Americans mark these communities. So do lower incomes and higher poverty rates. In **Baton Rouge, Louisiana,** I went to two bars just steps from each other existing in entirely separate racial worlds.

MONIED BURBS—286 counties, 69.1 million people. These places have higher than average levels of household income and educational attainment, and they tend to be closely split in presidential races. In **Los Alamos, New Mexico,** where one's value is measured by academic C.V., I sat sipping cabernet at one resident's hillside winery/distillery and talked about how the shaky global economy had created employment opportunities in Uzbekistan.

MORMON OUTPOSTS—44 counties, 1.7 million people. Located primarily in the Mountain West, these places have very high numbers of adherents to the Church of Jesus Christ of Latter-day Saints and are often rural and sparsely populated. I went to **Burley, Idaho,** and met the Mormon county commissioner, city manager, and newspaper editor, who explained how the city had held to its roots even as new immigrants arrived.

SERVICE WORKER CENTERS—663 counties, 31 million people. These places hold tourist centers or midsize towns where many people live without employee benefits and on the margins. Out in **Lincoln City, Oregon,** I walked the coastline looking for hand-blown glass floats hidden for the tourists and played in a poker game with the people who remain in town after the visitors have all gone home.

TRACTOR COUNTRY—311 counties, 2.3 million people. These places are white, rural, and remote, with sparse populations and farming and agribusiness as their economic base. In **Sioux Center, Iowa,** I visited the Tri-State Livestock auction house and listened as hog farmers chastised the media for talking about swine flu.

The first half of this book is a walk through each of those places and a look at how they represent their respective types in terms of demographics, employment, mores, challenges for the future, and other commonalities. The second half is more comparative. We look at how these places stack up and what may be in store for them by viewing them through three critical lenses: economics, politics, and culture. We examine what key indicators may tell us and use our knowledge of these places and the people in them to divine something of the future.

How do we know we got it right? We don't know for certain. Or, more to the point, there is no "right." A different analysis with different numbers might have yielded different community types. But, as we show in the appendix, we know that the groups we identified stand for something because when we filter the numbers we have—survey results and real data on things ranging from unemployment to public attitudes to store locations—through our twelve community categories, there are definite correlations and fault lines, not simply random distributions.

For example, look even at those two most oversaturated American commercial brands—Starbucks and Walmart—and you'll see recognizable breakdowns within our communities. Are these retailers ubiquitous? Yes, but not evenly so. If you're jonesing for a Caramel Macchiato, the Monied Burbs are your best bet, with 7.5 Starbucks per 100,000 people on average. If you're looking for the "always low prices" of Walmart, the Evangelical Epicenters are the place, with 3.2 Walmarts per 100,000 people on average. Is that simply because there are more people in the Burbs and more room to build big-box stores in the Epicenters? No. Those numbers are signs of something larger.

Consider Starbucks. The big cities are much more dense than the Burbs, but they have actually fewer Starbucks per capita. So the old saw about there being a Starbucks on every corner is more accurate outside of the cities than in them. As for Walmart, there are plenty of places that have more room than the Epicenters—Tractor Country, for instance—but the Epicenters are Walmart central. Why are those things true?

Because corporations, driven by dollars, don't like to take chances. Before they build, they consult their research—and their research tells them that Sam Walton's sprawling megastores do better in places like Nixa than in places like Ann Arbor. And Starbucks knows that its "proprietary buttery caramel sauce" will be the most welcome in the land of bigger homes and higher incomes. Marketing experts, in other words, have been viewing the United States through something like the Patchwork Nation prism for years. In that respect, they've been way ahead of red-state/blue-state journalists.

There are hundreds of other data points to examine and map out. Many of them break down in expected ways; others fall into place more counterintuitively. But together they create a comprehensive knowledge of the United States at a critical juncture in history.

LIMITS AND LESSONS

Before we begin, a few provisos.

We sorted all of the nation's 3,141 counties, but counties can be complicated places. Many are large and contain highly diverse populations, which could make categorization difficult. Look at Los Angeles County, California. It might be thought of as an Immigration Nation locale because of its high Hispanic population. Or it might be a Boom Town—the city of Los Angeles has added more than 150,000 people since 2000. But to us it seemed to fit best into the Industrial Metropolis category, because of its size, diversity, and economy. There were a handful of counties, about 5 percent, that were difficult to place into any category. In those cases, we simply used our best judgment in classifying them into the most likely and proximate category.

And we know that not everyone's experience is the same. You may live in a rural Boom Town county and believe that your experience is somewhat removed from the kind of life we describe people living in Eagle, Colorado. We are not suggesting that we have developed the one and only set of types that could be applied to the nation's counties, or that our representative places are perfectly representative. In a country as big and diverse as the United States, you could have a variety of alternative location schemes and still not account for every aspect of variability.

The places in our categories are not all the same. We know that every town and county has its own traits—historical, political, even culinary—that make it unique. But we believe that much can be learned by looking at the country according to our scheme. Our lens may not be flawless, but we believe it's extremely well suited to understanding the country in the early twenty-first century.

In 1981, Joel Garreau took a stab at organizing the United States in *The Nine Nations of North America*. He drew lines around broad areas of the country, creating new regions such as the Foundry, which includes all or parts of industrialized states like Michigan, New York, Pennsylvania, and Virginia. Or the Breadbasket, which includes all or parts of thirteen agricultural states stretching from Minnesota down to Texas.

Though there's some broad truth to Garreau's breakdown of the nation, how similar are Foundry cities like Philadelphia; University Park, Pennsylvania, the home of Penn State; and Mackinaw City, Michigan, where life revolves around the ferry to nearby tourist destination Mackinac Island? Not very. Philadelphia, a massive Industrial Metropolis, has illiteracy and poverty rates that would shock the generally well educated and prosperous residents of University Park, a Boom Town that has taken off as the influence of Penn State has grown. And people in neither of those places would fret over a rainy summer the way they would in Mackinaw, a Service Worker Center that survives on an influx of outside money.

Urban theorist Richard Florida, author of *The Rise of the Creative Class: And How It's Transforming Work, Leisure, Community, and Everyday Life*, and journalist Bill Bishop, author of *The Big Sort: Why the Clustering of Like-Minded America Is Tearing Us Apart*, have both written provocatively about the socioeconomic and cultural divides within American society, focusing on how different places are home to different types of people. Their work is fascinating in its examination of how and why people migrate and the impacts of those movements, but in neither case does it create a comprehensive framework for understanding the variety of different places within the United States.

Americans want that framework—or at least some kind of framework. That's why we so often lapse into thinking in the stereotypes created by that red and blue election-night map. We want to understand the parts of the country that seem foreign to us. The great failing of the blue/red view of the United States is that it expresses little beyond the lever someone pulled in a voting booth. It suggests that blue cities or counties or states are all blue for the same reasons. But they rarely are. In some communities elections are primarily about economics. In others they may be about religion or energy policy.

As the nation heads forward in an uncertain time, there's a lot we can learn from ourselves. The different community types within the Patchwork Nation can be instructive for one another. It may be that Tractor Country has some things it can teach the Industrial Metropolis. Or there may be larger warning signs in the path of the Boom Town or Immigration Nation counties that all of us should heed, no matter where we live.

And beyond all of that, beyond the data and the scenes of life from across the nation and the predictions about the future direction of the country, the community types outlined in these pages should serve at least one more purpose. Whatever changes—or lack of them—your community experiences, this book shows that there are other places going through some of the same highs and lows for some of the same reasons. And not just in a nearby town, but all across the country, perhaps in some places you may never have heard of before.

In other words: The place you live may be unique, but it's not alone.

BOOM TOWNS:
EAGLE, COLORADO

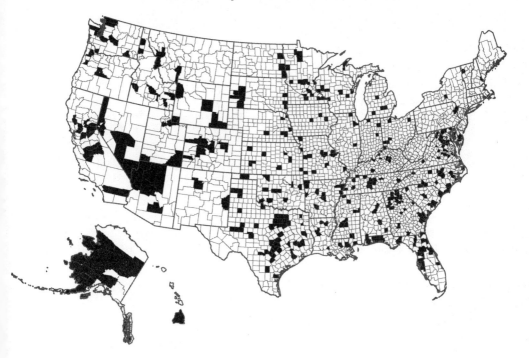

THE BUILT ENVIRONMENT

There may be no better summer day in the United States than a summer day in Eagle, Colorado. In an average year here there are 244 sunny afternoons, which in July top out only in the mid-eighties. And at 6,600 feet above sea level there's scant humidity. At night the mountain air can cool down into the fifties or lower. It's the ideal place to hike, bike, or fish, and for golfers it can feel like heaven: The surrounding Sawatch Range, with numerous peaks towering to more than ten thousand feet, makes a breathtaking backdrop for fairways, greens, and even bunkers.

That's what made the scene at Adam's Rib Ranch so disconcerting.

Under a brilliant blue July sky the eighteen-hole private club was empty, with nary an Izod-wearing soul to be seen out in the seventy-six-degree air.

Figure 1

BOOM TOWNS

a) PERCENTAGE OF PRESIDENTIAL VOTE OVER TIME

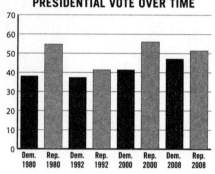

b) PERCENTAGE OF AGE DISTRIBUTION DATA

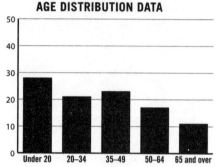

c) PERCENTAGE OF RACE/ETHNIC BREAKDOWN

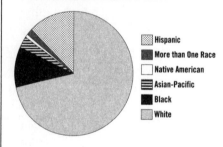

- Hispanic
- More than One Race
- Native American
- Asian-Pacific
- Black
- White

d) PERCENTAGE OF INCOME DISTRIBUTION DATA

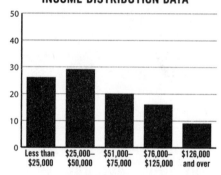

e) PERCENTAGE OF IMMIGRATION OVER TIME

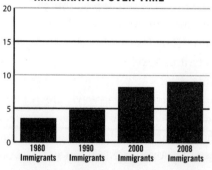

Driving through the facility was like touring an immaculately preserved ghost town. First there was the unmanned guardhouse, then the deserted putting greens and empty spec homes and housing lots, then the disused pool and unpopulated clay tennis courts at the forty-thousand-square-foot clubhouse. There I was finally greeted by a human being wearing an Adam's Rib Ranch golf shirt.

"Are you looking to play a round?" he asked, turning his attention away from the lawn. No, just looking for someone to talk to. "Inside," he said, and then went back to watering.

Inside the clubhouse, morning radio softly echoed through the empty space as club pro Eric Bradley explained the challenges the place has faced. Adam's Rib was developed in 2007, when people and money were flowing into Eagle and the surrounding area. The developers set a three-hundred-person ceiling on membership in their "wildly luxurious" club and sited ninety-nine large plots for homes on the grounds.

And now? "We're, um, building the membership," Bradley said without going into specifics. "We're really just starting."

The empty course is proof of that. The membership records of Adam's Rib aren't publicly available, but in Eagle the rumor was that the number of people who have so far ponied up the $150,000 deposit sits in the low double digits. Eleven, to be precise. And staffers willingly acknowledged that they hadn't yet sold a single home site—beyond the one atop a hill overlooking the course, which belongs to Adam's Rib's owner.

"There's plenty of good selections out here for $1.2 million," John Helmering, Adam's Rib sales manager told me. "That's just the land. Then you've got to build, too. It's a $4 or 5 million proposition to live here as an owner."

There was a time when those kinds of numbers made sense in Eagle, when growth seemed certain and swift.

In 2001 the town of Eagle issued the first building permits for an 1,800-acre parcel of land known as Eagle Ranch. Within six years Eagle Ranch the ranch had become Eagle Ranch the mixed-use housing and retail development. By 2008 the Rocky Mountain village had doubled in size from about three thousand to about six thousand people. And, as you would expect, it changed.

Before the development explosion, Eagle, county seat of rugged, sparsely populated Eagle County, had always felt something like a one-horse frontier town. It's the far western edge of development in what could be called greater Vail. The celebrated ski town is just 30 miles away along

Interstate 70. But the largest city in western Colorado, Grand Junction, is some 120 miles away, through the remote towns of Silt and Rifle and past a former Naval Oil Shale Reserve.

That remoteness attracted a certain type of people: those who wanted to get away, to live a quiet mountain life with neighbors they knew—or knew they wanted to avoid. In old Eagle, which sits on a bluff above the development, the big retail draw downtown is the Nearly Everything Store, which has offerings running the gamut from toiletries to fishing tackle. Just down the block is the Brush Creek Saloon, a dive bar that serves massive burritos and has a jukebox that plays Kenny Chesney's "She Thinks My Tractor's Sexy."

The Eagle Ranch development was intended to be a different animal. It built its own upscale "downtown" from scratch, with a Starbucks, a wine store, and a few higher-end restaurants. And it has attracted different people. Young wealthy families poured in, not hoping to get away, but hoping to remake. These strivers wield pricey strollers and eagerly volunteer to be room parents for the local elementary schools. They buy the latest high-tech outdoor gear and look to improve their training times. They came to get away from the bustle of the big city, but they still wanted to be able to buy a good latte nearby.

"We went from being a cowboy-boot community to being a hiking-boot community," said Arn Menconi, who served as an Eagle county commissioner during the boom.

From 2000 to 2006, Eagle and the 383 other Boom Town counties saw their population grow by an average of 12 percent, the most of any of our community types. The majority of them continued on that upward trajectory until the subprime mortgage crisis hit beginning in early 2007. Largely exurban in nature, these places typified the rapid, far-flung growth of the United States in the first half of 2000s. They were the places that saw building permits skyrocket and then struggled with their newfound diversity as Hispanics came to town along with the construction jobs.

In some of the biggest Boom Towns construction never seemed to stop. Clark County, Nevada, issued more than 31,000 building permits for new single-family homes in 2004. Riverside County, California, issued more than 30,000 permits for new single-family homes in 2005. But when the crash came, it came hard. Between June 2008 and June 2009 home foreclosures increased by 53 percent in the same places.

In Eagle, in the span of eighteen months, the biggest problems went from out-of-control growth and Latino poverty to falling property values and homeowner flight. At Adam's Rib, Helmering was left to look around the empty clubhouse wondering about the long-term viability of the Eagle housing market.

"When will it come back?" he asked himself. "Honestly, I think it's seven to ten years."

That's a lot of open tee times.

SPACE AVAILABLE

Housing mess aside, America's Boom Towns are (or at least were) pretty comfortable places economically. Their median household income is $7,000 above the national county average, and 11 percent of households in these communities earn more than $100,000 a year. Their poverty rate, 8.5 percent, is lower than average. Boom Towns have a few more people than most communities employed in steady occupations tied to education and government. And 7 percent of the people who live here are employed in professional or executive positions, the winners in the economy as it was.

Boom Towns are far younger than the nation at large, with 68 percent of their population under the age of fifty. There are a lot of young families who moved out here for streets that are a little less congested and homes that are a little bigger. And those families place a premium on a good education: 24 percent of the people here are enrolled in college, versus the national average of 16 percent.

They're also fairly conservative. George W. Bush won these counties by 14 percent in 2000 and by 17 percent in 2004. But the people here aren't necessarily among the evangelical-conservative base that helped Bush secure reelection. There are more Catholics and mainline Protestants in the Boom Towns than evangelicals.

At 84 percent white, Boom Town communities have fewer Caucasians than the typical U.S. county, which is 87 percent white. Their Hispanic population of 10 percent, meanwhile, is above the national county average. In fact, only three community types have a higher percentage of Hispanics. The Latino vote that went so heavily for Barack Obama in 2008, and so heavily against Republicans in general, mattered here: John McCain won the Boom Towns by only 5 percent. George W. Bush had won them by double digits.

In the next census, however, the Hispanic populations of these places may actually decline. A lot of Hispanics arrived in town as the building business was booming, and many have left as construction has slowed.

For years people in Eagle worried about keeping housing prices affordable for those and other lower-wage workers. In 2001 a family of three living in Eagle County needed to bring in more than $43,000 a year to get by without outside assistance.[1]

Local schools and police complained that their employees were priced out of the community they served. Menial laborers at the Vail and Beaver Creek resorts faced the same problem. Many of those who came to town for the building boom settled to the east of Eagle in Edwards, a long-time bedroom community for resort workers where one elementary school's Hispanic population grew to 90 percent. In Eagle County in 2008 Hispanics were the first priority as far as poverty relief and county aid were concerned.

And then the housing market abruptly cooled. Eagle, which had been living on a mix of tourism and construction, discovered just how important the second ingredient of that recipe was. Adam's Rib languished, and just down the road in Gypsum another golf course, Cotton Ranch, went into foreclosure. In late 2007 the median home price in Eagle was about $480,000. By September 2009 it was under $400,000, and there was a silent fire sale going on. Hundreds of homes were available in the small town, but people had stop putting up "For Sale" signs because of concern over what a street or a block full of them would look like.

Since the spring of 2009 several local churches have held a weekly "community dinner"—a free meal for those who need it—and offered bags of groceries for Eagle residents to take home. Not that many Hispanics have taken advantage of either service. "They've gone back to Mexico, or elsewhere," said Pastor Sid Spain of the United Methodist Church of Eagle Valley, which leads the effort. But for the young strivers who bought into the boom, picking up and moving elsewhere wasn't an option. They had homes they couldn't sell.

"In the beginning the construction people were feeling the impact because there was no new construction," Spain said. "But renovations—people were saying, 'Well, let's just fix up the kitchen.' Well, so that held for a few months. And then suddenly it went away, and . . . it all ground to a halt."

Kathy Heicher, former editor of the local weekly newspaper, has lived in Eagle for thirty-eight years. She finds the town's whipsaw fortunes shocking. "I have a lot of friends who are, oh, engineers, surveyors, stuff like that," she said. "They've always been so busy they couldn't get a day off. And now they're hurting—you know, several months without work."

Many in town told similar stories of how people involved in construction had been riding a wave. Those at the top of the industry were not just doing well—they were bringing in $200,000 or $300,000 a year. And they built their expectations for future income on those numbers. Now they're just trying to hold the line until things improve. For people who work, say, in the lumberyard, things have been even worse.

Yet even with the downturn, Eagle has weathered the hard times fairly well by Boom Town standards. Other places that got in on the rush of new building, such as Clark and Riverside counties, find themselves in more frightening situations because of their larger sizes. Clark County had tens of thousands for sale in fall of 2009, and tens of thousands more in some state of foreclosure. Behind those numbers are the collapse of entire neighborhoods and the loss of thousands of jobs in an industry that simply seized up.

"We're not Michigan," Heicher said, alluding to the foreclosed, boarded-up, and decaying Rust Belt properties whose vast numbers have made them an iconic image of the Great Recession. "We're not like that."

Indeed. You would never walk down the streets here and think, *This feels like Detroit.* Eagle bears the unmistakable stamps of money and newness. The four-screen Capitol Theater has a beautiful retro-styled marquee that protrudes over an old-fashioned ticket booth. The brick- and metal-work are brand spanking new—as is the rest of the street: the steakhouse, the upscale kids' store, and so on. Eagle Ranch Village is a New Urbanist's dream, full of walkable streets and homes with big porches, all centered around the bistros and boutiques of the downtown.

But a few years into its development a lot of the storefronts in that downtown are empty. Everyone was shocked when, without notice, the Starbucks closed in the fall of 2009. Across the street an entire building, the two-floor retail space called Building 6 by the developer, was empty. And farther down the way sat a 7,300-square-foot project, also empty, somewhat ironically called No Regrets.

WHAT WILL EVERYONE DO?

Of course, a lot of people in Eagle, particularly the newer residents, believe they have just been witnessing an economic hiccup. Soon, their mountain paradise will be perfectly Edenic once again.

"I think that there's still a level of—there's still a level of denial," said Cheryl Thomas, who works for Eagle County's Health and Human

Services Department. "I don't think they believe it's going to linger, that there'll be a turnaround. I mean, there's that kind of positive feeling. . . . And I think a part of that's the demographics here, because it is predominantly a thirtysomething community and only seven, eight percent of the population is sixty-five and older."

Heicher agreed—adding that youthful recklessness seems to have run rampant in Eagle. "My husband and I look at that a lot and say, 'You know, when we were thirty years old, we could not have moved into a brand-new house and lived that lifestyle.' And these people, they either all have trust funds or they're living way in debt. They're overextended, and you just don't see them cutting back all that much."

That analysis seemed spot-on during a visit to the Dusty Boot Steakhouse & Saloon on a crisp November night in 2009. It was a Tuesday, but the Texas-sized entrees and desserts flowed out of the kitchen to a sizable crowd in the dining room. The Boot is one of those places were you can dress casually but still order a $29 steak, and there were a lot of families with five- and six-year-olds eating pretty well. Of course, the Dusty Boot almost had to have been crowded. There aren't all that many dining options in a Boom Town during a bust.

There was also plenty of parking. Travis Barton, who once worked at a local lumberyard, told me that for many in Eagle eating out hasn't been an option recently. "Most people that I've met, including my parents and a lot of other people, work in the construction industry," he said. "I have personally a few friends who have lost their houses, and it's been a tough time, and we're all just trying to get through it. And the thing is, it's not like you can get up and move, because the whole country is this way right now."

Barton, who was born in Eagle, came back after college to cash in on the construction boom. He raked in good money for a few years as operations manager at the yard. But in early 2009, with a wife and two young kids at home, he saw the writing on the wall. Lumber orders had simply stopped. He took a job with Orkin pest control instead, which he said pays very well. More important, it's stable. "The thing is," he said, "God has blessed me, to be honest with you."

Of course, not everyone in Eagle can work for Orkin. When times were good almost a quarter of the jobs in town were tied to the construction industry. But the home-building market isn't primed to roar back anytime soon. There's plenty of housing stock still available nationally, and that's doubly true in Eagle and other Boom Towns. The employment market in Eagle County has been turning back toward that Rocky Mountain staple of tourism, with the hospitality industry doing more hiring than any other as of late 2009. In 2009 the Web site simplyhired.com listed the industries hiring the most workers in Eagle as bed-and-breakfast inns, hotels and motels, and resorts.

The relative isolation of many Boom Town communities leaves few other options. Even if they aren't as far off as Eagle, many of them are the outer, outer rings of suburbs of big metro areas—places where there was room for all the building that went on as they grew. There are some government jobs in these places, but not enough. About 17 percent of all the people are employed in government in these counties, a bit more than the national county average. And those aren't the same people who rushed in to stake their claims in Eagle Ranch Village, anyway. Their incomes are lower and their ways less free-spending.

As the United States negotiates the economic ups and downs of the next several years, newer, wealthier residents of Boom Towns like Eagle may find that the road back to the good life is long, indeed.

CAMPUS AND CAREERS: ANN ARBOR, MICHIGAN

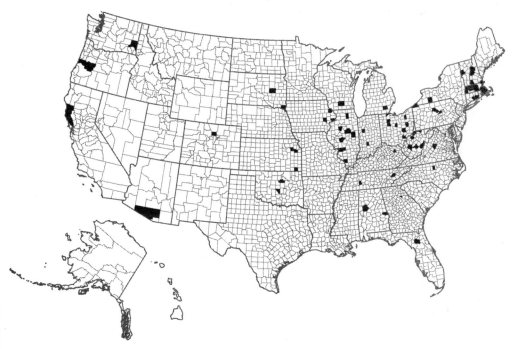

COMFORTABLE WITH A CHANGING WORLD

O n March 23, 2009, the citizens of Ann Arbor, Michigan, picked up their daily newspaper and learned of its impending demise. Advance Publications announced that it was closing the *Ann Arbor News*, founded in 1835, and replacing it with AnnArbor.com, a community Web site "complemented with a new print product two days a week."

If there were ever a place this might be expected to cause consternation, it's Ann Arbor. The city is home of the one of the country's celebrated "public Ivies," the University of Michigan. It has a highly educated population, with almost half of the adults in surrounding Washtenaw County having earned at least a bachelor's degree. And it boasts that there are more

Figure 2

CAMPUS AND CAREERS

a) PERCENTAGE OF PRESIDENTIAL VOTE OVER TIME

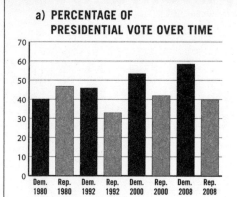

b) PERCENTAGE OF AGE DISTRIBUTION DATA

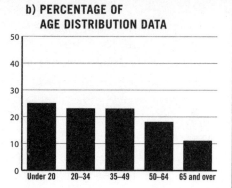

c) PERCENTAGE OF RACE/ETHNIC BREAKDOWN

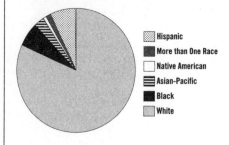

Legend:
- Hispanic
- More than One Race
- Native American
- Asian-Pacific
- Black
- White

d) PERCENTAGE OF INCOME DISTRIBUTION DATA

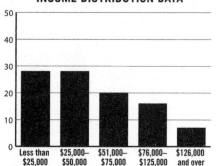

e) PERCENTAGE OF IMMIGRATION OVER TIME

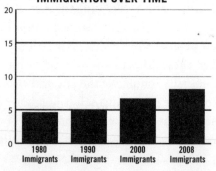

books sold per capita here than in any other U.S. city—an apocryphal statistic that hangs on the lips of many an Ann Arborite.

Besides, the *News* had been a part of life here for 174 years. How could the town that prides itself on being Michigan's intellectual hub be without a daily newspaper? Surely there would be protests.

But a funny thing happened on the way to the barricades: nothing. From the university dorms to the chamber of commerce to the city hall, the news of the *News'* demise was met not only with acceptance, but also with something a lot like pride.

Mayor John Hieftje saw it as proof that Ann Arbor was boldly charging ahead while others futilely tried to hold on to the past. "My view is, it was inevitable in one of the most Web-savvy cities in the country anywhere," he said. "I think we're gonna be on the leading edge of the wave learning how to cope with this, and I don't think that's a bad thing. I think it puts us ahead of the game because everybody else is going to go through this, as far as I can tell."

Down the street at the chamber, President Jesse Bernstein saw it as a kind of compliment. "The Newhouse folks picked Ann Arbor to be the model of the future," he said, referring to Advance's owning family, a force in American publishing since the 1920s.

Jane Coaston, a Michigan student headed off for a career as a journalist, greeted the development with disdain—for the newspaper: "Nobody reads the *News* anyway."

The voice of a community for the better part of two hundred years announces that it's shutting down, and no one seems troubled by it? Why? Because Ann Arbor, driven by research and a constant turnover of bright, young minds, takes great pride in leading the way. Newspapers? They're so twentieth century. And local newspapers? Why bother with them when, as many do here, you can read *The New York Times* on your BlackBerry? That's the way American publishing is moving, and wherever the nation is going, Ann Arbor is pleased to be there first.

That attitude is a hallmark of a Campus and Careers community, one of just seventy-one counties scattered in twenty-six states from coast to coast. Not every one of these counties holds an Ann Arbor or a University of Michigan, of course. Some, such as Sangamon County, Illinois, home of Robert Morris College, Springfield College, and a campus of the University of Illinois, contain collections of smaller schools with student populations drawn more from the region than from the nation. Some are more urban, such as Norfolk County, Massachusetts, which holds a slew of colleges including Babson and Wellesley. And some are very rural, like Beadle County, South Dakota, home of Huron University and a campus of the University of South Dakota. But even with those differences, on the whole these counties tend to follow the unique rhythms of the educational institutions in their midst.

The University of Michigan is a city campus. It could never be confused with, say, NYU, but it is situated in a town of more than 114,000, about one-third of them college students. School buildings stand amid the low-slung, three- and four-story structures that house the burrito shops, bars, cafés, bookstores, and tattoo parlors that typify a college town. Like other Campus and Career locales, Ann Arbor revels in its eggheadedness and cultural awareness. The elevator in the municipal parking structure downtown features not only Arabic numerals, but also Roman, Egyptian, and Hindu ones as well. The mural on the corner of State and Liberty streets features images of Woody Allen, Edgar Allan Poe, Hermann Hesse, Franz Kafka, and Anaïs Nin. Two theaters that show the latest foreign films and documentaries sit within a half block of each other downtown.

Ann Arbor may be a medium-sized city in southeast Michigan, but it has ambitions to being much more. "The quality of life here is really extraordinary," bragged Jesse Bernstein, president of the local chamber of commerce. "And when you look at music and the arts, we just opened up a truly incredible art museum. . . . They put an addition on it that blew me away. It is spectacular. The internal architecture and the exhibits are just incredible."

Hyperbole is easy for Bernstein. Promotion is his job, after all. But talk to other people in town and you soon get the message that as America's industrial base has receded nearby in blue-collar Detroit, the country's future has already come to wired, white-collar Ann Arbor. "I think we're as well positioned as anyplace in the U.S. to cope with change," Hieftje said. "We win all kinds of stuff, but I remember one that said we were in the top three or something in people who use the Internet."

Campus and Careers counties, in general, are further through the tech transition than most. More than 92 percent of Web users here have high-speed connections, according to a Pew Research Center Internet and American Life Project survey filtered through the Patchwork Nation community types.[2] That's the third highest among the twelve types. And it's not just how fast people here click, but how they click. Campus and Careers communities have the second-highest percentage of residents who regularly use social networking sites, behind only the Military Bastions,

according to another Pew poll from the spring of 2009.[3] That's significant, not because the future belongs to Facebook or Twitter, but because it
shows how Campus and Careers counties are full of early adopters of new
technologies.

In other words, while there's clearly a bit of braggadocio in Ann Arbor's "the future is ours" talk, there may also be a bit of truth. Consider
some of the locations of Google's offices around the country: Ann Arbor;
Boulder, Colorado; Cambridge, Massachusetts. All Campus and Career
locales. Residents in these places really are ahead of the curve—and not
just because they don't read the newspaper anymore.

LATTES AND LIBERALS

In a lot of ways America's Campus and Career counties are nice places to
be. The median household income in these communities isn't sky high, but
at $41,000 it's a good $4,000 above the national county average. Nearly 20
percent of households here have incomes of at least $75,000 a year, and the
poverty rate is three points below the national average of 11 percent. Starbucks sit in these communities at a rate of 4.4 per 100,000 people. That rate
is surpassed only in the big-city Industrial Metropolis counties and the
wealthier Monied Burbs and Boom Town communities—and it doesn't
account for other chains or the independently owned cafés that often oc-
cupy corners in Campus and Careers locales.

Lots of people here have time to linger over their lattes. More than
one-third of residents are enrolled in college, and a quarter of the residents
of Campus and Careers counties are employed in education in some way.
And behind all of that spare time and caffeinated bliss is some real economic stability. The people who live here hold the kinds of jobs that tend
to survive economic downturns. Even if budgets are trimmed at what's
almost always the area's largest employer, the local institute of higher
learning, the cuts are rarely catastrophic. Students don't disappear. Classes
still need to be taught. Facilities still need to be managed. That's one reason why even during the worst of the Great Recession, Campus and Career
communities remained below the national unemployment average by half
a percentage point or more.

Political debate flourishes in these places—just not left/right debate.
Politically Campus and Careers communities lean solidly left. Barack
Obama won them by 18 percent in 2008. In 2000 and 2004 Al Gore and
John Kerry won them by less, but still by double-digit margins. But the

most striking thing about politics in Campus and Careers communities is how politicized daily life is in these places. Voter turnout is regularly above the national average. In 2004 and 2008 only three community types had higher turnout than Campus and Careers locales—Tractor Country, the Emptying Nests, and the Monied Burbs. And beyond the votes, the story here is depth of involvement.

During the 2008 campaign the Democratic Party in Washtenaw County had so many volunteers that its door-knockers were sent to neighboring counties, said Hieftje, a party member. "We got to every place we wanted in Washtenaw, so we sent the volunteers here to other places," he explained. "The challenge was to find places to send them all." Andrew Grossman, former editor of the student-run *Michigan Daily*, joked that walking through campus before the 2008 vote was like running a gauntlet of clipboards: "You really couldn't walk four feet without someone asking if you were registered. They were everywhere."

When the pro-Obama tally was made official on election night, there was an impromptu parade through the streets of Ann Arbor. "People were marching and dancing and carrying drums," Hieftje recalled. "And people were just yelling and shouting and jumping up and down and carrying banners, and they had T-shirts on and things like that from the campaign."

Political involvement has a rich history at Michigan. John F. Kennedy announced the creation of the Peace Corps on the steps of the student union here in 1960, and the school is regularly among the top ten universities producing volunteers for the organization. In 1972 Ann Arbor voted onto its city council two members of the Human Rights Party, which, among other things, called for the immediate withdrawal of all U.S. military forces from foreign soil. That same year the town became one of the first to add sexual orientation to the list of items on which city contractors couldn't discriminate.

You won't find many opponents of gay marriage on the streets of Ann Arbor. "I think people have realized that if gay people get married, we're all okay. We're not trying to forcibly marry you. No one here takes that seriously," said Jane Coaston, editor of *The Michigan Review*, the *conservative* campus newspaper.

But in a college town full of activists, one issue reigns, according to Coaston: environmentalism. And that commitment has carried beyond the student population and into Ann Arbor at large. The city is ranked among the top twenty organizations in the nation—municipalities and businesses—producing on-site power by the EPA.[4] It's also one of the top twenty-five greenest cities in America according to *Popular Science* magazine, which based its rankings on a place's level of commitment to renewable energy sources, public transportation, green development practices, and recycling programs.[5]

It is a point of pride for Mayor Hieftje, who's made the environment a focus of his administration. From the hallway outside his third-floor office he pointed across to the Ann Arbor firehouse. "Those are the solar panels. We have the first solar fire station in Michigan," he said proudly. The panels don't power everything, but they can supply up to two hundred gallons of hot water a day to the firemen who live and work at the station—and that's a good start, said Hieftje. The farmers' market was also outfitted with panels. The streetlights were all converted to LEDs. And as the city worked to upgrade its city hall, it was with one eye on scoring a gold Leadership in Energy and Environmental Design certification. As of late 2009, there were more LEED platinum-certified buildings in the Ann Arbor area than there were in nine states.

Love of all things green is a key element to Campus and Careers communities. When we looked at surveys on environmental questions, Campus and Careers counties always scored at or near the top. When people here were read the statement "There need to be stricter laws and regulations to protect the environment," over a seventeen-year period more than 87 percent of them said that they completely or mostly agreed.[6] There was little movement in the numbers over that time.

THE BASE FOR THE NEW ECONOMY

As the nation retools itself to become whatever it will become, Campus and Career communities are primed to become economic drivers. Even among the perpetually in-fighting policy makers in Washington, there's a belief that the country needs to update itself and its economy with cutting-edge technologies in energy, transportation, and communications. Cutting-edge technologies involve research and development—and Campus and Careers locales are R&D hubs.

By September 2009, Ann Arbor alone had scooped up more than $100 million in federal money from the stimulus plan. There were awards from the National Science Foundation and the National Institutes of Health, as well as a $19 million pile of money from the Energy Department to explore new materials for solar cells.

Senior counsel in the Ann Arbor office of the international law firm

Miller Canfield, Paul Dimond is familiar with the machinations of Washington from his time as a special assistant to the president for economic policy during the Clinton administration. He believes that U of M and Ann Arbor are ready to reclaim the place they had in the national scene during the Cold War, when the government saw R&D as a key to national security. Back then, the Department of Defense funded academic research that it hoped would help the United States win the next war. Money poured into places like Bell Labs, the arm of AT&T that created the first transistor and hired university professors to do cutting-edge research.

Dimond is not a Michigan grad, but he has become a big booster. "I mean, we're right next to the EPA lab. The EPA lab is now doing all the CO_2 global-warming emission stuff," he explained. "Look, I'm just saying—look at the potential of a place like U of M. . . . Basically everybody's already here doing alternative-energy research for autos and transportation."

From 1945 through the sixties and even into the seventies, the money the U.S. government spent on research dwarfed what was spent by other major industrialized countries. In 1969, the United States put more than $25 billion into R&D. Combined, France, Japan, the United Kingdom, and West Germany spent just over $11 billion.[7] But after the end of the Cold War, federal funding of R&D began to dry up. Instead universities formed direct partnerships with corporations: Stanford with Exxon, the University of California Davis with Chevron, Berkeley with Intel.

As the Obama administration pumps money into the economy, government-funded R&D looks poised to make a comeback. The administration has promised that more than $1 billion will be spent on energy R&D alone, and the big universities are already cuing up for funding. Former Michigan president Jim Duderstadt formed a loose affiliation of researchers and institutions that he hopes are the beginnings of a hub-and-spokes system to do alternative-energy research of all kinds.

Discussion of climate change has taken on an ominous tone within the federal government of late—a tone that equals dollars. Multiple intelligence reports in recent years have warned of serious national security threats for the United States tied directly to global warming. Speaking at American University in April 2008, Defense Secretary Robert Gates compared climate change to jihadist extremism, failed states, and ethnic strife as a potential cause of terrorism. Even in hard times the federal government spends money on defense, and universities like Michigan are well situated to see a lot of that money.

Everyone here points to the 174-acre Pfizer campus on the outskirts of Ann Arbor that the university purchased in 2008 for $108 million. The goal is for it to become a major center for applied research—to produce the next generation of solar panels or car batteries or, really, anything that could store or produce electricity for the BlackBerries, iPhones, and laptops that seemingly everyone in town carries around. "This is a story that is somewhat unique because of Michigan's history and location," Dimond said. "But I don't think it's unfair to say if U of M does not make the crossing to whatever this future is that you envision, it's hard to imagine lots of places doing that."

There is in Ann Arbor a clear understanding that the role of the hometown university, and the role of universities in general, is changing. "Ten, twenty years ago university presidents didn't typically include the university's role in economic development as a cornerstone of their mission," said Cynthia Wilbanks, U of M's vice president for government relations. "I think today the expectation, especially for flagship institutions that carry the type of breadth and depth and research portfolio that we carry, encourage, stimulate and demand, is that we better be at the forefront of economic development."

That's clearly the role the university and Ann Arbor envision as theirs in the coming years. During her state-of-the-university address in 2009, Michigan president Mary Sue Coleman said that the university's research spending could grow to $2 billion by 2017. At the time of her speech it had just topped $1 billion.

Nothing is certain, of course. Not everyone favors federal spending. With or without government funding, however, Campus and Careers communities enjoy a lot of advantages. They are educated, adaptive, young, green, and relatively wealthy, with stable institutional employers propping them up. Whatever happens, it's hard to imagine a world in which those traits won't be beneficial.

EMPTYING NESTS: CLERMONT, FLORIDA

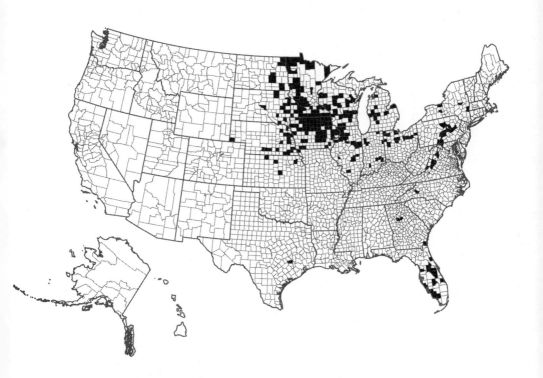

TWENTIETH-CENTURY HOLDOVERS

On a perfect February day in central Florida—sunny and in the mid-seventies—Clermont's movers and shakers piled into a dark, cool auditorium downtown for a rubber-chicken lunch to honor the town's Citizen of the Year. It was an impressive group: the mayor, the CEO of a big local cable company, a U.S. Olympian, and numerous doctors, lawyers, and real-estate types. All had come to pay tribute to local attorney Dennis Horton.

As the crowd tore into its breadbaskets, a local Eagle Scout stepped to the podium to lead everyone in a quiz. Every answer extolled the value of scouting—lessons learned, tonnage given to charity, accomplishments by various former scouts. The assembled dutifully answered, giving one

Figure 3

EMPYTING NESTS

a) PERCENTAGE OF PRESIDENTIAL VOTE OVER TIME

b) PERCENTAGE OF AGE DISTRIBUTION DATA

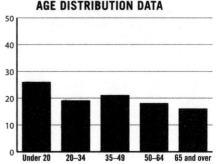

c) PERCENTAGE OF RACE/ETHNIC BREAKDOWN

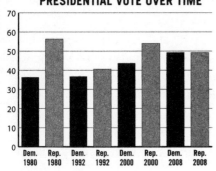

Hispanic
More than One Race
Native American
Asian-Pacific
Black
White

d) PERCENTAGE OF INCOME DISTRIBUTION DATA

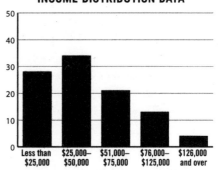

e) PERCENTAGE OF IMMIGRATION OVER TIME

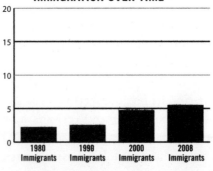

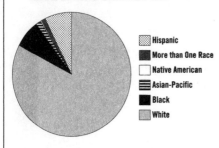

another good-natured ribbings as they did, then filled out their donation forms for the Boy Scouts of America.

Finally Horton was called to the front to accept his award, a sculpture of an eagle swooping out of the sky. And as he started in on his ode to Clermont, his voice caught. "It's just a beautiful place to live," Horton managed. "It's a special place."

The luncheoneers smiled and nodded: Of course it is.

In fact, Clermont, twenty or so miles west of Orlando in appropriately named Lake County, is special enough to have something of a national reputation. Close to 60 percent of its 200,000 residents are fifty or older, many retirees who have migrated from the Rust Belt. They are drawn to Kings Ridge, a two-thousand-plus-home gated community for the older set nestled among the greens and sand traps of two eighteen-hole golf courses. Or the smaller Summit Greens, which has another four hundred or so homes around the links behind its gates. With all of the Michigan State, Indiana, and Wisconsin grads walking the fairways here, you could hold a pretty good Big Ten alumni party come bowl season.

These newly minted Floridians have blended well with what many here call "Old Clermont"—the people who remember the hundreds of acres of orange groves that once surrounded the place and also tend to be closing in on their "active adult" years. The result is a city that has changed but dislikes change. Despite having seen rapid expansion over the past three decades, Clermont and Lake County like things the way they were.

"When I moved here, in 1975, there were about thirty-five hundred residents within the city limits," Horton recalled later in his office. "We had one high school that graduated between ninety and one hundred ten students a year, one elementary school, one junior high. We had one bank. We now have about thirty. We had one McDonald's. Now we have four or five. . . . We have two high schools . . . soon to be three. We now have a couple of junior highs. We have, I don't know, six or seven elementary schools."

And as far as Horton is concerned, it's all a bit much. He's been in town a long time now—long enough to be considered Old Clermont— though he's still one of those relocated midwesterners. He grew up in small Fowlerville, Michigan, and has never been a big-city guy. "I liked it back then because it was a simpler life, less traffic—the rural life, if you like rural," he said.

Ignore the massive spread of developments and Clermont can indeed feel like a throwback to a different era. The local leaders are members of the community's civic groups: two local Kiwanis Clubs—one meets in the morning, the other in the afternoon—a Lions Club, and a Rotary. And the city retains some of Florida's old-time roadside charm. The twenty-two-story Citrus Tower, built in 1956, "stands unrivaled as a majestic and monumental tribute to Central Florida's famed citrus industry and its lush subtropical groves." Next door there's the Presidents Hall of Fame, a wax-figure salute to the occupants of the Oval Office. Crammed full of miniatures of White House rooms, campaign paraphernalia, and assorted photos, the hall comes across a bit like the attic of a crazy aunt who's obsessed with the chief executive. Nine months into Barack Obama's presidency, the attraction's Web site still bragged, "You will be greeted by waxwork figures of the current President, George W. Bush, and his wife, Laura."[8]

LAKE COUNTY AND OTHER EMPTYING NESTS are among the nation's most conservative places—in terms of attitude and politics alike. The 250 counties that fall into the group voted for Bush for president by a margin of 10 percent in 2000 and 13 percent in 2004. Even when the stock market went south late into Bush's second term, destroying many Empty Nesters' investment portfolios, they weren't quite angry enough to pull the lever for a young African American senator from Chicago with a liberal voting record. The 2008 presidential vote was split, with both Obama and John McCain receiving 49 percent of the vote.

Like other Emptying Nests, Clermont proudly flies the banner of the status quo. Ray San Fratello shakes his head when he thinks about it. As president of the South Lake Chamber of Commerce, he consistently sees inflexibility on things like zoning and construction and roads. "They don't want . . . anything built around them," he said. "They don't want the roads improved because that'll bring more people. They don't want anything to do with schools 'cause they don't have to pay property taxes." That's particularly true of retirees who have come to town seeking a trouble-free paradise. "They get down here and all of a sudden they start to get some of the messes we had up there that they don't want any part of."

Their inflexibility, San Fratello suggested, filters into the community's broader culture.

"Part of it is, I think, religious," he said. "Part of it is just a natural conservative mood around here."

PULLING UP THE DRAWBRIDGE

With 35 percent of their populations age fifty or older, and 17 percent over sixty-five, Emptying Nests have a lot of older residents. But that's not their sole defining trait. Many of these communities are in the Midwest and full of people finishing up their time in the workforce as the industrial era winds down. Twenty percent of people here are employed in manufacturing, versus the national county average of 15 percent. Think of communities like those in Michigan and Ohio where the town auto industry is in full retreat. Or those in northern Minnesota where the work associated with mining is waning. Or in Iowa and Wisconsin and Pennsylvania where small manufacturers are disappearing.

Emptying Nests are solidly white and solidly middle class, with a 96 percent Caucasian population and a median household income about $2,000 higher than the national average. There are fewer people living in poverty here than elsewhere—about 6 percent of families versus 11 percent nationally. But how much longer that will be true is uncertain, given these communities' strong ties to so many fading industries.

Lake County is a hothouse version of an Emptying Nest. Over the past few decades active-adult communities have sprouted all over it. Leesburg, to the northwest of Clermont, has Legacy, the Plantation, and Royal Highlands. Mount Dora, to the northeast, has the Lakes. Even the Villages, the mother of all central Florida retirement developments with a population of 75,000, dips into Lake County. Kings Ridge and Summit Greens make up roughly a quarter of the population of the city of Clermont, but their sway is disproportionately large. Their residents vote in great numbers from on-site polling booths and have insinuated themselves into positions of local influence.

Take Jack Hogan, a Rust Belt retiree who sits on the city council. "We get a lot of people . . . they come down here with the idea they'll change something, like our development. They'll make it like New York City, and it's not going to be New York City," Hogan said. "And it's not going to be like Boston, and it's not going to be like Philadelphia. What it amounts to is, it's going to be more like suburban Grand Rapids, you know. And that I like. I prefer the laid-back."

Hogan is, unsurprisingly, from Grand Rapids, Michigan, where he worked as a television news director. You hear a lot of comments like his from the people who put him in office—but with their own hometowns subbed in.

So the seniors in Clermont work to hold the line on change and direct the agenda. They fight potential big-cityism by passing environmental rules aimed at limiting growth. They put stores, amenities, and government facilities where they want them. Hogan and the people of Summit Greens successfully fought to have the city's new firehouse located right next door. Now they get a response time of about four minutes rather than fifteen.

"It's my legacy," Hogan boasted.

That's all on the local level, of course. But in Clermont dislike of change extends to national issues, too. Naturally, retirees worry about changes that might affect things like health care and Social Security. And the late-2000s recession has meant that the insulation they had previously felt from the broader economy has worn thinner. Many older Americans sense that something big is coming down the pike and that they can't escape it, feelings that are particularly acute in Emptying Nests. They are places that see change, inevitable or not, as something to be staved off, not embraced. Clermont is a place where President Obama has been earnestly and frequently referred to as a socialist.

A lot of the retirees here, the sons and daughters of Chrysler, Ford, and General Motors, got out of the employment pool when retirement packages still included good health-care plans. They snap pretty quickly when you mention health-care reform. Hogan called the issue "a farce." Ray Goodgame, another city council member who lives in Knights Ridge, called it "horrible." More than 67 percent of those in Emptying Nests said that they disapproved of the way President Obama was "handling health care policy," according to a November 2009 survey by the Pew Research Center filtered though Patchwork Nation's twelve community types.[9] Clermont was where we heard the strongest anti–health care reform sentiment. The $455 billion in cuts to Medicare in the plan weighed heavy on minds here.

But as the dynamo of twentieth-century American manufacturing has wound down, so has Emptying Nesters' ability to isolate themselves from large-scale change. There are, for instance, a lot retirees in Clermont who rely heavily on 401(k) plans, especially among the younger set that started its golden years early. They are part of a crossover generation, the first to transition from a wholly employer-created safety net to a more unpredictable mixed bag of retirement-income sources—some pension, some investments, maybe some pieces of their old company. Many of them, suggested Goodgame, weren't experienced enough in money management to avoid suffering big losses when the Dow sank.

"These people, they watched their 401(k)s go up in value and . . . they were in this comfort zone. They didn't pay attention," he said. "Well what do you do now? There's a lot of them that are sacking groceries or doing anything they can." Grant Tribble, who works with Merrill Lynch in Clermont, said that a common joke among his retired clients is about taking a job as a greeter at Walmart. But the joke has been growing less funny.

According to a Pew Research Center survey taken in mid-2009, 75 percent of people aged fifty to sixty-four said that the stock market's downturn would make retirement harder. Even among those sixty-five and older, the number was 56 percent.[10]

How is it that these people had so much invested in the market when there were safer places for their money? Because many of them simply trusted their stock brokers—which wasn't a problem as long as their money kept growing, said Gary Clarke, a financial adviser with Ameriprise in Clermont.

"Tuesday I had an appointment with a lady that moved up from wherever she moved up from. She's sixty-eight years old. And she said, 'Would you come and look at what I got?' " Clarke said. "I look at it and say, 'You know, this is very aggressive. Not just for sixty-eight, but for twenty-one.' I said, 'Do you know how aggressive you are?' She said, 'Well no, I just kind of went along and did it.' "

WHEN THE MACHINE STOPS

Of all of the Patchwork Nation communities, Emptying Nests may be hardest to make predictions about. Because of their strongly conservative attitude, people in them will likely feel changes more acutely than the residents of other types of communities. But what will those changes be?

The national economic transformation will have a big impact on the manufacturing economies of the midwestern Emptying Nests. Jobs will be lost, and homes and people will probably move.

For the people still working here—still most of the population—there is not a lot to fall back on as manufacturing wanes. These communities are below the national county average in most all other categories of employment except education. Clermont relied on building, but that sector of the economy has dried up for the foreseeable future. It could be that old manufacturing bases could be retooled for things like green technologies. But if plants building, say, solar panels do come here, will there be enough of them to fill the void?

It's also not clear how the Emptying Nests will adapt to the technological changes sweeping through the United States—the act of e-mailing is a major accomplishment for many here. About 72 percent of people in the Emptying Nests never use social media sites, according to an April 2009 Pew Research Center study filtered through the twelve Patchwork Nation community types. That's not a perfect measure of technological competence, of course, but it is a reminder of how slowly changes in the broader culture come to these places.

There are real questions of what these places will look like culturally. What will happen to those large-scale developments designed specifically for living out one's golden years if retirement plans and 401(k)s don't bounce back fast enough? There will almost certainly be real estate for sale here, and depending on who moves into those homes, communities that are now Emptying Nests could change considerably. Migration patterns for new immigrants in recent years have shown a move toward inland and suburban locales. The Midwest, in particular, has experienced gains in its Latin American population, although the average Emptying Nest remains less than 10 percent Hispanic.

Clermont has recently seen an influx of people from more varied backgrounds than those of its Rust Belt retirees. The relatively cheap real-estate prices of central Florida, where a three-bedroom, two-bath home can be had for $150,000 or less, have brought young Hispanic families looking for a quiet place to raise their kids.

Mayor Harold Turville has lived in town his whole life. He's well aware that "international folks," as he called them, have been changing a city that had already changed since his days of childhood mischief in the orange groves. "I don't know whether they're citizens or with visa or what, but we do have a fairly large international community that lives here," he said. "I would say a high percentage from the Caribbean, and [though] not all [are] Hispanic, many are."

Turville wouldn't say it directly—though his comment about visas expresses a certain unease—but a lot of people in Clermont are unhappy with their new neighbors. The retirees and soon-to-be retirees who live here or came here have a very specific place in mind. Diversity isn't a big part of their mental picture. Kings Ridge promises a life "as diverse as you wish."[11] But it means recreationally: "Choose to take a dip in one of the three pools, soak the 'kinks' out in one of the two spas, relax and read a book in one of the four cabanas, or perhaps take part in one of the many games played in the multimillion-dollar clubhouse." The well-entertained retirees who adorn its Web site are nearly all white.

Mayor Turville will openly tell you that, as a lifelong resident of Clermont, he feels a need to limit the power of the growing "international community." He views the former midwesterners of Kings Ridge and Summit Greens as a buffer against newcomers from more exotic locales who may not have such conservative values. "I will tell you that they probably share more of my mother's and father's values than an awful lot of people that have come here from the Caribbean or from Mexico—or anywhere else, for that matter," he said.

The chamber of commerce's San Fratello explains Old Clermontian attitudes toward immigration more bluntly. "You know if you bring up an issue up like immigration, you'll hear pretty clearly, 'Send them back,'" he said. "There's nothing you can do about that except have time take its toll. Those people will eventually be gone."

There have already been signs of change around the margins. The city council has fresh blood in the form of Robert Thompson, who at twenty-eight years old is half the age of most of the other members. A son of Clermont, he has deep roots in the community, and seemingly everyone you talk to among the town's power brokers counts him as a friend—despite the fact that he's the most progressive voice in city politics. He worked hard for Obama in 2008 and made sure that people in town knew.

Among the people Thompson is friends with is Ann Dupee, former publisher of the local newspaper and an important player in the morning Kiwanis Club. She's also a columnist who writes about the way Clermont used to be for the small South Lake Press. She and Thompson like to talk and occasionally share a drink. "Oh sure, I love Ann," Thompson told me.

Dupee loves Thompson, too—just not enough to vote for him for anything above city council. "He's a Democrat," she said. "I don't know. Maybe if it was a county office, something where party politics doesn't matter. But I can't vote for a Democrat."

EVANGELICAL EPICENTERS: NIXA, MISSOURI

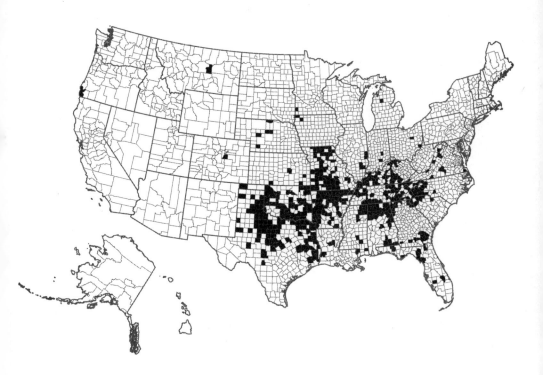

UTILITY BEFORE GOD

Shortly after 7:30 on a July evening during the Stained Glass Theatre's production of *From the Mountaintop*, angels descended to pull
"Cindy" from the audience. They brought her to the front of the
crowd and asked what had happened to her faith. Cindy had recently lost
her husband in a drunk driving accident and begun questioning why the
world is so unjust, and why she must endure such pain. Her life, the angels
said, was at a "point of crisis." She needed to make a decision about what
road she would take.

And to complicate matters, she had to deal with a group of fallen
angels on the other side of the stage. Costumed in goth makeup and red
and black Depression-era clothes, they looked like hell's version of the '80s

Figure 4

EVANGELICAL EPICENTERS

a) PERCENTAGE OF PRESIDENTIAL VOTE OVER TIME

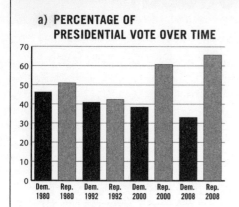

b) PERCENTAGE OF AGE DISTRIBUTION DATA

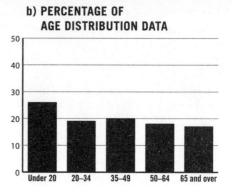

c) PERCENTAGE OF RACE/ETHNIC BREAKDOWN

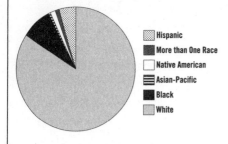

d) PERCENTAGE OF INCOME DISTRIBUTION DATA

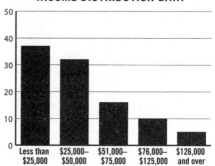

e) PERCENTAGE OF IMMIGRATION OVER TIME

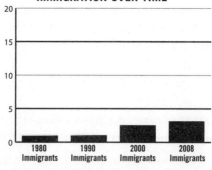

pop band Dexy's Midnight Runners. Life is empty, they told her, so she might as well turn her back on God and join them in embracing the substantial, if fleeting, pleasures of the world.

The "sometimes funny, sometimes musical, sometimes serious look at pain and suffering" that followed included each set of angels putting on a short play to try to win Cindy over, as well as some good-natured mugging to the crowd, particularly from the forces of darkness. Of course, the good angels won. Cindy got her life back on track. And the audience, an all-ages collection of two hundred or so faithful Christians, went wild. They even rose to give the cast a standing ovation, despite the poor to mediocre acting, singing, and dancing that had been the order of the evening.

That wasn't necessarily because the attendees didn't know bad acting when they saw it. They had come to this small theater next to a highway overpass in Ozark, Missouri, not only to be entertained, but also to be ministered to. The show began and ended with prayers that the play's moral would be heard and heeded, and the script was nothing if not on-message. There was no sarcasm. There were no winking pop-culture references or complicated mixed messages. *From the Mountaintop* was as advertised: a straightforward story about a woman's struggle with faith that typifies the Stained Glass mission of "serving Jesus Christ through the arts."

The company is very much a product of Christian County, Missouri. Christian and its largest city, Nixa, take pride in calling themselves "the buckle of the Bible Belt," though of course, there is a vast collection of cities and towns laying claim to this distinction. All around the area, businesses, cars, and people are adorned with the sign of the ichthys—better known to some as the "Jesus fish." The streets are lined with churches of assorted Protestant denominations—Baptist, Methodist, Church of Christ—as well as newer houses of worship such as the massive James River Assembly. The well-known evangelical denomination the Assemblies of God has its headquarters just up the road in Springfield.

When political commentators throw around the term "religious right," they have in mind the people who live in Christian and the 467 other counties that make up the Evangelical Epicenters. These places vote Republican consistently and heavily. In fact, of all of our twelve community types, only the Epicenters actually increased their percentage of Republican votes in 2008 over the previous presidential contest. People here weren't necessarily big fans of John McCain, but 66 percent of them voted for him anyway—in many cases because of his running mate. Here, they consider Sarah Palin one of their own.

"Can I tell you that I'm happy that [Barack Obama] didn't cancel all the prayer services? Yeah," said Pastor Gary Swearengin of the Nixa Church of the Nazarene. "Does that give me any hope? That's better than nothing." In other words, on January 21, 2009, Swearengin picked up his morning newspaper and was pleased not to see a story about the cancellation of all church services. He said this without a trace of irony.

"I didn't know what he was going to do," he explained.

Swearengin has ministered in town for twenty-three years. His two sons and two daughters have all attended Nixa High School. He's coached their sports teams. His political point of view typifies the city's as a whole. "It's all about where I submit to authority," he said. "I don't agree with everything about Obama. But will I submit to him as my president? Yes, I will. Until he asks me to do something that God told me not to, I will submit."

In Nixa and places like it the substantial religious community is leery of giving the secular one any more power than it has to. In these counties you don't want to schedule events on Wednesday nights if you can help it. For most Protestant denominations they are traditionally set aside for Bible study, something that's taken very seriously in the Epicenters. Forty-eight percent of the people who live in the Epicenters identify themselves as members of some evangelical congregation, according to the Glenmary Research Center Survey of Congregations from 2000. Only 38 percent of the population in these counties doesn't attend some form of church.

The Epicenters are very conservative communities, but conservative in their own particular way. Nixa is not wildly more conservative than Sioux Center, Iowa, our representative Tractor Country community. The Epicenters fell more into John McCain's column than Tractor Country in 2008, but only slightly—by 66 percent versus 64. And the two locations are in nearly complete agreement on their opposition to government spending put forward by the Obama administration. They both see it much more as "debt" than "investment," according to a Zogby International poll on that question.[12] In the Epicenters 72 percent see the expenditures as debt. In Tractor Country that percentage is 70 percent.

But look closely at Sioux Center and Nixa and you'll see places that are very different in their attitudes toward taxation and community spending, at least at the local level. When, for example, the public library burned down in Sioux Center the town built a $5 million Frank Lloyd Wright–inspired facility to replace it. In Nixa, which has about three times the population of Sioux Center, there is no library. "They don't support the library system because they don't find any value in it," said Ryan Bowling, editor of the weekly newspaper the *Nixa XPress*. "And they don't want their taxes to go up."

There are other signs of Nixa's antispending attitude. The town's roads mostly don't have shoulders or sidewalks. There has been little effort to revitalize the two or three blocks that make up the city's old downtown. Strip malls and chain restaurants constitute most of the options for commerce and dining. Like *From the Mountaintop*, Nixa is without flourishes.

"It's about convenience and practicality," said Bowling. "Nixa is an ugly-looking town. It really is. It's about, I think, sort of about doing things cheaper and about stretching your dollar as far as you can make it go." He pointed out the omnipresent utility poles that line the city's main drag, Massey Boulevard, which is also Missouri Highway 160.

"One-Sixty there is the ugliest road I've ever seen," he said.

THE CITY WITHIN THE CITY

With a median household income of about $31,500, Evangelical Epicenters are the second-poorest community type in the Patchwork Nation. Their poverty rate is just above the national average at 12 percent. Nearly 20 percent of the population here resides in a mobile home.

Spread around the South and the southern Midwest, these communities often survive on the money that comes from small factories and light production. Roughly 20 percent of their employment comes from manufacturing, well above the national average of 15 percent. At the same time, there are fewer than average professional or executive workers living in these counties, fewer people working for the government, and fewer working people in education.

There's not typically a lot of diversity here, although there is some in the southern setting. These places are 91 percent white, 6 percent African American, and only 5 percent Hispanic. Although they closely match the nation at large in terms of age, with a mix of young and old and about a quarter of their population under eighteen, the Evangelical Epicenters have fewer people enrolled in college than any other community type except for Tractor Country.

But what really makes the Epicenters stand out is their culture. These places are, for instance, more strongly opposed to abortion than any of our other community types. About 21 percent of the people in the Epicenters believe that abortion should be completely illegal, which is more than in any other type, according to a 2008 YouGov Polimetrix study filtered through Patchwork Nation's twelve community types. And 73 percent of people are opposed to allowing gay and lesbian couples to marry. Only Minority Central and Tractor Country communities are more opposed.

Those kinds of attitudes attract young families looking for communities with "strong values" to places like Christian County. In its case, proximity to the larger, amenity-laden communities of Springfield and Branson helps, too. Between 2000 and 2008 the area experienced sudden, explosive growth. Nixa ballooned from about twelve thousand citizens in 2000 to more than seventeen thousand in 2006. New roads and homes popped up with little attention paid to appearance or zoning. The city even splurged on a $4 million recreation and aquatic center complete with running track, pool, and water park—a clear sign of a community hoping to improve itself. Of course, it wasn't paid for by taxing individuals. A Walmart Supercenter came to town during the building boom, and the city put aside the revenue from the store's sales taxes for four years, then paid cash for the new facility.

The town, once a semirural village of a few thousand, has evolved into a bedroom community full of transplants from across the country, particularly western states such as California. Between 2006 and 2009 the Nixa school system added six hundred new students, leading to overcrowding and the construction of a new school for fifth and sixth graders. But the boom ended as the late-2000s recession set in.

"We lost our biggest employer, construction," said Sharon Whitehill Gray, director of the Nixa Area Chamber of Commerce. "Three years ago . . . we had over six hundred residential building permits. Last year we had thirty-four, and this year we've had four. That may actually be up a few—maybe six." The slowdown is evident on the back streets of the city, where weed-choked lots sit in front of empty homes and roads lead to nowhere.

The population and construction explosions aside, the city isn't fundamentally different from what it was fifteen years ago. It has changed without changing its ethos. "The growth sort of seems to have been fairly seamless," Bowling told me. "The newcomers, they knew what Nixa was like before they came here, and that's part of why they came here. I mean, with the James River Assembly headquarters being just down the road. Well, a lot of people knew what they were getting into."

Bowling noted that every week the *Nixa Xpress* has a lengthy listing of services at local houses of worship—about forty churches taking up about thirty column inches. And that's for a city of only 6.2 square miles.

The number of churches is a testament to the size and the strength of the religious community in the area. But it's also a reason why members of that community can have a tough time working together. "They, I think, just have their own agendas," Bowling said. "There are too many churches to pull them all together to try to unite behind one common cause. They are too small to do anything big alone, and then there are too many to do anything together." The religious community in Nixa is essentially a set of small tribes, each with its own chief.

The one big exception to that rule is the James River Assembly, a 370,000-square-foot, twenty-thousand-congregant megachurch in Ozark, just east of Nixa. Its Web site is clean, sleek, and almost corporate in feel, with music downloads, podcasts of recent sermons, and links to other, smaller sites the church also maintains. James River's lead pastors, John and Debbie Lindell, appear on the site grinning and in T-shirts, sitting together in front of an exposed-brick wall that could be inside a hip coffeehouse. They're the kind of spiritual leaders who draw young families looking for a more relaxed, up-to-date church environment. On Sundays thousands fill the assembly's main sanctuary—a cavernous arena with giant video screens on either side—to hear one of "the Preaching Team" provide context for modern life.

James River is more than just a modern church, though; it's almost a self-contained city. There's a café, a fitness center, and a huge play area for children. The last is impressive in its organization. Outside of it are fifteen computer terminals lined up to register kids aged four and under so that they can amuse themselves while Mom or Dad is faith-strengthening. It's the Evangelical Epicenter answer to the IKEA ball room, albeit with the adults involved in something a little more serious than furniture shopping.

Despite the New Age look and feel of James River the place, James River the church hews to the sixteen fundamental truths of the Assemblies of God, which include Judgment Day and "everlasting punishment in the lake which burneth with fire and brimstone" for the evil and the wicked. The all-important role of the church in "evangelizing the world" is another fundamental truth, one that the religious leaders at James River emphasize. "We're not trying to create our own Camelot or our little bubble of isolation. We want to make an impact," said Curt Cook, James River's senior associate pastor. "We are part of the community, and our desire and effort is to influence our community for better—you know, to make a difference. And that's why we do a project partnership at a school every year. As a matter of fact, we did two schools this last year."

The church does indeed do some community outreach, especially on holidays. Its annual I Love America celebration on July Fourth draws roughly one hundred thousand people. Other churches in Nixa don't have the money or the space to offer that kind of spectacle—not to mention lattes or ellipticals. But their houses of worship still stand as centers of power. That's true of all churches, of course. But it has special meaning in the Evangelical Epicenters, where the religious community is so strong.

MEGACHURCH AND STATE

The future for the Evangelical Epicenters looks to be one of retrenchment. Since 2008 the signs of disappointment and, at times, anger about the direction of the country have been impossible to miss in Nixa and the other Epicenters.

In September 2009, when President Obama wanted to address the children of America with what was essentially a stay-in-school pep talk, parents in Nixa said no thanks. Soon after the speech was announced, a local conservative talk radio host, Vincent David Jericho, devoted his entire broadcast to the topic. One caller suggested that the Obama speech smacked of Mao Tse-tung's efforts to brainwash the youth of China. Jericho explained that one of his concerns was that Obama would be portrayed as someone of great character who might say something that contradicts the words of a parent. "Now you have a very conflicted child who's trying to find out who's right," he said.

Whether children would watch the speech in the city's public schools quickly became a local controversy.

Nixa's schools are among the best in the state, in part because the large number of different congregations in the city has prevented the development of an extensive religious school system. They stand as a rare example of cooperative financial sacrifice, and parents in Nixa tend to be well attuned to what goes on in them. Attempting to alleviate parental concern over the speech, the school superintendent posted a message on the district's Web site. "Selected high school classes may end up presenting the 'President's speech-to-school children' in a course such as government, political science, etc.," he wrote. "We will make available the webcast link to all families who wish to access it on their own during non-school time."

Such tensions extend far beyond Nixa to the larger community of Evangelical Epicenters. In November 2009 a group of prominent Christian leaders issued something they called the Manhattan Declaration. The group included Eastern Orthodox and Catholic clergy, but the biggest force behind the declaration were evangelicals like the Rev. James Dobson, of Focus on the Family, a group dedicated to "cooperat[ing] with the Holy Spirit in sharing the Gospel of Jesus Christ with as many people as possible by nurturing and defending the God-ordained institution of the family and promoting biblical truths worldwide."[13]

The declaration expands upon three key concepts: "the sanctity of human life," "the dignity of marriage as the conjugal union of husband and wife," and "the rights of conscience and religious liberty." "Because [these ideas] are increasingly under assault from powerful forces in our culture, we are compelled today to speak out forcefully in their defense, and to commit ourselves to honoring them fully no matter what pressures are brought upon us and our institutions to abandon or compromise them," the authors asserted, inviting readers of the declaration to "sign" it online and then take action. Suggested next steps for signers include discussing the declaration at Kiwanis or Rotary meetings, blogging about it, and talking to your neighbors about it. The ultimate goal is to "build a movement" of "hundreds of thousands, perhaps millions."[14]

That movement is but one of many stands against what many in the Epicenters view as an increasingly misguided American culture. In October 2009, the leadership of the Assemblies of God, a Pentecostal faith headquartered in Springfield, Missouri, got in trouble with its own flock when it signed on to a resolution by the National Association of Evangelicals calling for immigration reform. The resolution says, among other things, that "our churches and communities have been blessed by immigrants, many of whom bring strong faith, entrepreneurial energy and family values that strengthen our future." It also calls for the government to overhaul its policies concerning visas, deportation, and citizenship.[15]

The document created so much turmoil within the church that AOG superintendent George Wood recorded a statement for the Web asking his own flock to keep the conversation civil. "When people . . . start swearing at our people who are answering the phone, you just have to say this is way overheated," he said.

What do stances like that mean for the future in the Epicenters?

The people here will likely not walk away from politics. The stakes for them are too high. "Rare is the occasion that we just sit around while God does all the work," reads the response to a question about striking a balance between "waiting on God" and taking personal action on the James River Assembly's Web site. "He expects us to live our faith and show what we believe."[16] For those in the Epicenters, that means trying to have an impact nationally, especially when it comes to social liberalization that they perceive as threatening to traditional family values. At the local level, elected officials who are part of the local culture will likely work to maintain it.

The Epicenters may see the construction of more James River Assemblies—places that essentially grow to become cities within cities, offering an ideal vision of a life lived spiritually rather than secularly. But even without them, the religious communities here will likely grow in their role as a counterbalance to government. It's not about money; it's about where the money goes. Consider the James River congregation's willingness to give thousands to build new facilities for the church, as well as those in the Epicenters' unwillingness to allow the federal government to increase its spending.

Those in the Evangelical Epicenters are holding the line against whatever changes threaten to transform the country in ways they believe are for the worse. They are the good angels at the Stained Glass Theatre trying to pull their fellow Americans onto the right path—and their mission is getting more important by the day.

IMMIGRATION NATION: EL MIRAGE, ARIZONA

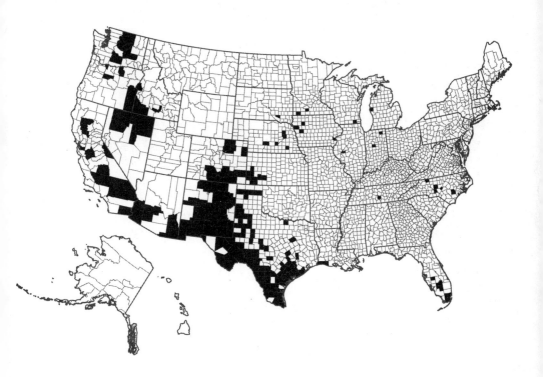

AMERICA EN ESPAÑOL

People generally like to be outside in El Mirage, Arizona. The area averages 290-plus sunny days annually. And though the midsummer can be blazingly hot, most of the year the climate is simply warm and dry. Even winter is generally light-jacket weather.

But whether it's 72 degrees out or 106, one thing can send much of El Mirage's population inside fast: the sight of a Maricopa County sheriff's car.

When a cruiser is spotted on a corner or in a parking lot, residents across town call one another with word that it might be a good idea to take a sick day or to postpone a trip to the store. Or to remind one another that, if you have to venture out, you should take your driver's license or other

Figure 5

IMMIGRATION NATION

a) PERCENTAGE OF PRESIDENTIAL VOTE OVER TIME

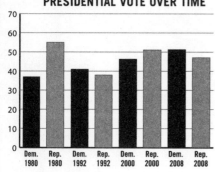

b) PERCENTAGE OF AGE DISTRIBUTION DATA

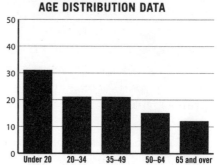

c) PERCENTAGE OF RACE/ETHNIC BREAKDOWN

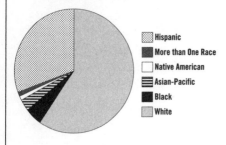

- Hispanic
- More than One Race
- Native American
- Asian-Pacific
- Black
- White

d) PERCENTAGE OF INCOME DISTRIBUTION DATA

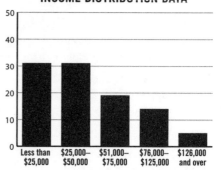

e) PERCENTAGE OF IMMIGRATION OVER TIME

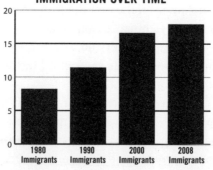

documentation. You never know when you might see police flashers in your rearview.

"You should see me. When I'm out and I see a sheriff's cruiser, I start shaking just because I'm Mexican," said Rachel Gomez, explaining the challenges for even a lifelong resident of El Mirage. "I mean, I wasn't born in Mexico. We've been here for three generations. But I'm Mexican."

Gomez is not just another local. She and her husband are well-known businesspeople in town, owners of the Rio Mirage Café restaurants—with two locations so far and more on the way, they hope. Still, Gomez got visibly nervous at even the mention of Maricopa County sheriff Joe Arpaio, who's made a reputation and career out of taking on illegal immigration. She sat up in her seat and leaned in to talk.

"You know, they'll pull you out," she said. "I feel like I'm in Iraq here. They'll pull you out of the vehicle, and if I don't have my purse, if I don't have my ID . . . I just get scared. I have heard stories that they just take you across the border at night."

Talk to most anyone with brown skin in El Mirage and you'll hear similar things.

Downtown in Phoenix Arpaio denied such claims. Sheriff Joe, as he's called, said that he doesn't seek out illegal immigrants. He and his deputies simply do their job out on the roads—pulling over speeders, arresting drunken drivers—with no attention paid to the ethnicity or race of those they stop.

"It's just another felony law that I'm enforcing," Arpaio said of his office's immigration arrests. "And we do everything else, too. We lock up dope peddlers, murderers, and everything. It happens to be a bigger problem right now coming across more of them."

For a lot of folks in El Mirage that's simply hard to believe. They've been pulled over or know people who've been pulled over for "DWH"—Driving While Hispanic. To them anything that Sheriff Joe says on the record to an out-of-town reporter means little. Their experience doesn't include what many Americans think of as the mainstream media. And all of that was before the passage of Arizona's new state immigration law SB 1070. The law lowered the barriers to Arpaio' s enforcement of that one particular felony by giving law enforcement officials the ability to pull aside anyone they suspected of being illegal immigrants. Any need for pretext to look at an individual's identification—speeding, a busted taillight, "erratic driving"—was gone. Shortly after the bill became law, Sylvia Rivera, a friend of Rachel Gomez, told us in exasperated tones, "The situation in the county was bad enough. Now I feel we live in a racist state as well. My Hispanic friends and family are not happy at all." Arpaio responded to the new law by announcing new plans to sweep the county for illegal immigrants. And while talk quickly began about finding ways to overturn the new law, even without it, the story for Latinos in Maricopa and in other Immigration Nation counties was well known by those that live there. Latinos like Rivera live in another United States, one that sits within the boundaries of the country but has its own culture and rules. In their America a lot of people speak a different language. They read different newspapers, listen to different music, and watch different television. And for them every traffic stop contains menacing possibility.

In El Mirage that's apparent right down to the actual structure of the city. There's an "old town" full of small, often beat-up structures where the Spanish speakers live and a "new town" full of larger, freshly landscaped homes where the Anglos live. The city represents the community type we call Immigration Nation in high relief.

The defining characteristic of these places is their large Hispanic populations: 44 percent of the 20 million people who live here are from Spanish-speaking backgrounds. Nationally that figure is only about 15 percent. Although Immigration Nation counties are scattered as far north as Minnesota and Michigan, the counties that fall into this group are primarily in the West and Southwest: San Bernardino County, California; Hidalgo County, New Mexico; Presidio County, Texas. In some of these places, residents who have a hard-line stance on immigration have tried to construct a wall between the United States and Mexico, to push through legislation making it illegal for landlords to rent to illegal immigrants, or to block public funding of centers for day laborers.

Such efforts seem particularly odd in El Mirage, because the Latinos got here first. They came to this arid, empty spot northwest of Phoenix in 1937, establishing what's now the city's downtown as a community for migrant workers employed on the farmland that once filled the surrounding landscape. They built their own homes, groceries, and restaurants. And because of El Mirage's remoteness, they were left alone. But over time greater Phoenix slowly rolled its way out toward the town, replacing the farmland with thousands and thousands of single-family homes and the giant Sun City retirement community. Eventually the sprawl surrounded the small community of Hispanic farmworkers with new housing developments— Rancho El Mirage, Dysart Park, Montana Blanca Estates.

Driving down Thunderbird Road, old El Mirage's main street, is driving right into the heart of that other United States. Store signs are in Spanish, sometimes with smaller English translations: *carnicería* ("butcher"), *almacén* ("grocery"). And there are a host of signs that read *envíos de dinero*: wire transfer. Those are the places where legal and illegal immigrants alike go to send money to Mexico. And there's a lot of that going on in El Mirage.

Much of the old town is populated by U.S. citizens, but there are also plenty of husbands and fathers who've come to the United States to make money to help their families back home across the border. Roy Delgado, a former mayor of El Mirage and a current city council member, told me that most everyone knows who's in town illegally. Many residents here don't begrudge the illegals their jobs in construction or in the backs of restaurants—but they draw the line at robbery and other crimes. "It's just those few that commit the crimes and break into the cars and have a bad effect on anyone who has the same skin color," Delgado said.

The result is that this former mayor gets distrustful looks from locals who don't know who he is and suspect he might be an illegal. His solution is to make people aware that he is a veteran. On his truck he has a prominently placed "Retired Army" bumper sticker, and when he goes out he wears his "Retired Army" baseball cap.

"It makes a difference," he told me. "It's really bad. . . . I was born and raised here. I mean, I defended [this country] for twenty years, and now I've got to wear this thing to identify who I am."

LIVING DAY TO DAY

Beyond their Hispanic populations, Immigration Nation counties tend to be less diverse than the nation as a whole. Their African American populations are only 3 percent compared to 9 percent across counties nationally. Most Hispanics identify themselves racially as white, since Hispanic has never officially been recognized as a racial category. As is often the case in places with a large minority group, there's a sharply divided electorate in Immigration Nation communities. George W. Bush won these counties by 5 percent in 2000 and by 9 percent in 2004. But GOP dominance slipped here with heightened Latino mobilization following the failed Border Protection, Anti-Terrorism, and Illegal Immigration Control Act of 2005, Republican-sponsored legislation that turned many Hispanics against the party. Barack Obama carried these places in 2008. The margin was slim, however: 51 percent for Obama, 48 percent for John McCain.

That divide is testament to the way immigration debate splits these places on the whole. In the early twenty-first century, a line has been drawn here between those who welcome immigrants and want to find a way to integrate them into the economy and those who feel inundated and overrun. Legal Hispanic residents of El Mirage may not like the way some of the illegals operate, but they share a heritage with them. When antagonistic Anglos lump all of the Hispanics in town together, that sense of kinship can be heightened.

In El Mirage, city hall and the local police generally have a more permissive take on immigration issues. But in the broader community of Maricopa County that's not the case. Sheriff Joe may say that he's enforcing one law among many where immigration is concerned, but he's gone to some impressive lengths to do so, regularly getting into skirmishes with local governments and police.

"There's this fight about jurisdiction," said one person involved in city government in the county. "He believes he has jurisdiction of the entire county inside city limits. The cities believe, 'It's our city; you don't come in.' He says, 'I have jurisdiction,' and you get into these big, gigantic pissing matches." In October 2008, for example, Arpaio's deputies raided the town of Mesa's city hall and library at 2 A.M. and arrested nine workers on immigration charges. Mesa mayor Scott Smith angrily told reporters that the town's city hall had been "violated by another government agency. I don't believe that's proper . . . and I believe that also crosses the line as to what law enforcement should do."[17]

Arpaio told me that he had some thirty thousand prisoners in the county jail on some form of immigration charge. "I see a problem from the international scope," he said. "I see the problem national. I see the political problem, which is the worst problem because they don't want to do nothing. But . . . I'm not the national sheriff. I'm just Maricopa County. So I'm taking care of the people that I work for, which is the four million [Maricopa residents]."

If Arpaio were the national sheriff? "You put 'em in jail. Then they'll say, 'We don't have enough jails. We don't have enough prosecutors.' Oh, really? . . . So you can put up temporary housing."

Those strong views have led to strong feelings both for and against Arpaio. He was reelected in 2008 with 56 percent of the vote. But below his nineteenth-floor office march a steady stream of protesters with signs calling him a racist or a fascist. In Immigration Nation, the feelings about immigration are very charged and very much split. Forty-eight percent of the population says it feels "the growing number of newcomers from other countries threatens traditional American customs and values." And that's in communities in which 44 percent of residents identify themselves as Hispanic.[18]

There are, of course, other challenges that face these places beyond coming to an agreement on immigration issues. The median household income here, about $34,000, is a good $3,000 below the national county average. The poverty rate, 14 percent, is 3 percent above the national average. And nearly one in five people in these counties lives in a mobile home—despite the fact that a three-bedroom, one-and-a-half-bathroom house can be had in old El Mirage for under $100,000, often for under $50,000.

There is no dominant industry in this swath of America. The percentages of people employed in education or in trades and services or as executives are fairly close to average. There are, however, two labor-related numbers that stand out in Immigration Nation. First, there are fewer people employed in manufacturing in this community type than in any other but Tractor Country. Second, nearly twice the proportion of people work in agriculture here as in the average county in the United States as a whole—13 percent versus 7 percent.

The median income in El Mirage is about $52,000, but that number is deceptive. There are many much lower incomes here that don't show up in surveys because they're part of an underground economy. Go to the corner of Dysart and Grand streets at six or seven in the morning and you'll find a line of workers looking for cars to jump into for a day's work. Others use one of the several businesses in town that place people in day jobs. Consequently, the number of people without health insurance here is high. In Maricopa County 22 percent of residents lack insurance, and that fits with Immigration Nation as a whole, in which the number is 23 percent. Nationally, it's just under 18 percent.

Rio Mirage Café owner Gomez wanted to give all of her staff health insurance—and to cover 75 percent of the cost. So in 2008 she selected a plan and let her employees vote on whether they wanted it. "All we needed was fifteen people to sign up so that they could have insurance," Gomez recalled. "But when you only make a hundred dollars a week as a busser or a server, a dishwasher . . . twenty-five percent can be the chunk of your check. Anyway, we got ten people to sign up."

Sylvia Rivera said that she's never had health insurance. Even her son's death from cancer hasn't changed her mind, despite the fact that he received treatment under the plan of his employer, Walmart.

A seamstress who owns her own business, Rivera doesn't bother with insurance because she knows she can go to the emergency room to get care if she has to. "To me, it's like you're gonna pay four or five hundred dollars a month on insurance," she said. "If you go to the hospital, they take you anyways, whether you have insurance or not, and then make arrangements for you to pay it back. So then why am I going to pay for years and years of all this insurance and then never use it?"

DOLLARS BUT NOT NECESSARILY ANY CHANGE

High numbers of uninsured, lots of low wages, and few manufacturing jobs—in some ways the communities of Immigration Nation are well prepared for the track the nation seems to be on. They at least have the benefit of having lived through a lot of it already. A lot of their population is familiar with getting by on less. As the American manufacturing base continues to shrink, these counties probably won't feel much of that pain.

It's not as if the economy here is recession-proof, however. In the Southwest especially, these counties experienced the downturn in the housing market firsthand. After all, there's a lot of empty land out here, and a lot of people were attracted to the warm, dry climate. El Mirage's population more than quadrupled in the first half of the 2000s as the denser core of Maricopa County sprawled toward it. Construction quickly became the major employer here as development after development spread to cover the land. But the jobs quickly vanished. Between 2002 and 2006 there were 4,600 new home building permits in the city. In 2007 there were only eighteen.[19] Today streets of finished homes give way to empty roadways. Blocks all over town have seen multiple foreclosures.

"It has been a disaster here. Housing was the economy, and it's gone," said one person with knowledge of the scene as he drove up and down the streets pointing out the unfinished projects and the foreclosures. Much of what was once agricultural land has been turned into housing that may not regain its value anytime soon.

Meanwhile, employment promises to remain a complicated issue because of the unique populations in these communities. The tensions over labor in Immigration Nation will likely intensify if economic times stay tough, especially if high unemployment endures in the long term. Many businesses here—construction companies, restaurants, retailers—have been built on the ability of employers to obtain very cheap labor from illegal immigrants. Whether that constitutes a betrayal of illegal workers or legal ones is at the heart of the immigration debate. Either way, the entire local economy is affected. A study of wages in Arizona by Harvard economist George Borjas found that the hiring of illegal immigrants has had a particularly dramatic effect on the wages of less-educated and inexperienced legal residents.[20] The report suggests that wages for high school dropouts in the state are about 5 percent lower than they would be without competition from illegal immigrants.

Of course, tough times for the U.S. economy may keep more potential illegal immigrants on the other side of the border. The 2008 American Community Survey showed that for the first time in forty years the immigrant population as a percentage of the total U.S. population remained essentially flat compared to the previous year.[21]

In Immigration Nation communities like El Mirage, however, the immigrants are already there. And those tough times have put new pressures on businesses that hire immigrants but don't go too far in checking paperwork. Nonimmigrant workers who wouldn't have been interested in bussing tables or washing dishes before the late-2000s recession now need whatever employment they can get. In April of 2008 the unemployment rate in Maricopa County was 3.1 percent. By November of 2009 it was about 8 percent.

In Laredo, Texas, in the Immigration Nation community of Webb County, a serious tightening of U.S. border security could essentially choke off a large part of the local economy. There the two local Walmarts have thrived on business from Mexicans coming across the border to shop in the United States—in part with money that U.S. citizens spend in their businesses in Nuevo Laredo in Mexico. Laredo's business community and government alike have a live-and-let-live attitude toward their neighbors to the south.

"In Texas there is an openness, a back-and-forth that goes culturally, economically," said Xochitl Mora Garcia, a spokesperson for the city of Laredo. "It goes familial, friendship-wise, between families and companies and businesses and individuals on both sides of the border."

But true border towns are a special case. And most Immigration Nation communities are more tense and more divided when it comes to crossing the border, regardless of how dependent their economies are on their immigrant populations. Arpaio's opinions are widely known because he holds a position of power. But there are people throughout Immigration

Nation who share his views: They want "the illegals" locked up and sent home, period.

And, as ever, there are those who don't. On Thursday, January 14, 2010, Sheriff Joe's Twitter feed read, "I will be closing down inmate visitation in all jails this Saturday in anticipation of a large scale protest outside of the jails."

INDUSTRIAL METROPOLIS: PHILADELPHIA, PENNSYLVANIA

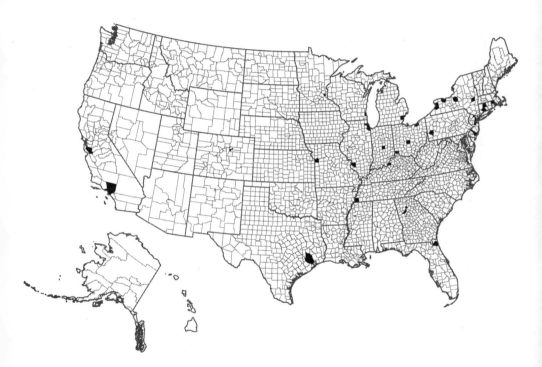

"A CITY OF NEIGHBORHOODS"

Ask a Philadelphian to describe his or her hometown and the response is more often than not something like this: "Philadelphia is a city of neighborhoods." The first time I visited, in December 2007, several interviewees told me this—never mind that the view is hardly unique to the City of Brotherly Love. People describe their hometowns this way in many big cities: Baltimore, Boston, Chicago, Cleveland, New York. Even Long Beach, California.

But that doesn't make it untrue.

Figure 6

INDUSTRIAL METROPOLIS

a) PERCENTAGE OF PRESIDENTIAL VOTE OVER TIME

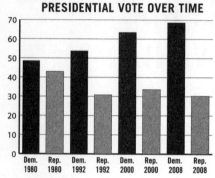

b) PERCENTAGE OF AGE DISTRIBUTION DATA

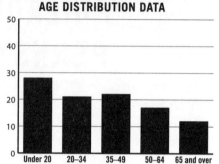

c) PERCENTAGE OF RACE/ETHNIC BREAKDOWN

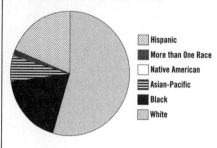

Hispanic
More than One Race
Native American
Asian-Pacific
Black
White

d) PERCENTAGE OF INCOME DISTRIBUTION DATA

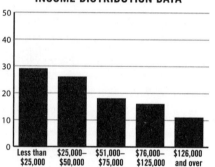

e) PERCENTAGE OF IMMIGRATION OVER TIME

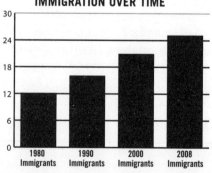

"You need a car to see the city," said Loree Jones, who was just finishing her time as the city's managing director. "People say Philadelphia is a city of neighborhoods, and it really is."

Indeed, if you're looking for an easy way to get a good feel for the city, take a drive up Germantown Avenue. The multiracial, multiethnic, multicultural tableau that is Philadelphia can't be easily broken down or explained. High-rises populated by the wealthy run into bungalows full of white blue-collar workers that bump against tenements holding struggling black families that give way to leafy streets full of young professionals. But Germantown Avenue, which runs northwesterly almost from the Delaware River right to the city's border, offers a look at a great number of the Philadelphias in Philadelphia.

Down near Girard Avenue, Germantown reveals Philadelphia's industrial past—"past" being the operative word. The street is lined with vacant apartment buildings and empty fields surrounded by barbed wire. On the corner of Oxford Street and Germantown the Gretz brewery's smokestack rises above the long-shuttered, graffiti-covered plant. This is Fishtown, a neighborhood that has been working-class since the nineteenth century.

A couple of miles later, at Broad Street, Germantown's sidewalks are alive with people, mostly poor and mostly African American, patronizing delis and pizza places and check-cashing joints. It's a familiar scene of urban grittiness—storefronts under old tin signs or bright plastic awnings, some still behind steel riot gates—that belies the area's name: Nicetown.

As you get closer to Philly's northern border, slowly, Germantown Avenue changes. The businesses are in better shape and aimed at a different clientele: There are wine shops rather than liquor stores and restaurants that serve Ethiopian food rather than ribs. The neighborhood called Mount Airy is a place in transition, full of historic buildings and impressive homes, but also well stocked with storefront churches and sketchy bars.

Finally, the street turns to cobblestone as it heads into the tony neighborhood of Chestnut Hill, home of antiques stores and organic groceries. The sidewalks here are tree lined, and Germantown bears all the hallmarks of an enlightened, upper-middle-class enclave—the kind of place where the color of your skin matters less than whether you're on track to make partner at the firm.

The entire trip, from the empty Gretz beer plant to Chestnut Hill Flower & Garden, covers less than eight miles. Along that segment of road, houses go for next to nothing—one near Fotterall Square sold for about

$3,000 in 2007—and appraise at well over $1 million, with a wide range of prices in between.

Germantown Avenue shows both the dynamism of and the challenges for Philadelphia and other Industrial Metropolises. Full of rich and poor, educated and illiterate, skilled and unskilled, these dense areas include the nation's biggest cities and about 54 million people, making them the third-most-populous community type in Patchwork Nation. How do you craft rules and create systems that work for all the people here? As the nation transitions economically, socially, and politically, how do you bring everyone along together? Can you?

Those are questions for the entire country, of course, but they have particular resonance in the forty-one diverse, complicated Industrial Metropolises. In Philadelphia the employment base is changing more by necessity than by choice. About 25 percent of the jobs in the city are in financial services and real estate, 36 percent in education and health, 18 percent in hospitality and retail, and only 14 percent in manufacturing, construction, wholesale, transportation, and utilities.

"For the first time in our history we've blown out that manufacturing base that would always go down more and come up slower," said Paul Levy, president and CEO of the Philadelphia Center City District. "They were good jobs, but they were globally no longer competitive jobs. I mean, if you want to build a wall around the United States or if you want to build a wall around Detroit, then you can maintain those. But you can't do that."

Beyond economic survival, though, the different neighborhoods in Philly have different agendas and different political allegiances. For the people out in Chestnut Hill or in wealthy Center City, quality-of-life issues like parks and retail options are big. For old-school ethnic white neighborhoods, debate revolves around maintaining the community's traditional character. For poor black areas, the biggest issues are crime and essential services. Education is a concern for everyone. But for some parents the worry is whether their kid can get an education that will get him or her into the University of Pennsylvania. For others it's whether their kid will come home at the end of the day unharmed.

There's been less white flight here than in other big metropolitan areas, and the population is split pretty evenly between white and black, at about 49 percent and 44 percent, respectively. Yet the racial tension is palpable, which compounds the challenge of uniting residents.

"In North Philly we had a black woman married to a white man, and people did nasty things," said Janet Ryder, director of labor participation for the AFL-CIO in Philadelphia. "We had another situation out of Southwest Philly, going towards the airport, same thing. They're putting graffiti on the houses. They threw something through the window. . . . So here you are in the twenty-first century, and you still see this kind of narrow-minded bullshit going on."

Ryder, who grew up in Philadelphia and still lives and works there, acknowledges that the city has become more diverse and tolerant since she was a child, in the fifties. But scan the headlines of recent Philly newspapers and you will discover a handful of stories about racial incidents—disputes about kicking people out of a pool or a club or police discrimination.

As the city's economic situation grew dire in the late-2000s recession, the city announced plans to close eleven library branches in less-wealthy neighborhoods, based on their low usage. The situation quickly blew up into a major fight, with the plan attacked as an assault on the city's poor. Those libraries' book-lending statistics may have been lower, their patrons said, but they provided a vital service for children as an after-school sanctuary. In the end the city was stopped by the courts.

Even with the closures Philadelphia would have had more libraries per capita than any other big city in the United States. Like many older Industrial Metropolises, Philly has a service system designed for its past, when it was wealthier and more populous. Today there are certainly bigger challenges on the horizon than choosing which library branches to close, but the incident shows how difficult it can be to manage a city of neighborhoods, each with its own population, power bases, and goals.

THE UNMANAGEABLE CITY?

Industrial Metropolises aren't all like Philadelphia County, which holds only the city of Philadelphia. Many, such as Wayne County, Michigan, or Cook County, Illinois, contain a major city as well as closed-in, old-money suburbs—in these cases Detroit and Chicago and such attendant areas as Grosse Pointe and the North Shore. That alters the demographics and raises the median income of those who live there, but it also underscores the disparities within this community type. The poverty rate in these counties, 11 percent, matches the national county average, but 8 percent of the households in Industrial Metropolises earned more than $125,000 annually. The national county average for that income level is only 3 percent.

That income difference isn't independent of race. The national county average shows a big difference between median incomes in black and white households: $28,000 for blacks versus $38,000 for whites. In Industrial Metropolises the gap is even wider: $33,000 for blacks versus $51,000 for whites. Because of that inequality, racial tensions tend to be heightened in these places, as they are in Philadelphia.

These counties are 67 percent white, while the national county average is 87 percent. They are also 25 percent African American, 15 percent Hispanic, and 6 percent Asian, far exceeding the national county averages of 9 percent, 7.5 percent, and 1 percent, respectively. Minority Central counties have more African Americans and Immigration Nation counties have more Hispanics, but the Industrial Metropolis is without question the most diverse community type in the Patchwork Nation.

That diversity extends to employment—most Industrial Metropolises aren't actually that industrial anymore, with the moniker referring mainly to a storied past. Only 11 percent of the jobs in these places are in manufacturing; nationally the number is 15 percent. The number of people holding professional or executive jobs in these counties, also 11 percent, is more than twice the national county average of 5 percent. Service-sector jobs, meanwhile, sit right at the national county average of 30 percent.

Industrial Metropolis counties often house multiple colleges and universities within their borders, and because of that there's a larger segment of the population seeking postsecondary education here than in the average U.S. county. A quarter of the adults in Industrial Metropolis communities are enrolled in college versus the national average of 16 percent. But the illiteracy rate here is sky-high, too. In Philadelphia it's 24 percent; in Chicago, 37 percent are illiterate; in Detroit, close to 50 percent.

Even with those stark contrasts, there's one way in which people in Industrial Metropolises are consistently on the same page: voting in presidential elections. This is landslide Democratic territory. Al Gore won the Industrial Metropolis communities by 29 percentage points in 2000. John Kerry took the counties by 27 percentage points in 2004. Barack Obama won them by an even larger margin, 37 percentage points, in 2008.

But that come-together moment every four years can't mask the day-to-day tensions in a lot of these places. In Philadelphia current mayor Michael Nutter gained election by running as the candidate of no one—not of the unions or the ministers, not of the black establishment, and certainly not of the ethnic whites. His constituency was primarily younger, wealthier, self-identifyingly post-racial Philadelphians. Other candidates split the ethnic votes, leaving Nutter to arrive in office to great fanfare in

2008. A respected African American city councilman, he was steeped in the local political scene—yet he'd also remained above it all.

"There was so much hope for Nutter because he wasn't owned by the unions, right? And he basically was a dark horse so we thought all these old allegiances would be moot, right?" said Sandy Shea, the opinion editor of the *Philadelphia Daily News.*

But that lack of a traditional political base has arguably been a problem, too. There was the library fracas. When Nutter needed the unions to make cuts to bring the city's budget in line, they refused to work with him. When he proposed a hike in property and sales taxes, 86 percent of residents opposed it.[22]

"Everybody's pissed at him," one city political insider told me anonymously. Others, including supporters of Nutter, asked me to turn off my recorder when they spoke about the current political climate.

The message was clear: The situation in Philadelphia was bad and getting worse.

How much that was due to Nutter, or due to the awful economic situation when he arrived in office, or due to an Industrial Metropolis's inherent resistance to unification is hard to say. "The thinking was, *Let's see what happens in the city if you get somebody who's nobody's man*," Shea told me. "But then you get slapped with a meltdown recession and I don't know. I mean, this is why it's hard to really pinpoint."

When I brought up the idea that the city might have irreparable structural problems—high poverty, high illiteracy—the political insiders I talked to strongly disagreed. After all, others have succeeded in other places.

"I think there have been a set of mayors who have proved that big cities are governable. I really do believe that," said the Center City District's Levy. "There was a series of books called *The Ungovernable City* or something like that, but that was in the seventies. And so it's incredibly hard, but it is not undoable."

John Saler, chairman of the law firm Stradley and Ronon's Government and Public Affairs Practice Group, said that Philadelphia's "structural problems" are really the way its municipal unions refuse to change how pensions are funded. Change the rules there, and the city will be on its way. A big supporter of Nutter's, Saler maintains that the city can be successfully managed—and that Nutter will do it.

When asked to describe how he might, both Saler and Levy cited a list of mayors of other big cities—Richard Daley in Chicago, Gavin Newsom in San Francisco. But they focused on New York City Mayor Michael Bloomberg.

He's a "folk hero at this point," said Saler. Levy called Bloomberg a man of "just extraordinary self-confidence who doesn't need to prove himself in the public arena."

MIDDLE-CHILD SYNDROME

It's hardly a surprise that Bloomberg is venerated in Philadelphia. New York weighs heavily on the minds of people in Philly. So does their southerly neighbor of Washington, D.C. Along the Amtrak corridor Philadelphia is the middle child. It's not the hub of finance and media that likes to think of itself as capital of the world. It's not the center of political power with its real designation as capital of the United States. It's not even Boston, with its prestigious universities and its image as capital of New England.

Philadelphia is a place that people pass by or over to get to one of those other places. If it were located anywhere else in the country, the sixth-largest city in the United States and its 1.4 million people would be a confident cultural force. But trapped between New York and Washington, Philadelphia suffers from a severe inferiority complex. Mention it to nearly anyone who knows the city and you'll get a knowing look or a nod or a story.

"Philadelphia is home to the most self-hating, self-loathing group of people in the world," said one native who insisted that his name not be revealed. "I love this city, don't get me wrong. It is beautiful. It has all the attributes. But . . . Philadelphians are only proud of Philadelphia if you're a New Yorker. They're not to each other. It's sort of like the Jews and the Irish or the Italians. 'You call me a what?' And blacks, too. It's like, 'I can call myself whatever I want. But you don't call me that.' That's the way Philadelphia is."

When we first visited Philadelphia, Mayor Nutter was about to take office. There was much excitement that the city was finally getting ready to emerge from the shadows of its East Coast neighbors. Several people used the phrase "world-class city" to describe where Philly was headed.

Of course, the recession came along just in time to derail that ambition—which might have been based on an unrealistic comparison anyway. The two big Industrial Metropolises near Philadelphia are exceptional. New York, because of its positions in finance and media and the arts, is truly unique, with a huge number of high-paying jobs to help fill city coffers with tax money. And Washington is a company town that will never lose its company. Its economy is likely only to grow in coming years.

For the majority of Industrial Metropolises the future will probably be more like Philadelphia's: a mixed bag of some good news and quite a bit of bad, with a lot of retrenchment and restructuring. The decline of American manufacturing has left these places large populations of under-skilled, undereducated people who don't really have a way to climb out of their circumstances. And in the big cities those populations are placed into fairly crowded circumstances, meaning that the problems feed on themselves. A few homes or streets of low wages and low skill sets is one thing. Strings of neighborhoods full of those kinds of homes or streets is another.

"Fixing those problems is going to take a while to do, but you basically unite or fold in education with job education," Saler told me. "And what I mean by that is not every kid out there is going to Princeton. Not every kid is going to Penn State. There are a lot of kids out there that need good training in the trades. . . . It is very long-term. And they've been trying to do it for a long time already."

Like those in other big cities, Philadelphia public schools have had some small successes—a handful are in the top fifty statewide.[23] But Philadelphia schools score poorly overall on the standardized Pennsylvania System of School Assessment. In 2009 only 32 percent of eleventh-grade students in Philly met or exceeded PSSA standards in math. Only 38 percent met or exceeded standards in reading. Only 15 percent met or exceeded standards in science.[24] Some individual schools in the city did better than those averages, of course. But many also did worse, and on the whole Philadelphia's scores trailed state averages by double digits. This is after decades of trying to right the listing ship of big-city schools.

And the task of improving the schools and the neighborhoods around them isn't getting any easier. Most of America's big cities are strapped for cash, and the federal government's debt is stacking up. At the same time, good jobs for those without good educations are getting harder to find. Manufacturing is going away and service jobs usually don't pay as well. Even if the public schools do switch their mission to trade training for some students, which trades? In a rapidly changing world, trade training will require frequent updating, which will require frequent investing—which brings things right back to . . . money.

What will be the economic drivers for the future Industrial Metropolis? White-collar jobs in regional and state headquarters? Will there be enough of them? What about the people who can't work those jobs? These are questions with no easy answers.

Things won't be all bad in Industrial Metropolis communities in the coming years, of course. There is that fraction of their population that not only likes city life but also can afford it on all levels—private schools, lots of square footage in relatively crime-free, well-serviced neighborhoods. The Industrial Metropolises display a compacted version of the worsening socioeconomic stratification that has afflicted the country as a whole. In 2005 the richest 300,000 Americans earned as much as the poorest 150 million, with an average income almost 450 times higher than their less prosperous counterparts. In 1980 the gap between richest and poorest was only about half that.[25]

If the future path of the United States is forked, with a few on the high road and a large number of people on the low road, the Industrial Metropolises already have a foot on it. Much may be learned from seeing how they navigate it.

MILITARY BASTIONS:
HOPKINSVILLE, KENTUCKY

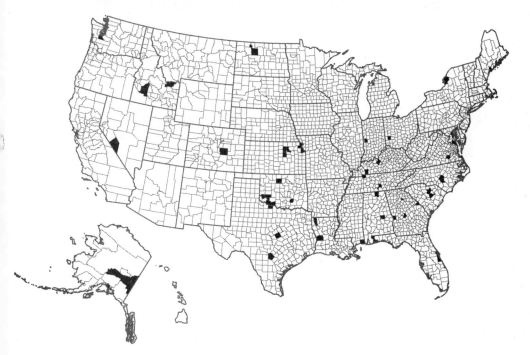

FROM COMBINES TO COMBAT READINESS

There was a time when the residents of Hopkinsville, Kentucky, didn't have much use for the hundred-thousand-acre neighbor now known as Fort Campbell—or, as the U.S. Army puts it, "the nation's premier power projection platform."[26] In the early twentieth century the city of ten thousand or so was an agricultural trade hub, a well-traversed stop on the Louisville & Nashville Railroad, and the seat of Christian County, which boasted seven banks, two colleges, and a newly established foundation determined to bring industrial manufacturing to the land of dark tobacco.

So when the state-line-straddling base opened, in 1942, the soldiers of what was then Camp Campbell were looked upon as troublesome interlopers. They were young men from elsewhere who were out of step with the

Figure 7

MILITARY BASTIONS

a) PERCENTAGE OF PRESIDENTIAL VOTE OVER TIME

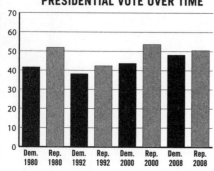

b) PERCENTAGE OF AGE DISTRIBUTION DATA

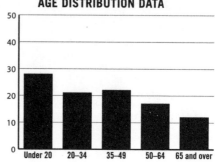

c) PERCENTAGE OF RACE/ETHNIC BREAKDOWN

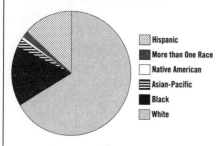

- Hispanic
- More than One Race
- Native American
- Asian-Pacific
- Black
- White

d) PERCENTAGE OF INCOME DISTRIBUTION DATA

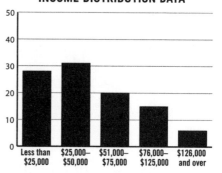

e) PERCENTAGE OF IMMIGRATION OVER TIME

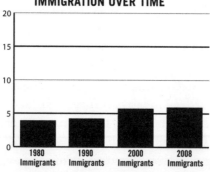

local community, easy marks for traffic tickets and other civic-coffer-padding infractions—and worse.

"You have to understand, this was a rural, isolated community up until 1942. A lot of fathers didn't want their daughters dating the soldier boys," Hopkinsville historian William Turner said. "It came to a head in 1952, when there were a number of incidents with soldiers being beaten by policemen for no real logical reason. And that led the military leadership to declare Hopkinsville off-limits for the troops for a few weeks."

That was then.

Today it's nearly impossible to imagine a bright future for Christian County without the base and the soldiers stationed there, who at thirty thousand strong roughly match the population of Hopkinsville itself. The passenger trains stopped coming long ago, replaced by massive CSX Transportation freight haulers that rumble through town without stopping. Bethel Woman's College is closed. Christian County's manufacturing, much of it tied to the auto industry, has dried up. There's still agriculture here—tobacco, of course, as well as wheat and corn—but not enough money-making around it to keep the area advancing economically. The median household income for the county is less than $34,000, beneath the national county average.

The murals in the city's Founder's Square area now serve mainly as a reminder of the businesses that have closed or moved away: the Hopkinsville Hoppers baseball team, 1903–1954; Dalton Brick Ovens, 1880–1950; and a series of downtown retailers, the last of which was shuttered in 1990. The only place in the city center that's reliably bustling is Ferrell's Snappy Service, a tiny greasy spoon specializing in hamburgers, chili, and pecan pie that seemingly the entire population of Hoptown frequents.

The real action is out on "the Strip": the retail shops, gas stations, and chain eateries that line U.S. Route 41, also known as Fort Campbell Boulevard. It's not exactly the Miracle Mile—there are five Waffle Houses on the twenty-five miles of road between Hopkinsville and Clarksville, Tennessee, just to the south of the base. But traffic is always heavy and the restaurants are always busy, especially in the tiny town of Oak Grove, Kentucky, which sits opposite Fort Campbell's main gate.

The home of the 101st Airborne is a giant that sits mostly out of sight to the west. But evidence of its existence is everywhere—in the small blue road signs that say things like GATE 7; in the stores like ATS Tactical Gear, which claims to be OUTFITTING THE WORLD'S FINEST WARRIORS!; and in such boys-will-be-boys businesses as the Cat West Showbar, which offers

TWO-FOR-ONE DANCES for soldiers on Tuesdays, and Jenna's Adult Novel-ties, which advertises a buy-two-videos-get-one-free deal under a WEL-COME HOME TROOPS banner.

Lap dances and adult novelties might not sit well with the culturally conservative residents of a place like Hopkinsville, where John McCain took 60 percent of the presidential vote in 2008 and George W. Bush won 66 percent in 2004. But as the city and Christian County have struggled in recent years, the big base down the road—and all of the business it drums up, morally objectionable and otherwise—has become something of a lifeline. Through the five rounds of base-realignment closures that began in 1988 as a way of streamlining the military, Fort Campbell has been a winner. In the last round, in 2005, it gained a combat brigade of several thousand soldiers. The base is now the third-most-populous army installation in the country, generating billions of dollars in contract work for businesses in neighboring towns.

"Fort Campbell has definitely become more important to the com-munity in a lot of ways, but especially the economy," said Jennifer Brown, editor of the *Kentucky New Era*, the local newspaper. "If we lost a brigade out of the base, it would have a major effect on us here."

If the city just north of the Tennessee border is becoming a twenty-first-century company town, it can rejoice in the fact that the company is growing. Military concerns following the conflicts in Afghanistan and Iraq have centered on the armed forces' being too small, not too large. As the military makes its big bases bigger, Hopkinsville and communities like it will be riding what is one of the surest waves in an unpredictable economy.

SMALL TOWNS, BIG MONEY

There are only fifty-five Military Bastion counties scattered across the country, with a combined population of about 8.4 million people. Not all of these communities are near behemoths like Fort Campbell, but what-ever the bases' size, they and the businesses that service them usually dom-inate the area.

The counties around military installations tend to be a bit more dense than some parts of America, but that's usually because of the base itself, which concentrates soldiers in a relatively small area. Many of the counties are actually quite rural, with a population concentrated just around the base gates. Obviously, bases need land on which their troops can train. But many of the nation's military posts are located in sparsely populated areas because Washington—or, more specifically, constituent-pleasing legislators in Washington—was hoping to develop small-town economies during the base-building boom in the first half of last century, particularly in the 1940s.

The result today is a group of places that are still evolving from small towns into big power-projection complexes, where old-boyishness and insularity survive even in the face of a constant influx of youthful, diverse outsiders. Military installations are magnets for twentysomething men and women, so military personnel, many of whom live off base, make nearby communities a bit younger than average: Only 28 percent of the people who live in Military Bastions are fifty or older. The bases also tend to make Military Bastions more racially diverse than the country as a whole. They are 79 percent white, 16 percent African American, and 7 percent Hispanic. That diversity in part comes with being near military installations that draw soldiers from across the country.

According to the military, racial diversity is a "readiness imperative critical to the success of the current and future Army."[27] But in Hopkinsville and other small towns situated near big bases, multiculturalism isn't always so exalted a concept.

That was made obvious one morning just before the 2008 election at Ferrell's Snappy Service. In the front of the diner, at the seven-seat counter, a row of African American patrons sat trading gossip. In Ferrell's back room, meanwhile, a few of the people who run the city rubbed elbows with local business owners. Every face was white.

When the conversation in the back of the restaurant turned to then senator Barack Obama, the crowd snickered. "I wonder how long before they have a bunch of cars parked all over the lawn," said Russell Holder, a retiree in his mid-seventies who had been coming to Ferrell's for breakfast for fifteen years. "They're going to be serving chitlins at the state dinners."

The assembled mostly smiled and tried to stifle their chuckles. Chuck Henderson, the seventy-something president and general manager of the *New Era* newspaper and a member of the Christian County Military Affairs Committee, shook his head and smiled. "That's Russell," he said indulgently.

When I noted the difference between the front counter and the back room, Henderson nodded. "Yeah," he said with a smile. "Some are friends. Some are county workers. Some are just freeloaders. I mean, you wonder how they get by." After we had talked politics for a bit, he said that I should hear what the people up front thought. He got up and returned with Lorenzo White, a thirty-eight-year-old African American construction worker.

White, who kept his head down while in the back room, repeatedly calling Henderson "Mr. Chuck," clearly felt out of place among so many local bigwigs. He explained that he supported Obama, but that the candidate would have a high hurdle to clear due to racism.

"Is that a problem in Hopkinsville?" I asked.

"Maybe not in this community," he told me. "But in this state race is huge."

The Rev. John Banks, head of the local chapter of the NAACP, was less diplomatic. "It just doesn't change here—not in Hopkinsville. Race relations haven't changed in thirty years," he told me. "You look down there at Clarksville, they've grown. They've changed. Not us. And we're not going to change."

That attitude is typical of Hoptowners, at least in one way: They have a lot of envy for their southern neighbors in Clarksville. There was a time when Hopkinsville was the area's big city. It was surpassed by Clarksville years ago in part because of that town's early willingness to embrace Fort Campbell. It welcomed the young soldiers when they first arrived, and Clarksville still has a better relationship with the base. About three-quarters of the soldiers who live off base live on the Tennessee side of the border. That state also held the advantage of having no state income tax, at least until 2009, when Kentucky passed a law exempting military personnel from taxation.

In 2004 Hopkinsville and Christian County decided that it was high time to reach out to the area's largest employer. So the chamber of commerce launched Operation Left Turn, a promotional campaign that asks soldiers to make the left out of the Fort Campbell's main gate into Christian County, rather than the right into Montgomery County, Tennessee.

Two-thirds of Fort Campbell personnel live off base. Once only about 13 percent of those lived in Christian County. Now about 25 percent do.

"You're talking a percent increase in military living off-post in Christian County that represents about thirteen hundred households," said Carter Hendricks, senior vice president of the Hopkinsville–Christian County Chamber of Commerce. "Times 2.9 is their average household size. So your population has just gone through the roof, and your per capita's probably come up because they're probably earning good money. So it's just a significant impact. So those are some of the ways we look at Fort Campbell's impact."

Any sizable modern military post—particularly a monster like Fort Campbell—has a profound economic influence on the surrounding community, and it goes beyond retail strips or off-base housing. Government money, such as the $110 million in stimulus funds Fort Campbell scored in 2009, occasionally falls from the sky. And large bases have a voracious need for contractors to help maintain and expand their facilities, which contributes significantly to the health of local economies. The median household income in Military Bastion counties is about $39,000, which beats the national median by some $2,000. The poverty rate in Military Bastions is slightly lower than the national rate, too—10 percent compared to 11.

About 7 percent of the people who live in Military Bastions typically work for the armed forces, compared with less than 1 percent nationally. But that number vastly understates the economic power the bases wield in these communities. "It's approximately $2 billion of contract work that happens at Fort Campbell annually, give or take," Hendricks noted. "And so we look at it."

And go after it. Two billion dollars is a lot of money anywhere, but in a place like Hopkinsville, where the median household income lags behind that of other Military Bastions by about $5,000, all that mowing and painting and electrical work are a means of economic survival. "As we look to the next fifteen to twenty years, or further out," said Hendricks, "as long as Fort Campbell maintains a strong position, as long as it's a growing installation or the installation that's not at least losing personnel, then we have always the stability on our regional economy."

WHEN THE COMPANY TOWN LOSES A FEW COMPANIES

There are, of course, some downsides to relying too heavily on the base down the road for Hoptown—and for any Military Bastion. Some company towns worry about layoffs; Hopkinsville and places like it worry about deployments. What the Defense Base Closure and Realignment Commission can giveth, war in Iraq or Afghanistan can taketh away.

From the 2003 buildup to Operation Iraqi Freedom until 2009, Christian County and the area around Fort Campbell watched as thousands of soldiers shipped out. At one point more than twenty thousand troops went to Iraq and Afghanistan, taking a good portion of the local economy with them. And military personnel stationed overseas aren't the only ones who aren't spending money at home. The families left behind, not knowing what the future might hold, make for particularly cautious consumers. The economic impact can be dramatic, particularly in the case of drawn-out conflicts like the one in Iraq.

"We got hit with the double whammy of the car business was marginal to start with, then fall comes along and people start to worry—and then we're in the midst of an eighteen-month deployment when the young people who buy lots of cars are gone or going," said Chuck Henderson, whose newspaper publishes a special edition for the base, the *Fort Campbell Courier.*

"The deployments just really rip the heart right out of ya. This community and the Clarksville community," Henderson explained. "In our case, our newspaper, I will tell you, we get hit from a down economy and then you put a deployment on top of that. And they don't much more than get back from a deployment and they start to get re-sent. . . . What's the natural reaction of a retailer? They stop promoting because [the troops] are all leaving."

You hear a lot about the new year-and-a-half deployments in Hoptown. The city was used to seeing its soldiers leave for a year at a time, but the longer tours, implemented in part because there are fewer soldiers in the new military and the operations being carried out overseas in the 2000s involve long-term occupations, have meant changes for the area. Some families and loved ones of the troops left town, having decided that they would rather be with other family members elsewhere than alone near the base during those anxiety-filled eighteen months. As the global war against terrorism continues and the military tries to do more with less, longer and more deployments will likely become more common.

Still, Fort Campbell offers Hopkinsville plenty of deployment-proof economic benefits. When the global recession hit hard in the late 2000s, Chrysler and General Motors needed to declare bankruptcy, but government work remained steady. "You know, those people on the base . . . have no reason to have felt the recession," Henderson said. "Their paychecks are still coming. Their combat pay is still coming. Their re-enlistment bonuses are still coming. Their wives, if they work . . . still have jobs at banks or wherever they're working part-time, I think. So that has helped, will continue to help."

The trade-off for Hopkinsville and other Military Bastions is short-term uncertainty for long-term stability. And despite what the Reverend Banks believes, Hopkinsville will probably change a good deal as it becomes more enmeshed with Fort Campbell. It was Fort Campbell's presence that led local Austin Peay State University to build a School of Technology and Public Management, which in part led the Hemlock Semiconductor Group to site a $1.2 billion polycrystalline-silicon-production facility in Clarksville. One thousand or so jobs will arrive with the plant, which opens in 2012 and will provide a key raw material for solar power generation. That in turn could lead to similar new ventures tied to Fort Campbell and, perhaps, to Hopkinsville.

One could imagine Hopkinsville and other evolving Military Bastions becoming high-tech communities built around the applied sciences and other military contracting. This is already the norm near some bases.

In 1997 a former U.S. Navy SEAL and a SEAL instructor grew dissatisfied with the Navy's training facilities and opened a private complex in North Carolina, not far from the numerous military installations in the Hampton Roads area of Virginia. That company, now called Xe, is better known by its original name of Blackwater USA—and is infamous for its involvement in several scandals during the Iraq War, including incidents in which its personnel allegedly fired upon civilians and smuggled prohibited weapons into the county in sacks of dog food.[28] But it still trains forty thousand people a year and provides hundreds of security contractors to the U.S. military.

In San Diego, near another Navy base, physicist Gene Ray founded Titan, a company that originally set out to improve missile-defense technology through the use of lasers. Purchased by the military contractor L-3 in 2005, Titan now specializes in providing communications technologies for the military and intelligence communities. It employs ten thousand people.

With an influx of dollars and people, Military Bastions could well become a Republican-leaning version of our Campus and Careers communities. Unlike the people attracted to a life in academia, those in the world of military contracting tend to hold more conservative views—particularly around politics and national defense. The places where they live could easily become the homes of a rejuvenated Republican Party, particularly if military issues play a role in coming elections.

In any case, what's left of the insular, old-time ways of Military Bastions communities will dissolve, as long as they continue to grow.

When leaders in Hopkinsville look down the road and see Clarksville's relationship with Fort Campbell, they see a model of the future. If they succeed with Operation Left Turn and other efforts to cozy up to the base, Hoptown will likely be a very different place in ten years' time: wealthier, better educated, and more defined than ever by the military culture it once shunned.

MINORITY CENTRAL: BATON ROUGE, LOUISIANA

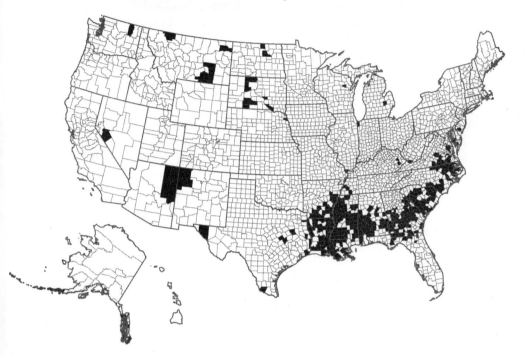

A TALE OF TWO CITIES

The Wine Loft in downtown Baton Rouge, Louisiana, is the kind of spot that attracts the young and climbing. It's dimly lit, with high ceilings and exposed brick and ductwork—the essence of minimalist, upscale chic. The booths in the back are surrounded by coarsely woven curtains that allow people to see without being seen. Even on a Tuesday night, ambient music burbled just below the conversation of a well-dressed crowd.

"We've been drinking sake," said a dapper young man as he flipped his hair back. He had led a group of six in the door and up to the bar. "What do you have like that—but with bubbles?"

He fit right in—and not just because he was out to have a good time

Figure 8

MINORITY CENTRAL

a) PERCENTAGE OF PRESIDENTIAL VOTE OVER TIME

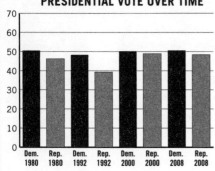

b) PERCENTAGE OF AGE DISTRIBUTION DATA

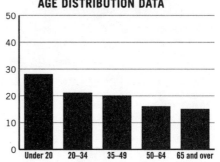

c) PERCENTAGE OF RACE/ETHNIC BREAKDOWN

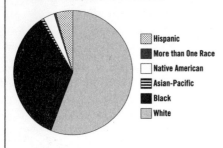

Hispanic
More than One Race
Native American
Asian-Pacific
Black
White

d) PERCENTAGE OF INCOME DISTRIBUTION DATA

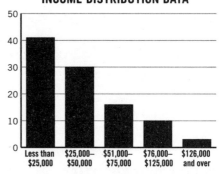

e) PERCENTAGE OF IMMIGRATION OVER TIME

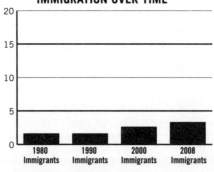

and spend some money. On this particular night everyone in the bar at 10:30 P.M. was white. Not just the man who wanted the bubbly sake, but also the couples at the end of the bar in jackets and short dresses and the waitress buzzing among the tables in an impossibly tight-fitting push-up top.

Just around the corner at the M Bar, the scene was very different, even if the venue is much the same.

The M Bar's crowd is young and climbing. Its brickwork is exposed. Its chic is minimalist and upscale. A set of low upholstered chairs runs along one side of the place; basic black stools line the other. On Tuesday at 11 P.M., as a DJ spun hip-hop near the bar, most of the seats were occupied by men in jackets and women in short dresses.

But the M Bar isn't the Wine Loft, and the main difference isn't that martinis are the house specialty. Here, everyone is black.

It's not surprising that there are such things as "white bars" and "black bars" in a city like Baton Rouge. After all, this is a town that, in 1953, held its own bus boycott almost three years before the more famous one in Montgomery, Alabama. The nation's first mass boycott challenging the Jim Crow South, it managed after just five days to change a city ordinance about where blacks could sit on the buses—although there were still restrictions.

What's surprising is that different worlds are living side by side in this metropolis of 227,000 that is 53 percent white and 44 percent black. The Wine Loft and the M Bar aren't on opposite ends of town or in different neighborhoods; they are a mere 150 feet apart. But they might as well be on different planets. In the state capital of Louisiana and the seat of East Baton Rouge Parish, the racial divide is so deep that not one white resident decided to stroll around the corner for a martini. And not one black resident chose to walk two-tenths of a mile for a glass of wine.

That's the story of Baton Rouge and the nation's other Minority Central communities: People of different races walk by one another on the street living in separate realities. For the most part, the white residents control these communities—the businesses, the politics—while the blacks are at the bottom of the social ladder. Most of these places are in the South, but there are also some Minority Central communities out West, counties that are primarily places with large Native American populations. Durham County, North Carolina; Jefferson Davis County, Mississippi; and Navajo County, Arizona, are all Minority Central communities.

Spend just a little time in Baton Rouge and it's impossible to ignore the fact that there are two distinct cultures coexisting around you. Sit on a street on a weekday and you'll see clutches of people of the same race going for coffee. Locals describe the city as divided geographically into white South Baton Rouge and black North Baton Rouge. There is a chamber of commerce and a black chamber of commerce. There are even two institutes of higher learning in town: predominantly white Louisiana State University in the south and Southern University, a historically black college, on the city's northern side.

Pat Felder, who sits on several boards and is very much a part of white, establishment Baton Rouge, told me that the goal of the city should be to "find a comfort zone with our racial divide." She recalled how she took a black acquaintance to lunch to talk to her about the problem.

"I said, 'If I were just to show up one Sunday morning at the door of your church, would I be welcomed? Would I feel comfortable? Would I think that you really wanted me there?' And she said, 'Probably not.' I said, 'But on the other hand, I can assure you if you show up at my church on any Sunday morning, and the person standing outside that's always there to greet is going to welcome you. They're going to say, "Please come in. Let me introduce you around."'"

That might happen, of course. But the question is, How would Felder's friend feel in that church? "Would I be welcomed?" and "Would I feel comfortable?" are very different questions. And many people in town see no contradiction in answering yes to the first and no to the second.

Cornelius Lewis, the black president of Gulf Coast BIDCO, a firm that provides money to small businesses, sees the divide as just part of the way things are in Baton Rouge. Lewis, who was born and raised in New Orleans, was taken aback when he first arrived in the capital, in the 1980s. The community was still dealing with race issues that seemed to be ancient history in the Big Easy. But after decades of living in Baton Rouge he's come to see things differently.

"You know, there are many whites, as well as many blacks, in this community that choose not to socialize or associate with the others for whatever reason. They're more comfortable," he said. "I think there's an element of fear. I think there's an element of the unknown. And they just choose not to. They're very comfortable being on their own.

"And I don't necessarily think there's anything wrong with that," he added.

The test, he suggested, is what racial division does to the individual. "If it stifles a person's movement or mobility because of this deep-down, deeply rooted disgust or dislike for another person, that's . . . pretty bad. But if I choose not to go to the Wine Loft, because I just don't feel comfortable there or whatever, then I won't go."

CLASS DIFFERENCES

Whites make up about 57 percent of the average Minority Central community; blacks, about 38 percent. But beyond proximity, not a lot unites the two groups. Indeed, looking at the statistics that define Minority Central communities is best done by breaking the numbers into separate racial categories.

For instance, the aggregate numbers indicate that the 13.5 million people who live here struggle financially. With a median household income of about $30,000, Minority Central communities are the poorest in the nation. Almost 20 percent of the families in them live in poverty.

But look at that first statistic by race. White households have a median income of about $36,000, close to the national average of around $37,000. Meanwhile, black households have a median income of only about $20,000. The only place where blacks have a lower median household income is rural, agricultural Tractor Country—and there aren't many blacks living there.

Minority Central communities are not built for the future economy. They also have a perpetually high unemployment rate and a lower than average number of residents enrolled in college. They rely more heavily than the average community on the waning manufacturing sector, which accounts for 18 percent of their jobs.

That last fact is evident looking at Baton Rouge's riverfront. Built along the Mississippi, it has been developed with an eye more toward utility than beauty. Getting to the water involves making it past the train tracks that run along the river, and the concrete steps on the bank offer little more than a view of the tugs and barges of a working port.

Like much of Louisiana, the city has done well in recent years thanks to the petrochemical giants that drill and refine down in the gulf. Every time you see a spike in your cost per tank, a little of that money floats its way into the parish of East Baton Rouge. And the greater Baton Rouge area was a surprise winner in the devastation that was Hurricane Katrina. When New Orleans was submerged, in 2005, a lot of people fled to the next big city along Interstate 10 West to make a new home. That influx of residents, who bought up the area's housing stock just as many thought the market was becoming glutted, helped Baton Rouge avoid many of the early pains of the late-2000s recession.

In some ways Baton Rouge is a less than perfect fit for the Minority Central category. Because it's a state capital, there are a lot of secure government jobs, but unlike the unreformed Louisiana of Huey Long's era, not just anyone can get one. The median household income in East Baton Rouge Parish was about $54,000 in 2007, much better than in Minority Central communities as a whole. But again, break that number down by race. White families in the parish brought in about $81,000 annually, while black families brought in less than $33,000. Even two average black families putting their incomes together could not equal what an average white family earned.

"We're not in the sixties, whereby I may stay on my side of the street and you stay on your side and we throw rocks at each other," said John R. Smith, community affairs director, at the Hollywood Casino in town. "But I still stay on my side of the street, and you still stay on your side of the street. We just don't throw rocks at each other. There's not that hostility, but there is the divide."

In a conference room in Southern's J.S. Clark Administration Building, Ed Pratt, a former reporter for Baton Rouge's *Advocate* newspaper, sat across from Smith and nodded. "Back during the mayor's race, a guy got up and they had a forum up here," he recalled. "And it was one of the greatest statements that anyone said. This old guy got up and said, 'You're not cutting any ribbons in our part of town.' And if you look around, the roads are being fixed, are being widened in South Baton Rouge."

Looking around does reveal a sometimes startling north/south divide, perhaps no more so than in a comparison between Southern and LSU. Southern's Scotlandville neighborhood is marked by poverty, dotted by boarded-up windows and beat-down machine shops, cheap fast-food franchises and even cheaper convenience stores. The campus sits next to a scrap-metal yard and is bounded by railroad tracks. It has a distinct lack of the big, verdant spaces that the word "university" conjures in the mind's eye.

But drive twenty minutes down the banks of the Mississippi and you'll find that ideal vividly on display at LSU. There the students jog around University Lake and play Frisbee on the immense Parade Grounds. The university golf course is nearby. And just off campus is a selection of real restaurants and bars offering such college-student mainstays as wings, pizza, and by-the-pitcher beer.

Pratt is assistant to the chancellor for media relations at Southern, and he can't help but take the disparity a bit personally. People, from the state government to the local businesses, treat the schools differently, he said—and it comes down to race.

"There's a street term—'You talk out of both sides of your mouth.' You say, 'We need these things, these schools. We got to have it.' But if it's black, 'We don't know.' Somehow or way it's inferior. It's something broken with it. It's tarnished," he said, shaking his head. "Case in point: Cox Communications has its name on a big ol' building down at LSU for the athletes. Not us. . . . And then you see other folk who are giving millions of dollars to LSU. You don't give us a million. . . . And the state is not going to be complete, and the city for sure is not going to be successful without bringing in the university."

Pratt acknowledges that LSU is the flagship of the state's university system. And that it's about twice as large as Southern in terms of enrollment. He doesn't expect things to be even. He just wonders if the differences have to be so stark.

Those sorts of differences assert themselves early in Baton Rouge. There are two K–12 school systems in East Baton Rouge Parish: a public, largely black system and a private, mostly white one. There are forty-four thousand kids in the East Baton Rouge Parish Schools System, 83 percent of them black. Many of them are struggling. In 2007 fewer than 60 percent of fourth and eighth graders were able to pass standardized Louisiana Education Assessment Program tests in English and math. In 2006 the dropout rate from grades nine through twelve was about 10 percent. More than 80 percent of students in the schools qualify for free or reduced-price lunch.

Better-off students, the majority of whom are white, have largely abandoned the public system, attending instead the dozens of private and parochial schools in the area. Enrollment at those institutions took off in the 1980s, after desegregation orders came down from the U.S. Justice Department. In 1980, the students in the East Baton Rouge schools were 60 percent white—that number is now about 10 percent. Today, in a city where the public schools are struggling immensely, you have schools like Runnels, a well-known private institution that proudly trumpets how its students regularly beat the state and national average ACT scores by several points. You have Episcopal High School, where well over 50 percent of the graduating class scored over 600 on the SATs. And a host of Catholic schools promising small class sizes and serious instruction: St. George, St. Aloysius, St. Thomas More.

What it all means is that the difference between black and white in Baton Rouge—of income, of opportunity—is drilled into the heads of those who live there as they grow up until it becomes just another part of life for them as adults. Many living here aren't sure whether it's a good thing, a bad thing, or simply the way things are.

Sitting in the Camelot Club, a dark wood, old-money hideaway high above downtown Baton Rouge, Pat Felder downplayed the power that such long-term conditioning might have over Baton Rouge's underprivileged. "Okay, I do not think that we need to continue to berate this issue [of slavery]," she said. "There were a lot of other people that had a lot of problems. They were not in maybe shackles but they were economically shackled. When the Irish came over here, you know, when the Italians came. So we're gonna need to get over it. If we could just eliminate that mind-set from the conversation."

Felder knows that her "get over it" comments are "easy for me to say." But she still maintains that it's the desire of blacks in the city to remain separate from whites that creates the divide. The strange thing about Baton Rouge is that there are plenty of blacks here who wouldn't necessarily disagree with her.

THE FUTURE IS BLACK AND WHITE

A lifelong Baton Rouge resident, Maxine Crump was the first black woman to live in the LSU dorms and the first black anchorwoman at WAFB-TV, a local CBS affiliate. Now in her sixties and project manager for a statewide microfinancing group, she marvels at how little Baton Rouge has changed.

"The lines have not blurred. I think blacks who've assimilated into the white culture can go to places that whites go to and feel totally comfortable. I'm one of those," she said. "Whites who feel totally comfortable with African American culture come to African American places. But there's not a blending of the culture."

That kind of hard, deep divide makes it challenging for Minority Central communities like Baton Rouge to come to a consensus on a host of issues—everything from education to poverty-relief programs—and that's doubly true in a time of tighter resources. Of all the Patchwork Nation's community types, Minority Central locales tend to be the most chronically split in electoral politics. In 2000, even with the first African American major-party presidential nominee in history and a high turnout by black voters, the vote in these places hardly changed at all. John McCain did about two percentage points worse than George W. Bush did in 2004; Barack Obama did about two percentage points better than John Kerry. Obama won Minority Central communities by a slim 1 percent—the same percentage by which Al Gore won them in 2000.

There are a range of issues—tax policy, business regulations, health care—that will indirectly and directly lead into discussions of race and class in America. In Minority Central communities class and income are inseparable from race. If the people who live in these places are unable to bridge their divide and engage one another in a more open way, it's easy to imagine them stumbling through the next decade enacting half measures to deal with problems as tensions rise. The people on both sides of the street who have "stopped throwing rocks at each other" may find reason anew to pick up stones.

That's not to suggest a brewing race war. But places like these could very well take steps backward. The relative prosperity of the past four decades has made it easier for people to live in different worlds and get along by essentially ignoring one another. In the coming years, if economic circumstances get tighter, those worlds will likely be forced to face each other directly. How they handle that new engagement will determine a lot about where they are headed.

What do you do, for instance, about the Baton Rouge public schools? The city's betterment at least to some extent relies on educating the poor and less fortunate, who are largely black. They need education and skills to climb out of their current economic situation. If they don't get it, they will need city, state, and federal aid. But the part of the city that has the resources to help the schools, which is mostly white, has for the most part opted out of the system. Raising taxes or channeling city or state money that could go elsewhere into the schools will not be an easy sell in South Baton Rouge.

Coming to an agreement on major issues is even more difficult in the few Minority Central counties in the West, where the divide is between whites and Native Americans. Those two populations technically do live in separate nations, and they often see the world through very different eyes. The challenge in all Minority Central counties is going to be convincing the two cultures that their fates are indeed connected. That won't be easy.

Even Crump, who helped break down the color barrier at LSU, is pessimistic about how much Baton Rouge can actually change in the coming years as far as race is concerned—even among the younger generation often touted as colorblind. "Like my nephews, for example. I have a nephew who's twenty and one who, I think, is twenty-five, and one who's thirteen, and they don't have friends who are white," she said. "When they were little boys they did, but they don't now." In Baton Rouge, that's the way it's always been.

MONIED BURBS:
LOS ALAMOS, NEW MEXICO

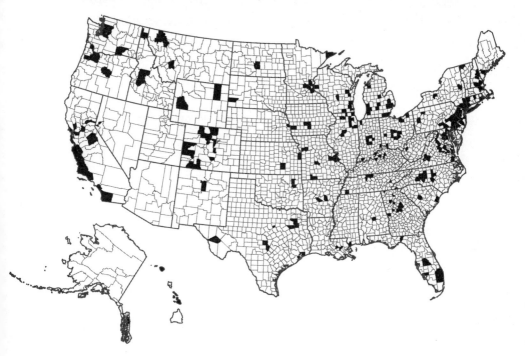

THE HIGH LIFE

For a certain type of person, Los Alamos, New Mexico, might seem almost too good to be true. The streets are clean, wide, and safe. The public schools are excellent, with more than 80 percent of Los Alamos High School grads going on to college.[29] And the high-desert views from nearly anywhere on the 7,200 feet above sea level are breathtaking. The ochre landscape surrounding the mesa-situated seat of Los Alamos County contains not only the centuries-old Native American cliff dwellings of Bandelier National Monument, but also the hiker- and cross-country-skier-ready natural areas of the Santa Fe National Forest and the Valles Caldera National Preserve.

In other words, those pursuing a family-friendly, outdoorsy lifestyle

Figure 9

MONIED BURBS

a) PERCENTAGE OF PRESIDENTIAL VOTE OVER TIME

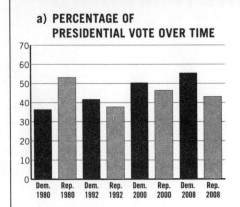

b) PERCENTAGE OF AGE DISTRIBUTION DATA

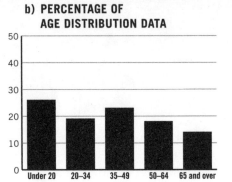

c) PERCENTAGE OF RACE/ETHNIC BREAKDOWN

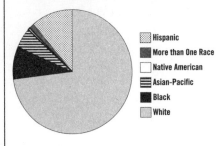

Hispanic
More than One Race
Native American
Asian-Pacific
Black
White

d) PERCENTAGE OF INCOME DISTRIBUTION DATA

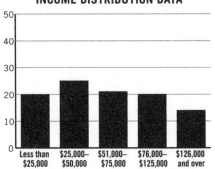

e) PERCENTAGE OF IMMIGRATION OVER TIME

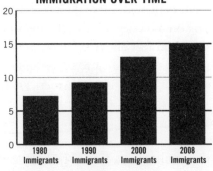

could do much worse. Los Alamos has a population of only twelve thousand, with about eighteen thousand in the surrounding county, so it has a small-town quality in addition to a spectacular setting and a full range of open-air activities. People in the coffee shops here don't just sit and read; they say hi to friends and neighbors who pass through or sit down for a longer chat. Plus, there's reasonably priced housing stock and still plenty to do when summer thunderstorms muddy the hiking trails. Santa Fe, the state's capital, and its celebrated arts scene are only thirty minutes down the highway, and without even getting in the car you can choose among visiting an aquatic center, an ice rink, and a science museum that features life-sized models of Fat Man and Little Boy.

The last of those attractions is a somewhat chilling reminder of the unusual history of Los Alamos. Born of the bomb, it was a nuclear-weapons research-and-development center off-limits to the general public until after World War II. But when Manhattan Project Scientific Director J. Robert Oppenheimer selected this isolated yet accessible site for the Los Alamos National Laboratory, he established what would become a very familiar type of community: the Monied Burbs. These 286 counties are the most populous of our twelve community types, with a combined population of some 69 million, which means they're what many people think of as everyday America. Denser than anything in the Patchwork Nation but the Industrial Metropolises, the often sprawling Burbs are full of well-off and well-educated residents who demand high-end amenities.

"There are a lot of people up here that aren't scientists, but the scientific community demands and makes sure the kids don't just have opportunities, but also take advantage of opportunities, from the day they're born 'til they get through postgraduate," Bill Enloe, chairman and CEO of Los Alamos National Bank, told me.

Yes, postgraduate. More than a third of the people who live in Los Alamos County, which comprises Los Alamos and the smaller town of White Rock, have a postgrad degree. More than 60 percent have a bachelor's. Ninety-six percent have a high-school diploma. Nationally, those figures are roughly 8 percent, 20 percent, and 86 percent, respectively. And all of that studying has paid off: The median household income in Los Alamos County is close to $80,000, situating its residents 116 percent above the national county average. In the Monied Burbs as a whole, the median household income hovers at about $51,000, so Los Alamos is extraordinary even among its class.

Los Alamos' biggest employer—known locally simply as "the Lab"—

provides jobs for about twelve thousand, making the county something of a Monied Burb terrarium. It's the home of a collection of brains gathered from around the country and the world who have the educations and the skills to go far. Elsewhere in the Burbs economic stability is drawn from nearby big cities, where a lot of Burbanites work in the industries that make those places move—manufacturing, for instance, or finance. These are the parts of the country encompassed by the adjective "metro": Westchester County in metro New York, Oakland County in metro Detroit, Montgomery County in both metro Philadelphia and metro Washington, D.C. They offer all the trappings of the happy middle- and upper-middle-class life to which many Americans aspire. These are the communities where you are most likely to find a Pottery Barn (seventy-three, nearly twice as many as in any other community type), a Starbucks (more than five thousand of them), or a Bloomingdale's (twenty-one out of thirty-eight locations).

Los Alamos is relatively spare by Monied Burb standards, remaining more or less true to Oppenheimer's vision of a place where sharp minds could be inspired by contemplation of the vast desertscape. Naturally, there's a Starbucks, as well as a few other coffee shops. There are a few nice restaurants, two hotels, and one big supermarket, but the nearest Whole Foods is in the bordering Monied Burb of Santa Fe. A lot of people in town say with a certain amount of pride how Los Alamos is different from other places, pointing out how its educated population often looks askance at the acquisitive nature of modern America. A quick drive around will show you this is more Subaru country than BMW land.

But that's not the whole story, said James Rickman, a communications officer at the Lab. "People aren't flashy around here. So you come into town and you're like, *Oh, it doesn't seem like that kind of place.* But if you sort of step back and look again, yeah—yeah, it is."

He paused and glanced around the café we were in. "Look at this place. The kids have all the latest gadgets. . . . I don't have data on this [pointing to his phone], but I would bet that probably at least eighty percent of the kids or more in the community have a computer. . . . It may even be one hundred percent. And most of them probably have their own computer, not like a family computer. A tremendous number have cars. Very few of them have jobs. They don't need to. It's a pretty nice life."

Rickman grew up on the mesa. His parents were both scientists at the Lab, but the academic life wasn't for him—at least not initially. He took time off after high school to kick around the rest of New Mexico, hiking and exploring and doing odd jobs. But he eventually went to college, began a career, and returned home to take his own job at the Lab. In his spare time he's the creative editor of *Mountain Flyer Magazine*, a bimonthly journal on mountain biking, a great love of his that's easy to enjoy in the area. The quality of life in Los Alamos, Rickman finally decided, is simply too good to give up.

When the late-2000s recession hit, however, that quality of life was threatened. Problems that usually afflicted other places came knocking on the doors of the Monied Burbanites' well-kept homes. Unemployment rose, topping out at nearly 10 percent. Foreclosure rates climbed, too. In August of 2009 they were the third-highest among our community types, behind only those in the Boom Towns and the Industrial Metropolises.

Even in Los Alamos people felt the pain. The housing market never went through a crazy boom here, but values had climbed nonetheless. Then, of course, they fell. Rickman said that when he wanted to refinance his house in 2009, he found it had lost 30 percent of its value. And life on top of the world has its own problems. The Lab can feel like a big security blanket of an employer, but it's so dominant here that just a few cutbacks could decimate the community. If even one hundred positions were cut, forcing people to look for similar high-tech work elsewhere, that might mean fifty or seventy-five homes on the market, all of them difficult to move if the Lab isn't hiring.

Rickman, for one, is glad he's not totally dependent on the Lab for his livelihood. His work with *Mountain Flyer* led Rickman and his wife to start what he calls a "PR- and advertising-type marketing firm."

"We started that up [in 2008] and actually showed a profit on paper," he said. "It makes you feel a little more comfortable."

CAPITAL CITIES

Beyond the education and income levels of their residents, the Monied Burbs are pretty close to average statistically. They're 88 percent white, 7 percent black, and 8 percent Hispanic, compared to the national averages of 86, 9, and 7. They're younger than the typically American county, but only slightly. The percentages of Burbanites employed in sectors such as education, government, and manufacturing are near the national county averages. Even their religious makeup seems unremarkable—a fifty-fifty mix of adherents and non-adherents, with believers spread pretty evenly among evangelicals, mainline Protestants, and Catholics.

But what a difference those education and income levels make. Many who live in the Burbs are very wealthy by U.S. standards. About 13 percent of households here have an annual income of more than $100,000. The national figure for that income level is only 6 percent. The segment of the population employed as professionals or executives in the Burbs is 9 percent, almost double the national average. The number of families living in poverty is, at 6 percent, almost half the national rate. You won't find too many trailer parks here, either. They house just 9 percent of the population in the Burbs, versus 15 percent in the average American county.

Like all counties, Monied Burbs hold a mix of people. But regardless of whether someone makes his or her living on the assembly line or behind a desk, there are a lot of good-sized incomes here, meaning these places are critical to driving the consumer economy. The Burbs can be robust even if the broader economy is weak. When there's a recession, these are the places that eventually pull the country out of it, or they have been in the past. People here shop. They eat out. They take trips. If they're struggling so much that they don't do those things, the whole economy is in trouble. During the Great Recession the problems in the Burbs were a sign that things had gotten very bad for just about everyone.

The country depends on the Monied Burbs in other ways, as well. This is where lots of people have the money to start businesses and the education to shape fields like science and law. People in the Burbs trade more stock more often than people in other community types—more often, in fact, than people in any type other than the Emptying Nests, where folks usually trade for different reasons. In short, the Burbs are where much of the nation's capital, intellectual and otherwise, resides.

Sitting on the front porch of Ron Dolin's house in Los Alamos, that couldn't have been clearer. As he leaned back in his chair, sipping a glass of cabernet and munching on a slice of brie, Dolin saw nothing on the distant desert horizon but boundless opportunity. At fifty he'd been working on and off for the Lab about twenty-five years. Along the way he acquired experience in a host of areas—everything from weapons engineering to international terrorism prevention. When the Bechtel Corporation won the contract to manage the Lab in the early 2000s Dolin was selected as one of six people at the facility to become a "Bechtel black belt." Black belts are people trained in the Six Sigma business management strategy that, in theory, allows them to take their management skills into any situation and improve it.

"So I'm already talking to Bechtel about maybe going over to Russia and help with the . . . the contract for the bio-weapons disarmament,"

Dolin said. "Or there's some work going on in London and some in Uzbekistan and—" He paused as his wife brought us a plate of grapes, then raised his glass. "Yeah, the world's my playground."

Of course, if Dolin ends up working overseas, he'll have to figure out what to do with his other business. The wine we were drinking is a product of the Don Quixote Distillery & Winery—which is to say, Dolin's home. Barrels of aging wine line the wall of his garage, and in a separate building out back sit stills that Dolin designed himself. Don Quixote makes wine, port, and blue-corn vodka, as well as brandy for a company in California.

"They give me the produce and I make the brandy for free, and I sell them back brandy for the going price in California," he explained. And voilà, Dolin the weapons engineer and terrorism expert is also the proprietor of a "boutique winery" and the first and only distillery in the Southwest. There's an advantage to being a distiller at 7,200 feet, he pointed out with a smile: Here alcohol boils at a temperature ten degrees cooler than it does most everywhere else.

In many ways, Dolin, like the Burbs community he lives in, has what lots of people want. He's using his education and experience to serve what he believes is a noble cause. He's making enough time for himself to pursue his own interests. And on top of all that, he's making a good living—and probably will continue to do so, no matter how much the economy is shaken up. People like Dolin and Rickman felt the ground tremble during the late-2000s recession, but their enviably constructed lives didn't come tumbling down.

"I think we're gonna see . . . a real different world," Enloe told me. "But . . . I think they think if you have the education and the brains, it'll work out. You know what I mean? That you'll be able to figure it out. The important thing's getting the tools."

There are, of course, some in Los Alamos who worry that they don't have those tools. David and Gillian Sutton own KRSN, a local AM radio station that aims to be the broadcast voice of the community. It offers morning interviews with local luminaries, coverage of high school sports, and real-estate and fishing reports, as well as music in a variety of genres. The Suttons don't consider themselves poor, David said, but they aren't making salaries in line with those of most people who work at the Lab.

Gillian described how the family's eldest child was forced to go to a friend's house to use a computer "'cause the schools expected him to have one at his disposal and we did not have one."

Particularly where their kids are concerned, she and her husband clearly feel pressure from the rest of the community to pick up the financial pace. Their response so far has been some degree of resistance. If the recession is followed by a sluggish recovery, at least a few other consumers in the consumer-packed Burbs will likely make the same choice. If enough of them do, that means a significant shift in how the U.S. economy functions. If enough Burbanites decide to resist keeping up with the Joneses, it could wildly transform consumer spending.

"Our kid's not going to get a cell phone at nine, she's not going to have a TV in her room, and she's not going to have a computer in her room," David said. "I mean, it's not like she's deprived. We do have another TV."

THE SWING SET

Money may not be everything, but in the Monied Burbs it affects almost everything—not only quality of life and expectations for the future, but also politics. Economic factors make the biggest difference for the voters in the Burbs for two reasons: First, the people in these places are among the least wedded to any particular political party, with 30 percent saying that they're Democrats, 28 percent Republicans, and 39 percent Independents.[30] (Although, the number of Independents shrinks down to about 13 percent when you ask people which party they "lean" toward.) Second, they're among the most attentive to the economy, with 54 percent of those living in the Burbs having some money in the stock market. That's six percentage points higher than the national average. And because these communities are relatively wealthy, not only are more people invested in the market, they're also invested in larger amounts.

For those reasons these communities hold large numbers of that highly prized political commodity, the swing voter. In 2000 Al Gore beat George W. Bush 50 percent to 47 percent in the Monied Burbs, in part because people here were doing well economically. The Dow rose from about 3,400 in January of 1993 to 10,700 in October of 2000, which meant tidy profits for those invested in the market. Burbanites saw no reason not to extend a Democratic dynasty that had helped them to increase their net worth, despite Gore's association with the embattled Bill Clinton.

In 2004 John Kerry defeated Bush only 50 percent to 49 percent in the Burbs. Why the gain for the GOP? At the time of the election the GDP was again on the upswing, and three years earlier Bush had pushed through a $1.3 trillion tax cut that benefited wealthier households. In 2008, with the stock market apparently in free fall, people in the Monied Burbs voted against the status quo. Barack Obama received 55 percent of the vote here, versus just 43 percent for John McCain. Given the community type's recent voting history, those numbers seem like an aberration—or so the Republican Party should hope. Burbs residents accounted for 4.1 million votes out of Obama's total margin of about 9.6 million.

Like the Monied Burbs in general, Los Alamos has swung in recent elections. In 2000 the county went heavily for Bush, voting for him by almost 16 percentage points. In 2008 it went for Obama, who won by 7 percentage points. Bush's anti-intellectual image—as well as the Iraq War—had worn on people in the area over the previous few years, but their decisions in the voting booth were mainly about the economy. We saw it in polling data as the election grew close, and I was in Los Alamos when the market began to plummet in 2008. The subject was on everyone's minds and lips. Lab workers and others in Los Alamos were dismayed when McCain suspended his campaign to rush back to Washington purportedly to get a handle on the economic crisis. Enloe told me it was a stunt. Rickman laughed about it.

Of course, future support for Obama from the people on the mesa is hardly guaranteed. They're watching closely—not only his handling of the recession and its aftermath, but also his approach to what they understand to be a large-scale economic restructuring. Rickman, a strong Obama supporter during the election, was considerably less enthusiastic when we talked.

"I think government should assist people who need assistance. But this idea of 'too big to fail.' I have friends who are businesspeople. If they make a crappy business decision, they don't get a bailout. But still, they got twenty employees or something that rely on them who are going be out of work if the place closes. And so they make decisions literally about, *Well, I'm gonna go behind a month on a mortgage payment and make payroll for my business and keep the place running instead of letting it fail.* The idea that I ran a business into the ground so I should get more money from the government to keep running it into the ground and pay myself four and a half million dollars—" He stopped and looked away. "It's just wrong."

Enloe agreed. "I think it's hard to have a true capitalistic society without allowing companies to go broke. I mean, you wind up with GMs; you wind up with Citibanks," he told me. "Too big to fail? If . . . the government doesn't make investors pay for the risk level, there's a problem. It won't work."

There's clearly turmoil in the Monied Burbs, and a large-scale, long-term economic restructuring could create even more. In Los Alamos, though the Lab has long been a stabilizing force in the area, there are some questions about its future. It remains primarily about nuclear weapons, with 55 percent of its budget going toward them. No other program line item in its $2 billion 2008 budget was even in the double digits. But nukes haven't been a growth industry since the end of the Cold War, and Obama has promised to reduce the country's nuclear stockpile. A few potential areas of growth for the Lab are non-proliferation, environmental management, and energy programs, which got a combined total of 19 percent of its 2008 funding.[31] And, of course, the facility is a government-run operation, so it made out fairly well in 2009—tens of millions of dollars in stimulus-package funds came flooding into town, some of them earmarked for energy projects.

Turning a big government lab is a lot like turning an ocean liner—or, for that matter, a big private-sector employer like an automaker. It takes many steps and many months. After years of very good times, the people on the mesa are looking for signs of what the future may hold for them. Federal budgets are scrutinized. Statements from Washington are decoded for their economic implications. As in many Monied Burbs, there have been a few things to worry about of late. Toward the end of 2009 a huge shopping-center project aimed at helping to build up and diversify the local economy came crashing down because the developer's main tenant was no longer interested in anchoring the project. Now the site is being cleared with no idea of what will happen to it.

It's enough to give even the self-assured people of Los Alamos pause.

"I think many people do realize that we are fortunate to have good-paying jobs when a lot of the rest of the nation is out of work," Rickman wrote in an e-mail early in 2010. "I think maybe for the first time in a long time, people in Los Alamos have gotten the sense that there's a cold, cruel world out there."

MORMON OUTPOSTS:
BURLEY, IDAHO

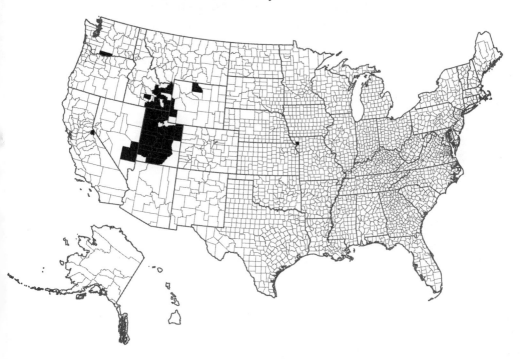

A MORAL MAJORITY

In the 1840s settlers traveling the Oregon and California trails began passing through what is now Cassia County, Idaho, by the thousands. If they paused, it was only to note the landscape of "immense rocky mountains, with not a particle of herbage or vegetation upon them," "worn, by the action of ages of elementary affluences, into strange and romantic forms."[32] Or to "dine hastily, on bread and water." Or to write their names in axle grease on one of the formations "resembling cottages . . . stooples and domes" that make up the forbidding valley still known as the City of Rocks.[33]

Cassia County was, in short, a stopover on the way to someplace better. It wasn't until 1866 that a group of cowboys from the East decided to

Figure 10

MORMON OUTPOSTS

a) PERCENTAGE OF PRESIDENTIAL VOTE OVER TIME

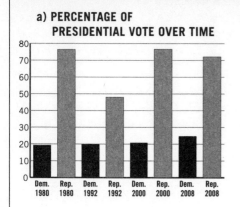

b) PERCENTAGE OF AGE DISTRIBUTION DATA

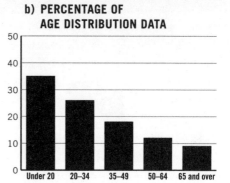

c) PERCENTAGE OF RACE/ETHNIC BREAKDOWN

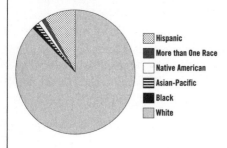

Hispanic
More than One Race
Native American
Asian-Pacific
Black
White

d) PERCENTAGE OF INCOME DISTRIBUTION DATA

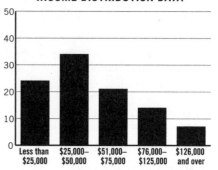

e) PERCENTAGE OF IMMIGRATION OVER TIME

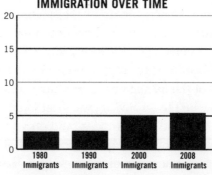

set up a small ranch in the area. Others trickled in slowly, unsure about how to make a living or worried that the local Indian tribes might make life difficult.

But all of that changed in 1879, when William C. Martindale, a member of the Church of Latter-day Saints, arrived with a group of settlers from Utah. Within a year church leaders in Salt Lake City had charged Elder Martindale with organizing a branch, or small congregation, in the area. By 1881 there were eighty LDS families in this desolate patch of southern Idaho, enough to merit the creation of a larger Mormon ward. Just six years later there were enough wards in Cassia to comprise a multicongregational stake. Half a century after LDS church founder Joseph Smith and his followers had been expelled from their planned New Jerusalem in Jackson County, Missouri, under threat of extermination, Cassia County had become not a stopover but a stop. For Mormon settlers, it was indeed someplace better: a community where they were free to practice their faith without prejudice or persecution.

Today there are more than one hundred Mormon stakes in Idaho, mostly in the southern part of the state. One is in Burley, the county seat of Cassia, just twenty miles north of Martindale's so-called mother stake.

According to the U.S. Census Bureau, there are 6 million Mormons in the United States. That's about 2 percent of the population. But more than half of Burley's nine thousand residents are members of the Church of Jesus Christ of Latter-day Saints. Five of the six members of the Burley City Council are LDS, as well as all three members of the Cassia County Commission. Judges, business owners, and journalists all gather at church on Sunday before meeting at work on Monday. In other communities Mormons might be a minority group looking for acceptance or approval or trying not to offend, but in Burley and other Mormon Outposts, they run the day-to-day affairs of government and civic life.

And the population they govern, in general, happily follows. After all, it's not as if Burley lives under Mormon law. There are a few bars in town, and the city even recently passed an ordinance allowing liquor by the drink to be sold on Sundays—albeit after a contentious debate.

Clay Handy, owner of Handy Truck Lines, is a third-generation resident of the Burley area. He is both an LDS church elder and a Cassia County commissioner. "We had a conversation last night at the city council, a couple was there that had just moved in, and they said, 'Wow, do you like have to be LDS to get involved in this community?' So yeah, it's pretty tight," he told me. "I think sometimes it can disenfranchise people that aren't LDS. But then, on the other hand, a lot of people like that. They like that value system, and that's why they're comfortable. They aren't LDS but are religious. There's . . . lots of heritage here, you know?"

"Heritage" might be called "traditionalism" or "conservatism" by some. And there is a kind of time-warp feel to Burley, a collection of used-car lots, diners, and small-town businesses that sit behind 1950s-era facades. In the past three presidential elections the Outposts have had the highest percentage of Republican votes of all Patchwork Nation types. In 2000 and 2004 they gave George W. Bush more than 76 percent of their votes. In 2008, they gave John McCain 72 percent. In Cassia County, McCain captured 81 percent.

Members of the Burley community, LDS and non-LDS alike, have grown up steeped in Mormon precepts, which overlap with core conservative values such as individual responsibility and the rule of law. In 2008 the church helped raise nearly half of the $40 million poured into support for California's Proposition 8 banning same-sex marriage. More than two-thirds of those who live in the Mormon Outposts oppose same-sex marriage and nearly 60 percent oppose allowing "gay and lesbian couples to enter into legal agreements with each other that would give them many of the same rights as married couples."[34]

"I think as long as you're not doing something that's offensive to the majority that you'll be treated well and embraced," Handy said of his hometown. "But if you come in and you don't—if you're too radical in your look, behavior, or language. I mean, there's a long list of things that can set people off—look, attitude, work ethic. There's a long list of things that is expected for a person being a good community member."

And if someone wants to change any of those things or bring a new perspective to Burley?

"That's not gonna happen," Handy suggested. "To begin with, they won't get anyone to go with them. And, you know, it's just not gonna happen."

NEW LAND, NEW PEOPLE

It's reasonable to wonder why Mormon Outposts merit their own community type. Many Outposts are, like the communities that make up Tractor Country, sparsely populated. And all have the strong religious faith of the Evangelical Epicenters. But the nation's Mormon communities grew differently than those other types of place—very deliberately, and often in deliberate isolation. Like Burley and Cassia County, many are the result of planned migration during the nineteenth century, when LDS president Brigham Young organized tens of thousands of followers into settling the Mormon "promised land" of the American West.

Of the 1.7 million people living in the forty-four Mormon Outposts, the majority reside in the Mountain West, particularly in Idaho, Montana, and Utah. They are neither rich nor poor, which makes them better off than the inhabitants of both Tractor Country and the Evangelical Epicenters, communities that are among the nation's least prosperous. The median household income in the Outposts is about $38,000, just slightly above the national county average of $37,000. The poverty rate, 9 percent, sits just under the national average of 11 percent. And the percentage of the population living in mobile homes is 16 percent in the Outposts versus 15 percent nationally.

Mormon Outposts on average are, behind Tractor Country, the second most rural community type, with only fifteen people per square mile. But a few of the more populous Outpost counties—Jefferson County, Idaho, or Utah County, Utah—have a suburban or exurban feel.

Besides the pervasive presence of the LDS Church, the most distinctive thing about Mormon Outposts is their ethnic composition. They are among the whitest places in the Patchwork Nation, with a population that averages 96 percent Caucasian. These places are only 2 percent Native American, 1 percent Asian-Pacific, and 0 percent African American. The typical Mormon Outpost is, however, 8 percent Hispanic, just above the national county average of 7 percent but clearly above the average for the other conservative, rural, and nearby white communities of Tractor Country and Evangelical Epicenters.

With 11 percent of the population working in agriculture, there are more people in farming in the average Mormon Outpost than in the average U.S. county. And it's the farms and fields that have helped insulate Burley from the rest of the world that have also brought the community's biggest change: the area's Hispanic population, originally attracted to Cassia County for agricultural work, has expanded from about 13 percent in 1990 to 18 percent in 2000 and to more than 23 percent in 2008. The overall population of Burley, however, hasn't grown more than 1 percent over the past fifty years.

That kind of demographic change should affect a place. But Burley and Cassia have felt barely a ripple. There isn't anger about illegal immigration or talk of how English is the nation's true language here.

Mark Mitton, Burley's city administrator, suggested that the main reason for the easy transition is that the area has long had a Hispanic population. "Even when I was growing up here there were migrant Hispanic workers. Now there are more residential ones," he said. "It's probably twenty to twenty-five percent by population now, depending which county you're looking at. But it was always ten to fifteen percent. It's always been a part of the total makeup of the community."

David Peña, a lawyer of Mexican heritage who grew up in Burley, told me there are no real tensions between the Hispanic community and the town or its Mormon power structure. "If you're asking me as far as how they get along with the LDS community, the LDS community is very embracive of anybody who comes here, any newcomers to the area," he said.

Indeed, the Mormon Church has done quite a bit to embrace local Hispanics. Burley has a ward just for its Spanish-speaking population, and nationally there are 350 such wards. LDS leadership has been aggressively reaching out to Latinos, emphasizing the faith's focus on family, and Hispanics are reportedly now joining the church faster than any other ethnic group.[35] That has introduced some tension to the LDS community. One of the principal tenets of the Mormon faith is that laws must be obeyed—including those concerning immigration. The twelfth of the thirteen LDS Articles of Faith is that "We believe in being subject to kings, presidents, rulers, and magistrates, in obeying, honoring, and sustaining the law."

In Cassia County it isn't the church's need for new members that attracts Hispanic immigrants, legal or otherwise. It's the potato and sugar-beet farms' need for workers. The result, Handy said, is that there are two different Latino populations in Burley. "You know, after they've been here a couple generations, they just fit. They just conform. They're just part of the community," he said. "The difficulty we have on a law enforcement basis isn't the people that live here. It's the people that are going through or are just here for a short time that are usually the problem."

Of course, separating those two groups isn't always easy—a cousin here or an uncle there may arrive in town to work with family members who are already a part of the community. And, of course, not all Mormons have the same attitude toward immigration. Down in El Mirage, Arizona, our representative Immigration Nation community, former mayor Roy Delgado talked about illegal immigrants who passed through Arizona heading north looking for work. Utah is a popular destination because of the LDS Church, he said. "If they join their religion, they try to get them what I call civil service jobs. For instance, this one guy came from South

America and migrated up there. . . . They got him a job at [Brigham Young University] in Provo, Utah."

THE BEEHIVE

Driving through Utah and Idaho, you will inevitably see images of bee-hives. They are on Utah state highway signs. They appear on Deseret Industries buildings—Mormon versions of Goodwill Industries thrift stores and rehabilitation centers—and in the logo of the Beehive Federal Credit Union, which serves LDS members in Idaho. The image was chosen as the emblem of Deseret, a proposed LDS state that would have encompassed parts of Arizona, California, Idaho, Nevada, and Utah and drew its name from a name for the honeybee used in the Book of Mormon. In 1881 Salt Lake City's *Deseret News* explained the hive as "a significant representation of the industry, harmony, order and frugality of the people, and of the sweet results of their toil, union and intelligent cooperation."

Harmony, order, union, intelligent cooperation—not bad things to build a community around. But they can be tricky in a democracy. Of all of the Patchwork Nation community types, Mormon Outposts express the most agreement on cultural issues like abortion, with two-thirds of the population believing it should be never be allowed or be allowed only in cases of rape, incest, or endangerment of the mother's life. But there are areas of disagreement. Immigration will likely be a hotly debated topic here in the coming years. And when the Mormon Church contributed to the fight for Proposition 8 in California, a small but vocal group of LDS members made their disagreement clear by creating the group Mormons for Marriage.

Jay Lenkersdorfer publishes the *Weekly News Journal*, Burley's newspaper, as well as the *Weekly Mailer*, "an upscale shopping guide" direct-mailed to homes in the area. Lenkersdorfer is Mormon and also a member of the city council, but he considers himself a newspaperman first and foremost. His papers contain mostly what you'd expect from small, local publications: city council news, police arrests, chamber of commerce headlines. But there's one unusual feature in the *Weekly Mailer* called "Sound Off," which features "unsigned editorial opinions."

"So people have an opportunity, anonymously, to say what's on their mind. Some people choose to sign it, and we'll allow them to sign it, but no one has to," Lenkersdorfer explained. The feature, he suggested, is necessary in the lockstep community of Cassia County. "People can say what they need to say without fear of reprisal. . . . What I find is that the people who have the greatest objection to this piece are the people in positions of power and influence. You know, we set up some rules. You just can't call and say, 'Hey, my neighbor Bob Johnson, he's sleeping with the other neighbor.' We don't allow that."

The reprisals people might face would likely be economic or social— "I won't work with your business" or "Your son won't be on the football team"—but they are very real possibilities. Lenkersdorfer suggested that this has less to do with Burley's being so heavily Mormon than with its being so small. Nonetheless, "Sound Off" does allow dialogue between Mormons and those living in Burley, Cassia, and the larger area who don't necessarily share all of their beliefs.

In July 2009 the *Weekly Mailer* took an advertisement for the "Naughty Burlesque Review" California Dolls, which was coming to perform in neighboring Minidoka County, an Immigration Nation community with a smaller percentage of Mormon residents than Cassia's. The next week the paper was chastised by readers in "Sound Off" for promoting pornography. One letter was signed by "A mom who has daughters." In a bar in the Minidoka County seat of Rupert, men laughed at the reaction as they sipped their beers.

"They're just ridiculously prudish," said one who isn't Mormon but has worked for many years in Cassia County, speaking on the condition of anonymity. No one should be surprised by the quieter tensions in the area, he suggested. "It's what you get anyplace where you have a large majority dominated by one belief. Whether it's Catholics or Republicans, they tend to foist their views on others. People don't talk about their differences much, but they are there."

For instance, the vast majority of Boy Scout troops in southern Idaho are sponsored by Mormon wards. "For any non-Mormon to participate they have to step out of their comfort zone because it's all run by the church. It is de facto exclusive," the bargoer said. When he was a boy, he went to a jamboree with a group of scouts sponsored by a Methodist church that felt like the "odd troop out."

Lenkersdorfer said that Burley, like the Mormon Church itself, has been growing more open to outsiders. "We're being taught a lot more tolerance as a religion, as a people. If you were in the early 1900s this was, *This is the way, the truth, the light.* And now a lot of what we're taught is . . . I guess not that that still isn't the case. But you know what? Live and let live."

Of course, that's easy to say as a Mormon living in a Mormon Outpost. It's hard to feel threatened when you're in control. And many of the Outposts have built pretty good walls around themselves.

But what happens when an issue is so big it makes it over the wall? What if it directly confronts LDS beliefs? The beehive would face a difficult test. It might already be doing so. Mormons for Marriage justified its opposition to the church by suggesting that LDS members "have been taught by prophets to never blindly obey."[36] *The Mormon Worker*, a journal concerned with the definitely subcultural world of "Mormonism and radical politics," argued in its August 2009 issue that the twelfth Article of Faith shouldn't be "a handy, isolated, general rule to cut short any further thinking or seeking of personal revelation."[37] But as issues such as immigration and same-sex marriage become more pressing, the numbers of Mormon faithful seeking personal revelation will likely increase. And their conclusions may not always be the same as their church's—or even their community's.

Even in their relatively remote locations and with their local governments stocked with like minds, the Mormon Outposts will probably find harmony, order, union, and intelligent cooperation difficult ideals to uphold in twenty-first-century America.

SERVICE WORKER CENTERS:
LINCOLN CITY, OREGON

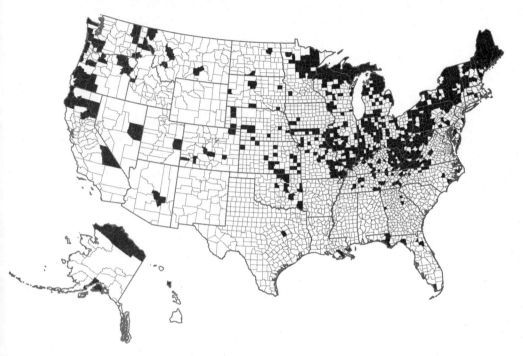

ON THE BEACH AND AT THE MARGINS

There's usually someone on the beach in Lincoln City, Oregon. Even on cold, wet winter days, solitary souls walk along the shore of the Pacific and gaze out at the water or up to the north, where the beach gives way to the rocky cliffs of Cascade Head, a UNESCO biosphere reserve that is home to 150-year-old stands of Sitka spruce and the endangered Oregon silver spot butterfly.

On sunny August days the coastline is packed. When the temperatures soar, hardier visitors stand and shiver knee-deep in the sixty-degree water, some fearlessly plunging under before running out again. Others walk and talk or look at the life in the tidal pools or just sit back and take in the sun. The space is wide and inviting, a natural draw.

Figure 11

SERVICE WORKER CENTERS

a) PERCENTAGE OF PRESIDENTIAL VOTE OVER TIME

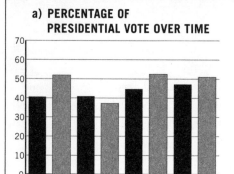

b) PERCENTAGE OF AGE DISTRIBUTION DATA

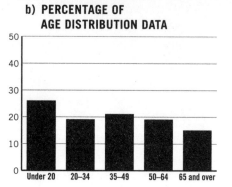

c) PERCENTAGE OF RACE/ETHNIC BREAKDOWN

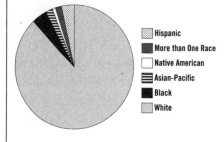

d) PERCENTAGE OF INCOME DISTRIBUTION DATA

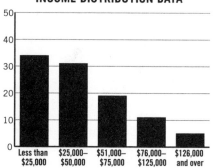

e) PERCENTAGE OF IMMIGRATION OVER TIME

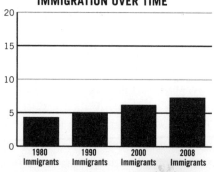

When the sun goes down the crowd hits the local restaurants or maybe the nearby Chinook Winds Casino to catch a show or try to strike it rich. But as long as the sun is out, the beach is the place to be.

The sandy stretch of oceanfront is, in a sense, Lincoln City's raison d'être. Every summer and fall it brings the life-giving draft of tourist dollars that allows many of the town's businesses to carry on. Lincoln City might exist without the beach and tourism, but it would be a very different place.

There are about 7,500 people in Lincoln City—and about 3,300 hotel rooms. On busy weekends the people filling those rooms, as well as the local beach-house rentals, campgrounds, and RV resorts, push the town's population to about thirty thousand. That makes for a place that lives not only in a seasonal boom-and-bust cycle, but also close to the margins.

All those hotels require a staff. The same is true of the gift shops, restaurants, and cafés that line the town's main drag, Oregon's Route 101. One might make a slightly better living if he or she could land a job at Chinook Winds—big tippers pass through the house once in a while, after all. But on the whole, jobs such as chambermaid, cash-register jockey, waiter, or barista aren't all that lucrative. They are hourly positions, many of them minimum wage—and Lincoln City, like the nation's other Service Worker Centers, has an army of them. There are places like Lincoln City all around the country. On the Atlantic Ocean there's Camden, Maine. On the Great Lakes, Cheboygan, Michigan. In all of them paycheck-to-paycheck is a way of life.

"There are a lot of people who just get by here," said Kip Ward, owner of the Historic Anchor Inn on Route 101. "And no one has health insurance. It can be pretty tough for people."

And when tourist season is over, Lincoln City goes into a state of semi-hibernation. After the water has turned too cold for even the most intrepid of swimmers, the town still serves as a commercial hub for the homes scattered throughout the woods in the rest of Lincoln County, on the western side of the Oregon Coast Range. People from the area come here to shop, bank, and go to the movies. But those businesses that cater to tourists shutter and wait for the stream of cars to return next year. Others try to run on one-half or even one-third of their high-season power.

The people left behind when the T-shirt-and-flip-flop-clad throngs leave listen to KBCH, a one-thousand-watt AM station that airs the play-by-play of the local high school basketball team. They call in to chat with Roger Robertson, whose catchall Tuesday-through-Friday morning show features giveaways and coupons from local businesses and, well, whatever people happen to call about. If you've lost something or seen something of interest, you're welcome to share it on the air.

And locals often stop by the Anchor Inn to commiserate with Ward about this or that. A former flophouse spruced up into a shabby-chic B and B, the Anchor serves as a congregation point and a hosting spot for local events. On most mornings Ward is in the kitchen in a flannel shirt and jeans talking not only with paying guests, but also with folks from around town.

"If I had to do this to make a living, it might get to me," he said. "It can be stressful, and it's hard to make a decent amount of money, but the way things are, I like it a lot." He also owns CICS Employment Services, a firm that does background checks on potential hires and pays a lot of his bills. But Ward clearly relishes the talks with visitors and neighbors he has at the Anchor. He's a central node in the communications structure of Lincoln City, and his thirty-two years in town have given him a good understanding of how it functions.

"We've always tried to manage our own affairs, and pretty well have managed over the long haul to shoot ourselves in the foot," he told me. There are projects that have been proposed and never finished—say, a road that would help ease traffic through town—and a lot of squabbles among the members of the city council. "The problem with a town that's so small, is that its resources are small, too. There isn't a lot of support."

The state of Oregon offers a little: The minimum wage here is $8.40 an hour, a full $1.15 over the national minimum of $7.25. But it's still an hourly wage, and the overwhelming majority of jobs that pay it don't offer much in the way of vacation, retirement plans, or health care. For many in Lincoln City, the last involves a trip to a free clinic in a small office downtown. Out at the twenty-five-bed Samaritan North Lincoln Hospital, a rambling one-story building just east of 101, about 40 percent of the patients are "self-pay"—meaning they are without insurance or have high-deductible plans that essentially offer only catastrophic coverage.

"A lot of the deductibles are in the five-thousand-dollar range. There are better options at higher tiers, but most can't afford those options," said Loretta Glaze, who works for Samaritan in quality improvement. "So it's out of pocket. It's self-pay." At Samaritan, she added, that often means no pay: "We collect less than fifty percent of those bills, between twenty-five and thirty-five percent."

What about the people who show up in the emergency room? "We don't have the lack of social graces to turn those people away—yet," Glaze said. "I don't know what it's going to be like in the future. It can't go on like that forever."

THE LARGESSE OF STRANGERS

There are more Service Worker Center counties than anything else in the Patchwork Nation—663 of them. But they aren't densely populated, so they are only the fourth most populous of our twelve community types, with about 31 million people total. Not all are places like Lincoln City, where Mom and Dad take the kids to the beach and couples spend the weekend getting away from it all. Some are isolated locales that survive solely on being the home of the local hardware, grocery, and department stores.

Communities like Aitkin, Minnesota; Amherst, Virginia; and the towns in Fremont County, Colorado, are the other part of small-town America, driven less by agriculture than by small-scale economic trade. The best way to think of Service Worker Centers is as places where you own the gas station, your friend owns the grocery store, and, maybe, the mayor owns the hardware store—and everyone trades money.

These places tend to lack a dominant industry that actually creates wealth, and it shows economically. The median household income in these communities is about $2,000 below the national county average—$35,000 versus $37,000. The biggest employer behind the service sector, which provides 31 percent of the jobs in the Service Worker Centers, is the local school system. The education sector employs 21 percent of the people who live here, though for the most part these counties aren't home to major research universities. There are some community colleges, some four-year colleges, and, of course, the K–12 schools that educate the kids in the towns that dot these counties. There's slightly more manufacturing in the Service Worker Centers than in the nation as a whole—about 17 percent of the jobs in these counties versus 15 percent nationally—but many of those jobs are in light manufacturing and not necessarily well-paying positions with benefits.

These communities are growing, but at a much slower rate than the rest of the country. Their population increased by only 2 percent between 2000 and 2006, while the national growth rate was about 6 percent. That makes Service Worker Centers older than the nation at large, with 34 percent of their population over the age of fifty. All of those low-paying jobs make Lincoln City and places like it less desirable places to live for a lot of younger people, no matter how spectacular the scenery or uncommon the wildlife.

"It's been rough on our infrastructure, because we're losing people," said Allyson Longueira, editor of the weekly Lincoln City *News Guard*. "We're losing people 'cause they're losing their jobs. . . . You know, it's very expensive to live up here."

Most everything that's sold in Lincoln City and other Service Worker Centers has to travel a long way to get there, so it costs more than it does elsewhere. Gas, for instance, is typically five to ten cents more per gallon in these communities than it is in the average U.S. county. And that cost is compounded by the fact that people living in these more isolated areas have to drive more to run errands and also earn lower incomes. The late-2000s recession, of course, drove those incomes even lower. Business owners in tight-knit small towns are often loath to cut the positions of people they know well. Instead they cut hours, unwilling to turn friends out with no income. The effect, however, can be nearly the same, as wages slow to a trickle.

All of that—higher unemployment, higher prices, a shrinking population—affects skilled employment at places like the schools and hospital. Qualified teachers and doctors look elsewhere. "People are moving away," Longueira said. "And people will not take jobs here."

The lower wages and tighter job prospects are part of why Service Worker Centers, which are 94 percent white, 3 percent African American, and only 2 percent Hispanic, aren't the uniform bastions of conservatism you might expect them to be. These places tend to be the economy's canaries in the coal mine. When things go bad, they go bad here first. Of all of our twelve community types, the Service Worker Centers almost always lead the pack in monthly unemployment rates, running ahead of the national county average by 1.5 to 2 percent.

Here, the recession didn't hit in the rarefied realms of the Dow and the 401(k) statement; it was a reality expressed in lost wages and jobs.

Yes, the Republican candidates for president won these communities in 2000, 2004, and 2008, but the vote tightened. George W. Bush won by 7 percent here in 2000 and by 12 percent in 2004. But John McCain took these places by a much narrower 4 percent in 2008. People in the Service Worker Centers promise to be a political wild card for the next decade. They are loosely tethered to political principles, vulnerable to bumps in the economy, and looking for solutions.

Ward and others in Lincoln City may hope that they can manage their own affairs, but they know to some extent that the town's future isn't really in its own hands. It has more to do with the broader state of the U.S. economy than anything else—in other words, whether people will have money to spread around, either for luxury items such as ocean-side vacations or for basics from the local hardware, grocery, and department stores.

Who will come to town, and how much will they spend? Those are and will be the most critical questions for the Service Worker Centers.

"If we can get them in at a discount rate, we give them customer service and a nice meal," Ward said. "We might make a few dollars, but what we hope to do is make a friend and a future customer. We notice that we're getting primarily middle-class people, and . . . they'll be back when we raise the rates, when the economy is good."

SOMETHING FOR—AND SOMETHING FROM—EVERYONE

Tourists have been coming to Lincoln City for more than seventy years, and they still arrive in waves on nice-weather weekends to go to the beach or play in nearby Devils Lake. At the latter, the state's parks and recreation department boasts, you can canoe or kayak or fish for rainbow trout or watch for bald eagles. And if you tire of any of those activities, "the nearby outlet mall, one of the largest in Oregon, is a short drive away."[38]

As with many vacation towns, Lincoln City's relationship with visitors is complicated. For the area's residents, those all-important dollar-bill-carrying carloads can make day-to-day life difficult. Most of the traffic into town—from Portland, two hours away, and Salem, about an hour—travels the two-lane Salmon River Highway, which can back up for miles. And then there are the lines at the stores and restaurants.

"When the town really gets packed in the summer, it's like you can't get anywhere," Ward complained.

A good tourist season, however, means that more money circulates around the community—more shifts and tips for waitresses, bartenders, and chambermaids, more knickknacks moving from the souvenir shops. And that money has a multiplier effect in town. Local people eat out more. They splurge at the grocery store. They improve their homes. One estimate in town is that every dollar spent in tourism goes around four times. Tourism is what bumps Lincoln City up into a different class of Service Worker Center, allowing it to be more than just a small, semi-urban hub for the rural population around it.

In the early twenty-first century, however, the town and its vacation-land image are in sore need of updating.

The businesses that line Highway 101—the taffy and candy shops, the pizza joints, the Christmas-all-year store—make for a certain kind of getaway. It's the type of trip you take with your family as a kid, on which your parents watch every dime. For many Oregonians this is a place to create a few sun-and-sea-tinged memories for the little ones on the cheap. But when the people of Lincoln City look eastward to Portland and Salem, they see a chance to draw in bigger money from wealthier people—young, childless professionals and empty nesters. For a community that needs outside dollars to grow and thrive, those people are very appealing.

So the town has been trying to retool itself to tap some of that money. It has built the Culinary Center in Lincoln City, where people can take cooking classes in a big kitchen loaded with stainless steel or witness a chowder-making contest "fashioned after the Iron Chef Competitions."[39] And it subsidizes the Jennifer L. Sears Glass Art Studio, where people can watch glass art being made or make their own. Both attractions are aimed at bringing in those other kinds of vacationers, and both have had limited success so far.

There have been lots of viewers at the glass studio, but not so many participants. A small "float," or hollow glass ball, costs $75 to make—and costs nothing to find on the beach, where the town hides more than two thousand of them for visitors to find every year. (It's a way of honoring the town's past, when glass floats from Japanese fishing boats washed up on the Lincoln City beach for real. Today the non-decorative version of this equipment is usually plastic.) The culinary center hadn't really caught on, either. In 2009 it was often closed for lack of attendees.

Meanwhile, residents like the Anchor Inn's Ward fumed about the money the city pays to help what they believe are gimmicky businesses, allowing long-timers to suffer in the process. "In the winter maybe they are blowing four floats a week, and the gas bill to keep the big furnace going can run up to ten thousand dollars monthly," he said, shaking his head at what he sees as environmental waste.

But bringing those out-of-towners who have more money to spend can mean so much for all residents, said Mayor Lori Hollingsworth, who had been feeling pressure from the community as unemployment numbers climbed during the recession.

"Ideally we would get more and more activities . . . and we're looking at some of those right now, what those would look like. . . . You know, a children's museum, a green-resource center, green motels, and how to make that a marketing tool," Hollingsworth told me, sitting at her kitchen table with pages of reports showing the town's struggle with revenue. Lincoln City's room-tax money was down about 5 percent. Construction was down 65 percent. Combined with the number of empty storefronts in town, that meant trouble with property taxes down the road.

"We're trying to connect the dots with the arts and the culture and tourism," Hollingsworth said. "You know, the arts and the culture and the economic-development tourism nugget."

Creating that nugget means making Lincoln City appealing to a dizzying array of demographics. September brings the new Iris Pride Festival, billed as "the first gay pride event on the Oregon Coast." November it's Antique Week, featuring sales, appraisals, and a scattering of "150 authentic antique Japanese glass floats" on the beach. March, "Oregon's best Indoor Kite Festival."[40] And so on throughout the year: a community-wide garage sale, a berry cook-off, a dog Olympics.

"You want everybody—the families, the working-class families, the oldsters, the double-income-no-kids," Hollingsworth explained. "We're always gonna be the beach. And, you know, I used to think, when people would talk about Lincoln City in that term, Well, how do you become more than that? Well, we don't have enough flexibility to become more than that. There's this little guy up there that does manufacturing and this other guy that does trucking or kites or something. But what's wrong with tourism? Tourism's pretty good."

TRACTOR COUNTRY: SIOUX CENTER, IOWA

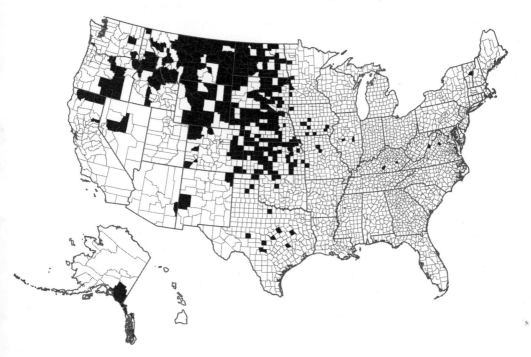

CROP CIRCLES

With a population of about 6,500 people, Sioux Center is the metropolis of Sioux County, Iowa. It has a movie theater, a mall, and a Walmart. There are a lot of options for dinner, too: a coffeehouse, a Mexican restaurant, and an Old West–themed place called Pizza Ranch. At Tofhers Restaurant & Lounge, you can even get a thick steak for just a bit more than you would pay for a meal at a fast-food joint, but they're here as well. A Hardee's, a McDonald's, and a Subway all line Sioux Center's Main Avenue, also known as U.S. Route 75.

But the city is more notable for its food-to-be than for its food. Sioux Center was founded and is still largely dependent on agriculture. Its tallest structure by far is the downtown grain elevator of the Sioux Center Farmers

Figure 12

TRACTOR COUNTRY

a) PERCENTAGE OF
PRESIDENTIAL VOTE OVER TIME

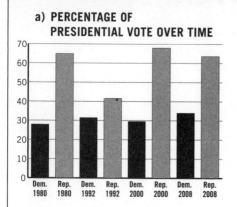

b) PERCENTAGE OF
AGE DISTRIBUTION DATA

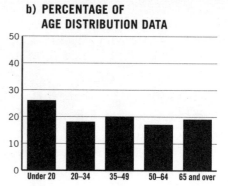

c) PERCENTAGE OF
RACE/ETHNIC BREAKDOWN

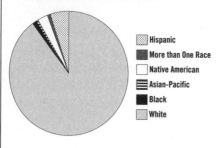

Hispanic
More than One Race
Native American
Asian-Pacific
Black
White

d) PERCENTAGE OF
INCOME DISTRIBUTION DATA

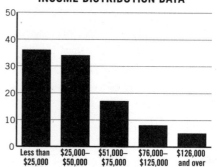

e) OPERCENTAGE OF
IMMIGRATION OVER TIME

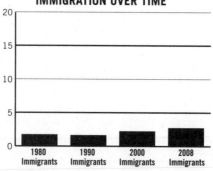

Co-Op Society. There's a farm-animal auction house complete with café. The first sign of civilization you see coming into town from the south is Hog Slat Inc., "World Leader in Swine Production Solutions." Take a quick left or right off of Main, and the rows of neat houses quickly give way to flatland dotted with livestock and crops of corn and soybeans.

Sioux is the leading pork-producing county in Iowa, and that fact is impossible to ignore on the streets of Sioux Center. On warm summer mornings you are greeted by the powerful smell of pig excrement as soon as you set foot outside. But the thousands of acres that surround Sioux Center aren't just a means of agricultural production. They are also a buffer that separates the town from the urban/suburban/exurban culture that predominates in much of the rest of the country.

There's no question that twenty-first-century information technology is, as Thomas L. Freidman has described it, a "flattener." Anyone in Sioux Center with an Internet connection can read *The New York Times* or click to TMZ.com to see what Britney has been up to. But just because anyone here can doesn't mean that anyone here will. In a close-knit farming community, many people aren't terribly concerned with what's going on in Los Angeles or New York. Neighbors are more likely to keep track of one anothers' lives, offering help when it's needed. And while people in some places feel pressure to keep up with the Joneses, residents of Sioux Center are more likely to feel pressure running in the opposite direction. Among farmers, frugality is proof of character.

"You buy a car when you have the money to buy a car, not just when you want a car," said Dennis Van Den Berg, who owns the local Furniture Mart.

The place where these people live looks different from a lot of the United States. Yes, there are three veterinary clinics downtown. But what differentiates the city more is what's not there. The Applebee's-industrial complex has not yet dented the community. The nearest Starbucks is an hour away—in South Dakota. For anyone who has traveled the country widely, eating the same never-ending pasta bowls over and over, the disparity is immediately noticeable.

Drive down Main Avenue and you won't see a single sign for Bank of America or Wells Fargo or Citibank. Instead there's Primebank, with offices in Sioux Center, Sioux City, and Le Mars, Iowa. There's American State Bank, of Sioux Center, Hospers, Granville, Alvord, and Hull, Iowa. And there's the First National Bank of Omaha. All are local or regional institutions with ties to and knowledge of the community. They don't make loans based simply on formulas or anonymous credit ratings. Their customers are neighbors and friends who come in to talk things over. It's the way business used to be done all over the United States, and in Sioux Center there's a certain amount of frustration over the fact that it's no longer done that way everywhere.

"'Bitter' maybe is a little harsh, but there are some upset feelings why some major businesses made some bad business decisions and it's affecting them, which affects everybody because agriculture is a large borrower of money, you know, top rate," said John Hansen, the Co-Op's grain manager. "In the eighties, we went through that here because everybody thought the land would keep going up and it was a bust. Bankers learned from that in the Midwest, and now there's not the leverage on land."

They learned in Sioux Center and the other faraway communities of Tractor Country, where they bank with people they know who largely avoid taking risks. But the rest of the nation didn't. And now, in the wake of the late-2000s recession, people here feel like they have been bailing out the Wall Street people and the McMansioners who wanted the good life and overleveraged themselves.

Tractor Country communities—places like Freestone County, Texas; Garden County, Nebraska; and Wheatland County, Montana—consistently scored low on our economic hardship index, which looks at gas prices, foreclosures, and unemployment. The housing market never collapsed in these places, and the unemployment rate never shot up, at least not like in the rest of the country. Month in and month out during the depths of the recession, unemployment here was four to five points below the national average. And Tractor Country is the least enmeshed of all our community types when it comes to the Troubles Asset Relief Program. Only 14 percent of the bank branches in these counties are affiliated with banks that took TARP money.

Eric Walhof, president of the First National Bank in Sioux Center, told me there's a reason for that. Many of the banks in Tractor Country don't like dealing with forms or credit scores, but with actual people whom bankers know personally—right down to the details of what their farms look like. "Small-town banking is all about relationships," Walhof said. "We know a lot of our people. We go to church with them. We see them at football games on Friday night. You're banking with your friends and neighbors."

PROGRESSIVE CONSERVATISM

Tractor Country can be thought of as the broad empty space in the middle of the United States. It comprises 311 counties, in a vast expanse of terrain mostly in Kansas, Nebraska, the Dakotas, and Montana, that together hold 2.2 million residents. And as the rest of the country grows, Tractor Country is getting even emptier. It lost about 2 percent of its population between 2000 and 2006, and it's the oldest of the twelve community types in the Patchwork Nation. Nearly 40 percent of the people here are age fifty or older, and 18 percent are sixty-five or older.

Tractor Country is also the least diverse of all our communities, a distinction it shares with the Mormon Outposts. The population of both community types is 96 percent white. But Tractor Country has begun to see an influx of Hispanics, who now represent 3 percent of the population here. They continue to arrive to work on the farms and for other agricultural businesses such as meat-packing facilities.

Like Sioux County, all Tractor Country communities rely heavily on working the land. Twenty percent of people here are employed in agriculture in some way, compared to only 7 percent for the average county nationwide. As a result, these aren't wealthy places. The median household income here is a modest $32,600, $4,400 less than nationally. But that might not be as painful in reality as it looks on paper. The cost of living in these communities is lower than average, too, particularly where housing is concerned. A five-bedroom, three-bath house with a two-car garage is only $250,000 in downtown Sioux Center, and the percentage of families living in poverty in Tractor Country is lower than the national average.

Still, the Co-Op's Hansen believes that the writing is on the wall for the area economically. The people here may still be driving pickup trucks here a decade from now, but fewer of them will be hauling farm equipment. When he arrived in Sioux Center, in the mid-nineties, someone's going into farming from scratch represented a real possibility. Land was relatively cheap at $2,500 or $3,000 an acre. It's about $7,000 now. And that's before purchasing the necessary machinery, all of which has become more expensive and technically complicated.

"Our company prided itself," he recalled. "We could take young farmers that wanted to get into farming, help them set up with the livestock operation, and they could generate enough income just to live on the farm, probably build up some equity and start to grow that way. But because of the cost of operation anymore, that's probably not the case anymore."

That economic escalation, combined with Sioux Center's changing demographics, is affecting the community in ways that reach far beyond the fields—albeit very slowly, at a pace befitting the town's special style of conservatism.

In the 2008 presidential race John McCain received 81 percent of the vote in Sioux County. In Tractor Country as a whole McCain earned 64 percent. George W. Bush captured 68 percent of the Tractor Country vote in 2000 and 68 percent again in 2004. There's little or no debate over things like abortion or same-sex marriage here because there aren't enough residents to argue the liberal side with any volume. And even if there were, they probably wouldn't. These close-knit communities don't welcome loud, open confrontation.

The people here not only didn't vote for Barack Obama; they also look at the spending under his administration and cringe. About 70 percent of the people who live in Tractor Country said that they view Obama administration government spending as "debt" rather than "investment," according to results from a Zogby International poll cross-tabulated by the Patchwork Nation community types.[41] But residents here don't necessarily frown upon all government spending—or at least on government spending at all levels. Because they are usually pretty remote, Tractor Country communities understand the need for residents to come together to improve local life with new ball fields or community centers or sewage-treatment plants. But always within reason and within budget.

The powers that be in Sioux Center embrace what might be called progressive conservatism. The city's mission is "to provide excellent municipal services and quality of life for our community through a spirit of progressive cooperation." To that end, the town has worked with both the state and local entities such as the Christian Reformed Church–affiliated Dordt College to fund what have to be considered major projects for a community of less than seven thousand people.

Sioux Center put $9 million into the All Seasons Center, a sixty-thousand-square-foot facility that includes a pool, an ice rink, and a senior center. And when kids put firecrackers into the book return and burned down the public library, the city built a new twenty-thousand-square-foot prairie-house-style replacement at a cost of $5 million. Both structures look as if they belong in much bigger, much more cosmopolitan settings.

"People here just don't sit around and wait for something to happen, you know. They go out and they make it happen," said Mayor Dennis Walstra, sitting with City Manager Paul Clousing in the town's compact city council chambers. "We have a lot of people with vision. And if we see a real need, we'll aggressively go after and try to fill that need. So we've got the facilities here. Our intent is to draw people to the community."

The city's latest mission is the Ridge golf club, a mixed-use development not far from Hog Slat Inc. Sioux Center officials see it as an opportunity to draw more people to town and have developed a master plan that includes 115 home lots as well as a forty-acre commercial park. As of late 2009, more than half of the residential lots had sold, and a Holiday Inn Express and the Center Fresh Eggs corporate offices had moved into the commercial area.[42]

It all sounds almost like, well, activist government. But you won't find many people here hoping to extend the powers of Washington.

"I would say we're pretty tried-and-true Republicans," Walstra told me. "That's maybe changed slightly, but we're pretty much Republicans."

"Yes, years ago, if you were a Democrat, you didn't want anybody to know about it. You were, and that was it. You just didn't say anything," Clousing added. "Now they've become more vocal and visible in the community."

Don King, an associate professor of political studies at Dordt College and one of those "more vocal and visible" liberals, said that most of the town's residents see the Obama administration as a bad dream—a reason to ignore the national news and focus on local issues. "They'll grumble, but to me it's like living in a time when there's so much less acknowledgment that Obama is even there," he explained. "There are people who are very openly critical. But a lot of other people just don't talk about it."

CLOSING THE DISTANCE

City Manager Clousing likes to say, "The best government is the one that is closest to the people." And the people in Sioux Center aren't just fiscally conservative.

Sioux Center has a strong Dutch heritage. The phone book still includes a lot of names that begin with "Van" and "Vander." The big religious debate in town is over which offshoot of the Dutch Reformed Church one is a member of: the Christian Reformed Church, which holds that the Bible is infallible, homosexuality "reflects the brokenness of our sinful world," and "Christians are not to reject dance but to redeem it, realizing that some forms of dancing are more difficult to redeem than others,"[43] or the more liberal Reformed Church in America.

Same-sex marriage and abortion are big motivators in Sioux Center and in Tractor Country in general. More than 80 percent of those who live in Tractor Country are opposed to laws legalizing gay marriage, according to a Pew Research Center poll cross-tabulated through Patchwork Nation's twelve types.[44] And 62 percent of those in Tractor Country believe that abortion should be illegal or only legal if the mother's life is endangered or true need can be established.

When the Iowa Supreme Court ruled in favor of same-sex marriages in 2009, people in Sioux Center shifted their attention to state politics. The overwhelming majority of residents were in favor of some plan to try and circumvent the ruling, including an amendment of the Iowa constitution. This despite the fact that Sioux was one of only three counties in the state in which no same-sex couples came forward to be married in the immediate aftermath of the ruling. ("I think there are people out there, but they just don't dare come forward," Walstra told me.)

"On an issue like that they're very engaged," King said. "People have said, 'Yeah, you're going way too far' and all this. So on those issues that are, I would say, really salient to [Sioux Center residents] because they see them as moral issues, they will engage. But at the same time, I think there are a lot of educated people who don't like the idea but at the same time recognize that it's going to be hard to fight this."

Even with their buffer zones of farmland, it seems, Tractor Country communities can't remain entirely isolated. The distance-collapsing technologies that have spread around the country have taken deeper root among the young—and that includes the young here. Broadband Internet connections may be more common in suburbia, but they exist in large numbers in Tractor Country. More than 76 percent of the homes here have high-speed Internet access, according to a survey by the Pew Research Center's Internet & American Life Project.

Pat O'Donnell, superintendent of the Sioux Center Community Schools, knows very well that the kids here aren't using the Web to check crop reports. "We try to use our firewall to stop things like Mob Wars on Facebook," he said. "So we block it, and they know how to get around it, and they do it quickly."

Facebook and the like have brought not only new knowledge to Tractor Country, but also a different set of attitudes. When younger residents grow up, they could bring their more outward-looking perspectives into, say, the decision-making process of the local city council—provided they stay, of course. Large urban environments have a strong pull for many of the youth here, especially as farming becomes more expensive and more difficult to break into.

The increasing migration of Hispanics into Tractor Country to work the as-yet abundant agricultural jobs will also have an impact. Sioux Center actually had a Cinco de Mayo parade a few years back, and Hispanics, obviously, will play a bigger role in town life as they grow percentage-wise. Their largely Catholic religious beliefs could be a particularly significant determinant, given that Tractor Country communities are now overwhelmingly Protestant.

But it's the changing nature of agriculture, with its higher barriers to entry and increasing consolidation, that will change the nature of life in these communities the most. The family-owned farms that were the foundation of Tractor Country have over the course of the twentieth century largely given way to industrialized agriculture. People here still work in agriculture, but many of them work in large dairies or meat-packing plants—or, in poultry- and pork-producing counties, as part of "vertically integrated" production systems, in which individual farmers, instead of owning animals, merely raise them for larger companies.[45]

Still, the communities of Tractor Country will likely remain among the least touched by what's to come in the new America. Internet or no Internet, family farming or factory farming, living in a small, conservative community that's tied to the land far removed from major media markets necessarily creates a culture different from that in much of the rest of the country. The impact of immigration may be a nudge toward a more multicultural perspective in these communities, but tradition remains strong here, and it won't be easily undone.

If, in the late 2000s, the United States is at the beginning of a shift from center-right to center-left, what will the residents of Tractor Country do? Will they engage or disengage? Even if they choose the latter, and even if life here does change the least, it may feel like it's changing the most.

THE ECONOMY

■ ■ ■

THAT DEPENDS ON WHAT "IT" IS

On October 11, 2008, *Saturday Night Live* aired a sketch that was destined to be only marginally hilarious. On the show's regular "Weekend Update" segment Kenan Thompson played a guest expert discussing the big financial news of the week: that the stock market had just posted two of its biggest one-day losses in history.

Was there any light at the end of the tunnel? he was asked.

"Well, there was a light, but now it's broken and someone needs to crawl down to the end of that tunnel and fix it," Thompson said. "I've been a financial analyst for sixteen years, and I've never seen it this out of control. They need to clamp it down and fix it. When I wake up tomorrow morning, it had better be fixed." As the skit went on Thompson's character grew more irate. "Take it one step at a time. Identify the problem and fix it! Identify the next problem and fix it! Repeat as necessary until it's all fixed!"

"You keep saying, 'Fix it,'" said host Seth Myers. "But how?"

"Fix it!"

"Fix what?"

"It! It needs to be fixed! Now!"

The bit devolved into Thompson's yelling, "Fix it!" over and over. The audience laughed hard—but nervously.

Thompson was giving voice to what a lot of people were thinking: *Can't we just get things back to how they were before?* Sure, the economy had shown some shakiness—rising foreclosures, the AIG bailout. But things had still seemed pretty good just before the tumble. The Dow had been locked into the 12,000 range. Gas prices had been up, but they had come back down. Banking on your home for your nest egg remained a reasonable proposition for the majority of Americans. And the word "tarp" referred only to something used to cover the infield in the event of rain.

No one knew what to do immediately after the crash because no one was completely sure what was wrong. What exactly needed to be fixed? The housing market? The stock market? Federal regulation? Our corporate culture? Our need for oil? The entire system suddenly seemed to be teetering. Thoughts of the Great Depression crept into people's minds. And behind everything was the worry that we didn't even know what "it" was.

There was a good reason for that. In a country as large and as diverse as the United States, when things go wrong in a big way—as they began to in the fall of 2008—they go wrong differently for different communities.

What "it" was, in other words, depended on where you lived.

Some parts of the country were in the midst of a foreclosure crisis. In others problems sprang from the disappearance of a company or an industry. And while some places saw the stock market crash as the last straw after years of tough times, others were experiencing a brand new 401(k) crisis. Naturally, the economic forces that shape Jefferson, Iowa, have long been quite different from those that shape New York City. But in a generally good economy we tend to forget that fact.

Cheap credit and a nationwide housing boom made it seem as though there was enough wealth to go around. Low gas prices allowed people to buy bigger homes farther from where they worked—provided they could stomach the time they spent in traffic. Wages had been essentially flat from

2003 on, but it was easy to get a new home-theater system or SUV with the help of credit card debt or a home equity loan.

That mode of living was wrecked by tightening credit, falling home values, and increasing job insecurity. A study by James W. Hughes and Joseph J. Seneca of the Edward J. Bloustein School of Planning and Public Policy at Rutgers postulates that the loss of 7.1 million jobs during the late-2000s recession means that the U.S. economy won't return to its precollapse strength until 2017. The average post–World War II recovery, by contrast, took just under three years.[46]

In every single community type in the Patchwork Nation—the rich and the poor, the urban and suburban and rural—the feeling was the same in 2009: *Things are different. The world is changing.* Greater than the Great Recession is the long-term economic restructuring that the whole country has been experiencing for decades.

The United States' economic power in the world has been diminishing since the country's postwar boom finally wound down, in the early 1970s. The fate of the world economy is no longer determined by the U.S.-led G7. It's determined by a long list of countries and economies, including smaller ones that are growing exponentially and have different concerns and goals than the United States does. By as early as 2027, Goldman Sachs has predicted, the combined gross domestic product of Brazil, Russia, India, and China could overtake that of the G7. That same year, China's economy could surpass the United States' as the world's largest.

In the long view things have actually been pretty bad for a while. Between 1972 and 2007 the productivity of the American worker grew 90 percent while his or her wages declined by 11 percent, according to University of Massachusetts professor of economics Robert Pollin.[47] Manufacturing accounted for more than 20 percent of the U.S. GDP in 1987. In 2009 it accounted for about 12 percent. The dominoes that began falling during the recession had been lined up for some time. As a nation we have been simultaneously transitioning to a service-and-information-based economy and dealing with an increasingly competitive global market—Thomas J. Friedman's "flat earth."

Although some might like to take comfort in the idea that that we're all in the same boat, we aren't really. Yes, nearly everyone in the United States has something to worry about right now, but the problems that keep people up at night in Lincoln City, Oregon; Sioux Center, Iowa; and Philadelphia are actually quite different.

As the larger restructuring continues, the number of people calling out, "Fix it!" will undoubtedly grow. But over time it will become clear just how different "it" is in the different communities of the Patchwork Nation. And, ultimately, that means any "fix" will not be easy to find. Different places will see different "fixes" leading in different directions.

THE MYTH OF THE "AMER.ECONOMY"

Here's a simple question: When did the late-2000s recession begin? There's a simple answer, of course. According to the powers that be at the National Bureau of Economic Research, the great trough began in December 2007. But that doesn't begin to capture the larger truth about what was happening around the country.

In January 2008, the people in Service Worker Center Lincoln City, Oregon, began to suspect that something wasn't right. They worried about summertime tourist revenue and talked of big changes coming. Meanwhile, in the Boom Town of Eagle, Colorado, folks thought that trouble would pass them by; they didn't feel the pinch until six months later. In Los Alamos, New Mexico, our representative Monied Burb, an understanding of the enormity of the problems came with the market crash in October. That the recession arrived in each place at a different time is an indicator of the many "its" that shape the economic realities of the Patchwork Nation—and of the many challenges the country will face in the future.

IT'S UNEMPLOYMENT

By July 2009 the size and scope of the recession were clear everywhere. Unemployment had climbed to 9.7 percent nationally, but that wasn't the whole story. In the Patchwork Nation, the rate ranged from 5.5 percent across Tractor Country to 12.1 percent across Minority Central communities. For places that had been teetering for some time, the recession was a final push. For some places higher unemployment is the norm. Add another few points to the number and a struggling economy becomes a serious crash.

There are three community types in particular for which unemployment and a lack of good jobs are the primary economic problems going forward. They were hit especially hard in the recession, and they are structurally bound to experience higher unemployment in the long term. (These numbers, we should note, were not unique to July 2009. Even as the economy slightly improved in late 2009 and early 2010, these disparities remained.)

Table 1. UNEMPLOYMENT RATE BY COMMUNITY TYPE—JANUARY 2008 AND JULY 2009

Community Type	January 2008	July 2009
Boom Towns	5.1	8.7
Campus and Careers	5.4	8.8
Emptying Nests	5.8	8.4
Evangelical Epicenters	5.7	9.9
Immigration Nation	5.4	8.8
Industrial Metropolis	5.8	10.3
Military Bastions	5.4	8.4
Minority Central	7.1	12.1
Monied Burbs	5.2	8.8
Mormon Outposts	4.5	6.5
Service Worker Centers	6.8	10.3
Tractor Country	4.6	5.5

Minority Central communities, heavily concentrated in the Southeast, are for the most part poor and rural. Even before the start of the recession, they had the highest unemployment rate in the country. In 2000, when much of the country was economically healthy, the unemployment rate in these 364 counties was 7 percent, slightly higher than the national county average. By July of 2009 their average rate was more than 12 percent.

These places never fully participated in the good times that came with the industrial revolution. There were manufacturing jobs here and there still are—they make up about 18 percent of the employment in Minority Central counties. But because of lower levels of union membership, wages never really climbed in these places the way they did up north. Minority Central locales are where companies went for lower labor costs before they went overseas. Now that even those low-paying jobs have begun to disappear, these places need to find a new engine for their local economies.

Our representative Minority Central community, Baton Rouge, Louisiana, is much better off than most because it's home to the state's government as well as to two universities. But even here there are gaping economic disparities between the white and black populations. The city is so divided that a 2007 study by Oxfam America found that Baton Rouge was simultaneously the best place to live in Louisiana and the worst: The average person in the wealthy white sections of the city "lives nearly half a decade longer, earns twice as much, is almost three times more likely to have a bachelor's degree, and is three times less likely to have dropped out of high school"[48] than the average person in the less prosperous black neighborhoods. These communities have not been well served for decades, and without better educational opportunities—only 14 percent of people are enrolled in college here versus 16 percent nationally—they are poorly positioned for the changes that are coming.

The same is true of the **Service Worker Centers**. These lightly populated counties simply don't have much to fall back on beyond small manufacturing and their ubiquitous service jobs. They don't offer the diverse labor markets or educated populace that high-tech employers crave. And their remote locations beyond even the exurbs work against them, as well. Transit centers and office parks are not big draws in the boondocks. Because it has few other choices, Lincoln City has attempted to strengthen its position as a tourist destination. As Mayor Lori Hollingsworth explained, there are "little guys" doing small business around Lincoln City and the hope is for something bigger. But tourism is the focus and "tourism's pretty good," she said.

Tourism does have its benefits, of course. It helps these places bring in outside dollars. But it has a few very big drawbacks for the next decade and beyond. First, anyplace dependent on tourism lives and dies by the amount of disposable income in the economy as a whole. People have to come to town to spend money at all the hotels, restaurants, and souvenir shops. If they don't, or they do but don't spend as much as they did before, stores and jobs will disappear. This has been the story in Lincoln City and the Service Worker Centers as a whole for the past several years. The unemployment rate in the Service Worker Centers went from 6.8 percent in January 2008 to 10.4 percent in July 2009.

Industrial Metropolis communities also witnessed a dramatic climb in unemployment during the recession, from 5.8 percent in January 2008 to 10.3 percent in July 2009. And their problems aren't going to go away now that the worst of the hard times are over. Although they contain a significant number of affluent and elite residents and are well positioned geographically, centered around major areas of commerce, whole parts of them are in danger of being left behind.

The education system in these places needs to be retooled, as people in the Industrial Metropolis of Philadelphia will tell you. And there's the difficult question of what the retooling would look like. The skills and trades that need to be taught so the next generation can get jobs are changing and will continue to change. Fixing unemployment here, in other words, requires an intense top-to-bottom reworking of how these places function, as well as a lot of ongoing maintenance.

The most difficult part of that challenge they face is the scale of the fixes needed. The size and diversity of these big urban places have long been a ·strength—they fill them with energy—but they're also something of a weakness, at least as the country goes through an economic shift. The individual counties in the Industrial Metropolis hold hundreds of thousands and often millions of people with different needs. Meeting all of them requires big solutions, in a time when those kinds of ideas will likely be especially hard to sell to the majority and when government coffers are very light.

IT'S THE HOUSING MARKET

For some parts of the Patchwork Nation the economic future comes down to one question: What do we build now? These places are or were heavily reliant on construction. And when that dried up with the housing crunch of 2008, it took away jobs for architects and masons, electricians and landscapers, roofers and carpenters. The impact on local economies has been enormous. Home values have dropped. Equity and disposable income have disappeared. In some places entire neighborhoods have been choked off.

A lot of communities got hit in the foreclosure crunch, but these economies took an especially hard blow. A return to where they were seems all but impossible in the near future. There's a lot of supply to go through before there's much demand for new building. Even a "boring" housing market, in which prices have settled into a sustainable range and properties move slowly but surely, is probably years off. Data from Moody's Analytics has suggested that the national median home price will climb back to $179,000 by late 2012. It was $180,000 in December 2008.[49]

And even a steady market probably won't be enough in places that were transformed by exponential housing growth prerecession. Builders got rich in these communities. Everyone who could drive a nail or wire a circuit was in demand all of the time, so companies involved in construction could hire more employees and charge more money and count on a calendar full of work year to year. Those who rode highest on the wave fell farthest in the crash, and for these places that means hardship.

That's especially true in the nation's **Boom Towns**. On average these places saw their populations increase by 14 percent between 2000 and 2006. Growth like that involves a lot of building and a lot of mortgages, so when the housing market went down nationally, it plummeted here. In January 2008, when the market was still essentially solid, the average foreclosure rate across the Boom Towns was 1.3 per 1,000 homes, not far from the national average. By December of 2009 it had spiked to 2.6. Most months in between, the Boom Towns were either at the top of the foreclosure heap or close to it.

Table 2. FORECLOSURES BY COMMUNITY TYPE, JANUARY 2008 VERSUS DECEMBER 2009

Community Type	Foreclosures per 1,000 Households January 2008	Foreclosures per 1,000 Households December 2009
Boom Towns	1.3	2.6
Campus and Careers	0.9	1.2
Emptying Nests	0.6	1.2
Evangelical Epicenters	0.3	0.5
Immigration Nation	0.7	1.4
Industrial Metro	2.4	2.7
Military Bastions	0.7	1.2
Minority Central	0.4	0.5
Monied Burbs	1.2	2.4
Mormon Outposts	0.3	3.3
Service Worker Centers	0.4	0.9
Tractor Country	0.1	0.3

Clark County, Nevada, home of Las Vegas, has been a poster child for Boom Town pain. In September 2009 one in every fifty homes there was in some state of foreclosure. In much smaller Eagle County, Colorado, there were five homes in some state of foreclosure in January 2008. By September of that year there were seven. By September 2009, there were thirty-one. But that doesn't show the full picture of current life in a six-thousand-person community like Eagle: the streets full of FOR SALE signs for the more than 180 houses on the market, plus a drop in median home value by 20 percent from the previous year.

The question is, Who would buy a home in Eagle now? It has the same blessing and curse of many Boom Towns. It's far removed from the city and the suburbs, so there are land and open space aplenty but not a lot of jobs. Living in the Boom Towns for most people involves either a long commute or a healthy stock portfolio. And given the likelihood of rising fuel prices and the fears the stock market has engendered over the past few years, these places are looking less desirable to most. Those houses will sit on the market for a longer time or their owners will take big hits when they sell. Either way, the net worth of these communities isn't going to reach 2008's heights for some time.

The counties of **Immigration Nation** also saw significant population growth between 2000 and 2006, about 11 percent overall. But unlike the Boom Towns, which are scattered far outside of major metropolitan areas, they are located primarily in the Southwest, which has seen a rapid influx of population for decades now. The communities that ballooned here did so around population centers such as Albuquerque, New Mexico; San Antonio, Texas; Denver; and Los Angeles. Because of this, they may be better set to emerge from the hard times.

Still, the numbers from these communities are troubling. In January 2008 Immigration Nation counties had 0.7 foreclosures per 1,000 homes. By August 2009 the number had climbed to 1.13 foreclosures per 1,000 homes and four months later, 2009 closed at a rate of 1.4 per 1,000. That's not terrible compared to elsewhere, but the decline in home values in these areas was. In the representative Immigration Nation community of El Mirage, Arizona, the median home price in September 2009 was down 42 percent from where it had been just twelve months earlier. In the surrounding county, Maricopa, it was down 25 percent. The economic climate in these places is likely to remain cold as long as the housing market does.

IT'S THE STOCK MARKET

The daily dealings on the trading floors of New York or London or Tokyo don't really matter to most people—unless, of course, they stray outside the norm and crash or skyrocket. There are, however, a few places where folks focus a bit more on the numbers at the top of the business page and the chatter on CNBC.

Table 3. STOCK OWNERSHIP AND TRADING HABITS BY COMMUNITY TYPE,
APRIL 2009 PEW RESEARCH CENTER VALUES SURVEY

Community Type	Percent Who Own Stock (Total)	Percent Who Trade Regularly	Percent Who Don't Trade Often
Boom Towns	53	6	47
Campus and Careers	45	4	41
Emptying Nests	54	10	44
Evangelical Epicenters	32	3	29
Immigration Nation	42	4	38
Industrial Metro	49	7	42
Military Bastions	48	6	42
Minority Central	37	3	34
Monied Burbs	54	8	46
Mormon Outposts	40	3	37
Service Worker Centers	45	3	42
Tractor Country	57	6	51

About 54 percent of the households in the **Monied Burbs** own stock in some way, whether directly or through 401(k)s or other retirement plans. People here are also among the most likely to trade stocks actively looking for gains—more than 8 percent of residents do. Of all the representative communities in the Patchwork Nation, the Monied Burb of Los Alamos was the most shaken when the stock market collapsed and the banking industry looked perilously weak. The financially savvy people here knew they were seeing an economic correction unfolding before them.

"The party is over for now here in America," James Rickman, who works at the Los Alamos National Lab, wrote in an e-mail in early 2009. "The market will eventually correct itself to account for the 'actual value' of America's assets. This likely will not be pretty or comforting. With or without a stimulus package, I see some very dark times coming to this nation and the world."

Even those with less apocalyptic takes on what was happening thought that a fundamental shift would follow the loss of all that wealth. Bill Enloe, president of the Los Alamos Bank, said that he saw "bad times ahead" for most of the country.

Of course, when the economy gets sick, it's the stock market that heals first, as it did in the Great Recession. Even as people in many parts of the country were wondering when things would fully turn around for them, many in the Burbs saw their troubles as history. They have the educations and the bank accounts to ride out tough times and get back on their feet quickly after the worst has passed.

Also high in stock ownership are the **Emptying Nests**, where about 54 percent of the population is invested in the market. About 10 percent of residents here trade actively—though that number no doubt comes in part from the fact that people in these communities scrambled to manage their investments after the market crash of October 2008. In Emptying Nest locales, where the population is older than the average American county's, the impact of the stock market crash was different. It's not just that massive amounts of wealth were lost; it's that there isn't time for investors to recoup what was lost.

In the Emptying Nest of Clermont, Florida, a surprisingly high number of people in and around town made risky and incorrect investment choices. "You'd be surprised how many people are invested. But the even more important point to it is that they literally are diversified wrong. And the asset allocations are way wrong," said Gary Clarke, a senior advisor at Ameriprise in Clermont. "I mean, just way overaggressive."

Unlike people in other community types, many in the Emptying Nests are either winding down their careers or have already retired. Making back what's been lost isn't going to be easy for them without a dramatic turnaround in the market.

IT'S SOMETHING ELSE

And then there are places where the economy's health will be determined by something else entirely—something that isn't a big part of the daily news coverage. For some places "it" will be big institutional investment and research funding, by the government or others. **Campus and Careers** and **Military Bastions** counties rely heavily on such money to fuel their economies.

In **Tractor Country** the health of the local economy may be determined by global demand for pork or beef or corn. These places have different concerns than the rest of the nation. The fear here, even as the recession was winding down most everywhere else, was that the hard times would continue as falling food-commodity prices began to compound over time. Smaller farmers had been hit particularly hard.

And there are some places, like the **Evangelical Epicenters**, where the "it" could be a combination of things. Those places are less wealthy than the average county, so small changes could shake them hard. Many of them sit in somewhat exurban or even rural areas, and they have been hit by foreclosures as well as unemployment fairly hard. Of course, in the Epicenters, cultural issues tend to be bigger drivers of opinion and political sentiment than the economy.

Obviously, the factors that drive the local economies of the Patchwork Nation are interconnected. A healthy stock market, for example, would help to restore employment—it would help put money in the pockets of people in Monied Burbs, who then might spend a bit more in the Service Worker Centers where they vacation. But even with this type of injection, the unemployment rate in Service Worker Centers will almost certainly remain high. It was even when times were good. And there are reasons to believe that the new good times won't be as good as the old good times.

SEEING AND BELIEVING

The next decade promises to be full of economic challenges and changes. When times were relatively smooth, the differences among the distinct economies of the Patchwork Nation were easy to put aside. An extended bumpy period will place the wants and needs of these locales in competition with one another. The people living in the Service Worker Centers and Minority Central communities got used to higher unemployment— but not double-digit unemployment for an extended period followed by a weak recovery. The people living in the Boom Towns weren't prepared for what's happened there, and the longer the housing market drags, the more unhappy they will become.

The late-2000s recession gave us a preview of some of the troubles ahead. As complete economic collapse loomed and the government rushed to prop up institutions and industries, two sentiments became common across the Patchwork Nation: *Why is there such a thing as "too big to fail"? And since the government is stepping in to help, where's* my *bailout?* Both express the idea of injustice in how the economy was being handled by the government. If we were all hurting, how come some got different treatment than others?

The recovery, such as it was, only emphasized the differences among the various community types. As the turnaround seemed to be arriving slowly in the fall of 2009, the media began debating whether another government stimulus package was needed. Much of that discussion fell along traditional liberal (yes, we do) and conservative (no, we don't) lines.

But political positions can be less important on such questions than where you live.

In February 2009 CNBC correspondent Rick Santelli responded to President Obama's plan to help people stuck in bad mortgages with a now infamous on-air rant. He asked whether it made sense for the government to "subsidize the losers' mortgages" rather than to "buy cars and buy houses in foreclosure and give them to people who might actually have a chance to prosper down the road." Although some borrowers clearly made bad choices, the foreclosure crisis wasn't just about "losers." It was about entire communities on the brink. Santelli saw it the way he did, at least in part, because he lives and works in one community type and doesn't experience what's happening in the others.

That's true of all of us, even if we aren't so acerbically vocal about it. The "American economy" in the news is just a collection of averaged numbers—stock values, home prices, jobs lost or gained. No one really experiences that economy. On the ground in the different community types within the Patchwork Nation, the economic numbers we experience are germane to our particular communities, and perhaps those next door, not a national average. Most of us observe and understand only the economic reality—the "it"—that immediately affects us. It's easy to mistake the problems you see where you live for problems that exist everywhere—to practice what psychologists call "projection." But the struggles of people in other places, although different, are no less real than yours.

Gary Shilling, an economic consultant who was among the first to predict the subprime mortgage crisis, is one of many who has looked ahead to see tough years requiring plenty of government intervention. "Economic growth in the bulk of the next decade will probably be slow—so slow that it will force the federal government to take continuing actions to prevent high and chronically rising unemployment," he wrote in his August 2009 newsletter.[50] But it's unlikely that the required actions will be the same for all of the Patchwork Nation. Some places may be in need of further housing assistance or jobs programs, while others may need little or nothing. Debate about whether the government should continue to take on debt will undoubtedly grow, and it could easily spin into louder talk of "losers."

That's why understanding the "its" of the twelve community types in the Patchwork Nation is so important. It's only through understanding their various local economies that you can get a grasp on what we think of as the American economy. And that grasp is important to have when it comes to devising economic policies that can help everyone.

Consider the home-buyers' tax credit. When, in November 2009, the federal government acted both to extend it and to expand it to include current homeowners who wanted a new primary residence, many people criticized the idea. In one typical op-ed, Simon Johnson and James Kwak, a professor at MIT and a Yale Law student who together blog about economics on a site called the Baseline Scenario, wrote in *The Washington Post* that any extension was "throwing good money after bad."[51] Prices had stabilized, they argued, but at values that were too high—about 20 percent over their values in 2000.

They may have been right—as long as the figures were viewed nationally. (Though finding the "right" value for anything can be a slippery proposition.) But the most important lesson that the Patchwork Nation teaches us is that national-level approaches can be too blunt for a highly segmented economy. Everyplace in the nation is not the same. Some places, like the housing-market-dependent Boom Towns, might have needed propping up for a little while longer; other places did not. Instead of applying income or employment thresholds to economic policies, the better way may be to look at geographic areas—and not just in relation to urban poverty or rural agriculture. The specifics of communities could matter as much or more than the specifics of individuals.

SO FAR AWAY—AND SO CLOSE

Given the complicated mix of economic realities that make up the Patchwork Nation, is there a simple way to understand the struggles these communities experience relative to one another? In a way, yes. Throughout our work on this project we have watched a few key indicators to create what we call an economic-hardship index, a measure of short-term economic pain in each of the twelve community types.

Six data elements went into its creation. Every month, for every county in the United States, we gathered gas prices for the previous month, the change in gas prices from two months ago to the previous month, an estimate of the percentage of monthly household spending dedicated to fuel consumption and car maintenance, the unemployment rate from two months ago (the release of those numbers lags), home foreclosures per one thousand homes in the previous month, and the change in home foreclosures per one thousand homes from two months ago to the previous month.

We condensed this information into one simple score for every county in the United States. We ranked those scores on a scale of 0 to 100, with the county with the least economic hardship receiving a score of 0 and the county with the worst receiving a score of 100. Finally, we sorted those counties into their appropriate Patchwork Nation community types to determine how different types of places were doing.

The graph below shows how the twelve Patchwork Nation types compared to a national average from September 2008, just before the stock market crash, to October 2009, when the economy began to turn around. The dotted line represents the national average. Each of the bars represents the range of the scores for each community type, with the black line in each bar representing each type's mean.

Places that might seem to have a lot in common turn out to look quite different on the hardship index. For instance, you might imagine that there would be a good deal of similarity between Tractor Country and the Service Worker Centers. Both community types are predominantly rural and usually far from metropolitan areas. Neither has even a hundred people per square mile. Both are at least 94 percent white and have

Figure 13. Hardship Ranges by Community Type

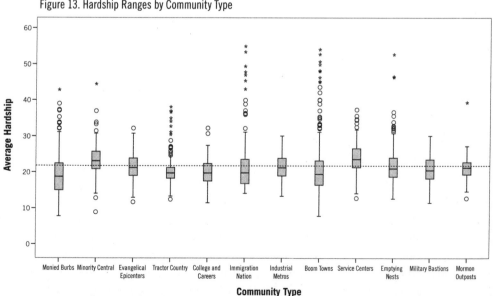

median household incomes below the national county average of about $37,000.

But their economic realities are starkly different.

The Service Worker Centers, although removed from the nation's most populous areas, are actually quite reliant on them. These places have little industry of their own, so they need a healthy broader economy to grow. Of all of the twelve community types, the Service Worker Centers consistently had the highest level of economic hardship during our study. Their mean hardship score over the deepest part of the recession was 23.3, versus the national average hardship score of 21.2.

In real-life terms in Lincoln City that meant painful off-seasons during which many local businesses closed, including longtime businesses that were presumed to be stable, such as the Kernville Steak and Seafood House. Its Web site reads, "Ordinarily in this space you'd be reading about the wonderful view, food and service we offered at 'The Kernville'. Unfortunately, as of January 31st, 2009, 'The Kernville' is closed. We hope that it'll be open again, but we don't know when that might be." As of early 2010, it had not yet reopened.

"You know, the locals are trying to keep this economy afloat in the down seasons," said Allyson Longueira, managing editor of the local weekly *The News Guard.* "When hotels aren't full, they're not giving their employees hours. When restaurants aren't full, they're not giving their employees hours. Same with the mall. The mall's not selling."

The people who should have been filling all of those hotels and restaurants and mall shops were visitors from larger metropolitan areas. So even though the Service Worker Centers are far away from such bigger, wealthier areas as the Monied Burbs geographically, they are closely tied to them economically. When the people in the Burbs trim their budgets, the Service Worker Centers feel it directly.

Not so for the communities of Tractor Country. These counties are similarly removed from those metro areas geographically, but they saw a different economic story unfold. Their economic hardship score of 19.3 is the second-lowest among the twelve community types.

Why is that?

Take the relatively low incomes of Tractor Country and add a cripplingly long economic trough and you should have a recipe for bad times. But the economies in Tractor Country counties, based heavily on agriculture, stand apart from those of the rest of the country. These places, so dependent on things like the price of a bushel of wheat or a head of cattle, tend to be somewhat immune to the daily ticks on Wall Street—or even stock market crashes.

When the nation's unemployment rate hovered near 10 percent in the fall of 2009, it was below 5 percent in the Tractor Country community of Sioux Center, Iowa. "I think Sioux Center has fared quite well through the struggles of the economy during the last year, especially some of the blue-collar industries hurt," said Steve Hoogland, editor of the *Sioux Center News.* "Have they gone through rough times? Absolutely. . . . But you see a lot of segments of the industry here in Sioux Center are doing well, you see new houses popping up. . . . Although the dairy prices have really tanked here recently, a number of the other agriculture things themselves have not hurt real bad. They've hung in there, let's put it that way. That's one of the reasons."

It's actually the big reason—and it held for most all of Tractor Country. Only the Monied Burbs experienced less economic hardship in the recession's darkest days. The Burbs had a similar average hardship score of 19, but for very different reasons.

Unlike Tractor Country, the Burbs actually suffered quite a lot during the Great Recession. Their unemployment rate got close to 10 percent. Their foreclosures, per capita, climbed to near the top of all the community types'. But they weathered the hard times better because of their higher incomes—they were insulated from truly terrible pain by their economic standing and their well-educated, highly mobile workforce.

Because of that, in terms of what the economy "felt" like, the average Monied Burb had a lot in common with the average Tractor Country county. They moved closer economically even if they remained as distant as ever geographically. That's not to say these places were suddenly siblings—there are few communities as different from each other as the Burbs and Tractor Country. But the hard times hit wealthy suburban America and agricultural rural America with about the same overall impact.

Just as the look at the different "its" in the Patchwork Nation shows how difficult "fixing" the economy will be over the long haul, the economic hardship index shows how many of our preconceived notions of metro and retro, urban and rural America are misguided. It's not just how much money you have or how close you are to a big metropolitan center that determines your economic fate; it's the economic drivers where you live, your home county's relative level of dependence on outside economic forces, and your community's economic values. Exactly the things, in other words, that aren't revealed in national-level figures.

LEARNING FROM TRACTOR COUNTRY

The inadequacy of the aggregate economic picture is also apparent when you look at the way household debt stacks up across the Patchwork Nation. Financial analysts and business writers often talk about the average American's overreliance on debt. The fear during the crunch was that the nation had built an unsustainable standard of living on credit cards—and now that the bills were coming due, there would be frightening consequences. People without jobs, or with lower-paying jobs, wouldn't be able to pay bills. Or perhaps they would be able to pay only bills, drying up consumer spending.

There's more than a little truth to that—broadly speaking. American consumer debt reached $2.6 trillion in 2008, with $972 billion of that credit card debt. That works out to over $8,000 per household. David Beim, a former banker who's now a business professor at Columbia University, told National Public Radio's Planet Money economic team in February 2009 that "we've been living very high on the hog. Our living standard has been rising dramatically in the last twenty-five years. And we have been borrowing much of the money to make that prosperity happen." Beim cited numbers showing that American consumer debt in 2009, $13 trillion, was equal to the U.S. GDP.[52]

That's a scary thought.

But look at how that debt was distributed in the Patchwork Nation— and how frightened people actually were about it. The table below reflects how people in our twelve community types felt about the credit card debt they carried before the economy truly destabilized. The analysis was built from pooled surveys conducted by the Pew Research Center for the People and the Press over an approximately two-year period before the 2008 market crash.[53]

For the most part, the greatest concern about holding too much credit card debt came from places where incomes are just above or just below the national median household income line, in the Military Bastions, Minority Central, and Immigration Nation. Lots of people in the relatively wealthy Boom Towns were worried about carrying too much debt, too. But in the Mormon Outposts and Tractor Country, where the median household income is below the national county average, fewer respondents expressed such concern.

Table 4. CREDIT CARD DEBT

Community Type	Percent Who Say They Owe Nothing on Credit Cards	Percent Who Say They Owe More Than They Can Afford
Boom Towns	19.4	22.5
Campus and Careers	23.9	18.6
Emptying Nests	28	18.7
Evangelical Epicenters	28.4	19.6
Immigration Nation	20.6	23.1
Industrial Metro	23.2	21.5
Military Bastions	22.8	30.2
Minority Central	23.7	28.2
Monied Burbs	19.4	20.2
Mormon Outposts	28	14.7
Service Worker Centers	20.9	22.4
Tractor Country	15.1	17.9

Sitting in the middle of the pack were the nation's large metropolitan areas, the Industrial Metropolises and the Monied Burbs. An optimist may see some hope there for the consumer side of the economy, which drives two-thirds of all spending in the United States. Those two places are responsible for a lot of that spending.

Keep in mind that these numbers were based on self-reports. The respondent was the one determining how much he or she can afford, and that's not inconsequential. It reflects his or her attitude toward debt—and that attitude has a lot to do with how much one spends in the consumer economy. But it gives us the whole picture of how debt was actually stacking up in our various locations.

The table below shows the percentage of bank branches in each one of the twelve Patchwork Nation counties that took Troubled Asset Relief Program money after the crash. The numbers, to some extent, express the different attitudes toward loan-making and finances in the different community types. These are local bank branches, places that make small-business as well as auto and personal loans. Whether they needed TARP money, intended to bail banks not only out of bad mortgages, but also out of bad loans and poor investments of many kinds, is in part a reflection of the debt troubles of the consumers they were serving.

Table 5. WHERE DID THE TARP MONEY GO?

Community Type	Percent of Branches Taking TARP Money
Boom Towns	46.9
Campus and Careers	37.1
Emptying Nests	33.8
Evangelical Epicenters	28.9
Immigration Nation	45.0
Industrial Metro	52.7
Military Bastions	45.2
Minority Central	36.9
Monied Burbs	48.1
Mormon Outposts	60.3
Service Worker Centers	33.8
Tractor Country	15.9

Look in particular at the number for Tractor Country, 15.9 percent. The banks here never made the same kinds of high-risk loans and investments that they did in other locations. Their attitude toward lending and risking money must be different.

Eric Walhof, president of the First National Bank in the Tractor Country community of Sioux Center, Iowa, said that loans at his bank are extremely personal. He knows the people who come in asking for money. He knows what they do for a living. If they are in agriculture, he's not only familiar with what they farm and what its commodity prices look like, but also with things like what kind of physical shape their property is in.

That works to his bank's—and Tractor Country's—advantage in two ways. First, Walhof has a very clear idea of the loan he's considering. Second, those seeking the loan know that he knows, which means that there's a high bar for going into his bank and asking for money in the first place. This is one area in which Tractor Country really stands apart from the rest of the country. Residents here are more hesitant to borrow than people elsewhere, and their general attitude toward debt—Don't take on more than you can handle—is deeply rooted in their communities. That's one reason foreclosures weren't a widespread problem here during the recession. You see a more conservative attitude toward debt in ways in these places as well.

When you get into some of these smaller communities, more removed from the big cities, you see a lot of advertisements for Dave Ramsey, a financial adviser and TV and radio media personality. In these communities, Ramsey seems to be something of a celebrity. It is sometimes difficult to open a newspaper or drive by five billboards without seeing his smiling, goateed face staring at you. Ramsey is a different kind of financial guru—less Jim Cramer than your frugal uncle who preaches savings as the way to wealth. His Web site shows pictures of Ramsey holding a fistful of hundreds, but it also shows him cutting up credit cards. He has built a small media empire around this message and it is one that resonates around Tractor Country.

More disconcerting are the places that have the most TARP-aided bank branches: the Industrial Metropolises, Monied Burbs, Boom Towns, and Mormon Outposts. Regardless of what people in these communities think about their debt loads, there are some serious problems.

There are twelve communities in the Patchwork Nation, but they don't all have the same impact on the economy as a whole. In terms of the nation's economic well-being, the Industrial Metropolises, Monied Burbs, and Boom Towns, all relatively wealthy and populous, have the most significance. And these numbers indicate that, in addition to being big debtors, these places also made a lot of bad bets. The implication is that for the nation to get its economic house in order, it's almost necessary that consumer spending drag for some time. First, these spendthrift communities have to pay off the debt they have—remember that more than 20 percent of people here said that they had too much credit card debt before the recession hit. Second, they have to find a new level of spending that's sustainable.

Does that mean a turnaround in consumer spending is a long ways off? Not necessarily, but there are certainly reasons to think so. Those wealthy community types that have the most influence over consumer spending have been shaken in this past recession. Many there lost their jobs. Others watched friends lose theirs. The tendency in those places may be to trim back spending a bit as a hedge against more hard times.

In fact, in terms of long-term stability, it could be best for those places to trim back. It might mean that the consumer economy would be slower to recover, but also that it would be rebuilt on a more solid economic foundation—one, perhaps, more like that of Tractor Country, where residents are reluctant to live beyond their means and banks are reluctant to help them do so. When more than a fifth of the people in the Patchwork Nation's three wealthiest community types say that they have too much debt, that's troubling—and that was before the economy turned truly bad. Given the rate of economic growth projected going forward, it's hard to imagine either spending or lending habits going back to where they were. Slower growth over the long term means fewer raises and fewer new jobs. That means that people will probably spend less, even in wealthier communities, just to keep debt levels where they are now.

And as Washington struggles to deal with that problem, a whole different set of issues may arise that would make large-scale policy changes likely impacts in the coming years.

THE RISE IN HARD FEELINGS AND NEW APPROACHES

If the American economy is changing in some broad, permanent way, what's ahead? There are no certainties, of course, but one likelihood is rising tensions.

The economic policies of the next decade could easily deepen existing cultural and attitudinal divides in the United States. Some people want the government to spend more; some want it to spend less. Some want a looser monetary policy; some want a tighter one. None of that's new. But those disparities will be exacerbated if more sluggish growth becomes the norm. Different places will seek different solutions. People living in the Service Worker Centers may look for direct government investment. Those living in the Monied Burbs may focus on cuts in capital gains taxes. Residents of the Military Bastions, whose local economies are dependent on large military bases, may be concerned about defense spending.

Remember that no matter what the government chooses to do, it will have less to spend. Washington has already incurred a massive debt over the course of the Iraq and Afghan wars and the bailouts that followed the financial industry's collapse. The amount stood at over $14 trillion in late 2009; it was less than $7 trillion in 2003. There will be hard choices to make in Congress and the White House, and there will be winners and losers in the government's attempts to improve the economy as a whole. Ideas that look very practical to people living in some places may seem extremely wrongheaded to people living elsewhere. We've already seen those kinds of discussions. Look at the home buyers' tax credit—nonsensical to some, but critical to others.

When you look at the economy through the Patchwork Nation framework, you wonder if it may behoove the U.S. government to reexamine how it handles economic policy, to tailor it more to places than to people. It's not an outlandish idea. Washington already looks at some geographic areas—for example, blighted sections of urban centers—as places that need special treatment. In 1974 the Department of Housing and Urban Development created the Community Development Block Grant program with the idea of targeting places, not people. The formula for CDBG grants looks at an area's poverty rate, population density, and housing stock. That's not completely different from what we have done with Patchwork Nation. But why should those measures come into play only in specific instances? Why not make them the standard for an assortment of policies—from housing tax credits to the duration of unemployment benefits to job retraining?

A place is more than a collection of individuals; it's a set of values, perceptions, and industries. And those things together create unique economic environments that, with the right analysis, can be grouped into specific types for which specific programs can be prescribed. That's not to say that the economic policy makers should adopt the Patchwork Nation scheme—we were trying to measure and analyze a lot more than just economics—but it may be a start. Maybe people who live in communities with an unemployment rate of X and a foreclosure rate of Y would be eligible for programs A and B. People living in places where the only real problem is foreclosures would be eligible only for program B.

Would the critics of extending the home buyers' tax credit feel the same way about it if it were targeted only to those places that were hammered by the foreclosure crisis?

When the economy dips, it's not just people who are hurting; it's places that are hurting. And not all of them hurt in the same way. It's far more complicated than urban and rural or black and white. If you lose your job in a relatively stable community, another probably won't be hard to find. If you lose it in a place that's teetering, you're likely looking at more time out of work. How easily could you find employment as a research assistant living in a Campus and Careers locale? What about as a master carpenter in a Boom Town? An approach to unemployment focused on people rather than places means that those two individuals will be treated the same. Should they?

One argument against an approach that organizes programs around types of community or community economic indicators is that it's unnecessary. If you create the right programs aimed at the right individuals, the right places will benefit anyway. That's to say, if more people are unemployed in Lincoln City than in Los Alamos, then government unemployment or retraining programs will necessarily give more help to the people of Lincoln City. But what if unemployment numbers remain high in Lincoln City? Historically, they have been, and a postrecession scenario featuring very slow economic growth wouldn't help. The problem is going to be getting and keeping the right programs in place. The Monied Burbanites, with their advanced degrees and large bank accounts, may sense by 2012 that the economy is largely "back to normal." But people in the Service Worker Centers may be feeling that things have only slightly improved since 2009. They will be looking for continuing responses from the government.

Could providing assistance or aid to people by community type create tensions? Absolutely. But they will exist under the current system anyway. If government assistance is granted, people in the communities where it's largely unneeded will criticize it as wasteful—and in some sense they will be right. If government assistance isn't granted, people in the communities who need it will feel their problems are being ignored—and in some sense they will also be right. Organizing government economic policies around communities would create winners and losers, too. All economic policies do. But will those policies be well devised for what's to come? Will they help the nation as a whole adapt to the changing global economy?

Naturally, the idea of making community indicators the basis of economic policy is an idea that would need a lot of further discussion and analysis. We have focused on using Patchwork Nation as a way to explore the differences in the United States, not as a way to build new systems of administering policy. But those differences all attest to the same thing: Dramatic economic changes of one kind or another are coming, probably sooner than we expect. The question is, What will they be where you live?

POLITICS

■ ■ ■

THE SEA CHANGE THAT WASN'T

I f you paid even the slightest attention to the news media in the hours and days following the election of Barack Obama as president, one idea was unavoidable: that America was a profoundly changed place.

The day of the election Adam Nagourney wrote in *The New York Times* that the 2008 campaign represented a "sea change for politics as we know it." Two days later, on November 5, Princeton professor Cornel West wrote in *U.S. News & World Report* that Obama's win had "ushered in a new era in American history and a new epoch in American politics." On November 7 columnist Michael Lind wrote on Salon.com a piece headlined "Obama and the Dawn of the Fourth Republic."

But the dawn never broke. The new epoch remained all too similar to the old epoch. Politics as we know it remained just that. As the first year plus of the Obama administration came to a close, expectations had come back to earth. The health-care reform plan that wound its way through Congress was dramatic but not the massive sea change many had expected—no government option, no big dip in the Medicare eligibility age. The Patriot Act appeared headed for renewal. The U.S. prisoner camp at Guantánamo Bay, Cuba, was to be closed, but the government continued the practice of "rendition"—removing suspects from their home countries without a trial. The military's "Don't ask, don't tell" policy toward gays and lesbians remained in place. Immigration reform hadn't yet been tackled. Gridlock reigned.

Some of this was inevitable. After all, truly changing politics isn't easy. But more to the point: Is that what Obama's election had really represented? Yes, voter turnout was higher than for the previous presidential election, but 61 percent wasn't a record. Yes, people aged eighteen to twenty-nine voted, but, again, not in record numbers. Their turnout was only 54 percent.

In fact, there was a much bigger jump in voter turnout between 2000 and 2004 than there was between 2004 and 2008. In 2004, 16 million more people voted for president than in 2000. In 2008 the number of voters was up by only 11 million versus 2004. In terms of voter engagement, the year of George W. Bush's reelection was arguably the bigger game changer than 2008, despite the outpourings of public—and media—enthusiasm inspired by the Obama campaign. Obama's seven-percentage-point victory was large, but it wasn't, historically speaking, enormous. Richard M. Nixon's margin was more than three times higher in 1972.

None of this is to downplay the significance of the 2008 presidential race. The election of an African American to the White House was a seminal event in U.S. history. And Obama's approaches to a long list of policies—from government spending to foreign relations—represented a significant departure from those of the Bush years. But the fact that the Republican Party had received a rebuke from voters didn't mean that there was widespread support for a specific idea about where the country should go next.

For all the attention we pay to them, presidential elections aren't usually the political fulcrums we make them out to be. They can be signs of something—satisfaction, disinterest, anger—but it's often hard to know what. As much as the media might present them as dramatic showdowns in which the public chooses a decisive new national direction, they're typically just a quadrennial temperature taking. Even on the rare occasions when they do signal some large-scale change, they're often a lagging indicator: The public chose a new course some time ago; the election simply proved it.

Given the challenges the United States faces at the beginning of the twenty-first century, proclamations about new eras in politics should be viewed with even more skepticism than usual. Who will be the winners and losers in the postrecession economy? Who will be the United States' new adversaries and allies? How far will social mores evolve internationally and at home? If the 2008 election marked anything, it was more likely the beginning of an especially turbulent time in U.S. politics, not the dawn of a new republic.

What does the American political landscape really look like in 2010? Different than before—but probably not as different as some imagined it would in November 2008.

The truth is, some parts of the country did change. But others didn't. The various community types in the Patchwork Nation have very different attitudes about politics, each shaped by a set of specific socioeconomic and cultural circumstances. It's difficult for one candidate or one election to alter the long-term mind-set of a place—in some cases extremely so.

Some community types enter each election cycle like new-car buyers going to a dealer's lot genuinely unsure of what they would like to buy. While they certainly house partisan voters with entrenched loyalties, they also hold unusually large numbers of independents who can be swayed by either major party. That's why the voters in such places—the portfolio-conscious Monied Burbs, for example—might be thought of as always on the market, looking to be won over with a good deal: the right candidate with the right approach to the right issues. From election to election, the particulars of the deal they're looking for can change, sometimes radically, but economic appeals are usually an important ingredient.

But other places never even go shopping. No deal can win over voters in these communities. When they want a new car, they march down to the dealer and go straight for the upgrade of their current model. They are so loyally partisan that they head into each election cycle more or less certain of what they will do. Well before the national conventions have confirmed party nominees, their minds will be made up. The only real question they face is whether they will feel strongly enough to go out and vote for their party and candidates of choice. The Evangelical Epicenters are the best example of this, but there are others.

Stable political attachments are hardly a new development. For all the media talk of swing states that accompanies each election, the fact is, the long-term voting patterns of most communities in the United States are pretty predictable. If they change, they do so slowly, in reaction to broad socioeconomic or cultural shifts over the course of a generation or more. Take, for instance, the community type we call Minority Central. In the 1950s and 1960s, many of those counties would have been part of the so-called Solid South, which had voted Democratic for decades. But changes in how the party approached civil rights moved these places to where they are now—very divided politically between their black and white populations and often leaning Republican due to low African American turnout.

Similarly, the social conservatism that's recently become a hallmark of at least portions of the Republican Party has had a big effect on the vote in the Evangelical Epicenters. In 1980 Jimmy Carter came within five points of winning these communities; in 2008 John McCain won them by more than thirty points. Other factors can change the politics of a place, too. In the most dynamic counties—those with big in- or outflows of population—who the voters are from election to election can a make huge difference. After all, counties are merely lines on a map. What happens within them depends on human beings.

For the sake of this discussion, we've picked a fairly limited period of time, the years 2000 to 2008, and a limited point of comparison, presidential elections. Why? There was no incumbent seeking reelection in 2000, and the current state of American politics—post–Cold War, postindustrial, highly polarized at the county level—was set. And presidential elections, in which regional party differences are diminished, and everyone is facing the same set of candidates, offer perhaps the best nationwide measure of political feelings and attitudes.

If you look at presidential elections in that time span, you quickly see that the list of community types that candidates have been fighting to win is short: the Monied Burbs, Immigration Nation, and Minority Central—and to a lesser degree the Boom Towns and Service Worker Centers. That doesn't mean that other, more predictable locations are unimportant. In these places, what matters is voter turnout and how it affects statewide margins, particularly in close elections, as we all found out in the 2000 presidential race.

In that election and those that have followed, what we've seen on those election-night maps is the result of a small number of voters who tipped a congressional district or a state red or blue. The community types that have long been politically untethered went this way or that. Or the places that have long been firmly tied to one particular party did so by a smaller or larger number of votes. That's it. Some combination of those factors has determined recent elections. That's hardly the stuff a sea change is made of.

NO SALE AT ANY PRICE

Four of our community types hold large numbers of voters with firm, even lopsided, party attachments. Some lean Democratic and some lean Republican, but in all cases the question in every election is one of margin.

When politicians in either party talk about the need to "bring out the base," they're speaking about voters who live in these communities. Their vote tends to be so one-sided that simply driving up turnout in some key locales can flip entire states. And as the parties attempt to remake themselves and discover their new identities—as the GOP is now—these loyalist places are the measuring stick for having gone too far.

Table 6. PERCENTAGE OF VOTES

Presidential Election	Industrial Metropolis	Tractor Country	Mormon Outposts	Evangelical Epicenters
2000				
Al Gore (D)	63	30	21	39
George W. Bush (R)	34	68	76	61
2004				
John Kerry (D)	63	30	18	34
George W. Bush (R)	36	68	80	65
2008				
Barack Obama (D)	68	34	25	33
John McCain (R)	31	64	72	66

Big, diverse, and urban, the Industrial Metropolis counties have long been a lock for the Democratic Party. They benefit more than other places from government largesse, receiving federal money for things like transportation services and poverty programs. They also contain high percentages of groups that have historically voted Democratic: minorities and the urban poor, as well as a notable affluent liberal population.

Through the last three presidential elections, the Industrial Metropolises have consistently given about two-thirds of their votes to the Democratic candidate. And that's having worked off a list of very different candidates in very different elections. Al Gore, running as a continuation of Bill Clinton's administration, garnered 63 percent of the vote in these counties in 2000. So did John Kerry, running as the anti-Bush four years later.

In 2008 these places went heavily for Obama for what would seem obvious reasons: Here was an African American who made his home in the Industrial Metropolis of Cook County, Illinois. But the margin of victory for Obama in these places—39 percentage points—also had much to do with disinterest in or dislike for the Republican challenger. McCain took only 6.5 million votes from these counties in 2008, whereas Bush had taken 7 million in 2004. That's an especially significant decline in a year when turnout was up in the Industrial Metropolises by about 2 million voters.

That should be a worry for the GOP. Somewhat tighter margins in the Industrial Metropolises could have helped McCain win a few more states. In Indiana, for example, McCain lost because of a solid defeat in Marion County (city of Indianapolis), where he captured twenty-two thousand fewer votes than Bush did in 2004.

The sheer exuberance for Obama in these places should be a concern for the Republicans, too. When Obama won, *Philadelphia Daily News* opinion editor Sandy Shea was overwhelmed by the reaction. "An impromptu group of kids came marching down Broad Street. I mean, it was like a parade," she said. "It was as big as the celebrations I saw when the Phillies won the World Series [earlier that fall], maybe bigger. It was just an outpouring of emotion." An army of young, enthusiastic voters could boost the Democratic margins here for some time and would seem to be a big Obama weapon in 2012.

How could the GOP make these places slightly more competitive? That's where things get complicated. Gaining a few votes in the Industrial Metros would probably mean taking positions that could hurt the party elsewhere.

Look at conservative **Tractor Country**. What ties these counties to the Republican Party is less economic than cultural. It's not about agricultural subsidies as much as it's about maintaining a small-town way of life—which includes resisting the influence of the federal government, often seen as a meddling, threatening outside force. Out of all our community types Tractor Country most strongly agrees with the statement "The federal government should run ONLY those things that cannot be run at the local level." Forty-one percent in these ruralmost burgs said that they completely agree with that statement, about 10 percent more than the national average.[54]

Since the 2000 presidential race there's been slightly more movement in Tractor Country than in Industrial Metropolises, but not much more. Bush won by the exact same margins here in 2000 and 2004—37 percentage points. In 2008 Obama closed the gap, if you can call it that, to only 30 percentage points. But these places seem to be in no danger of flipping for decades. Cultural issues such as abortion and same-sex marriage will probably be enough to keep them loyal to the GOP. To what degree might depend on how much the Republicans move toward the center on social issues in the hopes of capturing more votes in the populous Industrial Metropolises and Monied Burbs. Fewer than 1 million votes came from Tractor Country in 2008, but in a very tight race, turnout from these counties could be important in states such as Iowa, Minnesota, and Missouri—even Colorado.

The **Mormon Outposts** similarly see the conservative values that were their foundation as more closely aligned with the Republican than the Democratic Party. The margins of victory here for Bush in 2000 and 2004 were the most lopsided of those for any candidate in any of our communities: 55 and 68 percentage points, respectively. In 2008 things got measurably tighter, with McCain winning by a more modest 47 percentage points. Obama made gains both relative to his Republican opponent and to fellow Democrats Gore and Kerry, receiving 152,703 votes from the Outposts. That's 44,650 more than Gore got from these places in 2000 and 36,844 more than Kerry did in 2004.

The total number of votes from these counties has increased steadily over the past three presidential elections, accompanying rapid growth that has largely come from an influx of newcomers. The growth rate in these counties exceeds the national county average, and as they have expanded they have also become more diverse.

So could there ever be enough growth here to flip these places? If so, it would take a long time. The dominant culture in the Mormon Outposts is very conservative, both socially and fiscally. The better question might be, What happens if the Republican margin continues to slip in these places? The states where the Outposts hold the biggest shares of the population all went heavily for McCain. Idaho's tally was the tightest, with McCain capturing only 61 percent of the vote. But if areas such as Northern Utah continue to see an influx of new residents, the result could be a lessening of the Republican strength in these areas. Already Salt Lake County, a place many would probably assume is a Mormon Outpost, has had such rapid population growth that it fits our Boom Town category even better. And its voting patterns look very different from those of a traditional Mormon-dominated area. Obama won 48 percent of the vote in that county.

The **Evangelical Epicenters** are less likely to switch allegiances. Among all of the Patchwork Nation community types, these places are probably the most concerned with social issues. They're hardly wealthy, and they took a hit in the late-2000s recession, with unemployment rates that were consistently among the worst in the country. Yet there was no Republican backlash here. When it came time to vote in November 2008, the Epicenters supported McCain even more strongly than they had Bush.

These counties represent the only community type in which the GOP presidential candidate increased his margin of victory in each one of the last three elections. Bush beat Gore here by 22 percentage points in 2000. Bush beat Kerry by 31 points in 2004. And the Epicenters were completely immune to Obama's political charm in 2008. McCain won here by 32 points.

That's because the Evangelical Epicenters operate in their own political environment. They're the only community type that's produced both more voters and more Republican voters in every recent presidential race. Even as much of the rest of the nation took something of a leftward turn in the 2008 election, the Epicenters steered even harder to the right. How could this have happened with a Republican candidate who stirred such little enthusiasm from party faithful in other communities?

There were two big factors. First, as I heard firsthand in our representative Evangelical Epicenter community of Nixa, Missouri, there really was a great deal of preelection concern that Obama might secretly be a Muslim—or at least not a Christian. And in these communities 48 percent of residents identify themselves as evangelicals, many of whom believe it's their Christian duty to guide mainstream, secularized America onto the correct moral path. In Nixa there was genuine joy over the fact that Obama didn't cancel Sunday church services after his inauguration.

Second, there was Sarah Palin. A lot of America may have had qualms about her experience and her views, but she played very well in the Epicenters. In Nixa, chamber of commerce director Sharon Whitehall Gray told me, they called her "our Sarah." If the GOP puts a strong social conservative on the ticket in 2012, it could well bring out an even larger vote in these counties. There are already signs of a burgeoning conservative populism bubbling up in these locales, one that could be beneficial to the right kind of candidate.

WAITING FOR THE HARD SELL

There are a few places where campaigners might focus some effort, even against long odds. The Military Bastions, Emptying Nests, and Campus and Careers counties have a lot anchoring them to their respective attitudes and positions. But a certain positional change within a party or politician could be enough to switch their loyalties. People in each of these community types tend to focus on one or two policy areas—say, military spending or Social Security or climate change. If the parties change their stances on those issues, they could gain or lose support in these places.

Table 7. PERCENTAGE OF VOTES

Presidential Election	Military Bastions	Campus and Careers	Emptying Nests
2000			
Gore (D)	44	53	44
Bush (R)	54	42	54
2004			
Kerry (D)	43	55	43
Bush (R)	56	44	56
2008			
Obama (D)	48	58	49
McCain (R)	51	40	49

Sixty-two percent of those who live in the **Military Bastions** completely agree with the statement "I am very patriotic." That's the highest rate of agreement among all of the twelve Patchwork Nation community types, and that is a major reason why these places have sided firmly with the GOP. A 2009 Gallup survey found that current and former service members are more likely than civilian workers to be Republicans,[55] and that partisan tie clearly has an effect in these communities—even among those not actually in the military. There's a military culture in the Military Bastions that extends far beyond life on the military base itself.

In 2000 Bush beat Gore soundly in the Bastions, by ten percentage points. Between the flap over gays in the military and his record on Vietnam, Clinton had never been especially popular with soldiers and veterans. Those problems and the Monica Lewinsky scandal arguably hurt his vice president's efforts in these counties. And in 2004 Bush improved on his 2000 margin with a thirteen-point win over Kerry.

But 2008 was a surprise: The Republican margin in the Military Bastions shrank to about three points, in spite of John McCain's military pedigree.

Although Barack Obama never served in the military, he may have had one personal advantage in the Bastions: his race. African Americans make up about 17 percent of the armed forces and about 18 percent of the population in the Military Bastions, many of which are located in southern states. The African American population is higher only in Industrial Metropolis and Minority Central communities, and Obama won more than 95 percent of the black vote nationally.

Still, it's tough to imagine the Bastions switching columns. Early into the Obama presidency there was concern from people in our representative Military Bastion of Hopkinsville, Kentucky, over what they perceived as his slow action on Afghanistan. And even after the decision was made to put more troops into the fight, there were questions here about whether Obama had thought things through adequately. "They are talking about possibly moving some of these troops out pretty quickly," Chuck Henderson, a member of the local military-affairs committee, told us soon after the announcement. "You're going to run into problems with soldiers not having enough time between tours."

Time between tours means not only time spent among friends and family, but also money spent in places like Hopkinsville. Here, the national, somewhat theoretical issue of exactly how to fight the War on Terror is also the local, very real issue of economic survival. And there does seem to be a built-in skepticism about Democrats in these places. There will always be respect for the commander in chief in the Bastions—but for the time being, at least, also a preference for his belonging to the other party.

The older-than-average, whiter-than-average **Emptying Nests** tend to be conservative fiscally and socially, and they too respond most in elections to a specific set of national-cum-local issues: Social Security, Medicare, and retirement-related policies in general. Their votes generally go to Republicans, but if those areas are toyed with, they might swing.

Bush won these communities by ten percentage points in 2000, partly because of fallout from the Clinton–Lewinsky scandal. He had a thirteen-point edge over Kerry in these places in 2004, when national security issues and an apparently sound economy were uppermost in older voters' minds. In 2008, though, the Emptying Nests split their vote between McCain and Obama, with the Republican winning by only eleven thousand votes overall out of 5.5 million cast.

The biggest driver of the closeness of the vote here was probably the collapse of the stock market, which hit these communities surprisingly hard. Lots of people in these places, many of whom are no longer drawing salaries, have money in the market. And at their age they have little time to wait for their investments to bounce back after a crash. In 2008 they voted for some kind of change—any kind of change—that could improve their fortunes.

Overall, however, these communities' natural disposition tends toward holding the line. They're among the least comfortable in the Patchwork Nation with social changes and government spending. Only 23 percent in the Emptying Nests favor allowing same-sex marriage, and 71 percent see the Obama administration's spending as "debt," rather than "investment." There are, of course, differences between personal debt and government debt—individuals can't sell bonds to cover themselves or print money—but in the Emptying Nests the focus leans toward being careful and frugal. And numbers like those on gay marriage and debt—the third-lowest and second-highest among our types, respectively—denote attitudes that should keep these places in the GOP column.

With their youthful populations and progressive stances on issues like gay rights and climate change, **Campus and Careers** counties are, in terms of ages and political philosophy, the inverse of the Emptying Nests. Historically they've been joined closely to the Democratic Party. They're more attuned to social policy than economic issues, and their relative economic comfort, maintained by stable institutional employers in their backyards, only contributes to that tendency.

Gore won Campus and Careers counties by eleven percentage points in 2000. Kerry did equally well against Bush in 2004. But in 2008 Obama trounced McCain by eighteen percentage points in these places in part by aggressively courting the youth vote. Having "Hussein" as a middle name probably didn't hurt him in these multicultural places, either. Indeed, it may well have helped.

"I think, postelection, people just are less on edge," said Cynthia Wilbanks, vice president for government relations at the University of Michigan, the institution at the center of our representative Campus and Careers community of Ann Arbor. "I don't know if it's entirely [due to] a new administration, but I have to believe that the angst, anger, anxiety around some of the decisions and actions of the previous administration . . . really caused people just incredible amounts of pain."

Clearly, a significant portion of the nearly 5.8 million voters who turned out in Campus and Careers locales in 2008 shared that outlook. But should the libertarian wing of the Republican Party grow, there could be changes in the vote in these places. After all, these counties also produced some of libertarian-leaning presidential candidate Ron Paul's most fervent supporters. He scored points among them with not only his antiwar stance, but also his favoring of medical marijuana and same-sex marriage. As the GOP sorts through the many identities it could assume in the coming years, it could do well to keep in mind Paul's success in the Campus and Careers counties.

WINDOW SHOPPING

There are some communities that seem comfortable with their party affiliations on the whole but are willing to consider other options under certain circumstances. Both the Boom Towns and the Service Worker Centers lean to the right. However, as the past few elections have shown, a good-sized portion of their electorate can move toward either political party. That portion, which represents a million votes or so, can be of consequence in close national races.

Table 8. PERCENTAGE OF VOTES

Presidential Election	Boom Towns	Service Worker Centers
2000		
Gore (D)	42	45
Bush (R)	56	52
2004		
Kerry (D)	41	43
Bush (R)	58	55
2008		
Obama (D)	47	47
McCain (R)	52	51

Looking at election results in the **Boom Towns** over even just the past eight years can be problematic. The very nature of these places, which experienced explosive population growth very early in the twenty-first century, means that their populations have changed significantly over that span.

Nonetheless, the tendency in these counties is toward conservatism for a couple of reasons. First, the people living in the Boom Towns are a bit better off than those living in the average U.S. county. They're not necessarily rich, but many of them did move to these exurban locales because they wanted to keep more money in hand than they could in places where the cost of living is higher. Second, many people here came to these places specifically to get away from more densely populated, more liberal urban and suburban areas, in search of a better place to raise their families. Even if there isn't a large religious component to their beliefs, they favor a more "traditional" or "small-town" approach to life.

In 2000 the Boom Towns were the kinds of places where people weren't pleased about having to explain the conduct of the president to their kids. They went for Bush by fourteen percentage points. In 2004, with national security weighing heavily on people's minds post-9/11, they went even more heavily for Bush, by seventeen percentage points.

By 2008, though, the economy had turned nasty enough to make Boom Town residents worried. The foreclosure crisis was especially extreme in these places. Many employed in the building trades lost their jobs. In some communities property values declined across the board. Boom Towners still voted Republican, but they chose McCain over Obama by the relatively lean margin of five percentage points.

A few months after the election, Arn Menconi, the former county commissioner of Eagle, Colorado, our representative Boom Town, said he was worried about what was coming next. "What will we do here without construction? The jobs in the resort industry just don't pay enough. Things are going to change. People's attitudes toward growth and government are going to change."

But how? Two things will be critical for politics in the Boom Towns in the short term. If the housing market continues to drag, it could make people here more eager for government aid, pushing them to the left. Or it could make them angry about the federal government's inability to help, pushing them to the right. These counties have been "Tea Party" strongholds. More important, people will be moving—out of the Boom Towns and into them, to escape an oversaturated housing market or to take advantage of one. Which column those million or so votes go into could well depend on who leaves town and who arrives.

Like the Boom Towns, the **Service Worker Centers** are typically removed from big metropolitan areas and tend to be conservative. But their economic situation is very different. Their populations are essentially stable—they've barely climbed since 2000—and their residents' incomes are generally lower than the national county average, not higher.

As in the Boom Towns, two-thirds of people here see the Obama administration's spending as debt rather than investment. Conservatism in the Service Worker Centers, espoused by people who were born here and tend to stick around, is about the preservation of small-town values and a distrust of the outside influence of the federal government.

In 2000, in a very close national election, the Service Worker Centers sided with Bush by a solid seven percentage points. In 2004 they went for Bush by twelve percentage points. Obama made some real Democratic headway in the Service Worker Centers in 2008, however, cutting the GOP margin to just four percentage points. That probably has something to do with the fact that these counties were battered by the Great Recession earlier and harder than many other community types. But politics here is about more than economics, and those who voted with their pocketbooks weren't quite numerous enough to push the Service Worker Centers completely out of the Republican column.

Nonetheless, there's reason to believe that window shopping might become more widespread here. In Lincoln City, Oregon, our representative Service Worker Center, Kip Ward should serve as a warning to the GOP. Proprietor of the Historic Anchor Inn, he used to be a reliable Republican voter. But after living for many years in a town on the economic margins and witnessing the struggles of its poorer residents, he now considers himself an Independent—and one with some obviously Democratic leanings, at that. "I'm a free-market guy," he told me. "But I'm not free market as far as health care goes."

The people in the Service Worker Centers are potentially in harm's way as the impacts of the national economic restructuring become more pronounced. A recession is one thing. Five or more years of slow growth after a recession would be another—and it could very well change how some people here view their old political loyalties.

ALWAYS LOOKING FOR A DEAL

Three of our twelve community types contain voters in large numbers who, depending on their level of turnout and the issues at stake in a given election, can switch party allegiance relatively easily. That makes them a clear exception in the Patchwork Nation, but that similarity in voting habits doesn't mean they're all the same. Indeed, they're actually strikingly different. The economy is of most importance in the Monied Burbs, while the ethnic and racial makeup of who happens to vote drives the election results in the Immigration Nation and Minority Central communities. These community types are likely to be battlegrounds in the coming elections, but that, naturally, is nothing new.

Table 9. PERCENTAGE OF VOTES

Presidential Election	Monied Burbs	Immigration Nation	Minority Central
2000			
Gore (D)	50	46	50
Bush (R)	47	51	49
2004			
Kerry (D)	50	45	48
Bush (R)	49	54	51
2008			
Obama (D)	55	51	50
McCain (R)	45	48	49

Of all the community types in the Patchwork Nation, the **Monied Burbs** are probably the most politically crucial for two simple reasons: They're the most populous, and they're arguably the one least tethered to political ideology. More than people in other communities, the relatively wealthy Burbanites vote not primarily on cultural issues or community values, but on the economy. Whether they uphold the status quo or throw the bums out in an election year depends greatly on how well their stock portfolios are doing.

In 2000 those in the Monied Burbs weren't interested in punishing then vice president Gore for Bill Clinton's sex scandal. Gore beat Bush by three percentage points, in part because the swing voters here were enjoying a comfortable economic ride. The U.S. GDP grew at a rate of 5.1 percent in 2000, with much of the economic benefit going to the wealthier types who trade stocks. The Dow rose from about 3,400 in January of 1993 to 10,700 in October of 2000, which meant tidy profits for many in the Burbs.

In 2004 the Democratic advantage in the Monied Burbs essentially disappeared. One reason: The GDP was again on the upswing. And don't forget the $1.3 trillion tax cut that Bush pushed through Congress three years earlier, which benefited wealthier households. In 2008, with a slumping economy dominating the news, people in the Monied Burbs moved into Obama's camp. In fact, Burbs residents accounted for 4.1 million votes out of Obama's total margin of about 9.6 million.

When we first visited the representative Monied Burb of Los Alamos, New Mexico, a few people we met chuckled at the idea of a Democratic victory in the county, which had gone for Bush by six percentage points in 2004. But when the stock market turned south in the fall of 2008, the race here fundamentally changed. Obama wound up winning Los Alamos County by seven percentage points.

"When McCain went home from the campaign after the crash [and called for a postponement of the debates], the people around here just looked at it very strangely. It was just a defensive reaction that didn't make any sense. It seemed like he was lost and confused," said Kevin Holsapple, executive director of the Los Alamos Chamber of Commerce. "I talked to people, just regular people at the high school, other parents, and they just shook their heads."

The Independents in town, Holsapple said, had been interested in Obama before then. But the crash and McCain's reaction to it were the last straw for others.

In **Immigration Nation** communities the vote also changed dramatically in 2008 because of the economy and one other issue: the perpetually thorny topic of illegal immigration. These counties represent one of the most divided community types in the Patchwork Nation, with many of their Hispanic residents seemingly living in a different America than their non-Hispanic counterparts.

Bush won these places by five percentage points in 2000 and saw his advantage balloon to nine points in 2004. But Obama carried them by three percentage points in 2008. Why? Some insist that the Border Protection, Anti-Terrorism, and Illegal Immigration Control bill had a major impact in Immigration Nation counties. The bill, introduced by congressional Republicans in 2005, would have, among other things, classified illegal immigrants and those who aided them as criminals. That same year President Bush proposed a program that would have allowed millions of illegal immigrants to become legal guest workers before they were forced out of the country. Many conservatives rallied against him, and immigration became a source of internecine strife within the GOP, as it often has in the past.

It also blew up in Immigration Nation, where the vote has long been fairly evenly split. There are many people in these communities who clearly favor a hard-line approach. Witness the popularity of Sheriff Joe Arpaio and his desire to "put 'em in jail" in Maricopa County, Arizona, home of our representative Immigration Nation community of El Mirage. His supporters and other hard-liners tended to favor the Republicans' proposed legislation in 2005. But there were also many in Immigration Nation who opposed it—legal immigrants, and native-born Hispanics, who have friends and relatives who are illegal, as well as businesspeople who employ illegal immigrants.

Notably, there was no appreciable difference on immigration policy between Obama and McCain during the 2008 campaign, but those opposing Republican immigration reforms were nevertheless mobilized to vote against the Republican Party's candidate. Even some longtime supporters of the senator found it hard to side with a representative of the GOP in Immigration Nation counties when McCain's identity got muddled during the campaign. In El Mirage, Danny Arismendez, owner of Sun City Appliances, told me that he knew McCain fairly well, having chatted with him at Arizona State University football games.

"What you see on TV and who he's trying to cater to, that's not John McCain," Arismendez said in 2008. "I was all John McCain before, two years ago. But no one knows who he is anymore. People don't trust him."

It is honestly difficult to imagine how Republicans could appreciably better their prospects in these counties because much of their support comes from Anglos who are stalwart restrictionists favoring more conservative immigration policies. And while Latinos are not single-issue voters, in these locations, they do seem more animated by immigration policy concerns.

As in Immigration Nation, the vote in **Minority Central** communities has tended to be almost evenly split. Minority Central is not all black or even mostly black; it's about 37 percent black and 58 percent white as a whole. The great disparities of wealth and power between those two populations have long created anxieties over the allocation of jobs and resources as well as political control. The result is that these counties are full of cohesive voter blocs dug in very deeply on their respective sides. The overall vote sometimes goes to the Republicans and sometimes to the Democrats—but always by the thinnest of margins.

Through three very different elections based around very different topics and featuring very different candidates, the vote in Minority Central barely moved. In 2000 Gore won these counties by one percentage point. In 2004 Bush won them by three points. In 2008 Obama won Minority Central by one percentage point.

It doesn't take much to push these communities from one party's column to the other's. But the vote is so closely split that the best-case scenario for either is winning the Minority Central counties by maybe a couple hundred thousand votes. For these locales to really matter in a presidential election, the race would have to be breathtakingly close. Their predominant location, in southern states that reliably cast their Electoral College votes for Republicans, also marginalizes their influence.

WILL THERE BE A REALIGNMENT?

Observers have often searched for meaning in election results by asking whether a particular contest signaled an electoral realignment. A survey of the history of elections reveals that sweeping realignments hardly ever happen, and that smaller, more partial electoral movements are the norm—if there is movement at all. Major realignments are uncommon precisely because the nation is diverse, rarely reacting to the same set of candidates in the same way.

Of the twelve community types, only three are legitimately up for grabs in most elections—and not by large margins. Even elections that look like big wins are about peeling off a few voters from this community type and a few others from that one. In the 2008 presidential contest, the approximately 41 million votes cast in the Monied Burbs, Immigration Nation, and Minority Central represented just over a third of the national total.

So if 2008 wasn't an election that restructured American politics— and it clearly wasn't—is there one on the horizon? You may have to look pretty far into the future to see it. Historically, the number of truly transformative national elections has been very small. Some argue that the 1980 election signified a political realignment. Ronald Reagan won the White

House in a landslide and the Republican Party took control of the Senate for the first time in twenty-five years. Then again, the House of Representatives never changed hands, and the Senate returned to the Democrats just six years later. In retrospect, the actual *lasting* electoral changes wrought by the 1980 election are difficult to find.

Others point to the elections of 1964 and 1968. Race was clearly a significant factor in both of those civil-rights-movement-era races. African Americans lined up behind the Democratic Party in 1964 and remain there to this day. Some states in the industrial Midwest voted for Democratic candidate Lyndon Johnson after years of supporting Republicans— but so did most everywhere else. Johnson trounced Barry Goldwater. Only eight years later Republican Richard Nixon would trounce Democrat George McGovern.

Arguably, the last sea-change election in American politics was in 1932, when Franklin Roosevelt won the White House and set the Democratic Party on the road to holding it for five straight presidential elections. The Democratic share of the House exploded to nearly two hundred seats, and the party maintained control for fifty-eight of the next sixty-two years. The Democrats also took control of the Senate—and held on to it for forty-six of the next fifty years.

It doesn't take more than a few seconds to see the differences between that election and 2008. The Democrats gained some seats in 2008, twenty-one in the House and eight in Senate. But Roosevelt's initial days in the White House became a benchmark for accomplishment—they're where we get the idea of the critical first one hundred days of a presidency. Obama's time in the White House was marked by stagnating battles over major initiatives, from the stimulus package to health-care reform. And whereas the Democrats picked up congressional seats in FDR's first midterm election, in 1934, the question most analysts pose for 2010 is how many seats the Democrats will lose.

There was a large-scale reason for the sweeping change that came in 1932: the Great Depression. The unemployment rate was near 25 percent, and the party in power at the time, the GOP, had failed at every turn to shore up the economy ever since the stock market collapsed three years earlier. For all the justified concern we heard during the late-2000s recession, an unemployment rate that flirts with double digits pales next to what the country was going through in the early thirties.

In late 2008 it looked like a collapse might be coming, but it hadn't yet arrived. (And it was ultimately averted.) There wasn't a pervasive sense that politics needed a significant shift—a change, yes, but people simply wanted things "fixed." During the campaign Obama didn't propose dramatic solutions to America's problems. His ideas on everything from business regulation to health-care reform displayed cautious pragmatism. A selling point of his health-care plan was "If you have coverage, it won't change." Obama and his advisers named former World Bank chief economist Lawrence Summers director of the National Economic Council. In Timothy Geithner they chose a Wall Street man to be secretary of the treasury.

The cultural and socioeconomic circumstances of each of the twelve community types are what really decide most votes on Election Day, not a candidate's speech making or a strategist's planning. Truly changing voting patterns in the Patchwork Nation requires something far more epic than a serious but temporary recession. The terrorist attacks of 2001 couldn't do it. The economic teetering of 2008 couldn't do it.

Of course, that doesn't mean that a big change won't ever come. Indeed, one can see in the broader economic restructuring the seeds of political upheaval. Long-term instability in the coming decade could transform the American electorate even without some cataclysmic event. Gradually, economic stresses could prompt more locales to go shopping. Prolonged trouble in the housing market could seriously impact the Boom Towns. Slow economic growth could leave the Service Worker Centers in a perpetual state of recession. And those things combined with slow wage growth affect the ability of people in the Monied Burbs to save for college or retirement.

Those problems compounded over time might be enough to bump the various community types out of their historical patterns.

READING THE TEA PARTY LEAVES

Some believe we may already be seeing one impact of the prolonged trouble in the economy in the U.S. political scene in the Tea Party movement. The Tea Party groups have become a vocal presence in electoral politics since mid-2009, when the group's members began turning up at Democratic health-care reform town halls to decry big government spending and "socialism." They have also made their mark by attacking federal spending, particularly President Obama's stimulus plan.

Understanding the real power of the Tea Party movement is extremely difficult. In fact, "movement" may not even be the right word for the collection of quasi-independent quasi-grassroots conservative voter groups that have cropped up around the country. On their face, the Tea Party groups are a bunch of loosely affiliated local voter organizations fighting for limited federal government. But by spring of 2010 there were already signs of inherent tensions within their limited structure.

To raise its profile and show its power, the Tea Party Patriots, an organizing group for the Tea Party that calls itself the "Official Grassroots American Movement," held a national convention in Nashville in February of 2010 with keynote speaker Sarah Palin. But even before the meeting some members said they were worried that the event moved the Tea Party too close to becoming a partisan wing of the Republican Party. Others were upset that the cost to attend the convention, $549 a head, was moving the group away from its grassroots beginnings. "Let me be blunt: charging people $500.00 plus the costs of travel and lodging to go to a 'National Tea Party Convention' run by a for-profit group no one has ever heard of sounds as credible as an e-mail from Nigeria promising me a million bucks if I fork over my bank account number," wrote Erick Erickson, editor of Redstate.com, a prominent conservative blog affiliated with the Tea Party groups.[56]

What do the Tea Party groups really stand for? In the spring of 2010 anyway, they looked like a reenergized (and at times angry) home for the libertarian wing of the GOP. If you visited the Web site for Tea Party Nation, a "user-driven group of like-minded people who desire our God given Individual Freedoms which were written out by the Founding Fathers" in spring of 2010 you would find a lot of ads for the Libertarian Cato Institute. "We believe in Limited Government, Free Speech, the 2nd Amendment, our Military, Secure Borders and our Country!" the site proclaimed.[57]

There are elements in that list that could go over well in any number of the communities in the Patchwork Nation. So to get a better idea of where in our community types the Tea Party was drawing best, we looked at a list of some sixty-seven thousand members of those groups to see where they were coming from. (The numbers in bold are well above the national average statistically.)

Table 10. WHERE THE TEA PARTY DRAWS BEST

Community Type	Number of Tea Party Members per 10,000 People
Boom Towns	**3.3**
Campus and Careers	2.1
Emptying Nests	2.0
Evangelical Epicenters	2.5
Immigration Nation	2.3
Industrial Metropolis	0.9
Military Bastions	**2.8**
Minority Central	1.9
Monied Burbs	2.8
Mormon Outposts	**2.7**
Service Worker Centers	2.3
Tractor Country	**2.9**
NATIONAL FIGURE	2.4

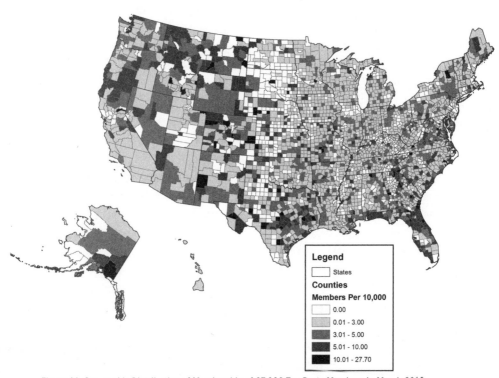

Figure 14. Geographic Distribution of Membership of 67,000 Tea Party Members in March 2010, by County

Of course, sixty-seven thousand people is not the entire Tea Party movement. Any list of "members" for a group as loosely connected as the Tea Party is bound to have shortcomings. And the number of Tea Party "supporters" is much bigger. Still, looking at that distribution, a few things immediately jump out. The groups are not, as many expected, a natural fit with the Christian Right of the GOP. The numbers show the Tea Party does well in rural Tractor Country, but not as well in the socially conservative, faith-based Evangelical Epicenters. And note the relatively high number of members in the Boom Towns and Military Bastions. Those places do tend to vote Republican, but they tend to have very different forces behind their votes than Tractor Country or the Epicenters, as noted earlier.

The distribution suggests that the Tea Party movement is young and still taking shape—it's an outlet for voter anger that does not (or at least not yet) have a true defining message. In Tractor Country the motivating Tea Party force may be distrust of Washington, a new form of prairie populism. In the Boom Towns, on the other hand, it may be a more specific impetus, the housing crunch. In those places there is anger about the bubble that burst and unease about what comes next.

It's worth noting, however, that the places where the economic pain has been the most dire—the Service Worker Centers, Minority Central, and, to some extent, the Evangelical Epicenters—were not prime movers in the early stages of the Tea Party's formation. And the swing-voting Monied Burbs don't seem to be displaying significant interest either.

The lack of interest in those places suggests a couple of possibilities. The Tea Party movement may have room for growth if it can find a way to bring more voters into its fold through embracing issues that might matter to people that live in those places. Or, if it cannot, its influence, much of it created by the news media, may be set to decline and perhaps relatively quickly. It is a curious mix of anger and issues without a lot of cohesion.

A NEW POPULISM?

The rise of the Tea Party groups and the media's coverage of them are only the latest stories in the discussion of a new populism in American politics. That conversation has been a part of U.S. political debate ever since Ross Perot's surprisingly successful presidential bid in 1992. After all, it's not hard to find both Republicans and Democrats who are dissatisfied with their respective parties, if not with the entire two-party system. But the talk has remained largely theoretical—a parlor game for the politically inclined.

Aside from Theodore Roosevelt's 1912 candidacy as a member of the Bull Moose Party, Perot's first effort, in which he garnered 19 percent of the popular vote, remains the high-water mark for recent nonmainstream presidential candidates. Four years later, running as a Reform Party candidate rather than an Independent, Perot received only about 8 percent of the popular vote. Others since—Pat Buchanan, Bob Barr—have essentially been sideshow attractions, although Ralph Nader was arguably a legitimate force, if not a victor, in 2000.

Even so, there are signs in the electorate of a growing populism beyond the rise of the Tea Party among some on the right. On the left you can see it in MoveOn.org, which began as an anti-Bush e-mail group but has since grown into a powerful liberal PAC. In fact, before the 2006 victories by the Democrats in Congress and the election of Barack Obama as president, most of the chatter about political populism was focused on the left.

If you look at past periods of populist swells—the 1880s and 1890s, the 1930s—you'll see obvious similarities to today. Both featured high unemployment and hard times, in rural America in the 1880s and 1890s and everywhere in the 1930s. And both were marked by significant cultural shifts, the former having to do with post–Civil War racial issues, the latter with pre-Depression immigration. Those problems echo through the current era, with its unsettled economy and growing fights over immigration and gay rights. All of that uncertainty and debate, combined with new communication technologies that allow for the easier organization of large numbers of people, create an atmosphere in which populist ideas and movements could flourish.

This is where any understanding of the future of American politics gets very messy. Populism makes for some strange bedfellows. Its key motivators—distrust of the powerful, distrust of outsiders—can manifest themselves in very different ways in different places. But they could also ally some unlikely combinations of community types, as we are seeing to some extent with the Tea Party groups now.

Take the first part of the populist equation: Is anger at the powers that be directed at the federal government or at big business? The following table shows how opinions on two statements from Pew Center for the People and the Press surveys about values, pooled together from surveys taken since 2000, were distributed across the Patchwork Nation.

Table 11.

STATEMENT: The federal government should run ONLY those things that cannot be run at the local level.

STATEMENT: There is too much power concentrated in the hands of a few big companies.

Community Type	Percent Who Completely Agree About Government	Percent Who Completely Agree About Big Companies
Boom Towns	30	33
Campus and Careers	28	33
Emptying Nests	30	36
Evangelical Epicenters	37	36
Immigration Nation	34	33
Industrial Metropolis	26	35
Military Bastions	32	32
Minority Central	32	40
Monied Burbs	29	31
Mormon Outposts	29	31
Service Worker Centers	31	36
Tractor Country	41	37

There's a lot of distrust of power, much of it clustered in community types that are either less wealthy than the national average overall or have high numbers of poor residents. And you can see a surprising coalition of places that show relatively high levels of distrust toward big business: Tractor Country and the Evangelical Epicenters, which both vote heavily Republican; the Industrial Metropolises, which vote heavily Democratic; and Minority Central communities, which vote for both parties almost equally. Strong distrust of the government is primarily limited to Tractor Country and the Epicenters, though the counties of Immigration Nation also score fairly high.

The Tea Party–based populist movement, then, aimed at government growth and trumpeting libertarian ideas, seems best built to unite a few elements of the Republican base—although it could push away some social conservatives. But a populist movement based more on anger at and distrust of the American business community could have broader cross-party appeal. And looking at these figures, it seems that such a movement could originate with equal ease on the right or the left.

What of the other element of populism, distrust of outsiders? Another question on the same Pew survey asked respondents about their attitudes toward immigration laws.

Table 12.

STATEMENT: We should restrict and control people coming into our country to live more than we do now.

Community Type	Percent Who Completely Agree
Boom Towns	46
Campus and Careers	41
Emptying Nests	48
Evangelical Epicenters	56
Immigration Nation	43
Industrial Metropolis	41
Military Bastions	46
Minority Central	55
Monied Burbs	42
Mormon Outposts	46
Service Worker Centers	49
Tractor Country	51

Admittedly, this is a broad way of viewing the immigration question— "more than we do now" can mean a whole range of things, from incremental restriction to keeping every last potential immigrant out. But the numbers are still notably high across the board. Again, the community types with some of the highest numbers are Tractor Country and the Evangelical Epicenters; those communities seem somewhat split on the Tea Party, but elements of them could be united around this issue by a different populist movement. However, the more politically moderate Service Worker Centers and the more politically split Minority Central counties also have high numbers. If you dip the bar a little lower, you also have the Boom Towns, Military Bastions, and Mormon Outposts. That's a significant group of communities, with lots of voters in lots of key places. And don't forget Immigration Nation. The counties score fairly low on this question, but it was anger about immigration in places like Maricopa County, a big Immigration Nation county that is also home to EI Mirage, that helped bring about Arizona's immigration law SB 1070. The law, which allows police in that state to demand identification of those suspected to be illegal immigrants, may wind up having a boomerang effect in some communities—stirring Latinos and more liberal voters to turn out conservatives—but the one thing it certainly promises to do is keep the issue alive as an intense one in American politics.

What does all of that mean? A larger upsurge of populism, bigger than the Tea Party groups, would probably bring what it always does: a big dose of anger from "the middle," however one chooses to define it, directed at the forces above and below. History offers a few possibilities of where that anger could take us as a nation.

The populist movement of the 1880s and 1890s led to some distinctly ugly moments in American history. In 1882 Congress barred Chinese immigrants from the country in response to riots and other expressions of anti-Chinese sentiment, much of it motivated by the belief that inexpensive Asian labor was costing Americans jobs. The 1890s saw the rise of barriers to keep African Americans out of polling places—things like literacy requirements and poll taxes. And there was plenty of general unrest: In 1894 alone seventeen "industrial armies" made up of unemployed workers marched on Washington demanding aid.[58]

The 1930s were very different, of course, with the hard times and unrest leading to new rules governing business and the construction of the social safety net that became the central feature of the New Deal.

We've seen some steps back from such legislation in twenty-first-century Washington. The extent of the new business regulation said to be needed during the late-2000s recession has been scaled back as the country has returned from the brink. Proposed fixes to Fannie Mae and Freddie Mac proved so contentious that they were held out of the initial bills concerning financial regulations—as were proposals to cap the interest rates credit cards may charge and to change the system in which corporations pay credit agencies for their ratings of the companies' abilities to raise or borrow money.

But enough extended hardship could reverse that attitude. And a large-scale populist movement would likely bring a push for much more dramatic measures such as capping executive pay. There's already anger over the money many CEOs make, and not just from regular Joes upset about the multimillion-dollar bonuses at AIG. In early 2010 New York attorney general Andrew Cuomo sent a letter to eight Wall Street firms that took federal bailout money, demanding to see their compensation plans.

That's anger directed at the top—the "Who's taking our money?" part of populism. In terms of anger directed at the bottom—aka "Who's taking our jobs?"—there's already turmoil around illegal immigration that will only grow if unemployment remains high over the coming years. There would undoubtedly be more proposals aimed at limiting immigration or at sending back people in the country illegally. The question is, How far will they get with those in power in Washington? There are already politicians who make a good living blasting loose immigration rules: Rep. Steve King in 2009 attended a constituent meeting in his district in Sioux Center, Iowa—some 1,200 miles from Mexico—and spent the majority of his time talking about the border fence. How many more like him will there be in 2015 or 2020 or 2025?

The stage appears to be set for some potentially big changes to take place over the coming years, beyond the Tea Party movement. A different antibusiness populist movement with an anti-immigration tinge could play a significant role in the coming decade of American politics. Such a movement could break down some of the historical differences among the twelve community types and create a kind of political realignment, particularly if it's coupled with a broader economic upheaval.

That, of course, would take time. In the short term we should expect some pretty rough waves—but no sea changes.

CULTURE

∎ ∎ ∎

WIRED TOGETHER, LIVING APART

In 1996, when the World Wide Web comprised a mere five hundred thousand sites, a group of academics gathered in Vienna, Austria, to talk about the implications of the new technology. The agenda was full of papers that considered the effects of the Web on individuals and, particularly, communities. One key notion, suggested by titles such as "CYBER-STADT: E.C.H.O. and the Growth of Virtual Communities" and "The End of Geography," was that the idea of place was becoming less important. In the latter essay, Annenberg Washington Program senior fellow Stephen Bates suggested that the proliferation of online groups built around common interests "won't mark the literal end of geography . . . but it will be a leap in that direction."

"We live in a world whose social institutions are rooted, historically and functionally, in geography," Bates wrote. "They pull us one way; the new technologies yank us in the opposite direction."[59]

That was before high-speed Internet service was commonplace. Before Wikipedia. Before YouTube. Before Facebook. The power of the Web has grown immeasurably since then.

Today you can live in rural Nebraska and have *The New York Times* as your morning newspaper. You can buy with equal ease from the Tractor Supply Co. and Neiman Marcus. You can communicate frequently and instantly with friends in Massachusetts, England, and China. You can, without too much investment or effort, live a life significantly freed from the bonds of locality.

So in a sense, Bates was right. Technology has, without question, made the world more customizable. When you travel the country you can even bring your own little individual bubble with you. And if you need to energize your iPod or yourself, you can buy a car charger at Walmart and the caffeine-loaded beverage of your choice at Starbucks—outlets whose on-the-road versions will be an awful lot like the ones back home.

Still, despite the twin rises of wi-fi-able individualization and brick-and-mortar homogenization, geographically definable cultures haven't disappeared from the United States—not yet, at least. Perhaps counterintuitively, many of the changes in American culture over the past twenty years haven't broken down the walls between the communities within the Patchwork Nation. They've built them higher.

The developments in communications technology, for instance, have been about personalization through growing variety, and individuals have more choices available than ever before. But the wider the range of choices—that is, the wider the range of potential niches—the narrower each becomes. Back in the days when ABC, CBS, and NBC dominated the airwaves, the people of Sioux Center, Iowa, and Philadelphia, Pennsylvania, clicked on their TV sets and were presented with more or less the same three prime-time options.

Now, thanks not only to Web sites such as Hulu.com, but also to cable and satellite services, the people in those cities have scores—even hundreds—of options. Look at the cable channels available in Sioux Center and Philadelphia and you'll notice some big differences. In Sioux Center, Country Music Television and the RFD-TV ("Rural America's Most Important Network") are in the basic package. In Philly you get E! and BET. The choices made in those different places grow out of and define their various cultures. The net effect is greater cultural distance between different communities, not less.

Marketing experts don't just understand that distinct community cultures exist; they do what they can to capitalize on that understanding, even when it comes to national chains. Whole Foods Market is a chain, but its individual stores are always in the same kind of neighborhood—fairly dense, educated, and wealthy or gentrifying, and they don't get there randomly. According to its Web site, Whole Foods' list of site-selection factors includes "200,000 people or more in a 20-minute drive time" and a "large number of college-educated residents."[60] Other criteria are more closely held.

"Culture," of course, is a hard thing to define, but a short look at some of its key characteristics—consumer habits and availability, media usage and attitudes toward faith—reveals much about the communities in the Patchwork Nation. Take something as simple as store locations. It's an oversimplification to say, "You are what you buy." But within that twenty-minute drive time you are to some extent what you *can* buy. Comparing a map of certain retailers' locations with a map of the twelve Patchwork Nation community types reveals some clear patterns.

$2 COFFEES AND $10 SHIRTS

Determining the exact number of Starbucks Coffee Company or Walmart locations in the United States can be a tricky proposition. What year—and what month—are you talking about? As of late 2009 there were about 11,000 Starbucks coffeehouses in the fifty states and about 3,800 Walmarts. In each case that's more locations than there are U.S. counties. Of the twelve representative communities in this book, ten have a Starbucks and eleven have a Walmart—and that includes Sioux Center and Burley, Idaho, two of our smallest towns.

But as ubiquitous as these two companies' stores can seem, their distribution is far from even across the Patchwork Nation. The placement of the nation's Starbucks and Walmart outlets is about more than just population density or income level. It's also indicative of cultural attitudes and preferences, as shown in the following table.

Table 13. NUMBER OF STARBUCKS AND WALMART LOCATIONS PER 100,000 PEOPLE, DECEMBER 2009

Community Type	Starbucks Locations per 100,000 People	Walmart Locations per 100,000 People
Boom Towns	6.0	2.0
Campus and Careers	4.3	1.7
Emptying Nests	2.5	2.3
Evangelical Epicenters	3.1	3.2
Immigration Nation	5.0	1.5
Industrial Metropolis	6.7	0.7
Military Bastions	4.4	1.8
Minority Central	1.9	2.6
Monied Burbs	7.5	1.3
Mormon Outposts	2.5	2.0
Service Worker Centers	2.0	2.2
Tractor Country	1.2	2.0

Look, for instance, at the Boom Towns versus the Monied Burbs. Both community types are more populous and wealthier than the average U.S. county. Both have a fairly high number of Starbucks locations per capita, and both hold lots of people with the means—and the desire—to fund a daily skinny vanilla latte. Theoretically, those same people could buy their share of Faded Glory button-downs, too. But whereas the Boom Towns contain 2 Walmarts for every 100,000 people—a figure above the national average of 1.7—the Monied Burbs contain only 1.3 stores for every 100,000 people.

Why is that? Means is part of it. People in the Monied Burbs make on average about $7,200 more per year than people in the Boom Towns, with 5 percent earning $150,000 or more. Burbanites certainly have less need to shop at a discount center than Boom Towners. But desire is part of it, too. Frugality may be hip in some places and on some items, but not everywhere and not on everything. In the Burbs, keeping up appearances matters more, especially at the wealthier end of the income spectrum.

It's not that people in the Burbs won't shop at Walmart. With some items it really doesn't matter: A box of Cheerios is a box of Cheerios regardless of the place of purchase. But with some items it does. In the case of clothing, price isn't necessarily the sole concern—ideas of quality and fashion and status matter, too. In some cases people don't want to buy a $10 shirt because everyone will know it's a $10 shirt. Politics may enter the equation, as well. In the liberal-leaning Burbs, people are more likely to be concerned with the attacks Walmart has faced—mostly from the left—about Chinese-made goods, worker treatment, and the impact of big-box retail on the environment.

Now contrast the Monied Burbs with the Evangelical Epicenters, which have the highest number of Walmarts per 100,000 people (3.2) but a comparatively lower number of Starbucks outlets. Wages are below average in these communities, and for many people spending $3 on a cup of coffee at Starbucks is a real luxury. A Walmart Supercenter, though, means jobs as well as "always low prices." In the Epicenters people are less concerned about how the service jobs at Walmart don't pay as well as white-collar work. There simply aren't as many of those other types of jobs to be had.

And when it comes to that $10 shirt, residents here are less worried about whether a $30 or $50 shirt would last longer or look better. Indeed, a $30 shirt might not even be an option. In our representative Evangelical Epicenter of Nixa, Missouri, residents are reluctant to spend even public money on anything but bare necessities. Walmart is a practical place, and that suits them fine.

The Monied Burbs hold about 69 million people, the Evangelical Epicenters about 14 million. Yet the Burbs have more than ten times as many Starbucks—5,182 versus 439—and less than twice as many Walmarts—892 versus 457. Marketers clearly recognize that they're dealing with different kinds of places in these two settings.

People in the Monied Burbs have a good chance of living near a Starbucks. People in the Boom Towns have a good chance of living near a Starbucks, a Walmart, and a Cracker Barrel Old Country Store. In fact, there are more Cracker Barrels per capita in the Boom Towns than anywhere else, and twice as many locations as in any other community type. The young families in these places appreciate a business that welcomes their kids and projects the kind of down-home traditionalism they fled more liberal, more urbanized areas to find. "A good meal at a fair price" served in what proudly proclaims itself "a museum of Americana" is exactly what they were looking for.

All national chains project certain attitudes and values that are meant to reflect those of the communities in which their stores are located. But the most obvious and extreme example may be Whole Foods. There are about 280 of the "natural and organic" supermarkets in the United States, with 246 of them clumped into just four community types: the Monied Burbs, the Industrial Metropolis, the Boom Towns, and the Campus and

Careers counties. Those types are all wealthier and better educated than the average U.S. county—and three out of four of them voted heavily for Barack Obama in 2008.

Whole Foods takes great pains to make its politics known. It offers copies of the *Utne Reader* in the checkout lane, and its Web site features stories such as one about how the company is helping "liberate Haitian micro credit clients from poverty."[61] Whole Foods has no mere mission statement. It has statements on "Our Core Values," "Our Quality Standards," and "Sustainability and Our Future," as well as a "Declaration of Interdependence" that discusses its support for sustainable agriculture, recycling, and "environmentally sound cleaning and store maintenance programs."[62]

In the summer of 2009 Whole Foods CEO John Mackey wrote an op-ed in *The Wall Street Journal* critical of President Obama's health-care-reform proposals. Outraged Obama supporters called for a boycott of the stores, and more than 22,000 people joined a group of Facebook users pledging to do so. Conservatives rallied behind Mackey and the store, pledging a "buycott." In the end the boycott/buycott had little effect. Whole Foods sales for that quarter were up 2.3 percent over the previous year—and not because Tea Party patriots marched to the registers with carts full of organic arugula.

Whole Foods has simply made sure that its stores are based in areas where the people want the things it offers. It doesn't try to be a store for everyone; it has identified a particular portion of the population that it aims to please. People shop at Whole Foods because it sells organic foods, certainly. But they also shop there because the *Utne Reader* is available at checkout and because they appreciate things like helping third-world debtors. Mackey's editorial wasn't a deal breaker for the majority of Whole Foods patrons, even if some of them disagreed with it. After all, at how many other supermarkets can you purchase grass-fed beef, flip through a story about green-collar jobs in the Midwest, and be assured that your shopping locally is having an impact globally?

In some communities that's a legitimate question. In others, it would never even be asked.

ARMS AND THE COMMUNITY AND *ARMS AND THE MAN*

No matter how the numbers break down, Whole Foods, Walmart, and Starbucks all mean something in the cultural shorthand of the contemporary United States—proof that the marketers, at least, have done their jobs

figuring out what local consumers want. What about even broader stereotypes? Guns and books may both be tools, but they're both potent cultural
symbols, too. Rural conservatives prefer the former, urban liberals the
latter—or so the supposition goes. But is that really true? After all, most
of our ideas about Red America and Blue America are oversimplifications.
Examining the number of gun shops versus the number of bookstores in
the Patchwork Nation reveals that this one is, too.

Table 14. GUNS AND BOOKS

Community Type	Gun Shops per 100,000 people	Bookstores per 100,000 people
Boom Towns	3.7	5.4
Campus and Careers	2.9	7.1
Emptying Nests	4.4	3.4
Evangelical Epicenters	5.5	1.5
Immigration Nation	2.6	2.5
Industrial Metropolis	1.0	3.3
Military Bastions	4.0	2.7
Minority Central	3.4	1.0
Monied Burbs	2.3	5.8
Mormon Outposts	4.5	1.7
Service Worker Centers	5.0	4.8
Tractor Country	10.1	3.8

You could draw a pretty decent correlation between voting patterns
in the 2008 presidential election and the gun shop–to–bookstore ratio.
The three community types that Obama won by the biggest margins—the
Industrial Metropolis, the Monied Burbs, and the Campus and Careers
communities—all have more than twice as many bookstores per capita as
gun shops. Conversely, the three community types that gave John McCain
his largest margins—the Mormon Outposts, the Evangelical Epicenters,
and Tractor Country—all have more than twice as many gun shops per
capita as bookstores.

But does that mean the stereotype that associates guns with Republicans and books with Democrats holds? Not exactly. Certainly not in the
longer term. Although it's true that the places with the highest numbers of
gun shops per capita have also tended to be the most right-leaning in the
Patchwork Nation in recent presidential elections, those with the highest
numbers of bookstores haven't been the most left-leaning. They include the

reliably liberal Campus and Careers counties, the swing-voting Monied Burbs, and the more conservative Boom Towns, Service Worker Centers, and Tractor Country locales. And the unshakably Democratic Industrial Metropolis, although it has the fewest gun shops per capita of any community type, also has relatively few bookstores.

Bookstore positioning is about cultures of education and reading, not necessarily leftist political cultures. Unsurprisingly, Campus and Careers communities have the largest number of bookstores per capita because of the educational institutions at their centers. They need places for students to buy and sell textbooks, as well as for teachers to purchase scholarly publications.

And what about gun shops? There are many more gun stores per capita in Tractor Country than anywhere else, but that's to be expected, too. There's a lot of land available for hunting in these isolated communities. Go to the Web site of the Sioux County Sportsman's Club and you can find a list of seventeen nearby hunting spots.

Indeed, population density is a very good determinant of gun availability. In almost all cases the more rural a place is, the higher its number of gun shops per capita. The Military Bastions, although they have the third-highest density of all of our twelve community types, also have a relatively high number of gun shops—obviously due to the military culture that dominates these places. The Immigration Nation communities are a more puzzling case: they aren't particularly dense, yet they have the third-lowest number of gun shops per capita among all community types.

Comparing the percentage of the population enrolled in college to the number of bookstores per capita yields even more discrepancies. Tractor Country, which has the lowest percentage of residents enrolled in college, also has the fourth-highest number of bookstores per capita. The Military Bastions and the Industrial Metropolis counties, in which 20 and 25 percent of the population is enrolled in college, respectively, have just 2.7 and 3.3 bookstores per capita.

Notice the sharp difference between Tractor Country and the Evangelical Epicenters in terms of retail access to books. These places have the two lowest percentages of residents enrolled in college in the Patchwork Nation and are close to each other in median household income. Yet there are more than twice as many general-interest bookstores per capita in Tractor Country as there are in the Epicenters. That may speak to how much free time people have in these locales or, more likely, how they choose to spend it. But it makes one thing clear: Our cultural shorthand isn't saying much.

Some rural conservatives, it turns out, like guns and books. And although just about all urban liberals don't like guns, not all of them like books as much as we believe they do.

INFLATING THE MEDIA BUBBLE

The decisions people make every day about what they read, watch, and listen to are about more than personal choice. Those selections are, in a sense, the way they choose to define reality. And in a world with satellite TV and radio and thousands of blogs and news Web sites, choosing what picture of the world you want to see is easier than ever. Even exactly what constitutes "news" is a personal choice in twenty-first-century America. For some people it's facts and figures presented with as little bias as possible. For others it's something that comes with a distinct point of view.

The table below shows what percentage of people in each of our community types said they listen to one of four national conservative radio personalities or to one of four types of National Public Radio programming. Besides the dominance conservative talkers have over the airwaves, it illustrates how personal media choices reinforce larger cultural milieus.

Table 15. FAVORITE TALK RADIO PROGRAMMING[63]

Community Type	Percent Who Say Conservative Talk	Percent Who Say NPR Talk
Boom Towns	50	13
Campus and Careers	37	25
Emptying Nests	55	13
Evangelical Epicenters	60	11
Immigration Nation	48	12
Industrial Metropolis	39	20
Military Bastions	52	16
Minority Central	53	14
Monied Burbs	41	17
Mormon Outposts	53	16
Service Worker Centers	54	13
Tractor Country	67	10

People who live in the most reliably Republican community types, the Evangelical Epicenters and Tractor Country, are the biggest fans of conservative talk radio. More than six in ten residents in these places said that their favorite radio program is hosted by Rush Limbaugh, Sean Hannity, Bill O'Reilly, or G. Gordon Liddy. The community types with the fewest conservative-talk listeners—Campus and Careers counties, the Industrial Metropolis counties, and the Monied Burbs—voted for Obama in the 2008 presidential race. More people in these places said that they listen to shows on National Public Radio—*Morning Edition, Talk of the Nation, All Things Considered,* and unspecified NPR programming—than in our other community types.

Note the relatively high number of NPR listeners in the Military Bastions. Why? Because, like it or lump it, NPR covers more foreign news than just about anyone on the radio. If you're waiting to be deployed or a loved one is deployed or you want to know when you may be losing ten thousand people from your customer base, foreign news is essential. The Bastions are conservative places, just like the Evangelical Epicenters and Tractor Country, where NPR listenership was lowest. But the people who live on and near the bases want information that concerns them—even if it's perceived, as it often is in these communities, as leaning leftward.

Consider a day's broadcast of both *All Things Considered* and *The Rush Limbaugh Show.* On January 7, 2010, *All Things Considered* presented "Tips for Making Sense of New Job Numbers," "Congress Creates Commission to Dig into Financial Crisis," "Mideast Water Crisis Brings Misery, Uncertainty," and "Experts Urge End to Mountaintop Mining," among other stories. On that same day the topics on *Limbaugh* included "Group Protests at the White House, Asks Obama to Reach Out to Rush," "Bam Slammed on Broken Promises," "State-Run Media Still Misses the Point on El Rushbo's Hospital Stay," and "Acrimony Roils Democrat Party."

There's a significant difference here: *All Things Considered* is a news program with coverage from all over the globe; *Limbaugh* is an opinion program about the partisan political struggle within the United States. Clearly, if many people in a particular community listen frequently to one or the other of those shows, the show is going to have an impact on how that place views the world. And in a media environment that includes much more than radio, members of those communities can reinforce their points of view with other news sources tailored just for them—say, the left-leaning *Huffington Post* or the right-leaning *Drudge Report.* In the twenty-first century, customization helps to confirm preconceptions.

OF COURSE, COMMUNITY ATTITUDES ALSO reveal themselves in experiences that to some extent resist personalization—sporting events and concerts and theater and cinema, all of which still bring groups of people together in one place at one time. The last offers a good way of studying community types because the matching of movies and places has already been done by marketers and theater owners hoping to maximize their products' return. Not everyone knows who John Waters is. Not everyone cares.

Box office revenue broken down by U.S. county isn't something that theater chains or movie studios or even ratings companies like Nielsen are eager to share. But looking at which movies have played in the twelve representative Patchwork Nation communities over the past few years offers some insights.

Less densely populated communities, obviously, have fewer choices. That comes with having fewer theaters. Going to the movies in these places means enjoying a pretty steady diet of standard Hollywood fare. But not always.

Consider the Fridley Theatres chain. Fridley has twenty-seven theaters based in small communities in Nebraska and Iowa—twenty-three of their twenty-seven theaters are located in some of the least densely populated of the twelve community types. Brian Fridley, who owns the chain, believes that choosing films for his theaters is more complicated than just following the national box office numbers. "In my towns we do best with family pictures," he told me. A look at the top ten movies in Sioux Center in 2009 versus the top ten in the nation as a whole shows what he means.

Table 16. TOP GROSSING FILMS IN 2009 FROM HOLLYWOOD.COM AND THE FRIDLEY THEATRES[64]

Nationally	Fridley Cinema 5, Sioux Center
Transformers: Revenge of the Fallen	The Blindside
Avatar	The Proposal
Harry Potter and the Half-Blood Prince	Paul Blart: Mall Cop
Up	Transformers: Revenge of the Fallen
The Twilight Saga: New Moon	The Twilight Saga: New Moon
The Hangover	Up
Star Trek	Couples Retreat
The Blindside	Alvin and the Chipmunks: The Squeakquel
Monsters vs. Aliens	Fast and Furious
Ice Age: Dawn of the Dinosaurs	Taken

A couple of things stand out on those lists besides Sioux Center's apparent love of the films of Sandra Bullock, who starred in both *The Blindside* and *The Proposal*. Where's James Cameron's blockbuster *Avatar* on the Sioux Center list? That film took a lot of criticism from the right for celebrating pantheism, and it was gone from this conservative Tractor Country community's screens by mid-January 2010, barely a month after its wide release. Meanwhile, *Alvin and the Chipmunks: The Squeakquel*, released a few days later, played on. And note the number 3 position of *Paul Blart: Mall Cop*, an inoffensive comedy about a mall security officer dealing with a hostage situation, on the Sioux Center list. Nationally, that film barely made the top twenty.

In the early days of 2010 visitors to the Fridley Web site saw an ad for a film called *To Save a Life*—weeks before it was released. The story of a popular high school kid who is shaken by an old friend's suicide, the movie was produced by New Song Pictures, the cinema arm of a Christian megachurch based in Oceanside, California. Why did Fridley publicize it so early? Why not the movies featuring big stars scheduled to open the same week—*Extraordinary Measures*, with Harrison Ford, and *Tooth Fairy*, with Dwayne "The Rock" Johnson? Because Fridley knew that *To Save a Life* would do well in its communities. One of the chain's biggest films of 2008 was the Baptist church–produced *Fireproof*. It didn't play in most Patchwork Nation communities, but it did more than $33 million at the box office.

Although everyone may have a chance to see films like *Avatar*, there are differences in what's shown in the twelve community types. The weekend of January 15, 2010, there were thirty-nine different offerings on the screens in and around the Campus and Careers community of Ann Arbor, Michigan, including foreign films like *Chance Pe Dance* and *Namo Venkatesa* and the Metropolitan Opera's live-in-HD performance of *Carmen*. There were fifteen films on the screens in and around the Military Bastion of Hopkinsville, Kentucky, all of them mainstream Hollywood fare. There were nine films playing in and around Sioux Center. And Mormon Outpost Burley had one film, the apocalyptic thriller *2012*.

Those differences reflect and impact how those communities see the world. But the size of a place isn't the only thing that matters when it comes to what's offered onscreen. For instance, despite all the people who live in the Industrial Metropolis of Philadelphia, on most weekends it doesn't have any more films available than Ann Arbor does—although it may be showing some different ones. And even among all of the choices in those two cities you would have had a hard time finding *Fireproof* in 2008. In Sioux Center the movie came back for a second run. Nearby at the James River Assembly megachurch there were special screenings of it. Meanwhile, in Immigration Nation counties in 2009, the science-fictional assimilation parable *District 9* played longer than most anywhere else.

NOT EVERY DIFFERENCE IN MEDIA CONSUMPTION is about worldview. Some are about a location's level of comfort with and access to new technologies. In the world of social media, the differences between community types are more about age and income than political belief or population density.

Table 17. FACEBOOK, TWITTER, AND MYSPACE USE, FALL 2009[65]

Community Type	Percent Who Said They Have Used Social Media Web sites "Ever"
Boom Towns	44
Campus and Careers	48
Emptying Nests	28
Evangelical Epicenters	43
Immigration Nation	41
Industrial Metropolis	47
Military Bastions	49
Minority Central	43
Monied Burbs	42
Mormon Outposts	41
Service Worker Centers	30
Tractor Country	19

The three places that use social media sites most often do so for different reasons. For people in the Military Bastions, social media have become a way to stay in touch with colleagues, friends, and loved ones stationed far away. And the Bastions, like Campus and Careers and Industrial Metropolis locales, contain a lot of young people. In each case, nearly half of the population is between twenty and forty-nine years of age. The three community types that use social networking sites the least are among the oldest in the Patchwork Nation: Tractor Country, the Emptying Nests, and the Service Worker Centers. In these places no more than 40 percent of the population is between twenty and forty-nine.

But social media use isn't all about age. The Minority Central communities are young, too, with 42 percent of their population aged twenty to forty-nine. But the people here don't use social media as much as people in other youthful community types. Why? The people of Minority Central counties also bring home the Patchwork Nation's lowest median household income, which limits their access to computer hardware and Internet service.

The numbers underscore the problems associated with what some call the digital divide. It's not that no one in Sioux Center, Iowa, or Lincoln City, Oregon, or Clermont, Florida, uses social media. It's that many there are being left behind. The current state of social media indicates that in the future they will be about information distribution as well as maintaining personal contacts. Facebook has become an organizing tool not just for individuals, but also for political groups. Look at the Whole Foods boycott of 2009 or, earlier, the Obama campaign of 2008. In the Massachusetts senate race to fill Ted Kennedy's seat, an early sign of upstart candidate Scott Brown's support was his number of Facebook fans. And Twitter has become a news feed in haiku for the most digitally connected—a way to share headlines and links to stories.

In an already fragmented media environment the digital divide threatens to do more than leave some people out of the tech loop. As important as community culture is already, its importance will grow in the next decade because of the social issues on the agenda. Things like immigration, same-sex marriage, the decline of the white majority, and the role of faith in politics promise to become increasingly divisive. Communities that seem politically similar today could, depending on how wired they are, end up looking very different tomorrow.

THE VIEWS FROM THE PEWS

Religion is, without question, one of the major cultural forces in the Patchwork Nation. But as important as it is in defining community values and attitudes, religion plays different roles in different community types. In Burley, Idaho, and other Mormon Outposts, one faith is so powerful that church services can lead into what are essentially impromptu city council meetings. In Evangelical Epicenters like Nixa, Missouri, religion is likewise a powerful personal motivator for many residents—but its effects on the municipality are lessened by the many different congregations that have a stake in the community. And in Industrial Metropolises like Philadelphia, among the most diverse places in the Patchwork Nation, there are so many different faiths that religion can be an even more divisive influence.

The level of religious adherence in a community is a key component of how that place functions because it directly impacts its power structure. It plays a big role in who can legitimately claim to speak for the citizenry. Yes, church leaders are always important, but they're most important where the pews are full and the words from the pulpit can mobilize a significant portion of the local populace.

Our measure of adherence here is fairly specific. These numbers in the table below originate from a comprehensive national survey of congregations carried out by the Glenmary Research Institute in Cincinnati, Ohio, estimating the number of people in each U.S. county as of 2000 who consider themselves to be members of a particular faith. We have added up all the numbers from various faiths to give us an estimated number of total adherents or believers of all major faiths with large numbers of followers in the United States. The data are not flawless, as some smaller congregations are missed, but the survey is widely used in research studies, and there are presently no alternatives that provide such full coverage for the entire nation. The Glenmary data are also consistent with other more recent surveys, such as the Pew Religious Landscape Survey, from 2007.

Table 18. GOING TO CHURCH

Community Type	Percent Adherents from All Major Faiths
Boom Towns	46.0
Campus and Careers	43.8
Emptying Nests	64.8
Evangelical Epicenters	62.0
Immigration Nation	62.0
Industrial Metropolis	53.9
Military Bastions	45.7
Minority Central	47.6
Monied Burbs	46.4
Mormon Outposts	72.3
Service Worker Centers	45.2
Tractor Country	62.7

When you summarize the numbers this way, one of the first things you see is that a clear-cut Red State/Blue State or rural/urban religious divide doesn't really exist. Some of the community types that went most heavily for Obama in the 2008 presidential race—the Monied Burbs and the Campus and Careers counties—score relatively low for religious adherence. Fewer than half of the people in those locales attend houses of worship regularly. But the community type that gave Obama his biggest margin of victory, the Industrial Metropolis, actually has more adherents than nonadherents.

The Boom Towns and Service Worker Centers, two community types in which McCain won by respectable margins, actually have as few religious adherents as or fewer religious adherents than many of the communities that voted for Obama. And Immigration Nation counties, which voted for Obama, have the same adherence rate as the Evangelical Epicenters, which voted for McCain in a landslide.

The two most populous community types in the Patchwork Nation, the Monied Burbs and the Boom Towns, have some of the lowest rates of religious adherence. And the fourth-most-populous community type, the Service Worker Centers, sits right alongside them. The votes in those places looked very different, but their residents' feelings about faith are fairly similar. In those types' representative communities—Los Alamos, New Mexico; Eagle, Colorado; and Lincoln City, Oregon—and their surrounding counties the adherence rates are all under 50 percent. In Lincoln County, Oregon, the adherence rate is only about 23 percent.

As the cultural issues on the front burner grow hotter, with candidates supporting some and opposing others, remember just how complicated the relationship between voting and religious adherence really is. The "religious vote" isn't easily characterized. The above table suggests it is not religious adherence that counts, per se, but the content of religious teaching, and the extent of religious observance. Religious affiliations in the Patchwork Nation's twelve community types are greatly varied, and the relative strength of one denomination or another in each has an impact on their respective cultures. There are differences even among places that look similar in terms of national voting patterns and numbers of adherents. The table below looks at some of the major Judeo-Christian traditions by community type, with the data again coming from the Glenmary Research Center survey of congregations.

Table 19. PERCENTAGE OF RELIGIOUS AFFILIATION BY COMMUNITY TYPE

Community Type	Evangelical Protestant	Mainline Protestant	Catholic	Mormon	Jewish
Boom Towns	20.1	10.6	12.2	2.1	2.5
Campus and Careers	11.8	13.6	16.3	0.7	8.0
Emptying Nests	14.9	30.3	19.1	0.3	0.7
Evangelical Epicenters	47.5	10.1	3.3	0.6	0.1
Immigration Nation	20.9	9.9	28.9	1.9	1.5
Industrial Metropolis	7.6	9.0	30.9	0.3	4.8
Military Bastions	24.7	11.3	7.9	1.4	3.2
Minority Central	30.6	9.5	6.7	0.5	0.8
Monied Burbs	13.9	11.5	18.4	1.0	1.2
Mormon Outposts	3.1	2.1	3.9	63.1	0.9
Service Worker Centers	16.1	13.8	14.4	0.8	0.1
Tractor Country	15.7	26.7	18.7	1.6	0.1

Look at the four community types with the highest percentages of adherents and you'll get some understanding of the different roles a religious community can play in places where the faith is an important community adhesive. In the Evangelical Epicenters it's not just that there are many adherents; it's that they come mostly from one particular faith tradition. Nearly half of the people who live in these places are members of some kind of Evangelical Protestant church, all of which share the key belief that faith and salvation are highly personal experiences.

That affects the local culture. Congregations here tend to be communities unto themselves, concerned foremost with the care of their own members. One pastor in our representative Epicenter of Nixa told us that his church doesn't have as much to give the greater community because there is so much need within his own congregation. That attitude is clearly shared by others: Nixa is full of churches and congregations, but they don't tend to organize into larger interfaith groups. That more personal understanding of God and religion may also have something to do with those places' attitude toward governing, which tends to put individual rights first.

Tractor Country, which looks a lot like the Evangelical Epicenters in terms of its vote, has a very different religious makeup. These small communities are a mix of different Christian sects. The percentage of evangelicals here is a fraction of what it is in the Epicenters, even though

Tractor Country has roughly the same number of religious adherents. These communities are mostly mainline Protestant, with a significant population of Catholics, as well. In general, these mainline churches are more open to ecumenical dialogue. They also tend have greater top-down organization than the evangelical denominations that predominate the Epicenters. It's easier to coordinate churches that have built-in power structures: It involves talking to fewer people.

Working together is an important part of life in agricultural Tractor Country. In our representative community of Sioux Center, people take an active interest in their neighbors' lives, helping out when they need to. In Sioux Center, a town of 6,500 people, many of whom are members of one or another offshoot of the Dutch Reformed Church, money is raised with relative ease and bond issues are passed to build things for the larger community. Here the community comes before the congregation.

Immigration Nation counties, by contrast, are deeply divided— ethnically, culturally, economically, politically, and religiously. They have a very high percentage of total religious adherents, but the distribution of those adherents among different faiths highlights the splits within these communities. In part due to their large Latino populations, Immigration Nation locales have the highest percentage of Catholics of any community type. But they also house a high percentage of Evangelical Protestants, who tend to be more conservative politically than their Catholic neighbors and who may find themselves opposed to the immigrant community on issues like social spending.

The Emptying Nests have the second highest percentage of adherents in the Patchwork Nation, but the influence of those worshippers on the community as a whole is diminished by two circumstances. First, the faithful are among a variety of different churches. Second, these are older-than-average counties. Churches full of elderly people are different from churches full of youngsters. The congregants are more likely to attend out of habit, and there's a difference between going to church for inspiration and going because you always have. You aren't going to find a lot of megachurches full of energetic young families looking to build a faith community. The Emptying Nests are not the Evangelical Epicenters. In the representative Emptying Nest of Clermont, the political system is run by older residents with an eye toward giving the aging the services they need. Here, being elderly trumps all other potential commonalities, religion included.

LOOKING FROM THE INSIDE OUT

Patterns of religious attendance, media consumption, and consumer marketing all reveal cultural differences within the Patchwork Nation. But how do those twelve different cultures view the larger national culture? The various community types have very different feelings about Hollywood's influence on morality, religion's role in government, and how gay and lesbian lifestyles should be treated by society as a whole.

When you look at how people in the twelve community types judge the impact of the entertainment industry on morality, what's most surprising is the lack of strong feelings regarding it in most of the Patchwork Nation. Despite the regular talk-show bubble-ups whenever the entertainment industry "crosses the line," concern over the power of the Hollywood boogeyman isn't particularly widespread. In only one of the twelve types are the majority of residents deeply concerned about the impact of the entertainment world on their values: the Mormon Outposts.

Table 20.

STATEMENT: I often feel that my values are threatened by Hollywood and the entertainment industry.[66]

Community Type	Percent Who Completely Agree	Percent Who Mostly Agree	Total Percent in Agreement
Boom Towns	21	24	45
Campus and Careers	18	22	40
Emptying Nests	19	25	44
Evangelical Epicenters	24	24	48
Immigration Nation	21	22	43
Industrial Metropolis	17	21	38
Military Bastions	19	25	44
Minority Central	20	25	45
Monied Burbs	18	24	42
Mormon Outposts	37	32	69
Service Worker Centers	20	25	45
Tractor Country	25	24	49

In Mormon Outposts, Tractor Country, and Evangelical Epicenters, 24 percent or more of respondents said that they "completely agree" that their values are in some way often under attack. But only in the Outposts do those people plus those who "mostly agree" equal more than half of the population—in this case, more than two-thirds of the population. The next highest level of unhappiness with Hollywood is only 49 percent, in Tractor Country. In the Industrial Metropolis and Campus and Careers counties, the Monied Burbs, the Military Bastions, and the Emptying Nests, the percentages of those who said that they completely agree don't reach even 20 percent, and the percentages of those who said that they mostly agree aren't significantly higher.

Mormon communities have often found themselves out of step with mainstream America, sometimes dangerously so. But why aren't the relatively conservative Emptying Nests and Military Bastions more worried about Hollywood's destructive influence? Their percentages are close to the more liberal Campus and Career counties and Monied Burbs. Some of that has to do with the media environments of these places. For instance, in the aging Emptying Nests, people might not be up on everything in the pop cultural media stream—remember these are among the least Web-savvy communities. And in the Military Bastions the large numbers of young men stationed at the nearby bases have a significant influence on the local media culture. They're the reason for the strip clubs in Hopkinsville. And if residents can tolerate those, they can tolerate the R-rated postapocalyptic violence of films like *The Book of Eli* and *Daybreakers*, both of which were playing in Hoptown the weekend of January 15, 2010.

But as the boundaries of what's permissible in entertainment are pushed in coming years, as they most likely will be, general indifference toward Hollywood morality might break down a little. If so, the Mormon Outposts won't seem so isolated anymore.

WHETHER PLACES OF WORSHIP SHOULD BE INVOLVED in social and political issues is a more complicated question than whether someone is a religious adherent. It's about whether religious influences should figure in how we conduct ourselves as a nation, politically and otherwise. Someone could be a nonadherent but still have enough respect for religious thought to believe that it should have some influence on the country. Conversely, someone could be a truly devoted religious follower but have a secular soul when it comes to the role of faith in the political sphere. You can see these kinds of differences in the way the twelve Patchwork Nation community types view this question:

Table 21.

QUESTION: Should churches and other houses of worship keep out of political matters or should they express their views on day-to-day social and political questions?[67]

Community Type	Percent Who Say Churches Should Keep Out	Percent Who Say Churches Should Express Their Views
Boom Towns	46	54
Campus and Careers	50	50
Emptying Nests	49	51
Evangelical Epicenters	39	61
Immigration Nation	48	52
Industrial Metropolis	49	51
Military Bastions	49	51
Minority Central	37	63
Monied Burbs	52	48
Mormon Outposts	55	45
Service Worker Centers	47	53
Tractor Country	47	53

A majority of people in only two community types believe that houses of worship should stay out of social and political matters—and it's hard to imagine two types more different than the dense, suburban, and not particularly religious Monied Burbs and the less-populous, often remote, and decidedly religious Mormon Outposts. And of the two, the Outposts feel stronger about keeping religion out of the public sphere. What's happening here?

In the case of the Burbs, the number is easy enough to understand: These communities tend to be less religious than others—this same survey finds than nearly 20 percent of people here are either atheist or agnostic, the highest percentage among all the types. In the case of the Outposts, though, there are a few more factors in play. Locally, the Church of Jesus Christ of Latter-day Saints doesn't have to step explicitly into civic affairs, because it's involved in them quietly, implicitly, in the form of community leaders who are LDS members.

On the national political stage, however, there's undoubtedly concern among Mormons about getting religion too involved in politics. The history of LDS conflicts with American governments goes back to the early days of the faith, and it accounts for some Outposts' intentionally remote locations. This is the other side of the separation of church and state—not to protect the state from the church, but to protect the church from the state. Mormons understand the importance of that.

Still, when California voted on gay marriage in 2008, money poured in from prominent Mormon families and individuals, and the church donated time and staff to help make sure the practice was banned. So there's at least one disconnect between the LDS Church and the people who live in the Outposts—or a feeling among the people in them that some issues are bigger than "day-to-day social and political questions."

What's notable about the rest of the community types in regard to this question is how much they're in agreement. Most lean slightly toward being in favor of churches weighing in on the events of the day, but there are two exceptions—the Evangelical Epicenters and the Minority Central counties—both of which strongly favor church involvement. Again, those are two very different community types. But they do share one important trait: They have the highest percentages of Evangelical adherents in the Patchwork Nation. These communities' attitudes about religious involvement in social and political matters is undoubtedly a reflection of Evangelical churches' mission to spread the word of God by sharing their beliefs.

IF THERE'S ONE ISSUE THAT'S guaranteed to involve Evangelicals in the cultural debates of the coming years, it's gay and lesbian rights as they relate to everything from serving openly in the military to same-sex marriage. Looking at the questions related to homosexuality in even their broadest context—whether that "way of life" should be accepted or discouraged—elicited a wide range of responses across the Patchwork Nation.

TABLE 22.

STATEMENT: Homosexuality as a way of life should be . . . [68]

Community Type	Percent Who Say It Should Be Accepted by Society	Percent Who Say It Should Be Discouraged by Society
Boom Towns	50	44
Campus and Careers	60	34
Emptying Nests	49	46
Evangelical Epicenters	30	65
Immigration Nation	55	38
Industrial Metropolis	60	34
Military Bastions	51	42
Minority Central	36	59
Monied Burbs	60	35
Mormon Outposts	29	67
Service Worker Centers	48	47
Tractor Country	45	50

The numbers defy easy explanation. For instance, attitudes about gay rights aren't solely dependent on religious adherence. It's true that people in the Evangelical Epicenters and the Mormon Outposts, two of the more strongly religious community types, believe that homosexuality should be discouraged—most certainly believe it's a sin. But people in the Industrial Metropolis counties, which contain many people who go to church regularly, are almost as strongly accepting of homosexuality. And in Tractor Country, which has an extremely high number of religious adherents, too, opinion is fairly closely divided. Once again, we take from this that it is religious teachings that matter, not whether people are religious.

Income also offers little insight into these attitudes. The residents of the Monied Burbs, the Industrial Metropolis, and the Campus and Careers counties have above-average median household incomes and are accepting of homosexuality. But people in the Boom Towns, also wealthy, are split. The Immigration Nation communities, which are less wealthy, are more accepting. There's no clear urban/rural divide on the question, either. Minority Central communities are denser than Service Worker Centers, but they're also less inclined to be accepting of gays and lesbians.

The one clear correlation is that the places that are most accepting of homosexuality all voted Democratic in the 2008 presidential election. Obama won by more than ten percentage points in all three of the communities where 60 percent of the population feels that "homosexuality as a way of life should be accepted." Given that relationship, gay rights could easily become a partisan talking point in upcoming campaigns. The populous, swing-voting Monied Burbs are an especially desirable election-year prize, and for the moment they seem to be joined with more liberal communities on this issue.

But there's a difference between "accepting" gays and lesbians and granting them things like the right to marry. If you look at the map of California's Proposition 8 vote of 2008, you'll see more than a few Monied Burbs that voted for banning gay marriage—as well as the Industrial Metropolis of Los Angeles County. I saw the same phenomenon in the representative Tractor Country community of Sioux Center, where people said they don't judge gays and lesbians but are far from pleased about the state of Iowa having allowed same-sex marriages.

"I don't think we're going to see too many marriage licenses around here," Mayor Dennis Walstra said just after the April 2009 court ruling, with a chuckle. He was right: By the end of the year there hadn't been a single same-sex marriage license issued in Sioux County.

The situation in Sioux County is similar to that in many places in the Patchwork Nation. Even if same-sex marriage became legal nationally, there probably wouldn't be long lines of gays and lesbians applying for licenses in communities like Burley or Nixa. In these areas same-sex marriage seems destined to remain a symbolic but powerful local issue.

COMMUNITY-TYPE TECTONICS

So, how does a churchgoing, Rush Limbaugh–listening, Walmart-shopping citizen of an Evangelical Epicenter relate to an agnostic, NPR-supporting, Starbucks-sipping Monied Burbanite—or vice versa? And even among community types that might appear similar on the surface there are differences underneath. Tractor Country and the Evangelical Epicenter communities may both vote Republican and listen to conservative talk radio, but their different religious backgrounds lead them in different directions on ideas of how the community should work together.

The number of truly common American cultural experiences is shrinking. Today there is no Uncle Miltie or Ed Sullivan—or even any "Must See

TV." Of the top forty most watched TV shows of all time, only one was from the last decade—the 2000 Super Bowl.[69] That may be why "events" like Michael Jackson's death or Tiger Woods's infidelities have become so big in the eyes of the media. They're bits of connective tissue. But those things plus trips to nearly ubiquitous chains like Walmart and Starbucks aren't much of a base on which to create a living national culture.

To residents of any number of the Patchwork Nation's twelve community types that may be welcome news. Why do we all have to live and breathe the same culture? After all, before Uncle Miltie there was . . . static. Or, perhaps, some small-time version of Uncle Miltie in the community playhouse or on the local radio station. The first nationwide radio broadcast didn't come until 1927. American communities were isolated from one another before then. Our national media culture hadn't existed for all that long before niche marketing, cable TV, and the Web began breaking it down.

But too many cultural divides can be problematic in terms of governance. The United States wasn't necessarily a better place back when it was so many cultural islands. Community standards weren't (and aren't) about simply upholding the best of local values. Sometimes they were (and are) about subtle and not so subtle discrimination. Cultural ideals spread through the national media at least created a baseline for the country to discuss and debate: *Is this what we are? Is this what we want to be?* Arguably, the civil rights movement needed the rise of the mass media to succeed.

Now there's not just national radio networks but Web radio. Common cultures can be localized, but they don't have to be. And they can be nationalized and localized at the same time—so similar communities in very different places can be experiencing the same media culture. That's what the Patchwork Nation's location boundaries mean in the modern media age. And that's what makes post-mass-media fragmentation different from pre-mass-media fragmentation. People and counties next door to each other can be absorbing very different news and entertainment.

Are we all drifting off to become numerous different cultures? To some extent we already have. But the twelve cultures of the Patchwork Nation aren't islands unto themselves. There are some important similarities between the Monied Burbs and, say, the wealthier parts of the Industrial Metropolis. The same is true of the Evangelical Epicenters and Tractor Country. It's hard to imagine a nation made up of twelve community cultures (or however many one identifies) that are entirely different from one another.

The best way of thinking about the individual cultures within the Patchwork Nation may be in terms of geology. Cultural plate tectonics are pushing some community types toward one another while pushing others away. Some divides will inevitably widen—but others will shrink. The question is, What will those alignments look like? Will they have to do with new cultural issues or new technologies? Will they mean more or fewer community types in the Patchwork Nations of the future?

One thing is certain: Whatever cultural Pangaea we have experienced in the past is long gone. The communities of the Patchwork Nation are headed in different directions because, in many ways, the people in them want to head in different directions—and because now, more than ever, they are not only free to go, they are being pushed that way.

Individually, people are choosing the kind of news and entertainment they want to see, read, and hear, but larger community predispositions underlie those individual choices to create different cultural settings. At the same time marketers and advertisers, armed with more exact data, better understand the different sets of targets, messages, content, and products that sell in Sioux Center and Philadelphia and everything in between. And the result is the community cultural differences that have always existed in the United States are not only being celebrated, they are being reinforced.

CONCLUSION

■ ■ ■

OUT OF MANY, MANY POSSIBILITIES

You land at an airport. You get your rental car. Maybe you grab a cup of coffee. Then you drive, sometimes a long way. When you reach your destination you look around and talk to people—and you realize, suddenly or slowly, that you're in a very different place than you were just that morning. People see different movies. Their political views are different. Their economies are different and they're in different states of health.

And the next week you land in another airport and visit another community and find that it looks and feels different not only from home, but also from the place you last visited.

For two and a half years, we traveled, we pored over data sets, read local media, and exchanged e-mails with informants and interviewees in scores of places. In the end, the research process has left us with some ambivalence. There was the exhilaration of having experienced the full measure of American diversity, of having visited each of the twelve community types that make up our Patchwork Nation. But there was also discouragement over just how diverse those places are. The differences among the twelve locations can sometimes seem as unbridgeable as they are fascinating.

A principal aim of this project was to get beyond the oversimplified red-state/blue-state model of the United States that we have become so familiar with as election analysts. Doing that during the late-2000s recession meant that we saw not one but twelve different recessions. Each place has its own set of economic problems. Increased regulation of the financial industry, stimulus-package funds—no one policy can address them all. Some communities—the undocumented-labor-dependent Immigration Nation, the tourist-dollar-chasing Service Worker Centers, the undereducated and underserved parts of the Industrial Metropolis and the Minority Central counties—can do only so well even in the best of times. In some places economic uncertainty has created political desperation, even rage. And in a few places, the recession was hardly noticed until the very late stages.

Looking at it all—the unemployment rates and the housing markets, the presidential votes and the political attitudes, the geographic concentrations of the Dittoheads and the National Public Radio connoisseurs—can make you wonder what actually holds the country together. Or what will hold it together in the future. When it comes to racial, religious, and technological divides, some communities seem destined to be left behind even after the rest of the country is moving forward again.

Discovering that the nation is divided and diverse is nothing new, of course. People have been plumbing these differences for meaning for generations, long before we lapsed into the easy generalizations of Red and Blue America. In the 1830s Alexis de Tocqueville toured the United States and wrote the two volumes of his *Democracy in America*, a font of insights into the American character. It takes only the smallest dip into this classic to discover that Tocqueville saw the country as a bundle of contradictions. Democracies like ours, he wrote, will "endure poverty, servitude, barbarism—but they will not endure aristocracy." At the same time he observed in America "the old aristocratic colours breaking through." He saw great potential in the United States in theory, but he also suggested that there's "no country in which there is so little independence of mind and real freedom of discussion."

Despite the apparently eternal relevance of Tocqueville, the United States is a very different place today than it was then. It's more populous and more diverse than it's ever been. Within a single metropolitan area you can experience any number of communities. The differences between some community types are particularly pronounced. How much do Philadelphia and Sioux Center, Iowa, really have in common? How about Nixa, Missouri, and Ann Arbor, Michigan? The twelve community types share a national government—but do they share a national identity? Sometimes that, too, seemed possible only in theory.

Traveling around the country for all of that time and talking with people in big cities and small towns and everywhere in between offered proof that American optimism had been shaken—but also that American optimism endured. Even if there's no national identity, there's a national mind-set. If we'd plotted on a graph the feelings expressed in conversations I had and e-mails I got over those thirty months, a sharp dip in positivity would have been visible as the recession worsened nationwide. People in some communities felt it earlier or later than others, but it hit everyone eventually. Yet discussion, both face-to-face and electronic, almost always came back to the belief that the nation would eventually emerge from its troubles—perhaps with a new outlook, but probably for the better.

Even in a time of immense change, that core conviction binds the country together across all the community types. James Rickman, a Los Alamos National Lab communications officer, can explain in great detail why he's worried for the future—of the economy, of the environment, of American politics. But he told me that when he talks to the scientists and theorists who work at the Lab, his mood inevitably improves. "When I look around here and I talk to some of these people, I just can't help but believe someone up here will save the world," he said one afternoon.

In Lincoln City, Oregon, Kip Ward, owner of the Historic Anchor Inn, wrote a blog post about the troubles he saw in his small oceanfront town in January 2010. "No storeowners I speak to are up over last year. And last year was a recession year that was way down from the other recession year, which was down from the prior recession year. It is now year number three and every day feels like a reminder of the seven hundred days prior," he wrote. "But most of us are still optimistic; after all spring is just around the corner. And with it opportunity knocks."

Those are people from two very distinctive locations—the high-salaried Monied Burb of Los Alamos and the living-on-tips Service Worker Center of Lincoln City. Yet their attitudes express a common idea: As bad as things are now, they will turn around; as Americans, we are still in charge of our destiny.

That belief in the power of individual effort and exertion toward goals is more widely and deeply held than you might expect. In 2008 the Pew Research Center for the People and the Press included in its survey on values a section that spoke directly to the idea of American optimism. It measured how people responded to two statements about succeeding in America: "Most people who want to get ahead can make it if they're willing to work hard" and "Hard work and determination are no guarantee of success for most people." The responses were uniformly positive in all twelve locations.

Table 23. SUCCEEDING IN AMERICA[70]

Community Type	Percentage Who Believe You Will Get Ahead If You Work Hard	Percentage Who Believe Work and Determination Are No Guarantee of Success
Boom Towns	71	28
Campus and Careers	62	36
Emptying Nests	67	31
Evangelical Epicenters	69	29
Immigration Nation	71	27
Industrial Metropolis	67	31
Military Bastions	73	26
Minority Central	74	25
Monied Burbs	68	30
Mormon Outposts	82	16
Service Worker Centers	66	32
Tractor Country	71	27

Consider everything you now know about the community types—the differences in their racial and ethnic composition, their economies, their political party loyalties—and those figures are truly remarkable. There's not a single community type in the Patchwork Nation in which fewer than two-thirds of respondents said that a person can succeed if he or she tries hard enough. Tellingly, residents of some of the poorest community types, full of people who are marginalized in our society, are among the most fervent believers in the American dream—people in Minority Central and Immigration Nation. The United States is, measurably, a nation of optimists.

How much of a national commonality is that? There are worse things to have as a foundation. People in each of the twelve community types may have different ideas of exactly what it means to "get ahead" or achieve "success," but they all believe that it can be done in the United States. That should be enough to make any of us exhilarated again by the breadth of American diversity—and to see the differences in the Patchwork Nation as opportunities as well as challenges.

For instance, what if the people living in the consumer-credit-driven Monied Burbs and Industrial Metropolises better understood the financial practices in Tractor Country communities like Sioux Center, where debt is seen as a burden to be taken on very cautiously? How might folks in Service Worker Centers far from the Mexican border feel about the immigration debate if they could better understand the economic impact of tightened border restrictions on Immigration Nation communities like El Mirage, Arizona? Could the single-minded communities of the Mormon Outposts or the Emptying Nests suggest new approaches to civic unity to the deeply divided places in Minority Central?

And remember, despite our differences, Americans as a whole are pretty tolerant too. We may live in starkly diverse communities—economically, politically, and culturally—but there are very few calls to political, ethnic, and racial violence these days, compared with times past. Surveys may report citizen dissatisfaction with this presidency, or that policy, but they are not so upset that they call into question the entire constitutional order. People are sufficiency supportive of the way their political institutions operate that elections continue to draw a large and active pool of voters. And the inevitable losers in these contests, while discouraged, do not turn their backs and give up, but resolve to compete again. Nonvoters, for their part, are not so much angry as they are apathetic.

None of this is to belittle the power of the different forces pulling at the Patchwork Nation. As the country redefines and remakes itself, those forces have the potential to create a truly divided and, in some ways, broken democracy. As the economy bumps along and the electorate lurches to find a new political equilibrium, frustration and fragmentation could rise to disturbing levels. People living in different communities could see starkly different problems and demand starkly different solutions. Cultural differences could be heightened through retrenchment, to the point that very few of the twelve community types understand one another at all.

But that's one possibility. It would be a mistake to look at this book as a portrait of a country cracking up. What it really shows is a picture of a complicated place in the midst of a transition.

You can't look at the twelve community types in the Patchwork Nation without thinking about time. The twelve community types aren't spinning apart; they're shifting, evolving. Some of them are moving farther apart as some of them move closer together. It's easy to imagine old community types splitting and new ones forming. What will the formerly growing and diversifying Boom Towns look like when the housing market finds a new normal? Will growing income disparities break the counties that now comprise the Monied Burbs into different socioecononomic types? What of the cities of the Industrial Metropolis that gave rise to the "American Century"? Will they reinvent themselves as the centers of the new economy or slide downward, pulled apart by their fractured populations—the very rich and the very poor? Or, perhaps, will the well-educated, research-driven communities assume an even bigger role as the nation looks to brainpower and technology as the building blocks of what comes next?

The changes that are already working their way through the country— economically, politically, and culturally—are going to mean different things in different places. Some are going to struggle—maybe mightily. And it's unlikely that there will be any locale left unaffected. Economically, the United States will no longer be unrivaled the way it was during the post–World War II boom years. Technological advances seem to be exacerbating the role of place and location in our lives, rather than diminishing them. Politically, these two forces will alter the political landscape by heightening contextual and centripetal forces, not centrifugal ones.

But we shouldn't look at the transitions the nation is facing and see only dark times ahead. Even if you're among the small minority of Americans who doesn't believe in American optimism, all the changes coming to the communities in the Patchwork Nation don't mean that the future looks bleak.

They mean, simply, that the future looks different.

APPENDIX

■ ■ ■

THEORETICAL AND METHODOLOGICAL BACKGROUND

The following pages are meant to offer an explanation of just how we arrived at the twelve community types and how we sorted through all the data we collected. This is where we "show our work." That being the case, this appendix is somewhat technical and the layperson may have difficulty following along.

Our goal here is to be as accurate and as transparent as possible about the system and approaches we used to identify and organize the community types that make up the Patchwork Nation. Our hope is that those with a background in statistical analysis will use this appendix to examine what we have done in these pages.

FIRST, OUR EFFORT IS ANCHORED in theoretical considerations originating from a long history of research on the nation's social and economic variability, and how that variation at the individual and local levels relates to political outcomes in major elections.[71] These works link the political tendencies of places chiefly to their socioeconomic composition, as voters' interests are commonly defined by their most observable social and economic characteristics.[72]

From previous research, we have learned that the variability of the national electoral landscape can be understood primarily by segmenting it according to well-recognized group distinctions that give rise to political beliefs and behavior. We can begin to understand the political responsiveness of places, then, by accounting for the voters' incomes, their work, their level of education, race and ethnic background, religious identity and practices, and age. In reviewing our work, readers will recognize many of the common characteristics that pollsters and pundits use on Election Night to break the national electorate into what they consider to be socially and economically relevant categories as they summarize the incoming election returns.

Readers should note that the county-level information we draw upon to categorize the nation into the twelve segments is not used as merely a poor substitute for individual-level information, as has been the case in research in which individual-level information has been in short supply. While we are certainly interested in individual voters, their lives, and their political decision making, we are also interested in the geographic settings in which individuals are making choices and living out those lives. The theoretical tradition on which this project builds is therefore sociological and "structural" in the broad sense that meaning is produced through local practices, and that human life is influenced by habits of local thought and action. People are not completely determined by their environments, but their position in space and time does limit their range of choices, steering them toward some courses of action, and away from others.

To be sure, counties are not the only relevant contexts for life experience; certainly people simultaneously live in households, cities, neighborhoods, school catchment areas, special utility districts, states, media markets, and other officially designated and unofficial geographies that shape patterns of public service, information flow, and human interaction. But research designed to set forth the variability of local environments must begin somewhere, and counties offer several advantages that make them excellent places to begin.

First, their boundaries are fairly fixed and continuous across time, making them practical measures of political, economic, and social context. New counties do occasionally emerge, for instance Broomfield, Colorado, and some disappear through consolidation, but this is a rare occurrence. The stability in boundary definition stands in contrast to many other geographic units, the borders of which are regularly altered with population growth and development. By using counties as a starting point, however, we do not mean to suggest that human interaction patterns are either as fully extensive as a county, or confined to county boundaries. Data on commuting indicate that some people's daily routines take them well beyond the confines of their home county, while others are limited to their immediate neighborhood.

Second, counties are commonly jurisdictions with governing authority and political power to shape the lives of their residents, structuring aspects of life (e.g., housing, schools, taxation, recycling, election administration) through law making and enforcement. Legally drawn boundaries take on great meaning precisely because of the social and economic activities that are encouraged, permitted, or prohibited within them.

Third, major political campaigns take counties seriously, treating them as individual units as they develop and target outreach efforts toward the achievement of strategic goals.[73] Finally, previous research across several social science fields has not only utilized county-level data extensively, but found it to be relevant as a contextual container of the life experience of residents.[74]

Avoiding Fallacious Inferences from Ecological Information

Any casual look at the red and blue maps in election coverage shows that the mapping of state-level patterns of political support does little to help us to understand the rugged terrain of locality. It is a fallacy to conclude that because Nebraska is usually a red state, all of the states' communities are Republican, or that because next-door Iowa is a competitive state, all of its constituent locales are, too. As we note in the Introduction, however, we do not want to take the opposite extreme and unhelpfully insist that every location is unique. One motivation for the research in this book is to move beyond overly general characterizations of locations and voters, while not giving up on social scientific generalization altogether. We are mindful of the fact that many distinctive attributes of places and their populations are not particularly relevant to the kind of political demands they come to express. Many apparently unique aspects of local environments can be safely ignored in research and analysis. There aren't just two kinds of places, but places are not infinite in variety, either.

Just as localities are more varied than states, individuals are different from the observations made at the county or municipal level, too. We cannot assume that because a county is 60 percent black, and that 56 percent of that county voted for the Republican candidate in a presidential election, that the black voters there voted Republican. Such patterns in county behavior may exist, but an African American majority voting for a Republican candidate would be rather unlikely in any *recent* U.S. election. Instead, it was probably the case that only the white voters cast votes in that election, and that African American turnout was very low. But looking only at the county-level data on the percentage won by the Republican candidate does not tell you exactly which voters went to the polls within that county.

To make such faulty inferences is to commit the *ecological fallacy*, in which a researcher makes an unjustified inference about individual behavior from the observation of aggregate (district, county, state) data.[75] Processes of aggregating individual data to larger units for analysis can obscure variability and details that aren't observable at the broader geographic level. Relationships for groups do not necessarily hold for individuals.[76]

Readers should note that counties are not just an inferior substitute for individuals as they have been in academic research where individual-level information has been unavailable. In this particular research, we are not interested simply in the behavior of individuals, but also in the behavior of places or settings in which individuals live.

We have digested a considerable amount and variety of data in writing this book, and we continue to do so for our related work online. Much of our data originate not from aggregated observations of counties or cities, or from standard government sources, but from large-scale surveys of individuals residing in these locations, data purchased from private sector specialists, as well as in-depth interviews at exemplar locations. Bearing in mind the variety and diversity of information sources we utilize, we are careful to talk about places, or locations, when we are discussing region-, county-, and city-level information, and individuals when we draw on polling data, surveys, or information originating directly from residents of the places under study. Organizing all of this multilevel material coherently is not easy, but fortunately ecological and individual relationships are not widely disparate in the numerous comparisons and tabulations that we draw upon where both have been available.

Data Collection

We started by gathering data from the U.S. Bureau of the Census in four general areas that would help us to gauge the socioeconomic aspects of counties that would be most relevant to contemporary political life.

1) Population size and density—traits that usually determine the peripheral or central status of locations in economic, media, and cultural terms. City size also determines electoral influence.
2) Income, occupation, and education—measures useful for evaluating the varying socioeconomic status of locations, vital for examining the geographic concentration of wealth and poverty.
3) Race and ethnicity—essential measures for assessing the racial and ethnic composition of counties, highly relevant to understanding levels of political activism and party support.
4) The age distribution—necessary measures for evaluating the uneven concentration of youthful, family-age, and elderly populations across the nation, sometimes due to retirement migration or the presence of universities and colleges.

A fifth area of interest relevant to explaining political outcomes was religion, knowing that political values often spring from moral codes, and that morality typically finds its source in religious instruction and indoctrination. Although the U.S. Census does not collect or record information on the religious affiliation of the nation's inhabitants, we did find a satisfactory source of data from the Glenmary Research Institute's decennial census of religious congregations.[77] This source is not perfect in every respect, but it does provide accurate information on the local presence of the major denominational groups within Christianity, as well as some non-Christian religious membership groups. Most auspiciously, the Glenmary survey reports congregation counts and membership tabulations at the county level for the entire nation. Although some small Christian denominations and other sectarian organizations do not participate in the survey and remain uncounted, a 100 percent count is not considered essential given the broad level of generalization and description we require.

Statistical Procedures

Once our initial data were collected, we used a statistical method called "principal components," often classified as a type of factor analysis, to guide our classification of counties. Factor analysis methods are commonly used in connection with attitude and opinion surveys when complex attitudes cannot be measured adequately by a single question, but are instead a product of several questions. Here we use factor analysis because socioeconomic contexts of the kind we are measuring across U.S. counties are thought to be the result of a number of indicators, not singular ones.

Factor analysis is mainly exploratory as we use it, and was not deployed so as to confirm the existence of clearly defined, a priori socioeconomic settings. We started with the theoretically relevant variables mentioned above, and moved from there to use principal components to evaluate the presence of a smaller number of underlying factors. Factors can be understood as condensed statements of the relationship among a larger set of variables.[78] Factors account for the variance and explain correlations among a set of variables (e.g., income indicators, race indicators, religion indicators).

Principal components is a particular type of factor analysis used to identify (or "extract") these factors. The first factor (technically called a "component" in principal components analysis) always explains the most variance in the correlation matrix of variables. If more than one factor emerges, the factors are ordered from highest to lowest in terms of the amount of variance they explain in that larger correlation matrix of socioeconomic variables.

Drawing upon U.S. Census and other data elements described above, the factor analysis methodology captures the extent of overlap in these items by mathematically identifying their interrelationship or common correlation (see Figure 15). We found that our socioeconomic and religious indicators pointed to an underlying structure of about twelve components, allowing us to reduce many socioeconomic indicator variables to just twelve basic factors, or location types. In this manner, factor analysis permitted us to take an extensive set of measures of economic, social, and religious importance and determine just how many basic factors or components were at their foundation.

Once several variables are found to indicate a single underlying factor, the principal components procedure produces a "factor score" derived from the weighted combination of the individual items that are highly associated with (or "load highly on") that factor. After exploratory analysis we found that in the vast majority of cases, the number of items we drew upon from our sources of county-level data produced a solution of between ten and fourteen uncorrelated factors, but most often twelve, that explained about 70 to 80 percent of the variance in the total matrix.

Consistent with statistical convention, we devoted serious attention only to factors with eigenvalues greater than 1. The scores from these factors were then utilized in our classification scheme of counties into twelve basic types. Readers should note that every county receives a score on each of the twelve factors, although when we then moved to designate a single best-fitting type to each county, we made those assignments categorically and exclusively. We used both the original interval-level scores, and our

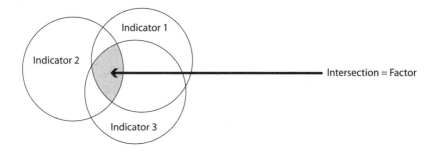

Figure 15. Depiction of the Measurement Overlap of Three Variables that Generate the Factor or Component Score in Factor Analysis

simplified categorical generalizations of those scores, in subsequent efforts to evaluate the validity of the typology. We would advise that the interval-level scores should be used in any advanced statistical analysis, such as regression analysis and its variants. To facilitate interpretation, these scores have been rescaled to run from 0 to 100.

Interpretation of the factor scores is guided by theory, but invariably contains a subjective component, involving an examination of the factor loadings of individual variables with the factor scores, and taking into account estimates of the influence of specific data items in shaping those scores. Careful scrutiny of the scoring of individual cases, coupled with detailed knowledge of individual cases, is essential to making reasonable distinctions, and advancing plausible classification.

The Twelve Community Types

Among the more clearly defined categories was one we interpreted as identifying upper-income counties situated within major metropolitan areas. These were often a mix of urban and suburban locations we dubbed, for simple descriptive purposes, **Monied Burbs**. Professions are a major occupational category, with low unemployment levels and little poverty. There is some religious diversity, including a Jewish presence. School enrollments are robust, signaling the presence of families with children. Residential tenure is shorter than average, an indication of residential mobility and new subdivisions developing on the metropolitan fringe. Our shorthand label for these locations does not fully capture their variation, but it does offer a convenient and abbreviated way to communicate about them. For illustration, we present a histogram of the distribution of scores for the Monied Burbs factor in Figure 16. Two counties that fit this category especially well are identified: Loudoun County, Virginia, located in the Washington, D.C., metro area, and Douglas County, Colorado, a collection of high-income suburbs on the metropolitan fringe situated south of Denver. In recent years, these were two of the top ten most affluent counties in the entire nation.

A second clearly defined county type can be characterized by their low income and minority populations—chiefly African American counties in the South's "Black Belt" region, along with scattered locations in the West with large Native American concentrations. While it may seem highly unusual to group counties on Native American Indian reservations with low-income black counties from the "Old South," statistically speaking, we observed that the living conditions are remarkably similar, especially with respect to basic indicators such as poverty, unemployment, occupational status, and educational attainment. After consideration, we decided on the shorthand descriptor **Minority Central** for these locations.

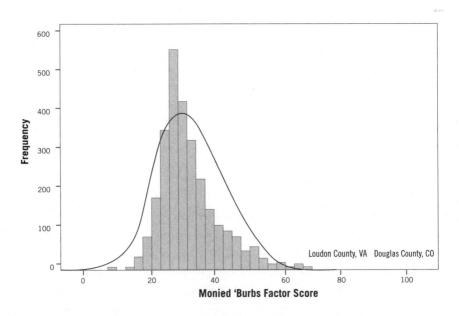

Figure 16. Histogram of Factor Scores for Monied Burbs for 3,141 Counties, Mean=31.0; SD=8

A third type that emerged from our analysis was a set of fast-growing, mainly midsize counties with sizable Evangelical populations. We should note that our research suggested that religious groups do not always stand out in relief across the nation's terrain—at least using counties as units of observation. Evangelical Christian adherents were prominent in the South and some parts of the West. Mormons were a major presence in the mountain states, and especially Utah and Idaho, reflecting long-standing settlement patterns dating to the 1850s. There was no particularly distinctive set of mainline Protestant, "Jewish," or "non-Christian" locales that stood apart. We use the terms **Evangelical Epicenter** to describe the counties with noteworthy Evangelical populations, and **Mormon Outposts** to describe the counties we grouped into the Mormon influence category.

The most rural and sparsely populated counties often stood out for either their diminutive population size or their agricultural occupational base, and often both. Although we decided to dub these locations **Tractor Country** for ease of description, it should be noted that sometimes sparse populations are a sign that agriculture is not at all viable, particularly in desert regions of the West. The job-related attribute common to this set of locales is the high percentage of people who are *self-employed*, but only a minority share is generally employed in farming.

College towns and locations, which we refer to as **Campus and Careers**, with especially youthful age distributions stood out distinctly, although they are not a particularly large group. These places can be described as having a larger than typical population of residents in the twenty-to-thirty-four age range, fewer elderly residents than the national average, high postsecondary enrollment, and a very large percentage of the population employed in education and educational services. Some of these locations also showed greater than average religious diversity, including the presence of non-Western religions.

The nation's most Latino counties, usually home to large and growing immigrant populations, appeared easy to identify in a sixth factor. These places included some larger cities and suburbs, and were concentrated primarily in the Southwest. Given the large percentage of Hispanic residents, these counties were home to larger than average Catholic populations. These locations were also poorer, on average, than other counties, with a younger age distribution. We have described these locations as **Immigration Nation**.

Big cities stood out as a seventh factor, and although their numbers are smaller, they are home to a large percentage of the U.S. population. In addition to their sheer size, counties such as Cook, Illinois, and the New York City boroughs are home to religiously diverse populations with elite residents topping out at the highest end of the income distribution. Although they are certainly not as industrial as they once were, they are presently described in our framework as **Industrial Metropolis**.

A set of cities of varying sizes, but with rapidly growing, increasingly prosperous populations emerged from our study to be labeled **Boom Towns**. These locales are predominantly located in the southern and western states, commonly home to recently settled and retirement-age populations, along with residents who profited, then lost, during the housing boom and bust of 2008 and 2009.

An expansive list of smaller counties, though not the smallest, fit into the **Service Worker Centers** category. These towns are home to family-age and retirement-age populations, but are usually not places attractive to younger adults. Service Center communities make great hometowns, truly wonderful places to grow up, but less wonderful places to live one's twenties and thirties. They stand out mainly for having typical small-town economies characterized by employment in retail trade, wholesale trade, and miscellaneous personal and business services. Residents are middle and lower middle income. Although more Catholic and mainline than Evangelical, and more Christian than not, no single Protestant denomination predominates.

A number of locations are particularly noteworthy for having large elderly populations and/or populations within ten years of retirement. In most cases, our **Emptying Nests** counties can be found in the warmer climates of the southern states, for instance, in the suburbs and exurbs of major cities in Florida. But in other cases, these are less affluent elderly populations, living on fixed incomes, in small and midsize midwestern towns that are losing population through the exodus of younger people who see a limited future locally.

Finally, a small but very distinctive final category emerging from our exploratory work is the **Military Bastions**, a small subset of counties primarily distinguished not simply by the proximity of a major military base or installation, but also by the heavy economic dependence on that installation in the local economy. Usually these are midsize counties characterized by large populations employed in trade and services supporting a local military base. The age distribution is younger and family age, reflecting the presence of military personnel. Residents are transient, middle- and lower-income earners.

Counties as Composites

To be sure, very few counties fit purely into one category or another. Counties are not consistent in size, and can be internally quite diverse, as Cook County, Illinois, serves to illustrate. Cook County is comprised not only of the city of Chicago, with its broad-ranging neighborhoods, but also a collection of fast-growing suburbs lying to the northwest, in and around O'Hare International Airport. Numerous other counties are also highly heterogeneous collections of sundry communities with individuals in assorted walks of life.

Then there are a handful of counties with tiny populations numbering less than one hundred, with the working adults employed in just one, two, or three occupations. Some might wonder how we can possibly compare such disparate settings, but our response is that the vast differences are exactly the point. Population density is part of what makes a place distinctive as a socializing environment. Two people may be similar in relevant respects, yet one resides in a city of 2 million, while another resides on a cattle ranch, five hours' drive from the nearest metropolitan area. Such contrasting residential contexts are real features of the U.S. landscape, having different cultural, economic, and political consequences for their residents. The goal is not to understand places that are artificially zoned off so as to be equal in population size, though such an approach might have research value, but to study communities as they are experienced and inhabited by their residents, and as they might be evaluated by potential movers, market researchers, businesses, and political campaigns. Comparing counties, some large and diverse, some small and simple, is one way to reach that goal, while underscoring our earlier caveat about the varying distances over which routine life may range.

The assignment of counties into the one best-fitting and exclusive category of each of the twelve community types was an arduous process for which there is no readily justified, off-the-shelf, statistical procedure. In our effort to choose the best classification for each county in conducting much of our analysis, there has been no substitute for a ground-level familiarity with the nation's demographic and economic geography. Judgment based on prior knowledge and further study of local conditions has been the primary resource we have drawn upon.

The statistical rankings of counties on the twelve factor scores were the most useful single piece of information in allotting counties to singular categories. Ordinarily, counties that ranked highest on a particular factor but did not rank as highly on others were assigned as members of the type on which they ranked the highest. For example, in Figure 16, there was little question that Loudoun County and Douglas County would be best classified as "Monied Burbs," although both also ranked highly on the "Boom Towns" factor given their high growth rates. In quite a few cases, we found that locations were ranked as high on one factor as they were on one, two, or even three other factors. Counties that fit into our "Industrial Metropolis" category often ranked high on the "Immigration Nation" factor. There was also considerable intersection between "Military Bastions" and "Service Worker Centers," and between "Service Worker Centers" with smaller populations and "Tractor Country," our most rural locales.

With no wooden rule to rely upon in assigning these hard cases to one type or the other, we proceeded on a case-by-case basis, looked at neighboring locations, and then examined similar locations in other states. On balance, we believe this procedure anchored in evidence from similar locations, mixed with impressions and judgment, produced good matches and satisfactorily resolved ambiguities. Nevertheless, we fully acknowledge that in many cases there is room to argue for a different classification than the one we utilized, and that forcing one category on a heterogeneous county surely risks oversimplification. Wherever possible, in statistical analysis by other scholars, the categorical scheme of classification should be replaced by the actual factor scores that offer interval-level rankings of each county on each of the twelve county types. We will make those available if others are interested in exploring them.

Validation of Classification Scheme

Any coding or classification scheme should be validated not only informally, asking if the scale or typology bears a reasonable resemblance to reality—the face validity test—but also using statistical methods. One way we do this in the context of this research is to gauge the statistical association of the twelve types to indicators not included among the original data used to produce the factor scores. Using geocoded survey data from surveys with unusually large samples allows us to assess, for instance, whether the counties we have coded as Evangelical Epicenters really do have a sizable plurality or majority of Evangelical adherents, as well as how observant they are. Locations are also highly distinctive for what they are not. By way of discriminant validity, then, one would not expect big cities or the Campus and Careers towns to have the highest percentages of Evangelical Christians, and in fact previous studies might lead us to expect them to have the most irreligious populations.

Validity tests using data from a large-scale survey, the *2004 National Annenberg Election Survey* (NAES), conducted throughout that year, appear in Table 24. This survey draws upon an unusually large sample; Annenberg researchers interviewed 80,500 citizens and noncitizens. Although such impressive samples do not allow us to represent each of the 3,140 counties in the nation, they can represent the counties as they are combined into the twelve community types. By blocking the respondents from counties of the same, then aggregating the survey responses from those locations as a group, we can assess whether the survey responses reinforce a meaning and definition of each location type.

Clearly the Monied Burbs locations stand out in Table 24 for having highly educated and affluent populations according to the NAES study. They are also home to the largest percentage of professionals of any of the twelve community types. The Minority Central counties have large black populations as reflected in the survey tabulations, but they also stand out as predominantly Protestant and low income. Note that surveys of these diverse counties will typically contain about 73 percent white respondents. Simply because they have large black populations does not mean they are majority black; they simply have a larger minority presence than other counties.

The Evangelical Epicenters are the most Protestant and born-again of the location types, as we would expect, and they are also very high in church attendance. Survey respondents from these counties are notably less well educated, but also predominantly white. Gun owners are common in the Evangelical Epicenter counties.

According to the Annenberg survey, Tractor Country locations are distinct for having high levels of self-employment, mainly in agriculture and trade, as well as white gun-owning populations. They are heavily Protestant, but do not claim to be born-again nearly as often as residents of the Evangelical Epicenters. Notably, these counties also contain the largest percentage of residents over age seventy.

It would appear that the Campus and Careers locations accurately pick up the largest percentage of residents with graduate and professional degrees from the Annenberg study, although there are several locations with equal-sized youth populations, including the Mormon Outposts and the nation's large cities. The Campus and Careers counties are similar to the

Table 24. TABULATIONS OF INDICATOR VARIABLES FROM SURVEY DATA WITH 12-COMMUNITY TYPOLOGY

	Boom Towns	Campus and Careers	Emptying Nests	Evangelical Epicenters	Immigration Nation	Industrial Metropolis	Military Bastions	Minority Central	Monied Burbs	Mormon Outposts	Service Worker Centers	Tractor Country	TOTAL U.S.
Education													
% Less than HS Diploma	6.6	5.2	7.0	11.4	10.4	7.4	6.7	11.2	5.3	4.0	9.0	7.2	7.3
% College Degree	22.0	20.5	16.6	14.6	18.3	22.9	18.9	15.5	23.7	20.1	15.3	13.8	20.3
% Grad/Prof Degree	14.2	19.5	10.3	8.6	12.9	17.6	14.1	9.9	18.2	14.0	10.0	7.6	14.6
Race and Ethnicity													
% Latino	7.6	3.9	4.0	2.8	25.4	12.3	10.0	3.9	6.6	6.2	2.1	2.5	7.6
% White	89.2	93.5	95.6	91.5	90.8	76.6	85.1	72.6	90.7	99.3	96.1	96.8	88.6
% Black	8.1	3.9	3.4	5.3	6.0	19.1	12.2	24.4	6.4	0.2	2.2	0.8	8.5
% Asian	1.4	1.5	0.4	0.2	1.7	3.4	1.3	0.6	2.2	0.2	0.3	0.4	1.6
% Born in U.S.	92.4	94.2	95.3	97.0	84.5	84.2	93.3	96.2	90.0	94.1	97.4	97.6	91.5
Religion													
% Attend Church Weekly+	42.6	35.5	44.9	54.7	41.5	38.1	44.2	53.8	36.7	62.2	40.9	44.4	41.3
% Never Attend	17.2	23.3	15.5	10.6	19.5	19.3	14.4	9.7	21.1	12.4	18.5	18.1	18.2
% Protestant	68.5	58.7	68.8	88.0	55.9	48.7	69.7	77.8	54.9	20.2	68.1	72.0	62.7
% Catholic	22.2	31.9	25.9	6.9	34.3	39.1	23.7	16.2	34.2	8.8	25.6	22.7	28.0
% Jewish	0.8	2.3	0.6	0.2	1.9	4.8	0.7	0.2	3.9	0.0	0.6	0.1	2.1
% Mormon	3.2	0.6	0.7	0.6	2.6	0.6	1.0	1.0	1.0	68.5	0.9	2.3	1.8
% Born-Again Christian	45.5	33.1	43.1	72.2	41.3	32.8	49.1	62.7	32.3	22.7	44.8	44.8	41.9
Culture													
% Gun Owners	43.0	34.2	43.7	62.7	38.8	20.5	42.7	54.4	30.8	54.8	51.4	69.3	39.0
% Know Gay/Lesbian	51.3	55.9	44.0	36.5	48.2	55.5	45.2	39.8	55.5	41.1	44.6	32.7	50.1

Age/Length of Residence													
% Age 18–25	10.1	9.4	7.7	7.9	**10.9**	10.5	10.2	9.3	7.8	**10.6**	8.0	7.6	9.1
% Age 60 and Older	23.0	25.1	**29.8**	29.7	23.9	21.5	24.1	26.0	24.4	19.5	28.1	**31.7**	24.8
% Age 70 and Older	10.9	11.9	**16.1**	13.6	12.0	10.7	11.4	12.5	12.0	9.3	14.0	**19.2**	12.2
% Lived 2 Years or Less	**30.7**	27.7	25.0	22.1	**29.9**	25.9	28.6	23.0	26.1	25.2	22.0	20.3	26.3
Occupation and Employment													
% Self-Employed	18.4	18.1	17.4	**19.9**	18.8	16.5	15.2	18.3	18.4	18.3	17.5	**25.7**	18.0
% Professional Worker	34.1	**37.9**	30.8	26.5	32.0	37.7	33.1	29.6	**38.8**	34.1	28.3	25.9	34.4
% Laborer	7.1	5.0	9.7	**11.1**	8.9	5.7	6.6	9.4	6.0	7.5	**10.0**	9.1	7.4
% Clerical Worker	10.6	10.5	9.5	10.1	10.9	**12.5**	11.8	10.3	10.9	**12.9**	11.3	11.9	11.1
% Service Worker	9.8	9.7	11.0	10.7	10.3	9.8	**11.4**	10.4	8.6	8.2	**11.5**	9.5	9.9
% Skilled Trades	9.8	10.0	10.2	12.2	10.4	8.7	8.9	**12.8**	9.1	12.2	12.0	**12.6**	10.0
% Semiskilled Workers	4.0	4.2	**6.4**	**7.9**	5.2	4.0	3.9	5.4	3.2	5.0	6.3	5.9	4.5
% Salespersons	6.0	**5.8**	5.2	5.3	5.2	**5.8**	4.8	4.8	5.6	4.7	4.7	4.0	5.5
% Business Owners	4.1	3.6	4.2	4.0	4.1	2.7	3.3	**4.4**	3.7	3.6	3.5	**6.9**	3.7
% Ever Served in Military	16.1	13.9	14.9	16.7	14.4	11.8	**21.8**	16.2	14.1	12.6	16.1	**18.2**	14.9
% Other Householder Served in Military	15.2	14.2	16.2	16.0	13.8	11.5	**18.7**	15.7	14.4	15.0	16.2	**16.5**	14.7
% Currently in Military	**3.9**	3.2	1.5	2.6	2.9	2.2	**9.5**	1.6	2.9	3.3	2.2	2.3	3.0
% Other Householder Currently in Military	**7.3**	5.4	4.0	5.7	6.5	5.6	**11.8**	7.1	5.7	6.5	6.3	5.8	6.4
Income													
% Earning $25,000 or Less	19.3	21.1	22.5	**28.4**	23.1	20.6	21.2	**28.3**	14.7	20.7	26.5	27.7	20.8
% Earning $100–150K	10.4	**11.2**	6.4	6.2	9.0	10.8	8.7	6.3	**13.7**	5.5	5.9	3.5	9.9
% Earning $150K and Up	6.6	6.1	3.7	3.3	5.6	**8.6**	3.5	4.4	**10.2**	2.8	3.4	1.8	6.7

Source: Tabulations from *2004 National Annenberg Election Survey.*

Note: Cell entries are percentages, with two highest percentages highlighted in each row.

Monied Burbs in that they have a professional workforce, although these counties do not have the same earning power. They are far less religious than other locations, and survey respondents from such places are more likely than those from other places to say they know a person who is gay or lesbian.

The Industrial Metropolis and Immigration Nation are similar in their ethnic diversity, but the big cities have far-better-educated and professional workforces, and consequently higher incomes. As we would expect if we had measured properly, the Boom Towns have the most recently settled populations, although the highly mobile Immigration Nation counties are almost equally transient, with Military Bastions not far behind.

Emptying Nests can be recognized in the survey data for having large percentages of residents in retirement, or nearing retirement. Unlike the Tractor Country locations, which also have large elderly concentrations, Emptying Nests residents are more mobile, reflecting retirement migration, and higher income and education levels. Emptying Nests do not have nearly the level of self-employment that can be found in Tractor Country (e.g., due to farming).

Military Bastions are distinguished in the survey for housing large shares of past and currently serving military personnel, while exhibiting higher levels of ethnic and racial diversity than other similar communities lacking a military presence. Locations are defined by what they are not, as well as by what they are. Many Military Bastions locations would be Service Worker Centers were it not for the military presence, as both have high percentages of employment in personal and business services and trade, a mix of pink-collar and blue-collar jobs, but little manufacturing, and fewer high-end professional jobs. The tabulations in Table 24 remind us that these community types are not founded on a single characteristic, but reflect the presence of some features and the absence of others.

Efforts to validate the twelve community types against other large-scale surveys produced similarly encouraging results, though we do not report those tabulations here. For instance, we used the 2008 *Cooperative Congressional Election Study,* conducted by YouGov/Polimetrix, which included nearly thirty-three thousand respondents, and found that the Evangelical Epicenters and the Mormon Outposts were the most religiously observant, and residents of the Campus and Careers and Monied Burbs locations were the least. Findings for ethnic diversity and military employment were similar, as were those for income, education, and age distribution. Similar efforts validated the typology against pooled survey data from the Pew Center for the People and the Press, finding results that are congruent with those described above.

Additional Evidence for Validity

The collected evidence from a number of large-scale surveys conducted between 2000 and 2008 suggests a high degree of construct validity for the twelve county types. We also conducted extensive validity tests drawing from other data sources that were not used to conduct the factor analysis that informed the typology. For example, we examined the geographic prevalence of certain types of church congregations, businesses and chain stores, geocoded to the street or zip code level. While these data, purchased from the most highly reputable list vendors, did not always provide information on congregation size, or business size and sales volume, we still found that the mere concentration and presence of larger numbers of these enterprises across counties was associated with predictable community characteristics.

Evangelical Epicenters, for instance, had far more Southern Baptist churches per household than the other locations, for example. Specific black Protestant denominations such as the African Methodist Episcopal and offshoot A.M.E. Zion congregations were more prevalent in the Minority Central communities and in the diverse Industrial Metropolis locales than they were elsewhere, again suggesting that our coding has more than just a surface plausibility.

Universities and colleges were also mapped to their precise street addresses, and we were able to inspect whether these educational institutions were more prominent in some locations—for example, our Campus and Careers counties—than in others. To be sure, colleges and universities can be found in all types of places, rich and poor, in all parts of the nation. Even so, a simple count of higher education institutions was positively and significantly associated with the Campus and Careers designation.

On the business front, we found more farms per household in Tractor Country, and vastly more crop acreage there than in the other counties. We found gunsmiths and gun dealers far more plentifully in Tractor Country and in the Mormon West than in the Monied Burbs or the Industrial Metropolis counties. The geography of retail trade was helpful in validating the twelve categories. Food purchases are an expression of culture, as well as economics. We looked at the nationwide locations of ethnic grocers, carefully mapping the communities where they were concentrated. If our typology is valid, we would have expected these enterprises to populate the big urban centers and the Immigration Nation counties. This is exactly the pattern we found, although remarkably we also found many ethnic grocers to be present in and around military bases, located in our Military Bastions counties. This also makes sense, as military personnel are a more diverse group than the nation as a whole and spend a great deal of time overseas acquiring a taste for ethnic food, and a number of U.S. military bases are well-known for their nearby ethnic and immigrant populations.

If our typology is valid, we might also expect that high-end grocers such as Whole Foods Markets would be located mostly in the Monied Burbs and in the major urban Industrial Metropolis locations, with a sprinkling perhaps in the Campus and Careers towns. This pattern was confirmed by our research based on store locations as of 2009 and 2010. The Monied Burbs did not express much interest in shopping at bargain grocers such as Walmart and have far fewer Walmart stores than one can find in Tractor Country, Minority Central, or the Evangelical Epicenters. Finally, as the foreclosure crisis developed in 2008 and endured through 2009, we were not surprised that the mortgage meltdown hit the rapidly growing Boom Towns most of all—again this was a predictable result if our typology accurately reflected ground-level conditions in residential mobility and housing development.

Other aspects of retail consumption proved to be interesting tests that confirmed the validity of our typology. In the chapter on culture, we discussed the locations of more than 4,100 bookstores nationwide, both the major chain outlets—Borders, Barnes and Noble, and Books-A-Million—as well as small regional chains, and the legions of small independently owned stores. An easy prediction would suggest that bookstores would be most prominent in those counties with well-educated populations, and among populations that possessed both the disposable income and leisure time to buy and read books. Sure enough, we did find that Campus and Careers locales ranked highest in book vending, and not far behind were the Monied Burbs. With low levels of literacy and income, the Minority Central locales were dead last. Tractor Country locations, with high literacy rates, but tiny populations and middling income, ranked high for the presence of diminutive independent booksellers, but hardly any of the big chain stores were located there—again a perfectly predictable geographic pattern based on the market size considerations that guide the decision making of major retailers.

Are Socioeconomic Settings Unchanging?

The upshot of these various investigations is that the twelve types we have identified and mapped appear to have strong construct validity using a variety of convergent and discriminant criteria drawn from contemporary sources. But we do not pretend that the way we have labeled counties today is the way they would have been labeled thirty years ago, or the way they would be thirty years from now, based on research using similar methods. Socioeconomic characteristics of counties, cities, and regions do not change overnight, but they are not permanent, either. For example, we suspect that if we were using data from 1960 or 1970, we would have a set of midsize counties identified with the presence of manufacturing and heavy industry. Durable goods manufacturing has gradually been replaced in the years since with the service economy. Growing up in the Akron, Ohio, of the early 2010s, is not like growing up in the Akron of the 1950s.

We fully acknowledge that our work is dependent entirely upon data drawn from the first decade of the twenty-first century, and developed on the basis of the features of socioeconomic life we ascertain to be theoretically relevant to contemporary politics. Just how permanent and enduring the present set of socioeconomic conditions will be is an empirical question, to be left to future investigation.

Finally, we would certainly not make the brash claim that the twelve-category typology is the only one possible even for contemporary times, using current data. While there may be one best way to segment the nation's counties, we do not make the wild claim that we have found it. Further research may want to include different measures, either more or fewer, and perhaps gather data from previous decades, knowing that a place's socioeconomic past can leave an enduring imprint. We have our own plans now under way to investigate the multiplicity of settings at a level of granularity well below the county, realizing that people are variably subject to multiple and overlapping contexts of influence. We welcome the efforts of others to understand the complex reality that is the variegated geography of the nation, and the captivating plurality of local environments in which the nation's residents live out their lives.

A MORE NUANCED VIEW OF THE PATCHWORK NATION

While the community-type maps in the first twelve chapters of this book show the best match for each of the nation's 3,141 counties, no place fits entirely into one type. Some Boom Town counties may have elements of Immigration Nation. Some Campus and Careers communities may have aspects of the Monied Burbs. The maps on the following pages offer a more nuanced view of the Patchwork Nation.

FIND YOUR COUNTY

Listed on the following pages are the 3,141 counties that make up the United States, alphabetically, by state. Next to each one we have used numbers to identify the two community types that are the best fit for each using the following key:

KEY TO CATEGORIES

1 = Monied Burbs
2 = Minority Central
3 = Evangelical Epicenters
4 = Tractor Country
5 = Campus and Careers
6 = Immigration Nation
7 = Industrial Metropolis
8 = Boom Towns
9 = Service Worker Centers
10 = Emptying Nests
11 = Military Bastions
12 = Mormon Outposts

For each county, the number that follows first is the best fit—the fit it falls into on the main map for Patchwork Nation. The second number is the designation that fits it next best. We are sharing this second-best fit to give a feel for the more subtle differences that define these complex places.

You can use this list to find your county and see how it falls into the Patchwork Nation system.

For a more interactive and exploratory experience, you can visit www .patchworknation.org. There not only can you see where your county fits; you can also map and sort through scores of other sets of numbers—including many we could not fit into this book and new data we have gathered and sorted since publication.

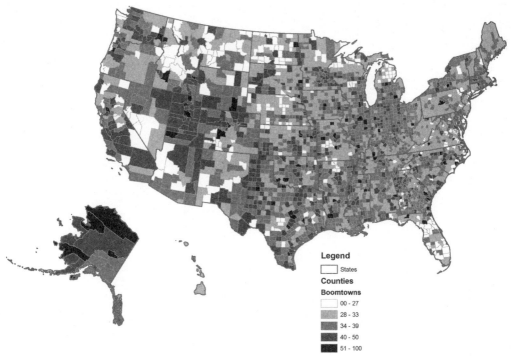

Figure 17. Boom Town Scores for U.S. Counties

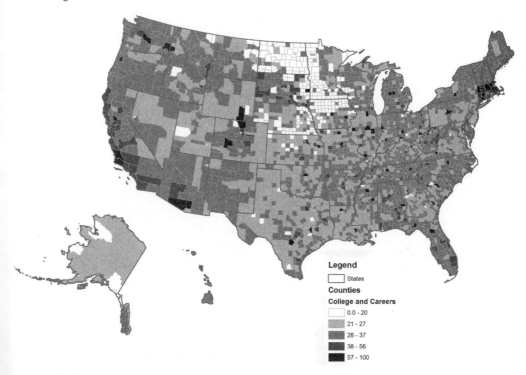

Figure 18. Campus and Careers Scores for U.S. Counties

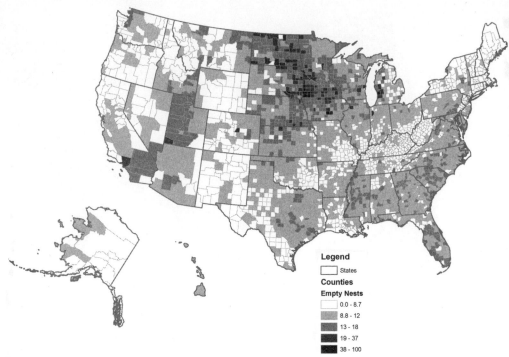

Figure 19. Emptying Nests Scores for U.S. Counties

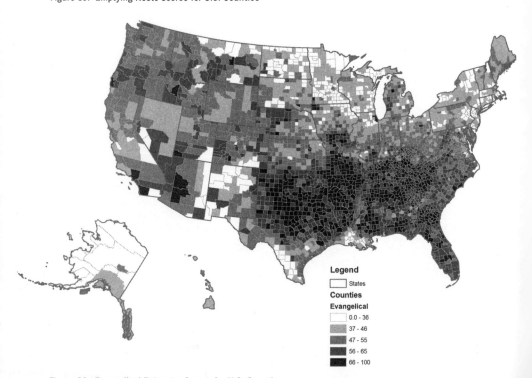

Figure 20. Evangelical Epicenter Scores for U.S. Counties

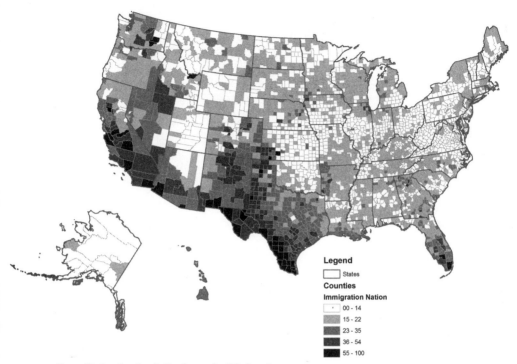

Figure 21. Immigration Nation Scores for U.S. Counties

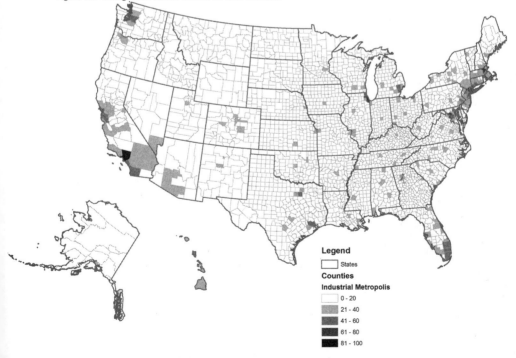

Figure 22. Industrial Metropolis Scores for U.S. Counties

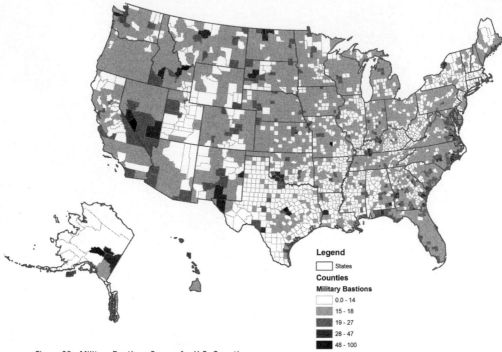

Figure 23. Military Bastions Scores for U.S. Counties

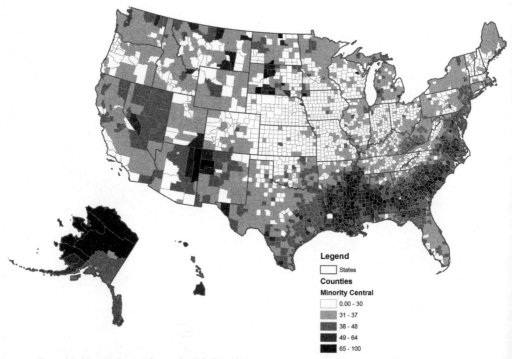

Figure 24. Minority Central Scores for U.S. Counties

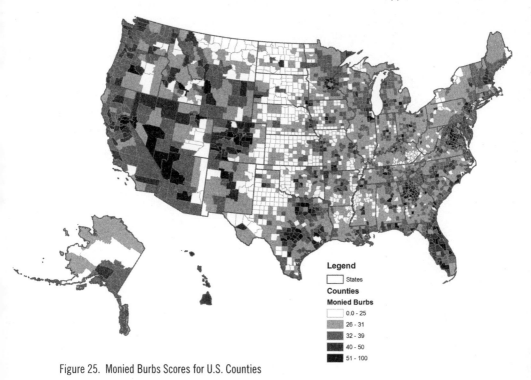

Figure 25. Monied Burbs Scores for U.S. Counties

Legend

☐ States

Counties

Monied Burbs

☐ 0.0 - 25
■ 26 - 31
■ 32 - 39
■ 40 - 50
■ 51 - 100

Legend

☐ States

Counties

Mormon Outposts

☐ 0.0 - 20
■ 21 - 40
■ 41 - 60
■ 61 - 80
■ 81 - 100

Figure 26. Mormon Outposts Scores for U.S. Counties

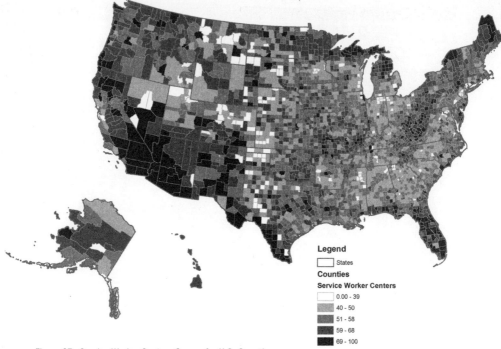

Figure 27. Service Worker Centers Scores for U.S. Counties

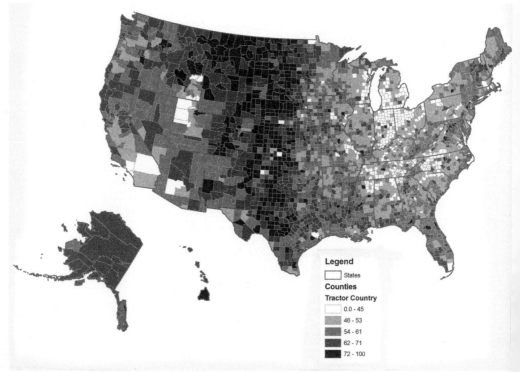

Figure 28. Tractor Country Scores for U.S. Counties

fips	county	totpop00	totpop06	chpop	Cat.10_1	Cat.10_2
1001	AL_ Autauga County	43,671	49,471	13.2	1	3
1003	AL_ Baldwin County	140,415	167,677	19.4	8	1
1005	AL_ Barbour County	29,038	28,056	-3.3	2	3
1007	AL_ Bibb County	20,826	21,653	3.9	2	3
1009	AL_ Blount County	51,024	56,118	9.9	3	2
1011	AL_ Bullock County	11,714	10,884	-7.0	2	6
1013	AL_ Butler County	21,399	20,749	-3.0	2	3
1015	AL_ Calhoun County	112,249	112,100	-0.1	3	2
1017	AL_ Chambers County	36,583	35,189	-3.8	2	3
1019	AL_ Cherokee County	23,988	24,530	2.2	3	10
1021	AL_ Chilton County	39,593	42,014	6.1	3	2
1023	AL_ Choctaw County	15,922	14,454	-9.2	2	3
1025	AL_ Clarke County	27,867	27,024	-3.0		3
1027	AL_ Clay County	14,254	13,789	-3.2	3	2
1029	AL_ Cleburne County	14,123	14,381	1.8	3	2
1031	AL_ Coffee County	43,615	45,892	5.2	3	10
1033	AL_ Colbert County	54,984	54,478	-0.9	3	2
1035	AL_ Conecuh County	14,089	13,107	-6.9	2	3
1037	AL_ Coosa County	12,202	10,971	-10.0	2	3
1039	AL_ Covington County	37,631	37,021	-1.6	3	2
1041	AL_ Crenshaw County	13,665	13,647	-0.1	3	2
1043	AL_ Cullman County	77,483	80,262	3.5	3	2
1045	AL_ Dale County	49,129	48,131	-2.0	8	3
1047	AL_ Dallas County	46,365	44,110	-4.8	2	3
1049	AL_ DeKalb County	64,452	67,540	4.7	3	2
1051	AL_ Elmore County	65,874	75,419	14.4	11	3
1053	AL_ Escambia County	38,440	37,728	-1.8	2	3
1055	AL_ Etowah County	103,459	102,905	-0.5	3	2
1057	AL_ Fayette County	18,495	18,207	-1.5	3	2
1059	AL_ Franklin County	31,223	30,750	-1.5	3	2
1061	AL_ Geneva County	25,764	25,686	-0.3	3	2
1063	AL_ Greene County	9,974	9,570	-4.0	2	3
1065	AL_ Hale County	17,185	18,342	6.7	2	3
1067	AL_ Henry County	16,310	16,625	1.9	2	3
1069	AL_ Houston County	88,787	95,193	7.2	3	2
1071	AL_ Jackson County	53,926	53,296	-1.1	3	2
1073	AL_ Jefferson County	662,047	654,344	-1.1	2	7
1075	AL_ Lamar County	15,904	14,750	-7.2	3	2
1077	AL_ Lauderdale County	87,966	87,496	-0.5	3	2
1079	AL_ Lawrence County	34,803	34,524	-0.8	3	2
1081	AL_ Lee County	115,092	125,220	8.8	5	8
1083	AL_ Limestone County	65,676	71,418	8.7	3	2
1085	AL_ Lowndes County	13,473	12,824	-4.8	2	7
1087	AL_ Macon County	24,105	22,431	-6.9	2	5
1089	AL_ Madison County	276,700	300,933	8.7	11	1
1091	AL_ Marengo County	22,539	21,634	-4.0	2	3
1093	AL_ Marion County	31,214	30,023	-3.8	3	2
1095	AL_ Marshall County	82,231	85,966	4.5	3	2
1097	AL_ Mobile County	399,843	400,929	0.2	2	3
1099	AL_ Monroe County	24,324	23,525	-3.2	2	3
1101	AL_ Montgomery County	223,510	220,334	-1.4	8	7

fips	county	totpop00	totpop06	chpop	Cat.10_1	Cat.10_2
1103	AL_ Morgan County	111,064	114,003	2.6	3	2
1105	AL_ Perry County	11,861	11,179	-5.7	2	7
1107	AL_ Pickens County	20,949	19,951	-4.7	2	3
1109	AL_ Pike County	29,605	29,794	0.6	2	3
1111	AL_ Randolph County	22,380	22,740	1.6	3	10
1113	AL_ Russell County	49,756	49,540	-0.4	2	3
1115	AL_ St. Clair County	64,742	74,163	14.5	8	3
1117	AL_ Shelby County	143,293	176,701	23.3	8	1
1119	AL_ Sumter County	14,798	13,610	-8.0	2	3
1121	AL_ Talladega County	80,321	80,334	0.0	2	3
1123	AL_ Tallapoosa County	41,475	40,670	-1.9	3	2
1125	AL_ Tuscaloosa County	164,875	169,770	2.9	5	8
1127	AL_ Walker County	70,713	70,076	-0.9	3	2
1129	AL_ Washington County	18,097	17,667	-2.3	2	3
1131	AL_ Wilcox County	13,183	12,853	-2.5	2	3
1133	AL_ Winston County	24,843	24,383	-1.8	3	10
2013	AK_ Aleutians East Borough	2,697	2,688	-0.3	2	11
2016	AK_ Aleutians West Census Area	5,465	5,423	-0.7	8	2
2020	AK_ Anchorage Borough	260,283	277,568	6.6	11	7
2050	AK_ Bethel Census Area	16,006	17,192	7.4	8	9
2060	AK_ Bristol Bay Borough	1,258	1,118	-11.1	8	3
2068	AK_ Denali	1,893	1,832	-3.2	11	3
2070	AK_ Dillingham Census Area	4,922	4,946	0.4	8	9
2090	AK_ Fairbanks North Star Borough	82,840	88,558	6.9	8	9
2100	AK_ Haines Borough	2,392	2,254	-5.7	4	1
2110	AK_ Juneau Borough	30,711	30,866	0.5	1	8
2122	AK_ Kenai Peninsula Borough	49,691	52,085	4.8	9	4
2130	AK_ Ketchikan Gateway Borough	14,070	13,311	-5.3	8	3
2150	AK_ Kodiak Island Borough	13,913	12,907	-7.2	8	1
2164	AK_ Lake and Peninsula Borough	1,823	1,579	-13.3	8	1
2170	AK_ Matanuska-Susitna Borough	59,322	80,174	35.1	8	9
2180	AK_ Nome Census Area	9,196	9,374	1.9	8	9
2185	AK_ North Slope Borough	7,385	6,740	-8.7	9	1
2188	AK_ Northwest Arctic Borough	7,208	7,676	6.4	8	9
2201	AK_ Prince of Wales-Outer Ketchikan Census Area	6,146	5,620	-8.5	2	9
2220	AK_ Sitka Borough	8,835	9,007	1.9	8	1
2232	AK_ Skagway-Hoonan-Angoon Census Area	3,436	3,128	-8.9	2	3
2240	AK_ Southeast Fairbanks Census Area	6,174	7,089	14.8	11	8
2261	AK_ Valdez-Cordova Census Area	10,195	9,912	-2.7	4	8
2270	AK_ Wade Hampton Census Area	7,028	7,577	7.8	8	6
2280	AK_ Wrangell-Petersburg Census Area	6,684	6,228	-6.8	4	9
2282	AK_ Yakutat	808	737	-8.7	4	3
2290	AK_ Yukon-Koyukuk Census Area	6,551	5,988	-8.5	8	9
4001	AZ_ Apache County	69,423	69,653	0.3	2	9
4003	AZ_ Cochise County	117,755	127,233	8.0	6	11
4005	AZ_ Coconino County	116,320	123,502	6.1	8	5
4007	AZ_ Gila County	51,335	51,241	-0.1	9	6
4009	AZ_ Graham County	33,489	32,839	-1.9	6	9
4011	AZ_ Greenlee County	8,547	7,480	-12.4	4	6
4012	AZ_ La Paz County	19,715	20,457	3.7	6	10
4013	AZ_ Maricopa County	3,072,149	3,721,082	21.1	6	7

fips	county	totpop00	totpop06	chpop	Cat.10_1	Cat.10_2
4015	AZ_ Mohave County	155,032	192,310	24.0	8	6
4017	AZ_ Navajo County	97,470	109,157	11.9	2	6
4019	AZ_ Pima County	843,746	930,391	10.2	5	1
4021	AZ_ Pinal County	179,727	245,236	36.4	8	6
4023	AZ_ Santa Cruz County	38,381	42,543	10.8	6	8
4025	AZ_ Yavapai County	167,517	204,078	21.8	8	10
4027	AZ_ Yuma County	160,026	185,094	15.6	6	8
5001	AR_ Arkansas County	20,749	19,997	-3.6	3	2
5003	AR_ Ashley County	24,209	22,739	-6.0	3	2
5005	AR_ Baxter County	38,386	40,795	6.2	3	10
5007	AR_ Benton County	153,406	193,277	25.9	8	10
5009	AR_ Boone County	33,948	36,072	6.2	3	10
5011	AR_ Bradley County	12,600	12,036	-4.4	2	4
5013	AR_ Calhoun County	5,744	5,537	-3.6	3	2
5015	AR_ Carroll County	25,357	27,138	7.0	3	6
5017	AR_ Chicot County	14,117	12,858	-8.9	2	4
5019	AR_ Clark County	23,546	22,725	-3.4	8	5
5021	AR_ Clay County	17,609	16,399	-6.8	3	2
5023	AR_ Cleburne County	24,046	25,504	6.0	3	10
5025	AR_ Cleveland County	8,571	8,987	4.8	3	2
5027	AR_ Columbia County	25,603	24,377	-4.7	2	3
5029	AR_ Conway County	20,336	20,673	1.6	3	10
5031	AR_ Craighead County	82,148	87,345	6.3	8	5
5033	AR_ Crawford County	53,247	58,173	9.2	3	2
5035	AR_ Crittenden County	50,866	52,081	2.3	8	2
5037	AR_ Cross County	19,526	19,224	-1.5	3	2
5039	AR_ Dallas County	9,210	8,377	-9.0	2	6
5041	AR_ Desha County	15,341	14,108	-8.0	2	6
5043	AR_ Drew County	18,723	18,649	-0.4	2	3
5045	AR_ Faulkner County	86,014	99,471	15.6	8	3
5047	AR_ Franklin County	17,771	18,240	2.6	3	10
5049	AR_ Fulton County	11,642	11,913	2.3	3	10
5051	AR_ Garland County	88,068	94,227	6.9	3	10
5053	AR_ Grant County	16,464	17,467	6.0	3	2
5055	AR_ Greene County	37,331	39,724	6.4	3	10
5057	AR_ Hempstead County	23,587	23,222	-1.5	3	2
5059	AR_ Hot Spring County	30,353	31,538	3.9	3	10
5061	AR_ Howard County	14,300	14,597	2.0	3	2
5063	AR_ Independence County	34,233	34,607	1.0	3	10
5065	AR_ Izard County	13,249	13,359	0.8	3	10
5067	AR_ Jackson County	18,418	17,612	-4.3	3	4
5069	AR_ Jefferson County	84,278	80,559	-4.4	2	3
5071	AR_ Johnson County	22,781	24,217	6.3	3	10
5073	AR_ Lafayette County	8,559	7,848	-8.3	2	3
5075	AR_ Lawrence County	17,774	16,866	-5.1	3	2
5077	AR_ Lee County	12,580	11,386	-9.4	2	7
5079	AR_ Lincoln County	14,492	14,081	-2.8	2	3
5081	AR_ Little River County	13,628	13,012	-4.5	3	2
5083	AR_ Logan County	22,486	22,827	1.5	3	6
5085	AR_ Lonoke County	52,828	62,410	18.1	1	3
5087	AR_ Madison County	14,243	15,231	6.9	3	10

fips	county	totpop00	totpop06	chpop	Cat.10_1	Cat.10_2
5089	AR_ Marion County	16,140	16,870	4.5	3	10
5091	AR_ Miller County	40,443	43,283	7.0	3	9
5093	AR_ Mississippi County	51,979	47,326	-8.9	8	2
5095	AR_ Monroe County	10,254	9,126	-11.0	2	4
5097	AR_ Montgomery County	9,245	9,251	0.0	3	10
5099	AR_ Nevada County	9,955	9,468	-4.8	2	3
5101	AR_ Newton County	8,608	8,307	-3.5	3	10
5103	AR_ Ouachita County	28,790	26,823	-6.8	2	3
5105	AR_ Perry County	10,209	10,413	2.0	3	10
5107	AR_ Phillips County	26,445	23,796	-10.0	2	4
5109	AR_ Pike County	11,303	10,907	-3.5	3	2
5111	AR_ Poinsett County	25,614	25,308	-1.1	3	2
5113	AR_ Polk County	20,229	20,119	-0.5	3	2
5115	AR_ Pope County	54,469	57,076	4.7	8	10
5117	AR_ Prairie County	9,539	8,927	-6.4	3	2
5119	AR_ Pulaski County	361,474	365,336	1.0	8	1
5121	AR_ Randolph County	18,195	18,438	1.3	3	10
5123	AR_ St. Francis County	29,329	27,508	-6.2	2	3
5125	AR_ Saline County	83,529	92,638	10.9	1	3
5127	AR_ Scott County	10,996	11,150	1.4	3	2
5129	AR_ Searcy County	8,261	7,978	-3.4	3	10
5131	AR_ Sebastian County	115,071	118,849	3.2	8	10
5133	AR_ Sevier County	15,757	16,602	5.3	3	2
5135	AR_ Sharp County	17,119	17,330	1.2	3	10
5137	AR_ Stone County	11,499	11,774	2.3	3	10
5139	AR_ Union County	45,629	43,597	-4.4	2	3
5141	AR_ Van Buren County	16,192	16,551	2.2	3	10
5143	AR_ Washington County	157,715	185,451	17.5	8	11
5145	AR_ White County	67,165	71,923	7.0	3	2
5147	AR_ Woodruff County	8,741	7,992	-8.5	2	4
5149	AR_ Yell County	21,139	21,298	0.7	3	6
6001	CA_ Alameda County	1,443,741	1,453,069	0.6	6	1
6003	CA_ Alpine County	1,208	1,119	-7.3	12	8
6005	CA_ Amador County	35,100	39,249	11.8	8	9
6007	CA_ Butte County	203,171	216,600	6.6	9	8
6009	CA_ Calaveras County	40,554	48,243	18.9	8	10
6011	CA_ Colusa County	18,804	21,730	15.5	6	8
6013	CA_ Contra Costa County	948,816	1,032,571	8.8	1	7
6015	CA_ Del Norte County	27,507	29,393	6.8	9	8
6017	CA_ El Dorado County	156,299	181,323	16.0	8	1
6019	CA_ Fresno County	799,407	896,018	12.0	8	6
6021	CA_ Glenn County	26,453	28,105	6.2	6	8
6023	CA_ Humboldt County	126,518	129,277	2.1	9	5
6025	CA_ Imperial County	142,361	160,663	12.8	6	8
6027	CA_ Inyo County	17,945	17,997	0.2	9	6
6029	CA_ Kern County	661,645	785,186	18.6	6	7
6031	CA_ Kings County	129,461	146,387	13.0	8	6
6033	CA_ Lake County	58,309	66,347	13.7	8	9
6035	CA_ Lassen County	33,828	35,248	4.2	9	8
6037	CA_ Los Angeles County	9,519,338	10,015,968	5.2	7	6
6039	CA_ Madera County	123,109	148,207	20.3	8	6

fips	county	totpop00	totpop06	chpop	Cat.10_1	Cat.10_2
6041	CA_ Marin County	247,289	249,030	0.7	1	7
6043	CA_ Mariposa County	17,130	18,360	7.1	1	9
6045	CA_ Mendocino County	86,265	88,608	2.7	5	6
6047	CA_ Merced County	210,554	248,555	18.0	6	8
6049	CA_ Modoc County	9,449	9,600	1.6	4	9
6051	CA_ Mono County	12,853	12,552	-2.3	6	8
6053	CA_ Monterey County	401,762	412,432	2.6	1	6
6055	CA_ Napa County	124,279	133,577	7.4	1	8
6057	CA_ Nevada County	92,033	99,957	8.6	1	9
6059	CA_ Orange County	2,846,289	3,016,262	5.9	1	7
6061	CA_ Placer County	248,399	330,459	33.0	8	1
6063	CA_ Plumas County	20,824	21,683	4.1	9	5
6065	CA_ Riverside County	1,545,387	2,044,771	32.3	8	6
6067	CA_ Sacramento County	1,223,499	1,383,416	13.0	1	7
6069	CA_ San Benito County	53,234	56,155	5.4	1	6
6071	CA_ San Bernardino County	1,709,434	2,028,926	18.6	6	7
6073	CA_ San Diego County	2,813,833	2,951,784	4.9	1	7
6075	CA_ San Francisco County	776,733	739,457	-4.8	1	7
6077	CA_ San Joaquin County	563,598	684,236	21.4	8	6
6079	CA_ San Luis Obispo County	246,681	258,149	4.6	1	8
6081	CA_ San Mateo County	707,161	705,238	-0.2	1	7
6083	CA_ Santa Barbara County	399,347	401,942	0.6	1	6
6085	CA_ Santa Clara County	1,682,585	1,727,431	2.6	7	1
6087	CA_ Santa Cruz County	255,602	249,778	-2.2	1	5
6089	CA_ Shasta County	163,256	182,024	11.5	9	10
6091	CA_ Sierra County	3,555	3,384	-4.8	4	10
6093	CA_ Siskiyou County	44,301	45,782	3.3	4	9
6095	CA_ Solano County	394,542	412,494	4.5	8	1
6097	CA_ Sonoma County	458,614	468,897	2.2	5	1
6099	CA_ Stanislaus County	446,997	514,801	15.1	6	8
6101	CA_ Sutter County	78,930	91,615	16.0	6	8
6103	CA_ Tehama County	56,039	62,657	11.8	6	8
6105	CA_ Trinity County	13,022	14,013	7.6	9	10
6107	CA_ Tulare County	368,021	424,051	15.2	6	8
6109	CA_ Tuolumne County	54,501	58,767	7.8	1	9
6111	CA_ Ventura County	753,197	801,832	6.4	1	7
6113	CA_ Yolo County	168,660	186,789	10.7	8	5
6115	CA_ Yuba County	60,219	69,651	15.6	8	6
8001	CO_ Adams County	348,504	397,377	14.0	6	8
8003	CO_ Alamosa County	14,966	15,519	3.7	6	5
8005	CO_ Arapahoe County	487,967	542,815	11.2	8	7
8007	CO_ Archuleta County	9,898	12,268	23.9	1	8
8009	CO_ Baca County	4,517	4,085	-9.5	4	9
8011	CO_ Bent County	5,998	5,576	-7.0	6	9
8013	CO_ Boulder County	270,199	264,352	-2.1	5	1
8014	CO_ Broomfield County	37,907	39,414	3.9	1	8
8015	CO_ Chaffee County	16,242	17,087	5.2	9	10
8017	CO_ Cheyenne County	2,231	1,920	-13.9	4	9
8019	CO_ Clear Creek County	9,322	9,196	-1.3	8	1
8021	CO_ Conejos County	8,400	8,741	4.0	6	9
8023	CO_ Costilla County	3,663	3,388	-7.5	6	9

fips	county	totpop00	totpop06	chpop	Cat.10_1	Cat.10_2
8025	CO_ Crowley County	5,518	5,406	-2.0	9	6
8027	CO_ Custer County	3,503	3,965	13.1	1	8
8029	CO_ Delta County	27,834	30,561	9.8	4	10
8031	CO_ Denver County	554,636	567,428	2.3	7	6
8033	CO_ Dolores County	1,844	1,831	-0.7	9	3
8035	CO_ Douglas County	175,766	264,748	50.6	1	8
8037	CO_ Eagle County	41,659	49,450	18.7	8	9
8039	CO_ Elbert County	19,872	23,230	16.9	8	3
8041	CO_ El Paso County	516,929	579,881	12.1	11	1
8043	CO_ Fremont County	46,145	48,440	4.9	9	8
8045	CO_ Garfield County	43,791	51,400	17.3	8	12
8047	CO_ Gilpin County	4,757	5,050	6.1	1	3
8049	CO_ Grand County	12,442	13,338	7.2	1	8
8051	CO_ Gunnison County	13,956	14,505	3.9	8	5
8053	CO_ Hinsdale County	790	781	-1.1	9	10
8055	CO_ Huerfano County	7,862	7,833	-0.3	6	10
8057	CO_ Jackson County	1,577	1,428	-9.4	4	6
8059	CO_ Jefferson County	525,591	530,004	0.8	1	7
8061	CO_ Kiowa County	1,622	1,437	-11.4	4	9
8063	CO_ Kit Carson County	8,011	7,612	-4.9	4	9
8065	CO_ Lake County	7,812	7,815	0.0	8	6
8067	CO_ La Plata County	43,941	48,529	10.4	1	8
8069	CO_ Larimer County	251,494	277,703	10.4	1	8
8071	CO_ Las Animas County	15,207	15,558	2.3	6	9
8073	CO_ Lincoln County	6,087	5,560	-8.6	4	3
8075	CO_ Logan County	20,504	20,877	1.8	9	4
8077	CO_ Mesa County	116,255	133,871	15.1	1	12
8079	CO_ Mineral County	831	945	13.7	1	10
8081	CO_ Moffat County	13,184	13,492	2.3	4	9
8083	CO_ Montezuma County	23,830	25,207	5.7	4	10
8085	CO_ Montrose County	33,432	38,789	16.0	1	8
8087	CO_ Morgan County	27,171	28,314	4.2	6	10
8089	CO_ Otero County	20,311	19,703	-2.9	6	9
8091	CO_ Ouray County	3,742	4,440	18.6	1	10
8093	CO_ Park County	14,523	17,286	19.0	8	3
8095	CO_ Phillips County	4,480	4,654	3.8	4	6
8097	CO_ Pitkin County	14,872	15,077	1.3	8	1
8099	CO_ Prowers County	14,483	13,977	-3.4	6	9
8101	CO_ Pueblo County	141,472	154,018	8.8	6	7
8103	CO_ Rio Blanco County	5,986	6,012	0.4	4	10
8105	CO_ Rio Grande County	12,413	12,420	0.0	6	4
8107	CO_ Routt County	19,690	21,854	10.9	1	8
8109	CO_ Saguache County	5,917	7,238	22.3	6	10
8111	CO_ San Juan County	558	578	3.5	4	10
8113	CO_ San Miguel County	6,594	7,292	10.5	8	1
8115	CO_ Sedgwick County	2,747	2,491	-9.3	4	6
8117	CO_ Summit County	23,548	25,222	7.1	1	8
8119	CO_ Teller County	20,555	22,279	8.3	1	8
8121	CO_ Washington County	4,926	4,610	-6.4	4	9
8123	CO_ Weld County	180,936	240,054	32.6	6	10
8125	CO_ Yuma County	9,841	9,903	0.6	6	9

fips	county	totpop00	totpop06	chpop	Cat.10_1	Cat.10_2
9001	CT_ Fairfield County	882,567	908,065	2.8	1	7
9003	CT_ Hartford County	857,183	884,909	3.2	7	1
9005	CT_ Litchfield County	182,193	191,601	5.1	1	5
9007	CT_ Middlesex County	155,071	164,569	6.1	5	1
9009	CT_ New Haven County	824,008	853,901	3.6	7	1
9011	CT_ New London County	259,088	266,902	3.0	5	1
9013	CT_ Tolland County	136,364	149,223	9.4	1	5
9015	CT_ Windham County	109,091	118,152	8.3	9	1
10001	DE_ Kent County	126,697	148,330	17.0	9	11
10003	DE_ New Castle County	500,265	525,194	4.9	1	7
10005	DE_ Sussex County	156,638	180,026	14.9	8	10
11001	DC_ District of Columbia	572,059	546,139	-4.5	7	1
12001	FL_ Alachua County	217,955	223,874	2.7	5	8
12003	FL_ Baker County	22,259	24,954	12.1	3	2
12005	FL_ Bay County	148,217	163,946	10.6	9	8
12007	FL_ Bradford County	26,088	28,558	9.4	9	3
12009	FL_ Brevard County	476,230	539,723	13.3	11	1
12011	FL_ Broward County	1,623,018	1,792,445	10.4	1	7
12013	FL_ Calhoun County	13,017	13,481	3.5	9	10
12015	FL_ Charlotte County	141,627	155,029	9.4	1	8
12017	FL_ Citrus County	118,085	137,555	16.4	8	10
12019	FL_ Clay County	140,814	176,949	25.6	8	11
12021	FL_ Collier County	251,377	315,769	25.6	10	1
12023	FL_ Columbia County	56,513	66,158	17.0	8	10
12027	FL_ DeSoto County	32,209	35,640	10.6	3	6
12029	FL_ Dixie County	13,827	14,979	8.3	3	10
12031	FL_ Duval County	778,879	830,490	6.6	7	1
12033	FL_ Escambia County	294,410	294,484	0.0	11	3
12035	FL_ Flagler County	49,832	83,102	66.7	10	8
12037	FL_ Franklin County	11,057	10,143	-8.2	3	9
12039	FL_ Gadsden County	45,087	46,730	3.6	2	3
12041	FL_ Gilchrist County	14,437	16,827	16.5	8	2
12043	FL_ Glades County	10,576	11,319	7.0	6	10
12045	FL_ Gulf County	13,332	14,605	9.5	9	3
12047	FL_ Hamilton County	13,327	13,870	4.0	2	3
12049	FL_ Hardee County	26,938	28,180	4.6	6	8
12051	FL_ Hendry County	36,210	40,735	12.5	6	2
12053	FL_ Hernando County	130,802	165,811	26.7	10	8
12055	FL_ Highlands County	87,366	97,463	11.5	10	6
12057	FL_ Hillsborough County	998,948	1,157,260	15.8	8	7
12059	FL_ Holmes County	18,564	19,200	3.4	3	2
12061	FL_ Indian River County	112,947	130,955	15.9	8	10
12063	FL_ Jackson County	46,755	49,927	6.7	9	3
12065	FL_ Jefferson County	12,902	14,578	12.9	1	3
12067	FL_ Lafayette County	7,022	8,230	17.2	3	8
12069	FL_ Lake County	210,528	291,197	38.3	10	8
12071	FL_ Lee County	440,888	570,480	29.3	10	1
12073	FL_ Leon County	239,452	245,496	2.5	8	11
12075	FL_ Levy County	34,450	38,663	12.2	3	10
12077	FL_ Liberty County	7,021	7,959	13.3	2	3
12079	FL_ Madison County	18,733	19,114	2.0	2	3

fips	county	totpop00	totpop06	chpop	Cat.10_1	Cat.10_2
12081	FL_ Manatee County	264,002	314,558	19.1	8	10
12083	FL_ Marion County	258,916	314,316	21.4	8	10
12085	FL_ Martin County	126,731	140,762	11.0	1	8
12086	FL_ Miami-Dade County	2,253,362	2,385,345	5.8	6	7
12087	FL_ Monroe County	79,589	74,329	-6.6	9	1
12089	FL_ Nassau County	57,663	66,033	14.5	8	1
12091	FL_ Okaloosa County	170,498	181,601	6.5	8	11
12093	FL_ Okeechobee County	35,910	40,466	12.6	3	10
12095	FL_ Orange County	896,344	1,049,713	17.1	10	7
12097	FL_ Osceola County	172,493	243,186	40.9	10	11
12099	FL_ Palm Beach County	1,131,184	1,286,060	13.6	1	7
12101	FL_ Pasco County	344,765	449,028	30.2	8	10
12103	FL_ Pinellas County	921,482	923,272	0.1	1	7
12105	FL_ Polk County	483,924	557,266	15.1	1	10
12107	FL_ Putnam County	70,423	73,924	4.9	9	10
12109	FL_ St. Johns County	123,135	170,338	38.3	8	1
12111	FL_ St. Lucie County	192,695	253,888	31.7	10	8
12113	FL_ Santa Rosa County	117,743	146,979	24.8	8	11
12115	FL_ Sarasota County	325,957	373,575	14.6	10	1
12117	FL_ Seminole County	365,196	408,022	11.7	8	1
12119	FL_ Sumter County	53,345	66,314	24.3	8	10
12121	FL_ Suwannee County	34,844	39,391	13.0	3	10
12123	FL_ Taylor County	19,256	19,782	2.7	9	2
12125	FL_ Union County	13,442	15,413	14.6	2	8
12127	FL_ Volusia County	443,343	497,450	12.2	8	10
12129	FL_ Wakulla County	22,863	29,228	27.8	8	10
12131	FL_ Walton County	40,601	52,229	28.6	8	3
12133	FL_ Washington County	20,973	22,588	7.7	3	10
13001	GA_ Appling County	17,419	17,979	3.2	3	2
13003	GA_ Atkinson County	7,609	8,059	5.9	3	6
13005	GA_ Bacon County	10,103	10,608	5.0	3	2
13007	GA_ Baker County	4,074	4,115	1.0	2	3
13009	GA_ Baldwin County	44,700	45,515	1.8	8	5
13011	GA_ Banks County	14,422	16,435	13.9	8	4
13013	GA_ Barrow County	46,144	63,285	37.1	10	8
13015	GA_ Bartow County	76,019	90,932	19.6	8	3
13017	GA_ Ben Hill County	17,484	17,472	0.0	2	3
13019	GA_ Berrien County	16,235	16,814	3.5	3	2
13021	GA_ Bibb County	153,887	154,301	0.2	8	3
13023	GA_ Bleckley County	11,666	12,328	5.6	2	3
13025	GA_ Brantley County	14,629	15,543	6.2	3	10
13027	GA_ Brooks County	16,450	16,318	-0.8	2	3
13029	GA_ Bryan County	23,417	29,793	27.2	8	3
13031	GA_ Bulloch County	55,983	63,471	13.3	8	2
13033	GA_ Burke County	22,243	23,324	4.8	2	3
13035	GA_ Butts County	19,522	21,071	7.9	2	3
13037	GA_ Calhoun County	6,320	5,892	-6.7	2	3
13039	GA_ Camden County	43,664	46,320	6.0	10	8
13043	GA_ Candler County	9,577	10,437	8.9	2	3
13045	GA_ Carroll County	87,268	108,238	24.0	8	3
13047	GA_ Catoosa County	53,282	61,956	16.2	1	10

fips	county	totpop00	totpop06	chpop	Cat.10_1	Cat.10_2
13049	GA_ Charlton County	10,282	10,748	4.5	2	3
13051	GA_ Chatham County	232,048	238,227	2.6	8	11
13053	GA_ Chattahoochee County	14,882	13,575	-8.7	11	3
13055	GA_ Chattooga County	25,470	26,576	4.3	3	2
13057	GA_ Cherokee County	141,903	192,720	35.8	8	11
13059	GA_ Clarke County	101,489	111,702	10.0	5	11
13061	GA_ Clay County	3,357	3,179	-5.3	2	3
13063	GA_ Clayton County	236,517	270,011	14.1	10	3
13065	GA_ Clinch County	6,878	7,036	2.3	2	3
13067	GA_ Cobb County	607,751	670,723	10.3	1	7
13069	GA_ Coffee County	37,413	39,930	6.7	2	3
13071	GA_ Colquitt County	42,053	44,161	5.0	3	2
13073	GA_ Columbia County	89,288	106,661	19.4	8	3
13075	GA_ Cook County	15,771	16,500	4.6	2	3
13077	GA_ Coweta County	89,215	114,089	27.8	8	3
13079	GA_ Crawford County	12,495	12,973	3.8	2	3
13081	GA_ Crisp County	21,996	21,932	-0.2	2	3
13083	GA_ Dade County	15,154	16,180	6.7	9	3
13085	GA_ Dawson County	15,999	20,426	27.6	1	3
13087	GA_ Decatur County	28,240	28,607	1.3	2	3
13089	GA_ DeKalb County	665,865	684,438	2.7	1	7
13091	GA_ Dodge County	19,171	19,575	2.1	2	3
13093	GA_ Dooly County	11,525	11,852	2.8	2	3
13095	GA_ Dougherty County	96,065	94,397	-1.7	8	5
13097	GA_ Douglas County	92,174	117,502	27.4	8	3
13099	GA_ Early County	12,354	12,016	-2.7	2	3
13101	GA_ Echols County	3,754	4,347	15.8	2	6
13103	GA_ Effingham County	37,535	49,110	30.8	8	3
13105	GA_ Elbert County	20,511	20,728	1.0	2	3
13107	GA_ Emanuel County	21,837	22,335	2.2	2	6
13109	GA_ Evans County	10,495	11,391	8.5	2	3
13111	GA_ Fannin County	19,798	22,070	11.4	3	10
13113	GA_ Fayette County	91,263	106,932	17.1	8	1
13115	GA_ Floyd County	90,565	94,396	4.2	3	2
13117	GA_ Forsyth County	98,407	148,101	50.5	8	1
13119	GA_ Franklin County	20,285	21,763	7.2	3	2
13121	GA_ Fulton County	816,006	946,645	16.0	7	1
13123	GA_ Gilmer County	23,456	28,026	19.4	8	10
13125	GA_ Glascock County	2,556	2,737	7.0	2	3
13127	GA_ Glynn County	67,568	72,609	7.4	2	3
13129	GA_ Gordon County	44,104	51,478	16.7	3	8
13131	GA_ Grady County	23,659	24,677	4.3	2	3
13133	GA_ Greene County	14,406	15,758	9.3	9	1
13135	GA_ Gwinnett County	588,448	752,586	27.8	8	1
13137	GA_ Habersham County	35,902	40,211	12.0	3	8
13139	GA_ Hall County	139,277	171,051	22.8	8	3
13141	GA_ Hancock County	10,076	9,497	-5.7	2	3
13143	GA_ Haralson County	25,690	28,763	11.9	3	4
13145	GA_ Harris County	23,695	28,626	20.8	1	3
13147	GA_ Hart County	22,997	24,371	5.9	3	2
13149	GA_ Heard County	11,012	11,398	3.5	9	3

fips	county	totpop00	totpop06	chpop	Cat.10_1	Cat.10_2
13151	GA_ Henry County	119,341	174,847	46.5	10	8
13153	GA_ Houston County	110,765	128,208	15.7	11	3
13155	GA_ Irwin County	9,931	10,305	3.7	2	3
13157	GA_ Jackson County	41,589	54,964	32.1	8	3
13159	GA_ Jasper County	11,426	13,434	17.5	1	10
13161	GA_ Jeff Davis County	12,684	13,218	4.2	3	2
13163	GA_ Jefferson County	17,266	16,758	-2.9	2	3
13165	GA_ Jenkins County	8,575	8,765	2.2	2	3
13167	GA_ Johnson County	8,560	9,351	9.2	2	3
13169	GA_ Jones County	23,639	27,346	15.6	1	3
13171	GA_ Lamar County	15,912	16,722	5.0	2	3
13173	GA_ Lanier County	7,241	7,642	5.5	2	6
13175	GA_ Laurens County	44,874	47,038	4.8	2	3
13177	GA_ Lee County	24,757	32,182	29.9	8	3
13179	GA_ Liberty County	61,610	58,350	-5.2	8	11
13181	GA_ Lincoln County	8,348	8,118	-2.7	2	3
13183	GA_ Long County	10,304	11,187	8.5	8	11
13185	GA_ Lowndes County	92,115	97,641	6.0	8	11
13187	GA_ Lumpkin County	21,016	24,989	18.9	8	3
13189	GA_ McDuffie County	21,231	21,896	3.1	2	3
13191	GA_ McIntosh County	10,847	11,046	1.8	2	3
13193	GA_ Macon County	14,074	13,577	-3.5	2	7
13195	GA_ Madison County	25,730	27,479	6.8	9	3
13197	GA_ Marion County	7,144	7,275	1.8	2	3
13199	GA_ Meriwether County	22,534	22,847	1.3	2	3
13201	GA_ Miller County	6,383	6,164	-3.4	3	2
13205	GA_ Mitchell County	23,932	23,646	-1.2	2	3
13207	GA_ Monroe County	21,757	23,950	10.0	1	3
13209	GA_ Montgomery County	8,270	9,005	8.8	2	3
13211	GA_ Morgan County	15,457	17,918	15.9	1	3
13213	GA_ Murray County	36,506	41,413	13.4	3	2
13215	GA_ Muscogee County	186,291	186,834	0.2	11	3
13217	GA_ Newton County	62,001	90,956	46.7	10	3
13219	GA_ Oconee County	26,225	30,606	16.7	8	1
13221	GA_ Oglethorpe County	12,635	13,687	8.3	2	3
13223	GA_ Paulding County	81,678	118,436	45.0	8	3
13225	GA_ Peach County	23,668	24,671	4.2	2	3
13227	GA_ Pickens County	22,983	29,106	26.6	8	3
13229	GA_ Pierce County	15,636	17,580	12.4	3	2
13231	GA_ Pike County	13,688	16,554	20.9	1	3
13233	GA_ Polk County	38,127	40,787	6.9	3	6
13235	GA_ Pulaski County	9,588	9,717	1.3	2	3
13237	GA_ Putnam County	18,812	19,827	5.4	1	3
13239	GA_ Quitman County	2,598	2,473	-4.8	2	3
13241	GA_ Rabun County	15,050	16,278	8.1	3	10
13243	GA_ Randolph County	7,791	7,212	-7.4	2	3
13245	GA_ Richmond County	199,775	193,953	-2.9	11	5
13247	GA_ Rockdale County	70,111	79,863	13.9	8	1
13249	GA_ Schley County	3,766	4,220	12.0	2	3
13251	GA_ Screven County	15,374	15,274	-0.6	2	3
13253	GA_ Seminole County	9,369	9,223	-1.5	2	3

fips	county	totpop00	totpop06	chpop	Cat.10_1	Cat.10_2
13255	GA_ Spalding County	58,417	61,645	5.5	2	3
13257	GA_ Stephens County	25,435	24,957	-1.8	3	2
13259	GA_ Stewart County	5,252	4,788	-8.8	2	6
13261	GA_ Sumter County	33,200	32,574	-1.8	2	3
13263	GA_ Talbot County	6,498	6,724	3.4	2	3
13265	GA_ Taliaferro County	2,077	1,783	-14.1	2	6
13267	GA_ Tattnall County	22,305	23,561	5.6	2	3
13269	GA_ Taylor County	8,815	8,801	-0.1	2	3
13271	GA_ Telfair County	11,794	13,459	14.1	2	3
13273	GA_ Terrell County	10,970	10,583	-3.5	2	3
13275	GA_ Thomas County	42,737	45,297	5.9	2	9
13277	GA_ Tift County	38,407	41,279	7.4	2	3
13279	GA_ Toombs County	26,067	27,680	6.1	2	3
13281	GA_ Towns County	9,319	10,476	12.4	8	10
13283	GA_ Treutlen County	6,854	6,540	-4.5	2	3
13285	GA_ Troup County	58,779	63,257	7.6	2	3
13287	GA_ Turner County	9,504	9,377	-1.3	2	3
13289	GA_ Twiggs County	10,590	10,135	-4.3	2	3
13291	GA_ Union County	17,289	20,203	16.8	8	3
13293	GA_ Upson County	27,597	27,842	0.8	2	3
13295	GA_ Walker County	61,053	64,522	5.6	3	2
13297	GA_ Walton County	60,687	79,068	30.2	8	3
13299	GA_ Ware County	35,483	34,332	-3.2	3	2
13301	GA_ Warren County	6,336	6,027	-4.8	2	3
13303	GA_ Washington County	21,176	19,474	-8.0	2	3
13305	GA_ Wayne County	26,565	28,707	8.0	3	2
13307	GA_ Webster County	2,390	2,247	-5.9	2	3
13309	GA_ Wheeler County	6,179	6,823	10.4	2	3
13311	GA_ White County	19,944	24,522	22.9	8	3
13313	GA_ Whitfield County	83,525	92,519	10.7	3	6
13315	GA_ Wilcox County	8,577	8,683	1.2	2	3
13317	GA_ Wilkes County	10,687	10,358	-3.0	2	3
13319	GA_ Wilkinson County	10,220	10,047	-1.6	2	3
13321	GA_ Worth County	21,967	21,973	0.0	2	3
15001	HI_ Hawaii County	148,677	171,644	15.4	8	12
15003	HI_ Honolulu County	876,156	910,533	3.9	9	7
15005	HI_ Kalawao County	147	118	-19.7	2	6
15007	HI_ Kauai County	58,463	63,257	8.2	1	9
15009	HI_ Maui County	128,094	141,632	10.5	1	8
16001	ID_ Ada County	300,904	353,041	17.3	8	7
16003	ID_ Adams County	3,476	3,579	2.9	9	10
16005	ID_ Bannock County	75,565	77,669	2.7	8	5
16007	ID_ Bear Lake County	6,411	6,088	-5.0	12	4
16009	ID_ Benewah County	9,171	9,237	0.7	9	3
16011	ID_ Bingham County	41,735	43,975	5.3	12	8
16013	ID_ Blaine County	18,991	21,126	11.2	8	1
16015	ID_ Boise County	6,670	7,538	13.0	1	10
16017	ID_ Bonner County	36,835	41,287	12.0	1	3
16019	ID_ Bonneville County	82,522	93,120	12.8	8	12
16021	ID_ Boundary County	9,871	10,761	9.0	4	3
16023	ID_ Butte County	2,899	2,728	-5.9	12	4

fips	county	totpop00	totpop06	chpop	Cat.10_1	Cat.10_2
16025	ID_ Camas County	991	1,061	7.0	4	3
16027	ID_ Canyon County	131,441	169,814	29.1	8	10
16029	ID_ Caribou County	7,304	7,010	-4.0	12	9
16031	ID_ Cassia County	21,416	21,016	-1.8	12	6
16033	ID_ Clark County	1,022	919	-10.0	11	10
16035	ID_ Clearwater County	8,930	8,282	-7.2	4	10
16037	ID_ Custer County	4,342	4,047	-6.7	4	10
16039	ID_ Elmore County	29,130	27,906	-4.2	11	6
16041	ID_ Franklin County	11,329	12,479	10.1	12	8
16043	ID_ Fremont County	11,819	12,082	2.2	12	10
16045	ID_ Gem County	15,181	16,480	8.5	9	8
16047	ID_ Gooding County	14,155	14,309	1.0	4	6
16049	ID_ Idaho County	15,511	15,645	0.8	4	10
16051	ID_ Jefferson County	19,155	22,142	15.5	12	8
16053	ID_ Jerome County	18,342	19,815	8.0	6	4
16055	ID_ Kootenai County	108,685	132,220	21.6	8	3
16057	ID_ Latah County	34,935	34,546	-1.1	8	9
16059	ID_ Lemhi County	7,806	7,881	0.9	4	10
16061	ID_ Lewis County	3,747	3,705	-1.1	9	4
16063	ID_ Lincoln County	4,044	4,644	14.8	12	6
16065	ID_ Madison County	27,467	31,333	14.0	12	8
16067	ID_ Minidoka County	20,174	18,653	-7.5	6	9
16069	ID_ Nez Perce County	37,410	37,887	1.2	9	10
16071	ID_ Oneida County	4,125	4,205	1.9	12	10
16073	ID_ Owyhee County	10,644	11,049	3.8	6	10
16075	ID_ Payette County	20,578	22,393	8.8	9	10
16077	ID_ Power County	7,538	7,795	3.4	12	6
16079	ID_ Shoshone County	13,771	13,153	-4.4	9	4
16081	ID_ Teton County	5,999	7,591	26.5	12	8
16083	ID_ Twin Falls County	64,284	70,220	9.2	12	8
16085	ID_ Valley County	7,651	8,622	12.6	1	10
16087	ID_ Washington County	9,977	10,090	1.1	6	10
17001	IL_ Adams County	68,277	67,254	-1.5	9	4
17003	IL_ Alexander County	9,590	8,680	-9.4	2	4
17005	IL_ Bond County	17,633	18,059	2.4	5	3
17007	IL_ Boone County	41,786	52,687	26.0	1	8
17009	IL_ Brown County	6,950	6,777	-2.4	9	3
17011	IL_ Bureau County	35,503	35,326	-0.5	10	9
17013	IL_ Calhoun County	5,084	5,229	2.8	9	10
17015	IL_ Carroll County	16,674	15,960	-4.2	10	4
17017	IL_ Cass County	13,695	13,962	1.9	6	9
17019	IL_ Champaign County	179,669	185,606	3.3	5	1
17021	IL_ Christian County	35,372	35,204	-0.4	9	10
17023	IL_ Clark County	17,008	17,066	0.3	10	3
17025	IL_ Clay County	14,560	14,092	-3.2	3	10
17027	IL_ Clinton County	35,535	36,261	2.0	9	3
17029	IL_ Coles County	53,196	50,920	-4.2	8	5
17031	IL_ Cook County	5,376,741	5,289,009	-1.6	7	1
17033	IL_ Crawford County	20,452	19,904	-2.6	9	4
17035	IL_ Cumberland County	11,253	10,979	-2.4	9	3
17037	IL_ DeKalb County	88,969	100,162	12.5	5	8

fips	county	totpop00	totpop06	chpop	Cat.10_1	Cat.10_2
17039	IL_ De Witt County	16,798	16,711	-0.5	9	3
17041	IL_ Douglas County	19,922	19,844	-0.3	10	3
17043	IL_ DuPage County	904,161	933,232	3.2	1	7
17045	IL_ Edgar County	19,704	19,205	-2.5	3	10
17047	IL_ Edwards County	6,971	6,739	-3.3	3	4
17049	IL_ Effingham County	34,264	34,564	0.8	9	3
17051	IL_ Fayette County	21,802	21,824	0.1	9	3
17053	IL_ Ford County	14,241	14,232	0.0	10	4
17055	IL_ Franklin County	39,018	40,078	2.7	9	10
17057	IL_ Fulton County	38,250	37,659	-1.5	9	10
17059	IL_ Gallatin County	6,445	6,167	-4.3	9	4
17061	IL_ Greene County	14,761	14,481	-1.9	9	10
17063	IL_ Grundy County	37,535	46,301	23.3	1	8
17065	IL_ Hamilton County	8,621	8,299	-3.7	9	4
17067	IL_ Hancock County	20,121	19,086	-5.1	9	10
17069	IL_ Hardin County	4,800	4,706	-1.9	4	10
17071	IL_ Henderson County	8,213	7,915	-3.6	9	10
17073	IL_ Henry County	51,020	50,661	-0.7	10	9
17075	IL_ Iroquois County	31,334	30,801	-1.7	9	4
17077	IL_ Jackson County	59,612	58,269	-2.2	5	8
17079	IL_ Jasper County	10,117	9,973	-1.4	9	4
17081	IL_ Jefferson County	40,045	40,598	1.3	9	3
17083	IL_ Jersey County	21,668	22,643	4.5	9	3
17085	IL_ Jo Daviess County	22,289	22,589	1.3	10	9
17087	IL_ Johnson County	12,878	13,379	3.8	9	3
17089	IL_ Kane County	404,119	493,097	22.0	1	8
17091	IL_ Kankakee County	103,833	109,179	5.1	1	5
17093	IL_ Kendall County	54,544	86,270	58.1	1	8
17095	IL_ Knox County	55,836	52,966	-5.1	9	5
17097	IL_ Lake County	644,356	714,310	10.8	1	7
17099	IL_ La Salle County	111,509	113,205	1.5	9	5
17101	IL_ Lawrence County	15,452	15,919	3.0	9	10
17103	IL_ Lee County	36,062	35,804	-0.7	10	9
17105	IL_ Livingston County	39,678	39,228	-1.1	10	9
17107	IL_ Logan County	31,183	30,527	-2.1	9	3
17109	IL_ McDonough County	32,913	31,689	-3.7	5	9
17111	IL_ McHenry County	260,077	312,515	20.1	8	1
17113	IL_ McLean County	150,433	160,175	6.4	5	8
17115	IL_ Macon County	114,706	109,943	-4.1	9	5
17117	IL_ Macoupin County	49,019	49,201	0.3	9	10
17119	IL_ Madison County	258,941	265,447	2.5	5	1
17121	IL_ Marion County	41,691	39,982	-4.1	9	5
17123	IL_ Marshall County	13,180	13,254	0.5	10	9
17125	IL_ Mason County	16,038	15,635	-2.5	3	4
17127	IL_ Massac County	15,161	15,356	1.2	9	4
17129	IL_ Menard County	12,486	12,697	1.6	4	9
17131	IL_ Mercer County	16,957	16,838	-0.7	10	9
17133	IL_ Monroe County	27,619	31,737	14.9	1	9
17135	IL_ Montgomery County	30,652	30,323	-1.0	9	10
17137	IL_ Morgan County	36,616	35,692	-2.5	9	3
17139	IL_ Moultrie County	14,287	14,569	1.9	10	3

fips	county	totpop00	totpop06	chpop	Cat.10_1	Cat.10_2
17141	IL_ Ogle County	51,032	54,900	7.5	1	9
17143	IL_ Peoria County	183,433	182,557	-0.4	5	7
17145	IL_ Perry County	23,094	22,968	-0.5	9	10
17147	IL_ Piatt County	16,365	16,841	2.9	4	3
17149	IL_ Pike County	17,384	17,153	-1.3	9	4
17151	IL_ Pope County	4,413	4,143	-6.1	9	4
17153	IL_ Pulaski County	7,348	6,720	-8.5	2	3
17155	IL_ Putnam County	6,086	6,058	-0.4	9	3
17157	IL_ Randolph County	33,893	33,213	-2.0	9	3
17159	IL_ Richland County	16,149	15,783	-2.2	9	4
17161	IL_ Rock Island County	149,374	147,886	-1.0	9	5
17163	IL_ St. Clair County	256,082	261,004	1.9	7	1
17165	IL_ Saline County	26,733	26,159	-2.1	9	4
17167	IL_ Sangamon County	188,951	193,355	2.3	5	1
17169	IL_ Schuyler County	7,189	7,103	-1.2	9	4
17171	IL_ Scott County	5,537	5,399	-2.4	10	4
17173	IL_ Shelby County	22,893	22,258	-2.7	10	4
17175	IL_ Stark County	6,332	6,160	-2.7	9	10
17177	IL_ Stephenson County	48,979	47,778	-2.4	10	9
17179	IL_ Tazewell County	128,485	130,740	1.7	1	3
17181	IL_ Union County	18,293	18,270	-0.1	9	4
17183	IL_ Vermilion County	83,919	82,235	-2.0	9	5
17185	IL_ Wabash County	12,937	12,522	-3.2	9	10
17187	IL_ Warren County	18,735	17,366	-7.3	9	5
17189	IL_ Washington County	15,148	14,842	-2.0	9	4
17191	IL_ Wayne County	17,151	16,787	-2.1	4	10
17193	IL_ White County	15,371	15,362	0.0	9	4
17195	IL_ Whiteside County	60,653	59,895	-1.2	10	9
17197	IL_ Will County	502,266	671,339	33.6	8	1
17199	IL_ Williamson County	61,296	64,173	4.6	9	10
17201	IL_ Winnebago County	278,418	292,200	4.9	9	7
17203	IL_ Woodford County	35,469	38,024	7.2	1	9
18001	IN_ Adams County	33,625	33,706	0.2	10	3
18003	IN_ Allen County	331,849	345,490	4.1	8	7
18005	IN_ Bartholomew County	71,435	74,201	3.8	10	3
18007	IN_ Benton County	9,421	8,911	-5.4	9	3
18009	IN_ Blackford County	14,048	13,778	-1.9	9	3
18011	IN_ Boone County	46,107	53,002	14.9	1	3
18013	IN_ Brown County	14,957	15,041	0.5	9	1
18015	IN_ Carroll County	20,165	20,434	1.3	9	3
18017	IN_ Cass County	40,930	39,995	-2.2	9	3
18019	IN_ Clark County	96,472	102,856	6.6	1	10
18021	IN_ Clay County	26,556	27,330	2.9	9	10
18023	IN_ Clinton County	33,866	34,067	0.5	6	3
18025	IN_ Crawford County	10,743	11,226	4.5	9	10
18027	IN_ Daviess County	29,820	30,358	1.8	9	4
18029	IN_ Dearborn County	46,109	49,404	7.1	1	9
18031	IN_ Decatur County	24,555	25,178	2.5	10	9
18033	IN_ De Kalb County	40,285	41,885	3.9	9	3
18035	IN_ Delaware County	118,769	115,277	-2.9	8	5
18037	IN_ Dubois County	39,674	41,146	3.7	9	6

fips	county	totpop00	totpop06	chpop	Cat.10_1	Cat.10_2
18039	IN_ Elkhart County	182,791	198,571	8.6	9	8
18041	IN_ Fayette County	25,588	24,782	-3.1	9	3
18043	IN_ Floyd County	70,823	72,410	2.2	9	2
18045	IN_ Fountain County	17,954	17,249	-3.9	9	3
18047	IN_ Franklin County	22,151	23,200	4.7	9	3
18049	IN_ Fulton County	20,511	20,696	0.9	9	3
18051	IN_ Gibson County	32,500	33,564	3.2	9	3
18053	IN_ Grant County	73,403	69,831	-4.8	9	3
18055	IN_ Greene County	33,157	33,519	1.0	9	3
18057	IN_ Hamilton County	182,740	250,060	36.8	1	8
18059	IN_ Hancock County	55,391	64,581	16.5	1	3
18061	IN_ Harrison County	34,325	37,217	8.4	9	8
18063	IN_ Hendricks County	104,093	130,981	25.8	1	8
18065	IN_ Henry County	48,508	46,961	-3.1	9	3
18067	IN_ Howard County	84,964	85,103	0.1	9	3
18069	IN_ Huntington County	38,075	38,102	0.0	9	3
18071	IN_ Jackson County	41,335	42,526	2.8	3	10
18073	IN_ Jasper County	30,043	32,105	6.8	10	9
18075	IN_ Jay County	21,806	21,484	-1.4	9	10
18077	IN_ Jefferson County	31,705	32,547	2.6	9	3
18079	IN_ Jennings County	27,554	28,479	3.3	9	10
18081	IN_ Johnson County	115,209	130,916	13.6	1	8
18083	IN_ Knox County	39,256	38,276	-2.5	9	5
18085	IN_ Kosciusko County	74,057	76,300	3.0	9	3
18087	IN_ Lagrange County	34,909	37,024	6.0	10	3
18089	IN_ Lake County	484,564	495,766	2.3	2	7
18091	IN_ La Porte County	110,106	110,744	0.5	9	3
18093	IN_ Lawrence County	45,922	46,461	1.1	9	10
18095	IN_ Madison County	133,358	130,145	-2.4	9	3
18097	IN_ Marion County	860,454	862,491	0.2	7	1
18099	IN_ Marshall County	45,128	47,193	4.5	9	3
18101	IN_ Martin County	10,369	10,312	-0.5	10	3
18103	IN_ Miami County	36,082	35,139	-2.6	9	3
18105	IN_ Monroe County	120,563	121,904	1.1	5	8
18107	IN_ Montgomery County	37,629	38,366	1.9	9	3
18109	IN_ Morgan County	66,689	70,162	5.2	1	3
18111	IN_ Newton County	14,566	14,508	-0.4	9	3
18113	IN_ Noble County	46,275	47,830	3.3	6	3
18115	IN_ Ohio County	5,623	5,900	4.9	9	3
18117	IN_ Orange County	19,306	19,791	2.5	9	10
18119	IN_ Owen County	21,786	22,767	4.5	9	3
18121	IN_ Parke County	17,241	17,258	0.1	11	3
18123	IN_ Perry County	18,899	18,959	0.3	9	10
18125	IN_ Pike County	12,837	12,611	-1.7	9	10
18127	IN_ Porter County	146,798	160,029	9.0	1	8
18129	IN_ Posey County	27,061	26,701	-1.3	9	3
18131	IN_ Pulaski County	13,755	13,785	0.2	9	10
18133	IN_ Putnam County	36,019	37,103	3.0	9	3
18135	IN_ Randolph County	27,401	26,507	-3.2	9	3
18137	IN_ Ripley County	26,523	27,755	4.6	10	9
18139	IN_ Rush County	18,261	17,748	-2.8	9	3

fips	county	totpop00	totpop06	chpop	Cat.10_1	Cat.10_2
18141	IN_ St. Joseph County	265,559	266,088	0.2	8	7
18143	IN_ Scott County	22,960	23,976	4.4	9	3
18145	IN_ Shelby County	43,445	43,793	0.8	3	1
18147	IN_ Spencer County	20,391	20,605	1.0	9	3
18149	IN_ Starke County	23,556	23,108	-1.9	9	3
18151	IN_ Steuben County	33,214	33,807	1.7	9	3
18153	IN_ Sullivan County	21,751	21,659	-0.4	9	3
18155	IN_ Switzerland County	9,065	9,847	8.6	9	3
18157	IN_ Tippecanoe County	148,955	155,388	4.3	5	8
18159	IN_ Tipton County	16,577	16,286	-1.7	9	3
18161	IN_ Union County	7,349	7,202	-2.0	9	3
18163	IN_ Vanderburgh County	171,922	173,173	0.7	9	7
18165	IN_ Vermillion County	16,788	16,596	-1.1	9	3
18167	IN_ Vigo County	105,848	102,098	-3.5	9	5
18169	IN_ Wabash County	34,960	33,556	-4.0	9	3
18171	IN_ Warren County	8,419	8,782	4.3	9	3
18173	IN_ Warrick County	52,383	57,257	9.3	1	3
18175	IN_ Washington County	27,223	27,899	2.4	9	3
18177	IN_ Wayne County	71,097	68,602	-3.5	9	3
18179	IN_ Wells County	27,600	28,082	1.7	9	3
18181	IN_ White County	25,267	24,245	-4.0	10	3
18183	IN_ Whitley County	30,707	32,462	5.7	9	3
19001	IA_ Adair County	8,243	7,767	-5.7	10	4
19003	IA_ Adams County	4,482	4,164	-7.1	9	4
19005	IA_ Allamakee County	14,675	14,773	0.6	10	9
19007	IA_ Appanoose County	13,721	13,668	-0.3	9	10
19009	IA_ Audubon County	6,830	6,365	-6.8	4	9
19011	IA_ Benton County	25,308	27,115	7.1	10	9
19013	IA_ Black Hawk County	128,012	125,728	-1.7	8	5
19015	IA_ Boone County	26,224	26,681	1.7	4	9
19017	IA_ Bremer County	23,325	23,762	1.8	10	4
19019	IA_ Buchanan County	21,093	20,976	-0.5	9	4
19021	IA_ Buena Vista County	20,411	19,945	-2.2	6	4
19023	IA_ Butler County	15,305	15,036	-1.7	10	9
19025	IA_ Calhoun County	11,115	10,339	-6.9	10	4
19027	IA_ Carroll County	21,421	20,918	-2.3	9	4
19029	IA_ Cass County	14,684	14,098	-3.9	10	9
19031	IA_ Cedar County	18,187	18,203	0.0	10	3
19033	IA_ Cerro Gordo County	46,447	44,288	-4.6	10	9
19035	IA_ Cherokee County	13,035	12,086	-7.2	10	9
19037	IA_ Chickasaw County	13,095	12,399	-5.3	10	9
19039	IA_ Clarke County	9,133	9,050	-0.9	9	10
19041	IA_ Clay County	17,372	16,788	-3.3	10	4
19043	IA_ Clayton County	18,678	18,203	-2.5	10	9
19045	IA_ Clinton County	50,149	49,566	-1.1	10	9
19047	IA_ Crawford County	16,942	16,805	-0.8	6	10
19049	IA_ Dallas County	40,750	54,540	33.8	1	8
19051	IA_ Davis County	8,541	8,574	0.3	9	4
19053	IA_ Decatur County	8,689	8,652	-0.4	9	4
19055	IA_ Delaware County	18,404	17,803	-3.2	10	9
19057	IA_ Des Moines County	42,351	40,530	-4.3	9	5

fips	county	totpop00	totpop06	chpop	Cat.10_1	Cat.10_2
19059	IA_ Dickinson County	16,424	16,839	2.5	10	4
19061	IA_ Dubuque County	89,143	91,794	2.9	5	9
19063	IA_ Emmet County	11,027	10,440	-5.3	10	4
19065	IA_ Fayette County	22,008	21,148	-3.9	10	9
19067	IA_ Floyd County	16,900	16,285	-3.6	10	9
19069	IA_ Franklin County	10,704	10,731	0.2	10	9
19071	IA_ Fremont County	8,010	7,695	-3.9	9	10
19073	IA_ Greene County	10,366	9,801	-5.4	10	9
19075	IA_ Grundy County	12,369	12,256	-0.9	10	4
19077	IA_ Guthrie County	11,353	11,452	0.8	4	9
19079	IA_ Hamilton County	16,438	16,097	-2.0	10	9
19081	IA_ Hancock County	12,100	11,726	-3.0	10	9
19083	IA_ Hardin County	18,812	17,818	-5.2	10	9
19085	IA_ Harrison County	15,666	15,868	1.2	9	10
19087	IA_ Henry County	20,336	20,342	0.0	10	5
19089	IA_ Howard County	9,932	9,628	-3.0	10	9
19091	IA_ Humboldt County	10,381	9,873	-4.8	10	4
19093	IA_ Ida County	7,837	7,254	-7.4	10	4
19095	IA_ Iowa County	15,671	16,077	2.5	10	9
19097	IA_ Jackson County	20,296	20,317	0.1	10	9
19099	IA_ Jasper County	37,213	37,385	0.4	10	3
19101	IA_ Jefferson County	16,181	15,954	-1.4	4	10
19103	IA_ Johnson County	111,006	117,751	6.0	5	8
19105	IA_ Jones County	20,221	20,456	1.1	10	4
19107	IA_ Keokuk County	11,400	10,984	-3.6	10	4
19109	IA_ Kossuth County	17,163	15,996	-6.8	10	9
19111	IA_ Lee County	38,052	36,592	-3.8	9	10
19113	IA_ Linn County	191,701	199,965	4.3	8	1
19115	IA_ Louisa County	12,183	11,611	-4.7	6	10
19117	IA_ Lucas County	9,422	9,692	2.8	9	10
19119	IA_ Lyon County	11,763	11,672	-0.7	3	9
19121	IA_ Madison County	14,019	15,354	9.5	4	10
19123	IA_ Mahaska County	22,335	22,409	0.3	10	4
19125	IA_ Marion County	32,052	32,994	2.9	10	4
19127	IA_ Marshall County	39,311	39,329	0.0	10	9
19129	IA_ Mills County	14,547	15,482	6.4	9	3
19131	IA_ Mitchell County	10,874	10,850	-0.2	10	9
19133	IA_ Monona County	10,020	9,396	-6.2	10	4
19135	IA_ Monroe County	8,016	7,828	-2.3	9	4
19137	IA_ Montgomery County	11,771	11,379	-3.3	9	10
19139	IA_ Muscatine County	41,722	42,902	2.8	10	9
19141	IA_ O'Brien County	15,102	14,232	-5.7	3	9
19143	IA_ Osceola County	7,003	6,597	-5.8	10	4
19145	IA_ Page County	16,976	16,272	-4.1	10	4
19147	IA_ Palo Alto County	10,147	9,621	-5.1	10	9
19149	IA_ Plymouth County	24,849	24,915	0.2	10	9
19151	IA_ Pocahontas County	8,662	7,765	-10.3	10	9
19153	IA_ Polk County	374,601	405,847	8.3	1	7
19155	IA_ Pottawattamie County	87,704	90,051	2.6	1	9
19157	IA_ Poweshiek County	18,815	18,896	0.4	10	4
19159	IA_ Ringgold County	5,469	5,219	-4.5	4	9

fips	county	totpop00	totpop06	chpop	Cat.10_1	Cat.10_2
19161	IA_ Sac County	11,529	10,493	-8.9	10	4
19163	IA_ Scott County	158,668	161,592	1.8	9	5
19165	IA_ Shelby County	13,173	12,452	-5.4	9	4
19167	IA_ Sioux County	31,589	32,317	2.3	4	9
19169	IA_ Story County	79,981	79,063	-1.1	8	5
19171	IA_ Tama County	18,103	17,907	-1.0	10	9
19173	IA_ Taylor County	6,958	6,524	-6.2	10	4
19175	IA_ Union County	12,309	11,982	-2.6	9	10
19177	IA_ Van Buren County	7,809	7,732	-0.9	10	4
19179	IA_ Wapello County	36,051	35,992	-0.1	9	10
19181	IA_ Warren County	40,671	43,562	7.1	1	9
19183	IA_ Washington County	20,670	21,398	3.5	4	5
19185	IA_ Wayne County	6,730	6,518	-3.1	4	10
19187	IA_ Webster County	40,235	38,593	-4.0	10	9
19189	IA_ Winnebago County	11,723	11,353	-3.1	10	9
19191	IA_ Winneshiek County	21,310	21,217	-0.4	10	4
19193	IA_ Woodbury County	103,877	101,743	-2.0	6	3
19195	IA_ Worth County	7,909	7,797	-1.4	10	4
19197	IA_ Wright County	14,334	13,482	-5.9	10	9
20001	KS_ Allen County	14,385	13,693	-4.8	3	10
20003	KS_ Anderson County	8,110	8,177	0.8	9	4
20005	KS_ Atchison County	16,774	16,770	0.0	11	9
20007	KS_ Barber County	5,307	4,915	-7.3	4	9
20009	KS_ Barton County	28,205	27,737	-1.6	9	6
20011	KS_ Bourbon County	15,379	14,904	-3.0	9	10
20013	KS_ Brown County	10,724	10,134	-5.5	4	9
20015	KS_ Butler County	59,482	63,027	5.9	1	9
20017	KS_ Chase County	3,030	3,104	2.4	4	9
20019	KS_ Chautauqua County	4,359	4,037	-7.3	4	10
20021	KS_ Cherokee County	22,605	21,352	-5.5	9	6
20023	KS_ Cheyenne County	3,165	2,914	-7.9	4	9
20025	KS_ Clark County	2,390	2,230	-6.6	4	9
20027	KS_ Clay County	8,822	8,650	-1.9	11	4
20029	KS_ Cloud County	10,268	9,726	-5.2	9	4
20031	KS_ Coffey County	8,865	8,617	-2.8	4	3
20033	KS_ Comanche County	1,967	1,956	-0.5	3	9
20035	KS_ Cowley County	36,291	34,753	-4.2	9	5
20037	KS_ Crawford County	38,242	38,252	0.0	8	5
20039	KS_ Decatur County	3,472	3,095	-10.8	4	9
20041	KS_ Dickinson County	19,344	19,206	-0.7	11	4
20043	KS_ Doniphan County	8,249	7,652	-7.2	4	5
20045	KS_ Douglas County	99,962	105,038	5.0	5	8
20047	KS_ Edwards County	3,449	3,261	-5.4	4	9
20049	KS_ Elk County	3,261	3,057	-6.2	4	10
20051	KS_ Ellis County	27,507	26,672	-3.0	8	5
20053	KS_ Ellsworth County	6,525	6,308	-3.3	4	9
20055	KS_ Finney County	40,523	39,044	-3.6	8	6
20057	KS_ Ford County	32,458	34,183	5.3	6	3
20059	KS_ Franklin County	24,784	26,369	6.4	9	3
20061	KS_ Geary County	27,947	23,886	-14.5	8	5
20063	KS_ Gove County	3,068	2,708	-11.7	4	9

fips	county	totpop00	totpop06	chpop	Cat.10_1	Cat.10_2
20065	KS_ Graham County	2,946	2,673	-9.2	4	9
20067	KS_ Grant County	7,909	7,402	-6.4	6	4
20069	KS_ Gray County	5,904	5,756	-2.5	6	9
20071	KS_ Greeley County	1,534	1,345	-12.3	4	9
20073	KS_ Greenwood County	7,673	7,211	-6.0	4	9
20075	KS_ Hamilton County	2,670	2,561	-4.0	6	9
20077	KS_ Harper County	6,536	5,968	-8.6	4	9
20079	KS_ Harvey County	32,869	33,821	2.9	9	10
20081	KS_ Haskell County	4,307	4,223	-1.9	6	4
20083	KS_ Hodgeman County	2,085	2,056	-1.3	4	9
20085	KS_ Jackson County	12,657	13,714	8.3	10	9
20087	KS_ Jefferson County	18,426	19,150	3.9	4	3
20089	KS_ Jewell County	3,791	3,286	-13.3	4	9
20091	KS_ Johnson County	451,086	515,484	14.2	1	7
20093	KS_ Kearny County	4,531	4,504	-0.6	6	9
20095	KS_ Kingman County	8,673	8,016	-7.5	9	4
20097	KS_ Kiowa County	3,278	2,914	-11.1	4	9
20099	KS_ Labette County	22,835	22,270	-2.4	5	10
20101	KS_ Lane County	2,155	1,859	-13.7	4	9
20103	KS_ Leavenworth County	68,691	73,538	7.0	11	9
20105	KS_ Lincoln County	3,578	3,393	-5.1	4	10
20107	KS_ Linn County	9,570	10,059	5.1	4	10
20109	KS_ Logan County	3,046	2,731	-10.3	4	9
20111	KS_ Lyon County	35,935	35,558	-1.0	8	6
20113	KS_ McPherson County	29,554	29,670	0.3	10	3
20115	KS_ Marion County	13,361	12,827	-4.0	3	9
20117	KS_ Marshall County	10,965	10,381	-5.3	4	10
20119	KS_ Meade County	4,631	4,618	-0.2	4	9
20121	KS_ Miami County	28,351	31,065	9.5	1	9
20123	KS_ Mitchell County	6,932	6,320	-8.8	10	9
20125	KS_ Montgomery County	36,252	34,513	-4.8	3	10
20127	KS_ Morris County	6,104	6,132	0.4	4	10
20129	KS_ Morton County	3,496	3,160	-9.6	4	9
20131	KS_ Nemaha County	10,717	10,381	-3.1	4	9
20133	KS_ Neosho County	16,997	16,552	-2.6	9	10
20135	KS_ Ness County	3,454	2,931	-15.1	4	9
20137	KS_ Norton County	5,953	5,587	-6.1	9	4
20139	KS_ Osage County	16,712	17,219	3.0	9	10
20141	KS_ Osborne County	4,452	4,005	-10.0	4	9
20143	KS_ Ottawa County	6,163	6,106	-0.9	4	10
20145	KS_ Pawnee County	7,233	6,679	-7.6	4	9
20147	KS_ Phillips County	6,001	5,410	-9.8	10	9
20149	KS_ Pottawatomie County	18,209	19,288	5.9	4	9
20151	KS_ Pratt County	9,647	9,507	-1.4	4	9
20153	KS_ Rawlins County	2,966	2,583	-12.9	4	9
20155	KS_ Reno County	64,790	63,553	-1.9	9	10
20157	KS_ Republic County	5,835	5,107	-12.4	4	10
20159	KS_ Rice County	10,761	10,443	-2.9	4	9
20161	KS_ Riley County	62,843	61,799	-1.6	11	5
20163	KS_ Rooks County	5,685	5,298	-6.8	4	10
20165	KS_ Rush County	3,551	3,376	-4.9	4	9

fips	county	totpop00	totpop06	chpop	Cat.10_1	Cat.10_2
20167	KS_ Russell County	7,370	6,752	-8.3	4	9
20169	KS_ Saline County	53,597	54,049	0.8	9	10
20171	KS_ Scott County	5,120	4,597	-10.2	4	9
20173	KS_ Sedgwick County	452,869	468,107	3.3	8	7
20175	KS_ Seward County	22,510	23,229	3.1	6	8
20177	KS_ Shawnee County	169,871	172,846	1.7	5	7
20179	KS_ Sheridan County	2,813	2,579	-8.3	4	9
20181	KS_ Sherman County	6,760	6,104	-9.7	9	4
20183	KS_ Smith County	4,536	4,080	-10.0	4	9
20185	KS_ Stafford County	4,789	4,469	-6.6	4	9
20187	KS_ Stanton County	2,406	2,168	-9.8	6	9
20189	KS_ Stevens County	5,463	5,441	-0.4	6	9
20191	KS_ Sumner County	25,946	24,599	-5.1	9	4
20193	KS_ Thomas County	8,180	7,464	-8.7	8	9
20195	KS_ Trego County	3,319	3,008	-9.3	4	9
20197	KS_ Wabaunsee County	6,885	7,023	2.0	4	10
20199	KS_ Wallace County	1,749	1,557	-10.9	4	9
20201	KS_ Washington County	6,483	5,933	-8.4	4	10
20203	KS_ Wichita County	2,531	2,272	-10.2	6	9
20205	KS_ Wilson County	10,332	9,758	-5.5	9	4
20207	KS_ Woodson County	3,788	3,572	-5.7	4	10
20209	KS_ Wyandotte County	157,882	155,832	-1.3	11	6
21001	KY_ Adair County	17,244	17,544	1.7	4	3
21003	KY_ Allen County	17,800	18,812	5.6	9	10
21005	KY_ Anderson County	19,111	20,673	8.1	3	8
21007	KY_ Ballard County	8,286	8,294	0.1	3	2
21009	KY_ Barren County	38,033	40,506	6.5	9	3
21011	KY_ Bath County	11,085	11,662	5.2	9	10
21013	KY_ Bell County	30,060	29,429	-2.1	9	4
21015	KY_ Boone County	85,991	110,515	28.5	8	1
21017	KY_ Bourbon County	19,360	19,989	3.2	3	7
21019	KY_ Boyd County	49,752	49,268	-0.9	9	10
21021	KY_ Boyle County	27,697	28,566	3.1	3	2
21023	KY_ Bracken County	8,279	8,667	4.6	3	10
21025	KY_ Breathitt County	16,100	16,047	-0.3	9	11
21027	KY_ Breckinridge County	18,648	19,358	3.8	3	10
21029	KY_ Bullitt County	61,236	70,541	15.2	1	3
21031	KY_ Butler County	13,010	13,426	3.2	3	10
21033	KY_ Caldwell County	13,060	13,017	-0.3	3	2
21035	KY_ Calloway County	34,177	35,330	3.3	8	5
21037	KY_ Campbell County	88,616	86,769	-2.0	9	8
21039	KY_ Carlisle County	5,351	5,277	-1.3	3	2
21041	KY_ Carroll County	10,155	10,520	3.5	8	3
21043	KY_ Carter County	26,889	27,287	1.4	9	3
21045	KY_ Casey County	15,447	16,383	6.0	3	2
21047	KY_ Christian County	72,265	69,533	-3.7	11	9
21049	KY_ Clark County	33,144	35,264	6.4	8	3
21051	KY_ Clay County	24,556	24,087	-1.9	2	4
21053	KY_ Clinton County	9,634	9,513	-1.2	3	6
21055	KY_ Crittenden County	9,384	8,932	-4.8	3	4
21057	KY_ Cumberland County	7,147	7,047	-1.4	9	2

fips	county	totpop00	totpop06	chpop	Cat.10_1	Cat.10_2
21059	KY_ Daviess County	91,545	92,868	1.4	9	3
21061	KY_ Edmonson County	11,644	12,068	3.6	9	3
21063	KY_ Elliott County	6,748	7,005	3.8	9	10
21065	KY_ Estill County	15,307	14,966	-2.2	9	10
21067	KY_ Fayette County	260,512	269,012	3.2	8	5
21069	KY_ Fleming County	13,792	14,703	6.6	9	2
21071	KY_ Floyd County	42,441	42,299	-0.3	9	3
21073	KY_ Franklin County	47,687	48,196	1.0	3	1
21075	KY_ Fulton County	7,752	7,077	-8.7	3	2
21077	KY_ Gallatin County	7,870	8,245	4.7	9	3
21079	KY_ Garrard County	14,792	16,843	13.8	9	3
21081	KY_ Grant County	22,384	24,722	10.4	3	8
21083	KY_ Graves County	37,028	37,809	2.1	3	2
21085	KY_ Grayson County	24,053	25,448	5.8	9	10
21087	KY_ Green County	11,518	11,502	-0.1	3	10
21089	KY_ Greenup County	36,891	37,330	1.1	9	10
21091	KY_ Hancock County	8,392	8,684	3.4	3	2
21093	KY_ Hardin County	94,174	97,357	3.3	11	3
21095	KY_ Harlan County	33,202	31,454	-5.2	9	2
21097	KY_ Harrison County	17,983	18,592	3.3	3	9
21099	KY_ Hart County	17,445	18,523	6.1	3	10
21101	KY_ Henderson County	44,829	45,605	1.7	3	2
21103	KY_ Henry County	15,060	15,939	5.8	3	10
21105	KY_ Hickman County	5,262	5,008	-4.8	2	4
21107	KY_ Hopkins County	46,519	46,536	0.0	3	2
21109	KY_ Jackson County	13,495	13,701	1.5	9	2
21111	KY_ Jefferson County	693,604	698,939	0.7	7	1
21113	KY_ Jessamine County	39,041	44,378	13.6	8	5
21115	KY_ Johnson County	23,445	24,231	3.3	9	10
21117	KY_ Kenton County	151,464	153,569	1.3	8	7
21119	KY_ Knott County	17,649	17,505	-0.8	2	4
21121	KY_ Knox County	31,795	32,297	1.5	3	2
21123	KY_ Larue County	13,373	13,818	3.3	3	2
21125	KY_ Laurel County	52,715	56,705	7.5	3	10
21127	KY_ Lawrence County	15,569	16,311	4.7	9	10
21129	KY_ Lee County	7,916	7,588	-4.1	9	2
21131	KY_ Leslie County	12,401	11,984	-3.3	9	2
21133	KY_ Letcher County	25,277	24,263	-4.0	9	3
21135	KY_ Lewis County	14,092	13,961	-0.9	9	2
21137	KY_ Lincoln County	23,361	25,397	8.7	3	10
21139	KY_ Livingston County	9,804	9,815	0.1	3	4
21141	KY_ Logan County	26,573	27,275	2.6	3	2
21143	KY_ Lyon County	8,080	8,161	1.0	3	2
21145	KY_ McCracken County	65,514	64,603	-1.3	3	9
21147	KY_ McCreary County	17,080	17,326	1.4	9	10
21149	KY_ McLean County	9,938	9,904	-0.3	3	2
21151	KY_ Madison County	70,872	79,278	11.8	8	5
21153	KY_ Magoffin County	13,332	13,488	1.1	2	4
21155	KY_ Marion County	18,212	19,008	4.3	9	2
21157	KY_ Marshall County	30,125	31,164	3.4	3	10
21159	KY_ Martin County	12,578	12,054	-4.1	9	2

fips	county	totpop00	totpop06	chpop	Cat.10_1	Cat.10_2
21161	KY_ Mason County	16,800	17,312	3.0	3	10
21163	KY_ Meade County	26,349	28,543	8.3	8	3
21165	KY_ Menifee County	6,556	6,814	3.9	9	2
21167	KY_ Mercer County	20,817	21,778	4.6	3	2
21169	KY_ Metcalfe County	10,037	10,334	2.9	3	10
21171	KY_ Monroe County	11,756	11,685	-0.6	3	2
21173	KY_ Montgomery County	22,554	24,592	9.0	9	10
21175	KY_ Morgan County	13,948	14,250	2.1	9	2
21177	KY_ Muhlenberg County	31,839	31,457	-1.2	3	2
21179	KY_ Nelson County	37,477	41,666	11.1	3	8
21181	KY_ Nicholas County	6,813	7,008	2.8	9	10
21183	KY_ Ohio County	22,916	23,790	3.8	3	2
21185	KY_ Oldham County	46,178	54,860	18.8	8	1
21187	KY_ Owen County	10,547	11,467	8.7	3	8
21189	KY_ Owsley County	4,858	4,745	-2.3	4	2
21191	KY_ Pendleton County	14,390	15,189	5.5	3	2
21193	KY_ Perry County	29,390	29,364	0.0	9	3
21195	KY_ Pike County	68,736	66,491	-3.2	9	2
21197	KY_ Powell County	13,237	13,911	5.0	9	2
21199	KY_ Pulaski County	56,217	59,703	6.2	3	10
21201	KY_ Robertson County	2,266	2,229	-1.6	9	10
21203	KY_ Rockcastle County	16,582	16,754	1.0	3	10
21205	KY_ Rowan County	22,094	22,174	0.3	5	2
21207	KY_ Russell County	16,315	17,146	5.0	3	10
21209	KY_ Scott County	33,061	40,761	23.2	1	3
21211	KY_ Shelby County	33,337	39,312	17.9	1	3
21213	KY_ Simpson County	16,405	17,181	4.7	3	10
21215	KY_ Spencer County	11,766	16,270	38.2	8	3
21217	KY_ Taylor County	22,927	23,786	3.7	3	4
21219	KY_ Todd County	11,971	11,951	-0.1	3	2
21221	KY_ Trigg County	12,597	13,575	7.7	3	10
21223	KY_ Trimble County	8,125	9,071	11.6	9	3
21225	KY_ Union County	15,637	15,492	-0.9	9	2
21227	KY_ Warren County	92,522	100,628	8.7	8	5
21229	KY_ Washington County	10,916	11,419	4.6	9	10
21231	KY_ Wayne County	19,923	20,405	2.4	3	2
21233	KY_ Webster County	14,120	14,151	0.2	3	2
21235	KY_ Whitley County	35,865	38,413	7.1	3	4
21237	KY_ Wolfe County	7,065	7,156	1.2	9	10
21239	KY_ Woodford County	23,208	24,406	5.1	1	7
22001	LA_ Acadia Parish	58,861	59,431	0.9	2	9
22003	LA_ Allen Parish	25,440	25,200	-0.9	2	3
22005	LA_ Ascension Parish	76,627	93,555	22.0	1	8
22007	LA_ Assumption Parish	23,388	23,105	-1.2	2	6
22009	LA_ Avoyelles Parish	41,481	42,036	1.3	2	3
22011	LA_ Beauregard Parish	32,986	35,104	6.4	3	2
22013	LA_ Bienville Parish	15,752	15,127	-3.9	2	3
22015	LA_ Bossier Parish	98,310	106,862	8.7	11	3
22017	LA_ Caddo Parish	252,161	251,498	-0.2	2	3
22019	LA_ Calcasieu Parish	183,577	185,721	1.1	2	5
22021	LA_ Caldwell Parish	10,560	10,546	-0.1	2	3

fips	county	totpop00	totpop06	chpop	Cat.10_1	Cat.10_2
22023	LA_ Cameron Parish	9,991	9,518	-4.7	6	9
22025	LA_ Catahoula Parish	10,920	10,345	-5.2	2	3
22027	LA_ Claiborne Parish	16,851	16,087	-4.5	2	3
22029	LA_ Concordia Parish	20,247	19,072	-5.8	2	3
22031	LA_ De Soto Parish	25,494	26,540	4.1	2	3
22033	LA_ East Baton Rouge Parish	412,852	410,665	-0.5	2	7
22035	LA_ East Carroll Parish	9,421	8,685	-7.8	2	6
22037	LA_ East Feliciana Parish	21,360	20,664	-3.2	2	3
22039	LA_ Evangeline Parish	35,434	35,736	0.8	2	6
22041	LA_ Franklin Parish	21,263	20,194	-5.0	2	6
22043	LA_ Grant Parish	18,698	19,849	6.1	3	2
22045	LA_ Iberia Parish	73,266	74,429	1.5	2	9
22047	LA_ Iberville Parish	33,320	32,143	-3.5	2	3
22049	LA_ Jackson Parish	15,397	15,052	-2.2	2	3
22051	LA_ Jefferson Parish	455,466	451,910	-0.7	2	7
22053	LA_ Jefferson Davis Parish	31,435	31,300	-0.4	2	9
22055	LA_ Lafayette Parish	190,503	198,428	4.1	8	7
22057	LA_ Lafourche Parish	89,974	92,187	2.4	9	6
22059	LA_ La Salle Parish	14,282	13,971	-2.1	3	2
22061	LA_ Lincoln Parish	42,509	42,000	-1.2	8	5
22063	LA_ Livingston Parish	91,814	112,167	22.1	8	3
22065	LA_ Madison Parish	13,728	12,312	-10.3	2	3
22067	LA_ Morehouse Parish	31,021	29,719	-4.2	2	3
22069	LA_ Natchitoches Parish	39,080	38,365	-1.8	8	5
22071	LA_ Orleans Parish	484,674	447,783	-7.6	2	7
22073	LA_ Ouachita Parish	147,250	147,946	0.4	8	3
22075	LA_ Plaquemines Parish	26,757	29,295	9.4	2	6
22077	LA_ Pointe Coupee Parish	22,763	22,267	-2.1	2	6
22079	LA_ Rapides Parish	126,337	128,659	1.8	2	3
22081	LA_ Red River Parish	9,622	9,368	-2.6	2	3
22083	LA_ Richland Parish	20,981	20,457	-2.5	2	3
22085	LA_ Sabine Parish	23,459	23,859	1.7	2	3
22087	LA_ St. Bernard Parish	67,229	65,069	-3.2	9	2
22089	LA_ St. Charles Parish	48,072	51,156	6.4	2	3
22091	LA_ St. Helena Parish	10,525	10,122	-3.8	2	3
22093	LA_ St. James Parish	21,216	21,089	-0.6	2	6
22095	LA_ St. John the Baptist Parish	43,044	47,072	9.3	1	2
22097	LA_ St. Landry Parish	87,700	90,274	2.9	2	9
22099	LA_ St. Martin Parish	48,583	50,479	3.9	2	9
22101	LA_ St. Mary Parish	53,500	50,818	-5.0	2	9
22103	LA_ St. Tammany Parish	191,268	226,007	18.1	8	1
22105	LA_ Tangipahoa Parish	100,588	108,042	7.4	2	8
22107	LA_ Tensas Parish	6,618	6,044	-8.6	2	4
22109	LA_ Terrebonne Parish	104,503	107,743	3.1	2	9
22111	LA_ Union Parish	22,803	22,889	0.3	2	3
22113	LA_ Vermilion Parish	53,807	55,640	3.4	2	9
22115	LA_ Vernon Parish	52,531	47,699	-9.2	11	2
22117	LA_ Washington Parish	43,926	44,910	2.2	2	3
22119	LA_ Webster Parish	41,831	41,258	-1.3	2	3
22121	LA_ West Baton Rouge Parish	21,601	21,530	-0.3	2	3
22123	LA_ West Carroll Parish	12,314	11,688	-5.0	2	3

fips	county	totpop00	totpop06	chpop	Cat.10_1	Cat.10_2
22125	LA_ West Feliciana Parish	15,111	15,208	0.6	2	3
22127	LA_ Winn Parish	16,894	15,818	-6.3	2	3
23001	ME_ Androscoggin County	103,793	108,763	4.7	9	10
23003	ME_ Aroostook County	73,938	73,605	-0.4	9	10
23005	ME_ Cumberland County	265,612	277,157	4.3	1	7
23007	ME_ Franklin County	29,467	29,923	1.5	9	10
23009	ME_ Hancock County	51,791	54,274	4.7	9	3
23011	ME_ Kennebec County	117,114	122,231	4.3	9	10
23013	ME_ Knox County	39,618	41,448	4.6	9	10
23015	ME_ Lincoln County	33,616	35,568	5.8	9	10
23017	ME_ Oxford County	54,755	57,263	4.5	9	10
23019	ME_ Penobscot County	144,919	147,887	2.0	9	5
23021	ME_ Piscataquis County	17,235	17,876	3.7	9	10
23023	ME_ Sagadahoc County	35,214	36,959	4.9	11	3
23025	ME_ Somerset County	50,888	52,202	2.5	9	10
23027	ME_ Waldo County	36,280	39,003	7.5	9	10
23029	ME_ Washington County	33,941	33,537	-1.1	9	10
23031	ME_ York County	186,742	204,652	9.5	9	5
24001	MD_ Allegany County	74,930	73,873	-1.4	9	10
24003	MD_ Anne Arundel County	489,656	515,455	5.2	11	1
24005	MD_ Baltimore County	754,292	794,932	5.3	1	7
24009	MD_ Calvert County	74,563	90,113	20.8	8	1
24011	MD_ Caroline County	29,772	32,632	9.6	9	3
24013	MD_ Carroll County	150,897	171,890	13.9	8	1
24015	MD_ Cecil County	85,951	100,874	17.3	1	8
24017	MD_ Charles County	120,546	142,796	18.4	8	1
24019	MD_ Dorchester County	30,674	32,051	4.4	2	9
24021	MD_ Frederick County	195,277	224,865	15.1	8	1
24023	MD_ Garrett County	29,846	30,039	0.6	9	10
24025	MD_ Harford County	218,590	244,477	11.8	8	1
24027	MD_ Howard County	247,842	273,855	10.5	1	7
24029	MD_ Kent County	19,197	20,174	5.0	9	10
24031	MD_ Montgomery County	873,341	937,541	7.3	1	7
24033	MD_ Prince George's County	801,515	854,833	6.6	1	7
24035	MD_ Queen Anne's County	40,563	46,379	14.3	8	1
24037	MD_ St. Mary's County	86,211	99,256	15.1	11	8
24039	MD_ Somerset County	24,747	25,981	4.9	2	5
24041	MD_ Talbot County	33,812	36,490	7.9	8	1
24043	MD_ Washington County	131,923	145,283	10.1	10	8
24045	MD_ Wicomico County	84,644	92,877	9.7	8	9
24047	MD_ Worcester County	46,543	49,050	5.3	9	3
24510	MD_ Baltimore city	651,154	637,697	-2.0	7	6
25001	MA_ Barnstable County	222,230	225,965	1.6	1	5
25003	MA_ Berkshire County	134,953	132,081	-2.1	5	9
25005	MA_ Bristol County	534,678	546,835	2.2	5	7
25007	MA_ Dukes County	14,987	15,641	4.3	1	9
25009	MA_ Essex County	723,419	740,960	2.4	5	1
25011	MA_ Franklin County	71,535	72,874	1.8	5	9
25013	MA_ Hampden County	456,228	463,756	1.6	9	1
25015	MA_ Hampshire County	152,251	153,963	1.1	5	1
25017	MA_ Middlesex County	1,465,396	1,463,316	-0.1	1	7

fips	county	totpop00	totpop06	chpop	Cat.10_1	Cat.10_2
25019	MA_ Nantucket County	9,520	10,186	7.0	1	8
25021	MA_ Norfolk County	650,308	654,985	0.7	5	7
25023	MA_ Plymouth County	472,822	496,928	5.1	5	7
25025	MA_ Suffolk County	689,807	653,588	-5.2	1	7
25027	MA_ Worcester County	750,963	788,979	5.0	5	7
26001	MI_ Alcona County	11,719	11,794	0.6	9	4
26003	MI_ Alger County	9,862	9,643	-2.2	9	10
26005	MI_ Allegan County	105,665	114,616	8.4	1	8
26007	MI_ Alpena County	31,314	30,381	-2.9	9	4
26009	MI_ Antrim County	23,110	24,570	6.3	10	4
26011	MI_ Arenac County	17,269	17,229	-0.2	9	10
26013	MI_ Baraga County	8,746	8,750	0.0	9	4
26015	MI_ Barry County	56,755	60,621	6.8	10	1
26017	MI_ Bay County	110,157	109,309	-0.7	9	6
26019	MI_ Benzie County	15,998	17,903	11.9	9	10
26021	MI_ Berrien County	162,453	162,775	0.2	9	2
26023	MI_ Branch County	45,787	46,228	0.9	9	3
26025	MI_ Calhoun County	137,985	139,194	0.8	9	3
26027	MI_ Cass County	51,104	52,089	1.9	9	3
26029	MI_ Charlevoix County	26,090	26,753	2.5	9	10
26031	MI_ Cheboygan County	26,448	27,543	4.1	9	10
26033	MI_ Chippewa County	38,543	38,972	1.1	9	5
26035	MI_ Clare County	31,252	31,675	1.3	9	10
26037	MI_ Clinton County	64,753	70,330	8.6	1	9
26039	MI_ Crawford County	14,273	15,249	6.8	9	10
26041	MI_ Delta County	38,520	38,398	-0.3	9	4
26043	MI_ Dickinson County	27,472	28,138	2.4	9	10
26045	MI_ Eaton County	103,655	108,275	4.4	1	8
26047	MI_ Emmet County	31,437	33,983	8.1	9	5
26049	MI_ Genesee County	436,141	445,865	2.2	2	7
26051	MI_ Gladwin County	26,023	27,291	4.8	9	10
26053	MI_ Gogebic County	17,370	16,748	-3.5	9	4
26055	MI_ Grand Traverse County	77,654	85,228	9.7	1	9
26057	MI_ Gratiot County	42,285	42,480	0.4	9	3
26059	MI_ Hillsdale County	46,527	47,207	1.4	9	3
26061	MI_ Houghton County	36,016	35,894	-0.3	8	9
26063	MI_ Huron County	36,079	34,517	-4.3	10	9
26065	MI_ Ingham County	279,320	278,832	-0.1	8	7
26067	MI_ Ionia County	61,518	64,863	5.4	9	8
26069	MI_ Iosco County	27,339	27,147	-0.7	9	4
26071	MI_ Iron County	13,138	12,267	-6.6	9	4
26073	MI_ Isabella County	63,351	66,396	4.8	8	9
26075	MI_ Jackson County	158,422	164,707	3.9	9	5
26077	MI_ Kalamazoo County	238,603	240,941	0.9	8	5
26079	MI_ Kalkaska County	16,571	17,259	4.1	9	3
26081	MI_ Kent County	574,335	601,073	4.6	10	7
26083	MI_ Keweenaw County	2,301	2,173	-5.5	9	4
26085	MI_ Lake County	11,333	12,211	7.7	9	10
26087	MI_ Lapeer County	87,904	94,568	7.5	1	9
26089	MI_ Leelanau County	21,119	22,270	5.4	1	9
26091	MI_ Lenawee County	98,890	102,854	4.0	1	5

fips	county	totpop00	totpop06	chpop	Cat.10_1	Cat.10_2
26093	MI_ Livingston County	156,951	186,230	18.6	8	1
26095	MI_ Luce County	7,024	6,758	-3.7	9	4
26097	MI_ Mackinac County	11,943	11,264	-5.6	9	10
26099	MI_ Macomb County	788,149	836,887	6.1	1	7
26101	MI_ Manistee County	24,527	25,207	2.7	9	4
26103	MI_ Marquette County	64,634	65,040	0.6	9	5
26105	MI_ Mason County	28,274	29,072	2.8	9	10
26107	MI_ Mecosta County	40,553	42,647	5.1	9	5
26109	MI_ Menominee County	25,326	24,956	-1.4	9	6
26111	MI_ Midland County	82,874	84,291	1.7	1	9
26113	MI_ Missaukee County	14,478	15,349	6.0	3	4
26115	MI_ Monroe County	145,945	156,101	6.9	1	3
26117	MI_ Montcalm County	61,266	64,363	5.0	10	8
26119	MI_ Montmorency County	10,315	10,462	1.4	9	10
26121	MI_ Muskegon County	170,200	177,063	4.0	10	7
26123	MI_ Newaygo County	47,874	50,449	5.3	10	3
26125	MI_ Oakland County	1,194,156	1,222,296	2.3	1	7
26127	MI_ Oceana County	26,873	28,664	6.6	6	10
26129	MI_ Ogemaw County	21,645	22,024	1.7	9	10
26131	MI_ Ontonagon County	7,818	7,283	-6.8	9	4
26133	MI_ Osceola County	23,197	23,768	2.4	10	3
26135	MI_ Oscoda County	9,418	9,171	-2.6	9	10
26137	MI_ Otsego County	23,301	24,903	6.8	9	10
26139	MI_ Ottawa County	238,314	259,131	8.7	1	4
26141	MI_ Presque Isle County	14,411	14,330	-0.5	9	4
26143	MI_ Roscommon County	25,469	26,177	2.7	9	10
26145	MI_ Saginaw County	210,039	208,485	-0.7	10	5
26147	MI_ St. Clair County	164,235	172,596	5.0	9	1
26149	MI_ St. Joseph County	62,422	63,225	1.2	9	3
26151	MI_ Sanilac County	44,547	44,865	0.7	9	10
26153	MI_ Schoolcraft County	8,903	8,856	-0.5	9	4
26155	MI_ Shiawassee County	71,687	73,306	2.2	9	3
26157	MI_ Tuscola County	58,266	58,576	0.5	9	3
26159	MI_ Van Buren County	76,263	79,349	4.0	1	9
26161	MI_ Washtenaw County	322,895	346,505	7.3	5	1
26163	MI_ Wayne County	2,061,162	1,988,031	-3.5	7	1
26165	MI_ Wexford County	30,484	32,282	5.9	9	10
27001	MN_ Aitkin County	15,301	16,312	6.6	9	10
27003	MN_ Anoka County	298,084	328,946	10.3	1	7
27005	MN_ Becker County	30,000	32,111	7.0	10	9
27007	MN_ Beltrami County	39,650	43,402	9.4	8	9
27009	MN_ Benton County	34,226	38,964	13.8	8	9
27011	MN_ Big Stone County	5,820	5,460	-6.1	4	9
27013	MN_ Blue Earth County	55,941	58,328	4.2	8	5
27015	MN_ Brown County	26,911	26,168	-2.7	10	9
27017	MN_ Carlton County	31,671	34,502	8.9	10	9
27019	MN_ Carver County	70,205	87,951	25.2	8	1
27021	MN_ Cass County	27,150	29,337	8.0	9	10
27023	MN_ Chippewa County	13,088	12,828	-1.9	10	9
27025	MN_ Chisago County	41,101	50,611	23.1	8	3
27027	MN_ Clay County	51,229	54,952	7.2	8	9

fips	county	totpop00	totpop06	chpop	Cat.10_1	Cat.10_2
27029	MN_ Clearwater County	8,423	8,476	0.6	9	4
27031	MN_ Cook County	5,168	5,375	4.0	1	10
27033	MN_ Cottonwood County	12,167	11,709	-3.7	10	4
27035	MN_ Crow Wing County	55,099	60,815	10.3	9	10
27037	MN_ Dakota County	355,904	389,554	9.4	1	7
27039	MN_ Dodge County	17,731	19,833	11.8	10	9
27041	MN_ Douglas County	32,821	35,719	8.8	10	9
27043	MN_ Faribault County	16,181	15,339	-5.2	10	9
27045	MN_ Fillmore County	21,122	21,270	0.7	10	4
27047	MN_ Freeborn County	32,584	31,978	-1.8	10	4
27049	MN_ Goodhue County	44,127	45,699	3.5	10	9
27051	MN_ Grant County	6,289	6,078	-3.3	4	9
27053	MN_ Hennepin County	1,116,200	1,122,457	0.5	1	7
27055	MN_ Houston County	19,718	19,971	1.2	10	9
27057	MN_ Hubbard County	18,376	18,953	3.1	9	4
27059	MN_ Isanti County	31,287	38,830	24.1	1	8
27061	MN_ Itasca County	43,992	44,610	1.4	9	5
27063	MN_ Jackson County	11,268	11,189	-0.7	10	9
27065	MN_ Kanabec County	14,996	16,387	9.2	10	8
27067	MN_ Kandiyohi County	41,203	41,563	0.8	10	9
27069	MN_ Kittson County	5,285	4,756	-10.0	10	4
27071	MN_ Koochiching County	14,355	13,869	-3.3	10	9
27073	MN_ Lac qui Parle County	8,067	7,482	-7.2	4	9
27075	MN_ Lake County	11,058	11,088	0.2	10	9
27077	MN_ Lake of the Woods County	4,522	4,447	-1.6	10	4
27079	MN_ Le Sueur County	25,426	28,011	10.1	10	9
27081	MN_ Lincoln County	6,429	6,005	-6.6	4	9
27083	MN_ Lyon County	25,425	24,678	-2.9	9	8
27085	MN_ McLeod County	34,898	37,069	6.2	10	9
27087	MN_ Mahnomen County	5,190	5,090	-1.9	9	10
27089	MN_ Marshall County	10,155	9,954	-1.9	10	9
27091	MN_ Martin County	21,802	20,904	-4.1	10	4
27093	MN_ Meeker County	22,644	23,382	3.2	10	4
27095	MN_ Mille Lacs County	22,330	26,320	17.8	10	4
27097	MN_ Morrison County	31,712	32,849	3.5	9	6
27099	MN_ Mower County	38,603	38,653	0.1	10	9
27101	MN_ Murray County	9,165	8,782	-4.1	10	4
27103	MN_ Nicollet County	29,771	31,083	4.4	8	5
27105	MN_ Nobles County	20,832	20,500	-1.5	6	4
27107	MN_ Norman County	7,442	6,957	-6.5	4	9
27109	MN_ Olmsted County	124,277	137,186	10.3	8	5
27111	MN_ Otter Tail County	57,159	57,762	1.0	10	9
27113	MN_ Pennington County	13,584	13,578	0.0	9	4
27115	MN_ Pine County	26,530	28,750	8.3	9	10
27117	MN_ Pipestone County	9,895	9,284	-6.1	3	9
27119	MN_ Polk County	31,369	31,416	0.1	10	9
27121	MN_ Pope County	11,236	11,246	0.0	10	4
27123	MN_ Ramsey County	511,035	491,854	-3.7	7	1
27125	MN_ Red Lake County	4,299	4,272	-0.6	9	10
27127	MN_ Redwood County	16,815	15,891	-5.5	10	4
27129	MN_ Renville County	17,154	16,711	-2.5	10	9

fips	county	totpop00	totpop06	chpop	Cat.10_1	Cat.10_2
27131	MN_ Rice County	56,665	61,880	9.2	8	9
27133	MN_ Rock County	9,721	9,495	-2.3	10	9
27135	MN_ Roseau County	16,338	16,609	1.6	10	4
27137	MN_ St. Louis County	200,528	196,671	-1.9	9	7
27139	MN_ Scott County	89,498	124,794	39.4	8	1
27141	MN_ Sherburne County	64,417	84,839	31.7	8	3
27143	MN_ Sibley County	15,356	15,160	-1.2	9	4
27145	MN_ Stearns County	133,166	144,031	8.1	8	5
27147	MN_ Steele County	33,680	36,243	7.6	10	9
27149	MN_ Stevens County	10,053	9,801	-2.5	8	9
27151	MN_ Swift County	11,956	10,377	-13.2	10	4
27153	MN_ Todd County	24,426	24,642	0.8	10	4
27155	MN_ Traverse County	4,134	3,788	-8.3	4	9
27157	MN_ Wabasha County	21,610	22,254	2.9	10	9
27159	MN_ Wadena County	13,713	13,662	-0.3	9	4
27161	MN_ Waseca County	19,526	19,350	-0.9	10	4
27163	MN_ Washington County	201,130	224,365	11.5	1	8
27165	MN_ Watonwan County	11,876	11,097	-6.5	6	4
27167	MN_ Wilkin County	7,138	6,694	-6.2	10	9
27169	MN_ Winona County	49,985	49,636	-0.7	8	5
27171	MN_ Wright County	89,986	113,978	26.6	1	8
27173	MN_ Yellow Medicine County	11,080	10,382	-6.3	10	9
28001	MS_ Adams County	34,340	31,619	-7.9	2	3
28003	MS_ Alcorn County	34,558	35,395	2.4	3	2
28005	MS_ Amite County	13,599	13,357	-1.7	2	3
28007	MS_ Attala County	19,661	19,508	-0.7	2	3
28009	MS_ Benton County	8,026	7,849	-2.2	2	3
28011	MS_ Bolivar County	40,633	38,212	-5.9	2	3
28013	MS_ Calhoun County	15,069	14,478	-3.9	3	2
28015	MS_ Carroll County	10,769	10,293	-4.4	2	3
28017	MS_ Chickasaw County	19,440	19,001	-2.2	2	6
28019	MS_ Choctaw County	9,758	9,427	-3.3	2	3
28021	MS_ Claiborne County	11,831	11,544	-2.4	2	5
28023	MS_ Clarke County	17,955	17,532	-2.3	2	3
28025	MS_ Clay County	21,979	20,897	-4.9	2	3
28027	MS_ Coahoma County	30,622	28,516	-6.8	2	3
28029	MS_ Copiah County	28,757	29,048	1.0	2	3
28031	MS_ Covington County	19,407	20,189	4.0	2	3
28033	MS_ DeSoto County	107,199	142,393	32.8	8	3
28035	MS_ Forrest County	72,604	75,466	3.9	8	5
28037	MS_ Franklin County	8,448	8,350	-1.1	2	3
28039	MS_ George County	19,144	21,569	12.6	3	2
28041	MS_ Greene County	13,299	13,099	-1.5	2	3
28043	MS_ Grenada County	23,263	22,829	-1.8	2	3
28045	MS_ Hancock County	42,967	47,230	9.9	1	10
28047	MS_ Harrison County	189,601	194,770	2.7	8	11
28049	MS_ Hinds County	250,800	248,653	-0.8	8	11
28051	MS_ Holmes County	21,609	20,970	-2.9	2	7
28053	MS_ Humphreys County	11,206	10,395	-7.2	2	4
28055	MS_ Issaquena County	2,274	1,827	-19.6	2	3
28057	MS_ Itawamba County	22,770	23,444	2.9	3	10

fips	county	totpop00	totpop06	chpop	Cat.10_1	Cat.10_2
28059	MS_ Jackson County	131,420	136,640	3.9	11	2
28061	MS_ Jasper County	18,149	18,001	-0.8	2	3
28063	MS_ Jefferson County	9,740	9,280	-4.7	2	7
28065	MS_ Jefferson Davis County	13,962	12,985	-7.0	2	7
28067	MS_ Jones County	64,958	66,476	2.3	3	6
28069	MS_ Kemper County	10,453	10,100	-3.3	2	4
28071	MS_ Lafayette County	38,744	40,652	4.9	8	5
28073	MS_ Lamar County	39,070	45,726	17.0	8	3
28075	MS_ Lauderdale County	78,161	76,795	-1.7	2	3
28077	MS_ Lawrence County	13,258	13,417	1.2	2	3
28079	MS_ Leake County	20,940	22,656	8.1	2	3
28081	MS_ Lee County	75,755	79,001	4.2	3	2
28083	MS_ Leflore County	37,947	36,144	-4.7	2	5
28085	MS_ Lincoln County	33,166	33,938	2.3	2	3
28087	MS_ Lowndes County	61,586	59,252	-3.7	8	2
28089	MS_ Madison County	74,674	87,023	16.5	8	1
28091	MS_ Marion County	25,595	25,297	-1.1	2	3
28093	MS_ Marshall County	34,993	35,728	2.1	2	3
28095	MS_ Monroe County	38,014	37,436	-1.5	2	3
28097	MS_ Montgomery County	12,189	11,743	-3.6	2	3
28099	MS_ Neshoba County	28,684	30,195	5.2	2	3
28101	MS_ Newton County	21,838	22,400	2.5	2	3
28103	MS_ Noxubee County	12,548	12,116	-3.4	2	7
28105	MS_ Oktibbeha County	42,902	41,242	-3.8	8	5
28107	MS_ Panola County	34,274	35,248	2.8	2	3
28109	MS_ Pearl River County	48,621	53,237	9.4	3	2
28111	MS_ Perry County	12,138	12,003	-1.1	2	3
28113	MS_ Pike County	38,940	39,416	1.2	2	3
28115	MS_ Pontotoc County	26,726	28,531	6.7	3	2
28117	MS_ Prentiss County	25,556	25,593	0.1	3	10
28119	MS_ Quitman County	10,117	9,373	-7.3	2	3
28121	MS_ Rankin County	115,327	134,760	16.8	8	3
28123	MS_ Scott County	28,423	28,710	1.0	2	3
28125	MS_ Sharkey County	6,580	5,857	-10.9	2	4
28127	MS_ Simpson County	27,639	28,083	1.6	2	3
28129	MS_ Smith County	16,182	16,061	-0.7	3	2
28131	MS_ Stone County	13,622	15,263	12.0	2	3
28133	MS_ Sunflower County	34,369	31,425	-8.5	2	3
28135	MS_ Tallahatchie County	14,903	14,009	-6.0	2	3
28137	MS_ Tate County	25,370	26,778	5.5	2	3
28139	MS_ Tippah County	20,826	21,269	2.1	3	2
28141	MS_ Tishomingo County	19,163	19,195	0.1	3	2
28143	MS_ Tunica County	9,227	10,448	13.2	2	8
28145	MS_ Union County	25,362	27,091	6.8	3	2
28147	MS_ Walthall County	15,156	15,491	2.2	2	3
28149	MS_ Warren County	49,644	48,899	-1.5	2	3
28151	MS_ Washington County	62,977	58,606	-6.9	2	3
28153	MS_ Wayne County	21,216	21,186	-0.1	2	4
28155	MS_ Webster County	10,294	10,004	-2.8	3	2
28157	MS_ Wilkinson County	10,312	10,144	-1.6	2	3
28159	MS_ Winston County	20,160	19,745	-2.0	2	3

fips	county	totpop00	totpop06	chpop	Cat.10_1	Cat.10_2
28161	MS_ Yalobusha County	13,051	13,436	2.9	2	3
28163	MS_ Yazoo County	28,149	27,834	-1.1	2	3
29001	MO_ Adair County	24,977	24,354	-2.4	9	5
29003	MO_ Andrew County	16,492	16,882	2.3	12	1
29005	MO_ Atchison County	6,430	6,207	-3.4	10	9
29007	MO_ Audrain County	25,853	25,626	-0.8	3	10
29009	MO_ Barry County	34,010	35,989	5.8	3	8
29011	MO_ Barton County	12,541	13,063	4.1	3	10
29013	MO_ Bates County	16,653	16,976	1.9	3	10
29015	MO_ Benton County	17,180	19,119	11.2	3	4
29017	MO_ Bollinger County	12,029	12,393	3.0	3	10
29019	MO_ Boone County	135,454	145,066	7.1	8	5
29021	MO_ Buchanan County	85,998	85,061	-1.0	9	3
29023	MO_ Butler County	40,867	41,615	1.8	9	10
29025	MO_ Caldwell County	8,969	9,290	3.5	3	10
29027	MO_ Callaway County	40,766	42,684	4.7	8	3
29029	MO_ Camden County	37,051	39,951	7.8	1	10
29031	MO_ Cape Girardeau County	68,693	71,846	4.5	8	9
29033	MO_ Carroll County	10,285	10,200	-0.8	3	10
29035	MO_ Carter County	5,941	5,891	-0.8	9	2
29037	MO_ Cass County	82,092	96,162	17.1	8	3
29039	MO_ Cedar County	13,733	14,241	3.7	3	10
29041	MO_ Chariton County	8,438	8,036	-4.7	4	10
29043	MO_ Christian County	54,285	70,238	29.3	3	8
29045	MO_ Clark County	7,416	7,293	-1.6	10	4
29047	MO_ Clay County	184,006	205,728	11.8	1	8
29049	MO_ Clinton County	18,979	20,963	10.4	9	3
29051	MO_ Cole County	71,397	72,904	2.1	9	3
29053	MO_ Cooper County	16,670	17,327	3.9	9	10
29055	MO_ Crawford County	22,804	23,984	5.1	9	10
29057	MO_ Dade County	7,923	7,835	-1.1	3	10
29059	MO_ Dallas County	15,661	16,556	5.7	3	10
29061	MO_ Daviess County	8,016	8,053	0.4	3	4
29063	MO_ DeKalb County	11,597	12,068	4.0	9	3
29065	MO_ Dent County	14,927	15,210	1.9	3	10
29067	MO_ Douglas County	13,084	13,671	4.4	3	2
29069	MO_ Dunklin County	33,155	32,528	-1.8	3	10
29071	MO_ Franklin County	93,807	99,934	6.5	1	9
29073	MO_ Gasconade County	15,342	15,831	3.1	3	10
29075	MO_ Gentry County	6,861	6,519	-4.9	9	4
29077	MO_ Greene County	240,391	253,413	5.4	8	5
29079	MO_ Grundy County	10,432	10,350	-0.7	3	4
29081	MO_ Harrison County	8,850	8,917	0.7	3	4
29083	MO_ Henry County	21,997	22,630	2.8	3	10
29085	MO_ Hickory County	8,940	9,386	4.9	3	10
29087	MO_ Holt County	5,351	5,043	-5.7	4	9
29089	MO_ Howard County	10,212	9,983	-2.2	4	9
29091	MO_ Howell County	37,238	38,887	4.4	3	10
29093	MO_ Iron County	10,697	10,274	-3.9	9	10
29095	MO_ Jackson County	654,880	661,628	1.0	7	1
29097	MO_ Jasper County	104,686	111,768	6.7	8	10

fips	county	totpop00	totpop06	chpop	Cat.10_1	Cat.10_2
29099	MO_ Jefferson County	198,099	216,507	9.2	1	3
29101	MO_ Johnson County	48,258	51,025	5.7	8	5
29103	MO_ Knox County	4,361	4,099	-6.0	3	10
29105	MO_ Laclede County	32,513	35,109	7.9	3	10
29107	MO_ Lafayette County	32,960	33,153	0.5	9	3
29109	MO_ Lawrence County	35,204	37,388	6.2	3	10
29111	MO_ Lewis County	10,494	10,120	-3.5	3	4
29113	MO_ Lincoln County	38,944	49,637	27.4	8	3
29115	MO_ Linn County	13,754	12,926	-6.0	3	10
29117	MO_ Livingston County	14,558	14,258	-2.0	9	3
29119	MO_ McDonald County	21,681	23,243	7.2	3	10
29121	MO_ Macon County	15,762	15,660	-0.6	3	4
29123	MO_ Madison County	11,800	12,242	3.7	3	10
29125	MO_ Maries County	8,903	9,099	2.2	3	10
29127	MO_ Marion County	28,289	28,465	0.6	9	3
29129	MO_ Mercer County	3,757	3,569	-5.0	3	10
29131	MO_ Miller County	23,564	24,887	5.6	9	10
29133	MO_ Mississippi County	13,427	13,786	2.6	9	10
29135	MO_ Moniteau County	14,827	15,127	2.0	3	10
29137	MO_ Monroe County	9,311	9,346	0.3	9	4
29139	MO_ Montgomery County	12,136	12,172	0.3	9	10
29141	MO_ Morgan County	19,309	20,647	6.9	3	10
29143	MO_ New Madrid County	19,760	18,310	-7.3	9	3
29145	MO_ Newton County	52,636	56,147	6.6	3	10
29147	MO_ Nodaway County	21,912	21,702	-0.9	8	5
29149	MO_ Oregon County	10,344	10,408	0.6	3	4
29151	MO_ Osage County	13,062	13,522	3.5	9	6
29153	MO_ Ozark County	9,542	9,439	-1.0	3	10
29155	MO_ Pemiscot County	20,047	19,230	-4.0	3	2
29157	MO_ Perry County	18,132	18,651	2.8	9	10
29159	MO_ Pettis County	39,403	40,456	2.6	3	6
29161	MO_ Phelps County	39,825	42,469	6.6	8	9
29163	MO_ Pike County	18,351	18,847	2.7	9	10
29165	MO_ Platte County	73,781	83,346	12.9	8	3
29167	MO_ Polk County	26,992	29,445	9.0	3	10
29169	MO_ Pulaski County	41,165	43,717	6.2	3	8
29171	MO_ Putnam County	5,223	5,182	-0.7	3	10
29173	MO_ Ralls County	9,626	9,915	3.0	9	3
29175	MO_ Randolph County	24,663	25,511	3.4	3	10
29177	MO_ Ray County	23,354	24,052	2.9	1	8
29179	MO_ Reynolds County	6,689	6,555	-2.0	9	4
29181	MO_ Ripley County	13,509	13,917	3.0	9	10
29183	MO_ St. Charles County	283,883	338,502	19.2	8	1
29185	MO_ St. Clair County	9,652	9,704	0.5	3	10
29186	MO_ Ste. Genevieve County	17,842	18,163	1.8	9	3
29187	MO_ St. Francois County	55,641	63,136	13.4	9	10
29189	MO_ St. Louis County	1,016,315	998,645	-1.7	1	7
29195	MO_ Saline County	23,756	23,227	-2.2	3	10
29197	MO_ Schuyler County	4,170	4,309	3.3	3	10
29199	MO_ Scotland County	4,983	4,928	-1.1	3	10
29201	MO_ Scott County	40,422	41,251	2.0	9	10

fips	county	totpop00	totpop06	chpop	Cat.10_1	Cat.10_2
29203	MO_ Shannon County	8,324	8,422	1.1	3	4
29205	MO_ Shelby County	6,799	6,771	-0.4	3	4
29207	MO_ Stoddard County	29,705	29,681	0.0	10	3
29209	MO_ Stone County	28,658	31,160	8.7	1	3
29211	MO_ Sullivan County	7,219	6,761	-6.3	3	4
29213	MO_ Taney County	39,703	43,737	10.1	1	8
29215	MO_ Texas County	23,003	24,788	7.7	3	10
29217	MO_ Vernon County	20,454	20,530	0.3	4	10
29219	MO_ Warren County	24,525	29,704	21.1	8	3
29221	MO_ Washington County	23,344	24,156	3.4	9	5
29223	MO_ Wayne County	13,259	13,224	-0.2	9	10
29225	MO_ Webster County	31,045	35,491	14.3	3	10
29227	MO_ Worth County	2,382	2,131	-10.5	3	4
29229	MO_ Wright County	17,955	18,344	2.1	3	10
29510	MO_ St. Louis County	348,189	348,344	0.0	7	6
30001	MT_ Beaverhead County	9,202	8,666	-5.8	4	9
30003	MT_ Big Horn County	12,671	13,215	4.2	2	9
30005	MT_ Blaine County	7,009	6,546	-6.6	4	9
30007	MT_ Broadwater County	4,385	4,526	3.2	4	10
30009	MT_ Carbon County	9,552	9,925	3.9	4	10
30011	MT_ Carter County	1,360	1,306	-3.9	4	9
30013	MT_ Cascade County	80,357	78,775	-1.9	4	5
30015	MT_ Chouteau County	5,970	5,396	-9.6	4	9
30017	MT_ Custer County	11,696	11,110	-5.0	4	9
30019	MT_ Daniels County	2,017	1,805	-10.5	4	9
30021	MT_ Dawson County	9,059	8,618	-4.8	4	9
30023	MT_ Deer Lodge County	9,417	8,945	-5.0	9	4
30025	MT_ Fallon County	2,837	2,663	-6.1	4	9
30027	MT_ Fergus County	11,893	11,396	-4.1	4	9
30029	MT_ Flathead County	74,471	84,581	13.5	1	8
30031	MT_ Gallatin County	67,831	80,667	18.9	8	5
30033	MT_ Garfield County	1,279	1,179	-7.8	4	10
30035	MT_ Glacier County	13,247	13,626	2.8	2	6
30037	MT_ Golden Valley County	1,042	1,184	13.6	4	10
30039	MT_ Granite County	2,830	2,970	4.9	4	10
30041	MT_ Hill County	16,673	16,219	-2.7	4	5
30043	MT_ Jefferson County	10,049	11,390	13.3	1	8
30045	MT_ Judith Basin County	2,329	2,160	-7.2	4	10
30047	MT_ Lake County	26,507	28,658	8.1	4	9
30049	MT_ Lewis and Clark County	55,716	58,696	5.3	9	10
30051	MT_ Liberty County	2,158	1,951	-9.5	4	9
30053	MT_ Lincoln County	18,837	19,286	2.3	9	4
30055	MT_ McCone County	1,977	1,776	-10.1	4	9
30057	MT_ Madison County	6,851	7,418	8.2	4	10
30059	MT_ Meagher County	1,932	1,972	2.0	4	10
30061	MT_ Mineral County	3,884	4,110	5.8	9	8
30063	MT_ Missoula County	95,802	100,275	4.6	8	9
30065	MT_ Musselshell County	4,497	4,464	-0.7	4	10
30067	MT_ Park County	15,694	16,001	1.9	4	10
30069	MT_ Petroleum County	493	444	-9.9	3	9
30071	MT_ Phillips County	4,601	4,088	-11.1	4	9

fips	county	totpop00	totpop06	chpop	Cat.10_1	Cat.10_2
30073	MT_ Pondera County	6,424	6,075	-5.4	4	9
30075	MT_ Powder River County	1,858	1,647	-11.3	4	9
30077	MT_ Powell County	7,180	6,988	-2.6	4	9
30079	MT_ Prairie County	1,199	1,056	-11.9	4	9
30081	MT_ Ravalli County	36,070	40,160	11.3	8	10
30083	MT_ Richland County	9,667	9,107	-5.7	4	9
30085	MT_ Roosevelt County	10,620	10,619	0.0	2	9
30087	MT_ Rosebud County	9,383	9,183	-2.1	2	9
30089	MT_ Sanders County	10,227	11,257	10.0	4	10
30091	MT_ Sheridan County	4,105	3,435	-16.3	4	9
30093	MT_ Silver Bow County	34,606	32,728	-5.4	9	5
30095	MT_ Stillwater County	8,195	8,452	3.1	4	9
30097	MT_ Sweet Grass County	3,609	3,697	2.4	4	10
30099	MT_ Teton County	6,445	6,104	-5.2	4	9
30101	MT_ Toole County	5,267	4,937	-6.2	4	9
30103	MT_ Treasure County	861	660	-23.3	4	10
30105	MT_ Valley County	7,675	7,039	-8.2	4	9
30107	MT_ Wheatland County	2,259	1,982	-12.2	4	9
30109	MT_ Wibaux County	1,068	930	-12.9	4	9
30111	MT_ Yellowstone County	129,352	137,479	6.2	9	8
31001	NE_ Adams County	31,151	33,445	7.3	9	10
31003	NE_ Antelope County	7,452	6,914	-7.2	4	9
31005	NE_ Arthur County	444	361	-18.6	4	9
31007	NE_ Banner County	819	740	-9.6	4	10
31009	NE_ Blaine County	583	457	-21.6	9	6
31011	NE_ Boone County	6,259	5,686	-9.1	4	9
31013	NE_ Box Butte County	12,158	11,177	-8.0	9	3
31015	NE_ Boyd County	2,438	2,236	-8.2	4	9
31017	NE_ Brown County	3,525	3,244	-7.9	4	10
31019	NE_ Buffalo County	42,259	43,754	3.5	8	5
31021	NE_ Burt County	7,791	7,375	-5.3	10	4
31023	NE_ Butler County	8,767	8,556	-2.4	9	10
31025	NE_ Cass County	24,334	25,997	6.8	9	3
31027	NE_ Cedar County	9,615	8,953	-6.8	4	9
31029	NE_ Chase County	4,068	3,788	-6.8	4	9
31031	NE_ Cherry County	6,148	6,077	-1.1	4	9
31033	NE_ Cheyenne County	9,830	10,030	2.0	9	4
31035	NE_ Clay County	7,039	6,609	-6.1	10	9
31037	NE_ Colfax County	10,441	10,192	-2.3	4	6
31039	NE_ Cuming County	10,203	9,597	-5.9	10	4
31041	NE_ Custer County	11,793	11,297	-4.2	4	9
31043	NE_ Dakota County	20,253	20,132	-0.6	8	6
31045	NE_ Dawes County	9,060	8,436	-6.8	9	5
31047	NE_ Dawson County	24,365	24,615	1.0	6	4
31049	NE_ Deuel County	2,098	1,967	-6.2	4	9
31051	NE_ Dixon County	6,339	6,193	-2.3	10	4
31053	NE_ Dodge County	36,160	36,071	-0.2	10	9
31055	NE_ Douglas County	463,585	492,159	6.1	8	7
31057	NE_ Dundy County	2,292	2,096	-8.5	4	9
31059	NE_ Fillmore County	6,634	6,295	-5.1	4	9
31061	NE_ Franklin County	3,574	3,395	-5.0	4	9

fips	county	totpop00	totpop06	chpop	Cat.10_1	Cat.10_2
31063	NE_ Frontier County	3,099	2,711	-12.5	4	9
31065	NE_ Furnas County	5,324	4,917	-7.6	4	9
31067	NE_ Gage County	22,993	23,153	0.7	10	4
31069	NE_ Garden County	2,292	1,889	-17.5	4	9
31071	NE_ Garfield County	1,902	1,801	-5.3	4	10
31073	NE_ Gosper County	2,143	1,989	-7.1	10	4
31075	NE_ Grant County	747	655	-12.3	4	10
31077	NE_ Greeley County	2,714	2,431	-10.4	4	9
31079	NE_ Hall County	53,534	55,267	3.2	6	9
31081	NE_ Hamilton County	9,403	9,564	1.7	4	9
31083	NE_ Harlan County	3,786	3,385	-10.5	4	9
31085	NE_ Hayes County	1,068	1,003	-6.0	3	4
31087	NE_ Hitchcock County	3,111	2,908	-6.5	4	9
31089	NE_ Holt County	11,551	10,650	-7.8	4	9
31091	NE_ Hooker County	783	747	-4.6	4	9
31093	NE_ Howard County	6,567	6,700	2.0	4	9
31095	NE_ Jefferson County	8,333	7,811	-6.2	10	4
31097	NE_ Johnson County	4,488	4,751	5.8	10	4
31099	NE_ Kearney County	6,882	6,717	-2.4	10	9
31101	NE_ Keith County	8,875	8,224	-7.3	9	4
31103	NE_ Keya Paha County	983	876	-10.8	3	4
31105	NE_ Kimball County	4,089	3,735	-8.6	10	4
31107	NE_ Knox County	9,374	8,751	-6.6	4	9
31109	NE_ Lancaster County	250,291	266,561	6.5	8	1
31111	NE_ Lincoln County	34,632	36,075	4.1	9	4
31113	NE_ Logan County	774	755	-2.4	4	10
31115	NE_ Loup County	712	649	-8.8	3	4
31117	NE_ McPherson County	533	489	-8.2	3	9
31119	NE_ Madison County	35,226	35,199	0.0	6	9
31121	NE_ Merrick County	8,204	7,990	-2.6	4	9
31123	NE_ Morrill County	5,440	5,122	-5.8	4	10
31125	NE_ Nance County	4,038	3,667	-9.1	4	9
31127	NE_ Nemaha County	7,576	7,023	-7.3	4	9
31129	NE_ Nuckolls County	5,057	4,690	-7.2	4	10
31131	NE_ Otoe County	15,396	15,521	0.8	10	9
31133	NE_ Pawnee County	3,087	2,845	-7.8	4	9
31135	NE_ Perkins County	3,200	3,078	-3.8	4	9
31137	NE_ Phelps County	9,747	9,351	-4.0	10	4
31139	NE_ Pierce County	7,857	7,624	-2.9	10	4
31141	NE_ Platte County	31,662	31,555	-0.3	6	9
31143	NE_ Polk County	5,639	5,365	-4.8	10	9
31145	NE_ Red Willow County	11,448	10,944	-4.4	9	4
31147	NE_ Richardson County	9,531	8,652	-9.2	4	9
31149	NE_ Rock County	1,756	1,526	-13.1	4	9
31151	NE_ Saline County	13,843	14,168	2.3	6	10
31153	NE_ Sarpy County	122,595	142,583	16.3	8	11
31155	NE_ Saunders County	19,830	20,670	4.2	9	4
31157	NE_ Scotts Bluff County	36,951	36,694	-0.7	4	10
31159	NE_ Seward County	16,496	16,777	1.7	9	5
31161	NE_ Sheridan County	6,198	5,524	-10.8	4	9
31163	NE_ Sherman County	3,318	3,088	-6.9	4	10

fips	county	totpop00	totpop06	chpop	Cat.10_1	Cat.10_2
31165	NE_ Sioux County	1,475	1,431	-2.9	4	10
31167	NE_ Stanton County	6,455	6,496	0.6	10	4
31169	NE_ Thayer County	6,055	5,375	-11.2	4	9
31171	NE_ Thomas County	729	611	-16.1	4	9
31173	NE_ Thurston County	7,171	7,437	3.7	4	6
31175	NE_ Valley County	4,647	4,320	-7.0	4	9
31177	NE_ Washington County	18,780	19,936	6.1	1	8
31179	NE_ Wayne County	9,851	9,196	-6.6	8	5
31181	NE_ Webster County	4,061	3,719	-8.4	4	10
31183	NE_ Wheeler County	886	818	-7.6	4	9
31185	NE_ York County	14,598	14,425	-1.1	4	9
32001	NV_ Churchill County	23,982	24,910	3.8	4	8
32003	NV_ Clark County	1,375,765	1,768,566	28.5	8	7
32005	NV_ Douglas County	41,259	47,256	14.5	8	1
32007	NV_ Elko County	45,291	46,425	2.5	6	9
32009	NV_ Esmeralda County	971	781	-19.5	11	4
32011	NV_ Eureka County	1,651	1,393	-15.6	6	2
32013	NV_ Humboldt County	16,106	17,406	8.0	6	3
32015	NV_ Lander County	5,794	5,189	-10.4	4	3
32017	NV_ Lincoln County	4,165	4,571	9.7	12	8
32019	NV_ Lyon County	34,501	51,512	49.3	8	3
32021	NV_ Mineral County	5,071	4,975	-1.8	2	10
32023	NV_ Nye County	32,485	43,210	33.0	8	4
32027	NV_ Pershing County	6,693	6,360	-4.9	6	9
32029	NV_ Storey County	3,399	4,381	28.8	1	10
32031	NV_ Washoe County	339,486	397,412	17.0	8	7
32033	NV_ White Pine County	9,181	9,296	1.2	9	4
32510	NV_ Carson City	52,457	55,929	6.6	1	8
33001	NH_ Belknap County	56,325	62,325	10.6	1	9
33003	NH_ Carroll County	43,666	48,009	9.9	1	10
33005	NH_ Cheshire County	73,825	78,169	5.8	5	9
33007	NH_ Coos County	33,111	34,013	2.7	9	10
33009	NH_ Grafton County	81,743	86,135	5.3	5	9
33011	NH_ Hillsborough County	380,841	406,181	6.6	1	8
33013	NH_ Merrimack County	136,225	149,025	9.4	9	8
33015	NH_ Rockingham County	277,359	298,275	7.5	1	5
33017	NH_ Strafford County	112,233	120,612	7.4	8	5
33019	NH_ Sullivan County	40,458	43,503	7.5	9	10
34001	NJ_ Atlantic County	252,552	276,146	9.3	7	3
34003	NJ_ Bergen County	884,118	909,074	2.8	1	7
34005	NJ_ Burlington County	423,394	454,534	7.3	1	7
34007	NJ_ Camden County	508,932	523,051	2.7	7	1
34009	NJ_ Cape May County	102,326	98,192	-4.0	9	1
34011	NJ_ Cumberland County	146,438	156,181	6.6	2	5
34013	NJ_ Essex County	793,633	791,428	-0.2	7	1
34015	NJ_ Gloucester County	254,673	282,236	10.8	1	9
34017	NJ_ Hudson County	608,975	605,178	-0.6	7	6
34019	NJ_ Hunterdon County	121,989	131,899	8.1	1	7
34021	NJ_ Mercer County	350,761	371,164	5.8	1	7
34023	NJ_ Middlesex County	750,162	800,080	6.6	7	1
34025	NJ_ Monmouth County	615,301	639,434	3.9	1	7

fips	county	totpop00	totpop06	chpop	Cat.10_1	Cat.10_2
34027	NJ_ Morris County	470,212	496,000	5.4	1	7
34029	NJ_ Ocean County	510,916	563,900	10.3	9	1
34031	NJ_ Passaic County	489,049	501,450	2.5	7	1
34033	NJ_ Salem County	64,285	67,370	4.8	1	9
34035	NJ_ Somerset County	297,490	325,172	9.3	1	7
34037	NJ_ Sussex County	144,166	154,674	7.2	1	5
34039	NJ_ Union County	522,541	534,476	2.2	7	1
34041	NJ_ Warren County	102,437	111,530	8.8	1	5
35001	NM_ Bernalillo County	556,678	613,009	10.1	6	7
35003	NM_ Catron County	3,543	3,362	-5.1	4	10
35005	NM_ Chaves County	61,382	62,091	1.1	6	9
35006	NM_ Cibola County	25,595	27,801	8.6	6	2
35007	NM_ Colfax County	14,189	13,563	-4.4	6	9
35009	NM_ Curry County	45,044	45,672	1.3	8	6
35011	NM_ DeBaca County	2,240	1,997	-10.8	6	9
35013	NM_ Dona Ana County	174,682	192,588	10.2	6	5
35015	NM_ Eddy County	51,658	50,986	-1.3	6	9
35017	NM_ Grant County	31,002	29,652	-4.3	6	5
35019	NM_ Guadalupe County	4,680	4,259	-9.0	6	9
35021	NM_ Harding County	810	729	-10.0	6	10
35023	NM_ Hidalgo County	5,932	5,077	-14.4	6	2
35025	NM_ Lea County	55,511	56,790	2.3	6	9
35027	NM_ Lincoln County	19,411	21,276	9.6	6	10
35028	NM_ Los Alamos County	18,343	18,783	2.4	1	5
35029	NM_ Luna County	25,016	27,019	8.0	6	10
35031	NM_ McKinley County	74,798	72,128	-3.5	2	5
35033	NM_ Mora County	5,180	5,070	-2.1	6	10
35035	NM_ Otero County	62,298	63,412	1.7	6	10
35037	NM_ Quay County	10,155	9,071	-10.6	6	4
35039	NM_ Rio Arriba County	41,190	40,643	-1.3	6	9
35041	NM_ Roosevelt County	18,018	18,157	0.7	8	6
35043	NM_ Sandoval County	89,908	111,548	24.0	8	1
35045	NM_ San Juan County	113,801	127,618	12.1	2	8
35047	NM_ San Miguel County	30,126	29,423	-2.3	6	9
35049	NM_ Santa Fe County	129,292	141,925	9.7	1	6
35051	NM_ Sierra County	13,270	12,638	-4.7	6	10
35053	NM_ Socorro County	18,078	18,195	0.6	6	5
35055	NM_ Taos County	29,979	31,761	5.9	6	9
35057	NM_ Torrance County	16,911	17,534	3.6	6	9
35059	NM_ Union County	4,174	3,837	-8.0	4	6
35061	NM_ Valencia County	66,152	69,516	5.0	6	10
36001	NY_ Albany County	294,565	298,515	1.3	7	1
36003	NY_ Allegany County	49,927	50,582	1.3	5	11
36005	NY_ Bronx County	1,332,650	1,358,507	1.9	7	6
36007	NY_ Broome County	200,536	196,280	-2.1	9	5
36009	NY_ Cattaraugus County	83,955	82,157	-2.1	9	10
36011	NY_ Cayuga County	81,963	81,671	-0.3	9	5
36013	NY_ Chautauqua County	139,750	136,069	-2.6	9	10
36015	NY_ Chemung County	91,070	88,951	-2.3	9	5
36017	NY_ Chenango County	51,401	52,004	1.1	9	10
36019	NY_ Clinton County	79,894	82,754	3.5	9	5

fips	county	totpop00	totpop06	chpop	Cat.10_1	Cat.10_2
36021	NY_ Columbia County	63,094	63,819	1.1	10	9
36023	NY_ Cortland County	48,599	48,629	0.0	8	5
36025	NY_ Delaware County	48,055	47,789	-0.5	9	10
36027	NY_ Dutchess County	280,150	297,631	6.2	1	9
36029	NY_ Erie County	950,265	928,091	-2.3	7	1
36031	NY_ Essex County	38,851	38,581	-0.6	9	10
36033	NY_ Franklin County	51,134	51,239	0.2	9	11
36035	NY_ Fulton County	55,073	55,920	1.5	9	10
36037	NY_ Genesee County	60,370	59,145	-2.0	9	5
36039	NY_ Greene County	48,195	50,275	4.3	9	10
36041	NY_ Hamilton County	5,379	5,214	-3.0	9	6
36043	NY_ Herkimer County	64,427	64,047	-0.5	9	4
36045	NY_ Jefferson County	111,738	117,350	5.0	11	8
36047	NY_ Kings County	2,465,326	2,515,470	2.0	7	6
36049	NY_ Lewis County	26,944	26,726	-0.8	9	6
36051	NY_ Livingston County	64,328	64,363	0.0	9	5
36053	NY_ Madison County	69,441	70,427	1.4	9	5
36055	NY_ Monroe County	735,343	733,565	-0.2	7	1
36057	NY_ Montgomery County	49,708	49,089	-1.2	10	9
36059	NY_ Nassau County	1,334,544	1,332,947	-0.1	1	7
36061	NY_ New York County	1,537,195	1,619,217	5.3	7	1
36063	NY_ Niagara County	219,846	217,264	-1.1	9	7
36065	NY_ Oneida County	235,469	234,550	-0.3	9	5
36067	NY_ Onondaga County	458,336	458,940	0.1	7	5
36069	NY_ Ontario County	100,224	105,735	5.5	1	5
36071	NY_ Orange County	341,367	377,540	10.6	1	9
36073	NY_ Orleans County	44,171	43,386	-1.7	9	5
36075	NY_ Oswego County	122,377	123,722	1.1	9	5
36077	NY_ Otsego County	61,676	63,247	2.5	9	5
36079	NY_ Putnam County	95,745	101,121	5.6	1	5
36081	NY_ Queens County	2,229,379	2,257,888	1.2	7	6
36083	NY_ Rensselaer County	152,538	156,446	2.5	9	5
36085	NY_ Richmond County	443,728	470,001	5.9	6	7
36087	NY_ Rockland County	286,753	293,038	2.1	1	7
36089	NY_ St. Lawrence County	111,931	112,064	0.1	9	5
36091	NY_ Saratoga County	200,635	217,562	8.4	1	8
36093	NY_ Schenectady County	146,555	150,522	2.7	9	5
36095	NY_ Schoharie County	31,582	32,596	3.2	9	10
36097	NY_ Schuyler County	19,224	19,372	0.7	9	10
36099	NY_ Seneca County	33,342	34,810	4.4	9	10
36101	NY_ Steuben County	98,726	98,577	-0.1	9	5
36103	NY_ Suffolk County	1,419,369	1,478,469	4.1	1	7
36105	NY_ Sullivan County	73,966	77,410	4.6	9	5
36107	NY_ Tioga County	51,784	51,429	-0.6	9	5
36109	NY_ Tompkins County	96,501	100,640	4.2	5	1
36111	NY_ Ulster County	177,749	183,729	3.3	9	5
36113	NY_ Warren County	63,303	66,331	4.7	9	5
36115	NY_ Washington County	61,042	63,823	4.5	9	10
36117	NY_ Wayne County	93,765	93,623	-0.1	10	9
36119	NY_ Westchester County	923,459	944,303	2.2	1	7
36121	NY_ Wyoming County	43,424	42,749	-1.5	9	3

fips	county	totpop00	totpop06	chpop	Cat.10_1	Cat.10_2
36123	NY_ Yates County	24,621	24,986	1.4	10	9
37001	NC_ Alamance County	130,800	141,773	8.3	1	3
37003	NC_ Alexander County	33,603	35,962	7.0	3	2
37005	NC_ Alleghany County	10,677	10,830	1.4	9	10
37007	NC_ Anson County	25,275	25,746	1.8	2	3
37009	NC_ Ashe County	24,384	25,330	3.8	3	10
37011	NC_ Avery County	17,167	17,580	2.4	9	2
37013	NC_ Beaufort County	44,958	46,128	2.6	2	5
37015	NC_ Bertie County	19,773	19,343	-2.1	2	4
37017	NC_ Bladen County	32,278	33,057	2.4	2	3
37019	NC_ Brunswick County	73,143	93,238	27.4	8	10
37021	NC_ Buncombe County	206,330	220,685	6.9	3	5
37023	NC_ Burke County	89,148	89,242	0.1	3	2
37025	NC_ Cabarrus County	131,063	153,121	16.8	1	8
37027	NC_ Caldwell County	77,415	79,109	2.1	3	10
37029	NC_ Camden County	6,885	9,582	39.1	1	3
37031	NC_ Carteret County	59,383	63,248	6.5	1	3
37033	NC_ Caswell County	23,501	23,380	-0.5	2	3
37035	NC_ Catawba County	141,685	153,189	8.1	1	3
37037	NC_ Chatham County	49,329	59,048	19.7	1	3
37039	NC_ Cherokee County	24,298	26,115	7.4	3	4
37041	NC_ Chowan County	14,526	14,606	0.5	2	3
37043	NC_ Clay County	8,775	9,988	13.8	1	10
37045	NC_ Cleveland County	96,287	97,963	1.7	3	2
37047	NC_ Columbus County	54,749	54,536	-0.3	2	3
37049	NC_ Craven County	91,436	91,084	-0.3	8	9
37051	NC_ Cumberland County	302,963	297,200	-1.9	11	7
37053	NC_ Currituck County	18,190	24,278	33.4	8	10
37055	NC_ Dare County	29,967	33,768	12.6	8	9
37057	NC_ Davidson County	147,246	155,124	5.3	1	2
37059	NC_ Davie County	34,835	39,949	14.6	1	3
37061	NC_ Duplin County	49,063	52,102	6.1	6	2
37063	NC_ Durham County	223,314	244,942	9.6	8	5
37065	NC_ Edgecombe County	55,606	53,771	-3.3	2	3
37067	NC_ Forsyth County	306,067	329,689	7.7	1	7
37069	NC_ Franklin County	47,260	55,522	17.4	8	3
37071	NC_ Gaston County	190,365	197,518	3.7	3	5
37073	NC_ Gates County	10,516	11,478	9.1	2	3
37075	NC_ Graham County	7,993	7,992	0.0	9	2
37077	NC_ Granville County	48,498	53,805	10.9	2	3
37079	NC_ Greene County	18,974	20,040	5.6	2	6
37081	NC_ Guilford County	421,048	448,028	6.4	8	7
37083	NC_ Halifax County	57,370	55,565	-3.1	2	5
37085	NC_ Harnett County	91,025	105,832	16.2	11	8
37087	NC_ Haywood County	54,033	56,280	4.1	3	10
37089	NC_ Henderson County	89,173	98,527	10.4	3	10
37091	NC_ Hertford County	22,601	23,435	3.6	2	6
37093	NC_ Hoke County	33,646	42,770	27.1	8	2
37095	NC_ Hyde County	5,826	5,356	-8.0	9	6
37097	NC_ Iredell County	122,660	144,103	17.4	1	8
37099	NC_ Jackson County	33,121	35,489	7.1	9	5

fips	county	totpop00	totpop06	chpop	Cat.10_1	Cat.10_2
37101	NC_ Johnston County	121,965	150,557	23.4	8	3
37103	NC_ Jones County	10,381	10,318	-0.6	2	6
37105	NC_ Lee County	49,040	56,878	15.9	6	10
37107	NC_ Lenoir County	59,648	57,644	-3.3	2	5
37109	NC_ Lincoln County	63,780	70,989	11.3	1	3
37111	NC_ McDowell County	42,151	43,216	2.5	3	2
37113	NC_ Macon County	29,811	32,346	8.5	3	10
37115	NC_ Madison County	19,635	20,300	3.3	3	10
37117	NC_ Martin County	25,593	24,339	-4.9	2	3
37119	NC_ Mecklenburg County	695,454	818,626	17.7	8	1
37121	NC_ Mitchell County	15,687	15,699	0.0	3	2
37123	NC_ Montgomery County	26,822	27,374	2.0	6	2
37125	NC_ Moore County	74,769	82,623	10.5	1	3
37127	NC_ Nash County	87,420	91,974	5.2	2	3
37129	NC_ New Hanover County	160,307	184,639	15.1	8	11
37131	NC_ Northampton County	22,086	21,326	-3.4	2	4
37133	NC_ Onslow County	150,355	148,980	-0.9	9	8
37135	NC_ Orange County	118,227	119,034	0.6	5	1
37137	NC_ Pamlico County	12,934	12,705	-1.7	11	2
37139	NC_ Pasquotank County	34,897	39,384	12.8	2	5
37141	NC_ Pender County	41,082	47,878	16.5	8	10
37143	NC_ Perquimans County	11,368	12,297	8.1	9	10
37145	NC_ Person County	35,623	37,273	4.6	3	2
37147	NC_ Pitt County	133,798	144,210	7.7	8	5
37149	NC_ Polk County	18,324	19,227	4.9	3	10
37151	NC_ Randolph County	130,454	139,511	6.9	6	3
37153	NC_ Richmond County	46,564	46,737	0.3	2	11
37155	NC_ Robeson County	123,339	128,925	4.5	2	6
37157	NC_ Rockingham County	91,928	92,375	0.4	9	3
37159	NC_ Rowan County	130,340	134,924	3.5	1	8
37161	NC_ Rutherford County	62,899	63,751	1.3	3	2
37163	NC_ Sampson County	60,161	63,469	5.5	2	3
37165	NC_ Scotland County	35,998	37,742	4.8	2	11
37167	NC_ Stanly County	58,100	59,005	1.5	3	2
37169	NC_ Stokes County	44,711	46,073	3.0	9	3
37171	NC_ Surry County	71,219	72,397	1.6	6	2
37173	NC_ Swain County	12,968	13,324	2.7	9	3
37175	NC_ Transylvania County	29,334	29,620	0.9	3	10
37177	NC_ Tyrrell County	4,149	4,113	-0.8	2	4
37179	NC_ Union County	123,677	171,950	39.0	8	11
37181	NC_ Vance County	42,954	43,638	1.5	2	3
37183	NC_ Wake County	627,846	775,316	23.4	8	1
37185	NC_ Warren County	19,972	19,709	-1.3	2	7
37187	NC_ Washington County	13,723	13,240	-3.5	2	4
37189	NC_ Watauga County	42,695	42,192	-1.1	8	5
37191	NC_ Wayne County	113,329	114,354	0.9	9	1
37193	NC_ Wilkes County	65,632	67,104	2.2	3	2
37195	NC_ Wilson County	73,814	76,521	3.6	2	3
37197	NC_ Yadkin County	36,348	37,713	3.7	9	3
37199	NC_ Yancey County	17,774	18,232	2.5	3	2
38001	ND_ Adams County	2,593	2,378	-8.2	4	9

fips	county	totpop00	totpop06	chpop	Cat.10_1	Cat.10_2
38003	ND_ Barnes County	11,775	11,003	-6.5	4	9
38005	ND_ Benson County	6,964	7,050	1.2	2	9
38007	ND_ Billings County	888	812	-8.5	4	9
38009	ND_ Bottineau County	7,149	6,691	-6.4	4	9
38011	ND_ Bowman County	3,242	2,999	-7.5	4	9
38013	ND_ Burke County	2,242	1,992	-11.1	4	9
38015	ND_ Burleigh County	69,416	74,730	7.6	1	9
38017	ND_ Cass County	123,138	132,030	7.2	8	1
38019	ND_ Cavalier County	4,831	4,203	-13.0	4	9
38021	ND_ Dickey County	5,757	5,431	-5.6	4	9
38023	ND_ Divide County	2,283	2,097	-8.1	4	9
38025	ND_ Dunn County	3,600	3,388	-5.8	4	9
38027	ND_ Eddy County	2,757	2,590	-6.0	4	9
38029	ND_ Emmons County	4,331	3,673	-15.1	4	9
38031	ND_ Foster County	3,759	3,591	-4.4	10	4
38033	ND_ Golden Valley County	1,924	1,686	-12.3	4	9
38035	ND_ Grand Forks County	66,109	65,537	-0.8	8	5
38037	ND_ Grant County	2,841	2,595	-8.6	4	9
38039	ND_ Griggs County	2,754	2,455	-10.8	4	9
38041	ND_ Hettinger County	2,715	2,475	-8.8	4	9
38043	ND_ Kidder County	2,753	2,403	-12.7	4	9
38045	ND_ LaMoure County	4,701	4,253	-9.5	4	9
38047	ND_ Logan County	2,308	2,009	-12.9	4	9
38049	ND_ McHenry County	5,987	5,367	-10.3	4	9
38051	ND_ McIntosh County	3,390	2,929	-13.6	4	9
38053	ND_ McKenzie County	5,737	5,616	-2.1	4	9
38055	ND_ McLean County	9,311	8,387	-9.9	4	9
38057	ND_ Mercer County	8,644	8,249	-4.5	4	9
38059	ND_ Morton County	25,303	25,532	0.9	4	9
38061	ND_ Mountrail County	6,631	6,506	-1.8	4	9
38063	ND_ Nelson County	3,715	3,419	-7.9	4	9
38065	ND_ Oliver County	2,065	1,767	-14.4	4	9
38067	ND_ Pembina County	8,585	7,867	-8.3	10	9
38069	ND_ Pierce County	4,675	4,163	-10.9	4	9
38071	ND_ Ramsey County	12,066	11,283	-6.4	9	4
38073	ND_ Ransom County	5,890	5,743	-2.5	10	4
38075	ND_ Renville County	2,610	2,392	-8.3	4	9
38077	ND_ Richland County	17,998	17,124	-4.8	8	9
38079	ND_ Rolette County	13,674	13,897	1.6	2	6
38081	ND_ Sargent County	4,366	4,133	-5.3	10	9
38083	ND_ Sheridan County	1,710	1,397	-18.3	4	9
38085	ND_ Sioux County	4,044	4,205	3.9	9	2
38087	ND_ Slope County	767	695	-9.3	4	9
38089	ND_ Stark County	22,636	21,987	-2.8	4	6
38091	ND_ Steele County	2,258	1,978	-12.4	4	9
38093	ND_ Stutsman County	21,908	20,602	-5.9	10	9
38095	ND_ Towner County	2,876	2,468	-14.1	4	9
38097	ND_ Traill County	8,477	8,317	-1.8	4	9
38099	ND_ Walsh County	12,389	11,472	-7.4	10	4
38101	ND_ Ward County	58,795	54,916	-6.6	11	5
38103	ND_ Wells County	5,102	4,472	-12.3	4	9

fips	county	totpop00	totpop06	chpop	Cat.10_1	Cat.10_2
38105	ND_ Williams County	19,761	19,172	-2.9	4	9
39001	OH_ Adams County	27,330	28,703	5.0	9	10
39003	OH_ Allen County	108,473	105,738	-2.5	9	5
39005	OH_ Ashland County	52,523	54,552	3.8	10	9
39007	OH_ Ashtabula County	102,728	103,365	0.6	9	10
39009	OH_ Athens County	62,223	61,642	-0.9	5	9
39011	OH_ Auglaize County	46,611	47,511	1.9	10	9
39013	OH_ Belmont County	70,226	69,064	-1.6	9	4
39015	OH_ Brown County	42,285	44,659	5.6	9	3
39017	OH_ Butler County	332,807	355,068	6.6	8	1
39019	OH_ Carroll County	28,836	29,223	1.3	9	10
39021	OH_ Champaign County	38,890	39,833	2.4	9	3
39023	OH_ Clark County	144,742	142,317	-1.6	9	8
39025	OH_ Clermont County	177,977	192,747	8.3	1	8
39027	OH_ Clinton County	40,543	43,036	6.1	9	8
39029	OH_ Columbiana County	112,075	110,520	-1.3	9	10
39031	OH_ Coshocton County	36,655	36,877	0.6	9	10
39033	OH_ Crawford County	46,966	45,530	-3.0	10	9
39035	OH_ Cuyahoga County	1,393,978	1,321,807	-5.1	7	1
39037	OH_ Darke County	53,309	52,986	-0.6	9	3
39039	OH_ Defiance County	39,500	39,073	-1.0	10	9
39041	OH_ Delaware County	109,989	157,424	43.1	1	8
39043	OH_ Erie County	79,551	78,530	-1.2	9	1
39045	OH_ Fairfield County	122,759	141,299	15.1	1	8
39047	OH_ Fayette County	28,433	28,389	-0.1	9	10
39049	OH_ Franklin County	1,068,978	1,094,849	2.4	7	1
39051	OH_ Fulton County	42,084	43,246	2.7	9	1
39053	OH_ Gallia County	31,069	31,435	1.1	9	10
39055	OH_ Geauga County	90,895	95,747	5.3	1	9
39057	OH_ Greene County	147,886	152,511	3.1	8	5
39059	OH_ Guernsey County	40,792	41,005	0.5	9	4
39061	OH_ Hamilton County	845,303	803,900	-4.9	7	1
39063	OH_ Hancock County	71,295	73,729	3.4	5	9
39065	OH_ Hardin County	31,945	32,296	1.1	5	9
39067	OH_ Harrison County	15,856	15,975	0.7	9	10
39069	OH_ Henry County	29,210	29,506	1.0	10	9
39071	OH_ Highland County	40,875	42,907	4.9	9	10
39073	OH_ Hocking County	28,241	29,084	2.9	9	10
39075	OH_ Holmes County	38,943	41,605	6.8	3	4
39077	OH_ Huron County	59,487	60,472	1.6	9	10
39079	OH_ Jackson County	32,641	33,798	3.5	9	10
39081	OH_ Jefferson County	73,894	70,358	-4.7	9	10
39083	OH_ Knox County	54,500	59,090	8.4	9	10
39085	OH_ Lake County	227,511	233,316	2.5	1	10
39087	OH_ Lawrence County	62,319	63,748	2.2	9	10
39089	OH_ Licking County	145,491	156,957	7.8	1	10
39091	OH_ Logan County	46,005	46,517	1.1	9	3
39093	OH_ Lorain County	284,664	300,450	5.5	1	7
39095	OH_ Lucas County	455,054	446,480	-1.8	5	7
39097	OH_ Madison County	40,213	41,693	3.6	1	3
39099	OH_ Mahoning County	257,555	255,117	-0.9	10	7

fips	county	totpop00	totpop06	chpop	Cat.10_1	Cat.10_2
39101	OH_ Marion County	66,217	65,818	-0.6	10	9
39103	OH_ Medina County	151,095	169,465	12.1	1	8
39105	OH_ Meigs County	23,072	23,231	0.6	9	10
39107	OH_ Mercer County	40,924	41,240	0.7	9	6
39109	OH_ Miami County	98,868	102,382	3.5	1	3
39111	OH_ Monroe County	15,180	14,617	-3.7	3	10
39113	OH_ Montgomery County	559,062	545,490	-2.4	11	7
39115	OH_ Morgan County	14,897	15,004	0.7	9	10
39117	OH_ Morrow County	31,628	34,629	9.4	5	3
39119	OH_ Muskingum County	84,585	85,896	1.5	5	9
39121	OH_ Noble County	14,058	14,148	0.6	9	10
39123	OH_ Ottawa County	40,985	41,705	1.7	10	9
39125	OH_ Paulding County	20,293	19,470	-4.0	9	3
39127	OH_ Perry County	34,078	35,392	3.8	9	10
39129	OH_ Pickaway County	52,727	53,714	1.8	1	9
39131	OH_ Pike County	27,695	28,054	1.3	9	2
39133	OH_ Portage County	152,061	155,949	2.5	8	5
39135	OH_ Preble County	42,337	42,504	0.3	9	3
39137	OH_ Putnam County	34,726	34,989	0.7	9	6
39139	OH_ Richland County	128,852	127,708	-0.8	9	10
39141	OH_ Ross County	73,345	75,554	3.0	9	5
39143	OH_ Sandusky County	61,792	61,737	0.0	10	9
39145	OH_ Scioto County	79,195	76,505	-3.4	9	10
39147	OH_ Seneca County	58,683	57,296	-2.3	9	6
39149	OH_ Shelby County	47,910	48,748	1.7	10	9
39151	OH_ Stark County	378,098	381,232	0.8	10	7
39153	OH_ Summit County	542,899	547,286	0.8	5	7
39155	OH_ Trumbull County	225,116	218,338	-3.0	9	10
39157	OH_ Tuscarawas County	90,914	91,841	1.0	5	9
39159	OH_ Union County	40,909	46,733	14.2	1	8
39161	OH_ Van Wert County	29,659	29,146	-1.7	10	3
39163	OH_ Vinton County	12,806	13,508	5.4	9	10
39165	OH_ Warren County	158,383	203,272	28.3	8	1
39167	OH_ Washington County	63,251	62,127	-1.7	9	1
39169	OH_ Wayne County	111,564	113,815	2.0	10	5
39171	OH_ Williams County	39,188	38,666	-1.3	10	3
39173	OH_ Wood County	121,065	124,818	3.1	8	5
39175	OH_ Wyandot County	22,908	22,753	-0.6	10	4
40001	OK_ Adair County	21,038	22,159	5.3	9	6
40003	OK_ Alfalfa County	6,105	5,627	-7.8	4	9
40005	OK_ Atoka County	13,879	14,477	4.3	3	2
40007	OK_ Beaver County	5,857	5,314	-9.2	4	9
40009	OK_ Beckham County	19,799	18,813	-4.9	3	4
40011	OK_ Blaine County	11,976	13,367	11.6	3	2
40013	OK_ Bryan County	36,534	38,133	4.3	3	10
40015	OK_ Caddo County	30,150	30,247	0.3	3	4
40017	OK_ Canadian County	87,697	101,655	15.9	8	3
40019	OK_ Carter County	45,621	47,443	3.9	3	9
40021	OK_ Cherokee County	42,521	44,869	5.5	8	5
40023	OK_ Choctaw County	15,342	15,271	-0.4	3	2
40025	OK_ Cimarron County	3,148	2,737	-13.0	3	9

fips	county	totpop00	totpop06	chpop	Cat.10_1	Cat.10_2
40027	OK_ Cleveland County	208,016	227,481	9.3	5	8
40029	OK_ Coal County	6,031	5,640	-6.4	11	6
40031	OK_ Comanche County	114,996	111,396	-3.1	8	5
40033	OK_ Cotton County	6,614	6,596	-0.2	11	3
40035	OK_ Craig County	14,950	15,257	2.0	3	10
40037	OK_ Creek County	67,367	68,584	1.8	9	10
40039	OK_ Custer County	26,142	25,425	-2.7	8	4
40041	OK_ Delaware County	37,077	39,394	6.2	3	10
40043	OK_ Dewey County	4,743	4,556	-3.9	3	9
40045	OK_ Ellis County	4,075	3,926	-3.6	3	4
40047	OK_ Garfield County	57,813	56,682	-1.9	11	10
40049	OK_ Garvin County	27,210	27,263	0.1	3	4
40051	OK_ Grady County	45,516	50,399	10.7	3	10
40053	OK_ Grant County	5,144	4,692	-8.7	4	9
40055	OK_ Greer County	6,061	5,878	-3.0	11	4
40057	OK_ Harmon County	3,283	3,080	-6.1	3	4
40059	OK_ Harper County	3,562	3,286	-7.7	3	4
40061	OK_ Haskell County	11,792	12,206	3.5	3	2
40063	OK_ Hughes County	14,154	13,826	-2.3	3	10
40065	OK_ Jackson County	28,439	26,015	-8.5	8	3
40067	OK_ Jefferson County	6,818	6,432	-5.6	3	2
40069	OK_ Johnston County	10,513	10,188	-3.0	3	2
40071	OK_ Kay County	48,080	45,812	-4.7	9	4
40073	OK_ Kingfisher County	13,926	14,410	3.4	4	9
40075	OK_ Kiowa County	10,227	9,867	-3.5	11	3
40077	OK_ Latimer County	10,692	10,651	-0.3	3	4
40079	OK_ Le Flore County	48,109	49,729	3.3	3	10
40081	OK_ Lincoln County	32,080	32,382	0.9	3	10
40083	OK_ Logan County	33,924	37,309	9.9	9	10
40085	OK_ Love County	8,831	9,208	4.2	3	2
40087	OK_ McClain County	27,740	30,921	11.4	3	10
40089	OK_ McCurtain County	34,402	34,010	-1.1	9	4
40091	OK_ McIntosh County	19,456	19,899	2.2	3	10
40093	OK_ Major County	7,545	7,265	-3.7	3	4
40095	OK_ Marshall County	13,184	14,779	12.1	3	10
40097	OK_ Mayes County	38,369	39,723	3.5	3	8
40099	OK_ Murray County	12,623	12,981	2.8	3	4
40101	OK_ Muskogee County	69,451	70,900	2.0	3	9
40103	OK_ Noble County	11,411	11,188	-1.9	3	4
40105	OK_ Nowata County	10,569	10,859	2.7	3	10
40107	OK_ Okfuskee County	11,814	11,334	-4.0	9	10
40109	OK_ Oklahoma County	660,448	688,316	4.2	8	3
40111	OK_ Okmulgee County	39,685	39,753	0.1	3	2
40113	OK_ Osage County	44,437	45,530	2.4	9	3
40115	OK_ Ottawa County	33,194	32,962	-0.7	3	9
40117	OK_ Pawnee County	16,612	16,815	1.2	3	10
40119	OK_ Payne County	68,190	69,414	1.7	5	8
40121	OK_ Pittsburg County	43,953	44,782	1.8	9	3
40123	OK_ Pontotoc County	35,143	35,494	1.0	8	3
40125	OK_ Pottawatomie County	65,521	68,515	4.5	3	9
40127	OK_ Pushmataha County	11,667	11,667	0.0	3	4

fips	county	totpop00	totpop06	chpop	Cat.10_1	Cat.10_2
40129	OK_ Roger Mills County	3,436	3,387	-1.4	3	4
40131	OK_ Rogers County	70,641	82,182	16.3	1	8
40133	OK_ Seminole County	24,894	24,872	0.0	3	10
40135	OK_ Sequoyah County	38,972	41,180	5.6	9	10
40137	OK_ Stephens County	43,182	43,222	0.0	3	9
40139	OK_ Texas County	20,107	20,122	0.0	8	6
40141	OK_ Tillman County	9,287	8,409	-9.4	2	4
40143	OK_ Tulsa County	563,299	571,721	1.5	8	1
40145	OK_ Wagoner County	57,491	65,332	13.6	1	3
40147	OK_ Washington County	48,996	48,935	-0.1	3	9
40149	OK_ Washita County	11,508	11,515	0.0	3	4
40151	OK_ Woods County	9,089	8,422	-7.3	8	4
40153	OK_ Woodward County	18,486	19,177	3.7	3	4
41001	OR_ Baker County	16,741	16,190	-3.2	9	10
41003	OR_ Benton County	78,153	78,230	0.1	8	5
41005	OR_ Clackamas County	338,391	373,755	10.4	1	7
41007	OR_ Clatsop County	35,630	37,323	4.7	9	8
41009	OR_ Columbia County	43,560	48,855	12.1	1	10
41011	OR_ Coos County	62,779	65,546	4.4	9	10
41013	OR_ Crook County	19,182	22,792	18.8	1	8
41015	OR_ Curry County	21,137	22,708	7.4	3	4
41017	OR_ Deschutes County	115,367	147,940	28.2	8	10
41019	OR_ Douglas County	100,399	105,261	4.8	9	10
41021	OR_ Gilliam County	1,915	1,793	-6.3	4	1
41023	OR_ Grant County	7,935	7,246	-8.6	4	10
41025	OR_ Harney County	7,609	6,795	-10.7	4	6
41027	OR_ Hood River County	20,411	21,538	5.5	6	9
41029	OR_ Jackson County	181,269	197,495	8.9	9	5
41031	OR_ Jefferson County	19,009	20,226	6.4	6	8
41033	OR_ Josephine County	75,726	81,610	7.7	9	10
41035	OR_ Klamath County	63,775	66,816	4.7	9	12
41037	OR_ Lake County	7,422	7,223	-2.6	4	9
41039	OR_ Lane County	322,959	337,417	4.4	5	1
41041	OR_ Lincoln County	44,479	46,591	4.7	9	10
41043	OR_ Linn County	103,069	110,300	7.0	9	10
41045	OR_ Malheur County	31,615	31,403	-0.6	6	3
41047	OR_ Marion County	284,834	308,613	8.3	1	7
41049	OR_ Morrow County	10,995	11,591	5.4	6	8
41051	OR_ Multnomah County	660,486	670,633	1.5	1	7
41053	OR_ Polk County	62,380	72,971	16.9	1	8
41055	OR_ Sherman County	1,934	1,746	-9.7	4	9
41057	OR_ Tillamook County	24,262	25,574	5.4	9	10
41059	OR_ Umatilla County	70,548	74,165	5.1	9	8
41061	OR_ Union County	24,530	24,437	-0.3	9	12
41063	OR_ Wallowa County	7,226	6,985	-3.3	4	10
41065	OR_ Wasco County	23,791	23,586	-0.8	9	10
41067	OR_ Washington County	445,342	511,056	14.7	8	1
41069	OR_ Wheeler County	1,547	1,393	-9.9	4	10
41071	OR_ Yamhill County	84,992	93,624	10.1	8	9
42001	PA_ Adams County	91,292	101,505	11.1	9	10
42003	PA_ Allegheny County	1,281,666	1,223,215	-4.5	7	1

fips	county	totpop00	totpop06	chpop	Cat.10_1	Cat.10_2
42005	PA_ Armstrong County	72,392	70,006	-3.3	9	4
42007	PA_ Beaver County	181,412	176,406	-2.7	9	10
42009	PA_ Bedford County	49,984	50,042	0.1	9	10
42011	PA_ Berks County	373,638	401,618	7.4	1	9
42013	PA_ Blair County	129,144	126,504	-2.0	9	10
42015	PA_ Bradford County	62,761	62,530	-0.3	9	10
42017	PA_ Bucks County	597,635	624,379	4.4	1	7
42019	PA_ Butler County	174,083	182,782	5.0	1	9
42021	PA_ Cambria County	152,598	147,280	-3.4	9	10
42023	PA_ Cameron County	5,974	5,559	-6.9	9	10
42025	PA_ Carbon County	58,802	62,824	6.8	10	4
42027	PA_ Centre County	135,758	140,541	3.5	5	9
42029	PA_ Chester County	433,501	481,454	11.0	1	2
42031	PA_ Clarion County	41,765	40,295	-3.5	9	10
42033	PA_ Clearfield County	83,382	82,531	-1.0	9	4
42035	PA_ Clinton County	37,914	37,352	-1.4	5	9
42037	PA_ Columbia County	64,151	65,012	1.3	10	9
42039	PA_ Crawford County	90,366	89,204	-1.2	9	10
42041	PA_ Cumberland County	213,674	224,892	5.2	1	5
42043	PA_ Dauphin County	251,798	253,705	0.7	9	7
42045	PA_ Delaware County	550,864	556,272	0.9	1	7
42047	PA_ Elk County	35,112	33,233	-5.3	9	6
42049	PA_ Erie County	280,843	279,220	-0.5	5	7
42051	PA_ Fayette County	148,644	146,388	-1.5	9	10
42053	PA_ Forest County	4,946	6,730	36.0	1	10
42055	PA_ Franklin County	129,313	139,700	8.0	10	5
42057	PA_ Fulton County	14,261	14,732	3.3	10	4
42059	PA_ Greene County	40,672	40,181	-1.2	9	5
42061	PA_ Huntingdon County	45,586	45,860	0.6	9	10
42063	PA_ Indiana County	89,605	88,338	-1.4	9	5
42065	PA_ Jefferson County	45,932	45,703	-0.5	9	10
42067	PA_ Juniata County	22,821	23,553	3.2	10	9
42069	PA_ Lackawanna County	213,295	209,915	-1.5	9	5
42071	PA_ Lancaster County	470,658	493,262	4.8	9	8
42073	PA_ Lawrence County	94,643	92,286	-2.4	9	10
42075	PA_ Lebanon County	120,327	126,775	5.3	1	9
42077	PA_ Lehigh County	312,090	335,712	7.5	1	7
42079	PA_ Luzerne County	319,250	313,376	-1.8	9	6
42081	PA_ Lycoming County	120,044	118,018	-1.6	10	1
42083	PA_ Mc Kean County	45,936	43,951	-4.3	9	10
42085	PA_ Mercer County	120,293	119,189	-0.9	9	10
42087	PA_ Mifflin County	46,486	46,081	-0.8	10	4
42089	PA_ Monroe County	138,687	167,282	20.6	8	5
42091	PA_ Montgomery County	750,097	776,672	3.5	1	7
42093	PA_ Montour County	18,236	17,950	-1.5	9	5
42095	PA_ Northampton County	267,066	292,239	9.4	1	9
42097	PA_ Northumberland County	94,556	92,185	-2.5	10	9
42099	PA_ Perry County	43,602	44,930	3.0	10	9
42101	PA_ Philadelphia County	1,517,550	1,455,065	-4.1	7	6
42103	PA_ Pike County	46,302	58,500	26.3	8	10
42105	PA_ Potter County	18,080	17,607	-2.6	9	10

fips	county	totpop00	totpop06	chpop	Cat.10_1	Cat.10_2
42107	PA_ Schuylkill County	150,336	147,407	-1.9	10	9
42109	PA_ Snyder County	37,546	38,060	1.3	10	4
42111	PA_ Somerset County	80,023	78,421	-2.0	9	10
42113	PA_ Sullivan County	6,556	6,336	-3.3	9	6
42115	PA_ Susquehanna County	42,238	42,210	0.0	9	10
42117	PA_ Tioga County	41,373	41,422	0.1	9	10
42119	PA_ Union County	41,624	43,544	4.6	5	9
42121	PA_ Venango County	57,565	55,740	-3.1	9	10
42123	PA_ Warren County	43,863	41,618	-5.1	9	10
42125	PA_ Washington County	202,897	207,684	2.3	9	1
42127	PA_ Wayne County	47,722	51,163	7.2	9	10
42129	PA_ Westmoreland County	369,993	367,439	-0.6	9	5
42131	PA_ Wyoming County	28,080	28,154	0.2	9	1
42133	PA_ York County	381,751	415,586	8.8	1	8
44001	RI_ Bristol County	50,648	53,411	5.4	1	9
44003	RI_ Kent County	167,090	173,693	3.9	1	7
44005	RI_ Newport County	85,433	83,490	-2.2	1	9
44007	RI_ Providence County	621,602	647,151	4.1	7	6
44009	RI_ Washington County	123,546	130,164	5.3	1	5
45001	SC_ Abbeville County	26,167	25,830	-1.2	2	3
45003	SC_ Aiken County	142,552	151,294	6.1	2	3
45005	SC_ Allendale County	11,211	10,830	-3.4	2	3
45007	SC_ Anderson County	165,740	176,854	6.7	3	2
45009	SC_ Bamberg County	16,658	15,727	-5.5	2	4
45011	SC_ Barnwell County	23,478	23,292	-0.7	2	3
45013	SC_ Beaufort County	120,937	140,960	16.5	8	1
45015	SC_ Berkeley County	142,651	151,747	6.3	8	3
45017	SC_ Calhoun County	15,185	14,969	-1.4	2	3
45019	SC_ Charleston County	309,969	333,220	7.5	2	7
45021	SC_ Cherokee County	52,537	53,732	2.2	3	2
45023	SC_ Chester County	34,068	32,768	-3.8	2	3
45025	SC_ Chesterfield County	42,768	43,362	1.3	2	3
45027	SC_ Clarendon County	32,502	33,397	2.7	2	3
45029	SC_ Colleton County	38,264	39,635	3.5	2	3
45031	SC_ Darlington County	67,394	67,184	-0.3	2	3
45033	SC_ Dillon County	30,722	30,885	0.5	2	3
45035	SC_ Dorchester County	96,413	117,688	22.0	8	11
45037	SC_ Edgefield County	24,595	25,553	3.9	2	3
45039	SC_ Fairfield County	23,454	23,968	2.1	2	3
45041	SC_ Florence County	125,761	131,880	4.8	2	3
45043	SC_ Georgetown County	55,797	61,229	9.7	1	3
45045	SC_ Greenville County	379,616	411,610	8.4	3	1
45047	SC_ Greenwood County	66,271	67,996	2.6	2	3
45049	SC_ Hampton County	21,386	21,213	-0.8	2	3
45051	SC_ Horry County	196,629	235,927	19.9	8	3
45053	SC_ Jasper County	20,678	21,588	4.4	2	3
45055	SC_ Kershaw County	52,647	57,354	8.9	11	3
45057	SC_ Lancaster County	61,351	63,122	2.8	3	2
45059	SC_ Laurens County	69,567	70,203	0.9	2	3
45061	SC_ Lee County	20,119	20,747	3.1	2	3
45063	SC_ Lexington County	216,014	238,710	10.5	1	3

fips	county	totpop00	totpop06	chpop	Cat.10_1	Cat.10_2
45065	SC_ McCormick County	9,958	10,053	0.9	2	3
45067	SC_ Marion County	35,466	34,794	-1.8	2	3
45069	SC_ Marlboro County	28,818	27,587	-4.2	2	3
45071	SC_ Newberry County	36,108	37,328	3.3	2	3
45073	SC_ Oconee County	66,215	69,834	5.4	3	2
45075	SC_ Orangeburg County	91,582	92,054	0.5	2	3
45077	SC_ Pickens County	110,757	113,666	2.6	8	3
45079	SC_ Richland County	320,677	340,949	6.3	8	7
45081	SC_ Saluda County	19,181	18,892	-1.5	2	3
45083	SC_ Spartanburg County	253,791	268,808	5.9	3	2
45085	SC_ Sumter County	104,646	104,590	0.0	11	3
45087	SC_ Union County	29,881	28,293	-5.3	2	3
45089	SC_ Williamsburg County	37,217	35,091	-5.7	2	7
45091	SC_ York County	164,614	195,904	19.0	8	3
46003	SD_ Aurora County	3,058	2,879	-5.8	4	9
46005	SD_ Beadle County	17,023	15,648	-8.0	5	4
46007	SD_ Bennett County	3,574	3,595	0.5	2	9
46009	SD_ Bon Homme County	7,260	7,031	-3.1	10	9
46011	SD_ Brookings County	28,220	27,619	-2.1	8	5
46013	SD_ Brown County	35,460	34,543	-2.5	10	9
46015	SD_ Brule County	5,364	5,162	-3.7	4	9
46017	SD_ Buffalo County	2,032	2,122	4.4	2	6
46019	SD_ Butte County	9,094	9,411	3.4	4	10
46021	SD_ Campbell County	1,782	1,505	-15.5	4	9
46023	SD_ Charles Mix County	9,350	9,230	-1.2	2	9
46025	SD_ Clark County	4,143	3,718	-10.2	4	9
46027	SD_ Clay County	13,537	12,873	-4.9	5	8
46029	SD_ Codington County	25,897	25,981	0.3	9	4
46031	SD_ Corson County	4,181	4,359	4.2	2	9
46033	SD_ Custer County	7,275	7,888	8.4	1	9
46035	SD_ Davison County	18,741	18,731	0.0	10	9
46037	SD_ Day County	6,267	5,700	-9.0	4	9
46039	SD_ Deuel County	4,498	4,269	-5.0	10	9
46041	SD_ Dewey County	5,972	6,203	3.8	9	4
46043	SD_ Douglas County	3,458	3,270	-5.4	6	9
46045	SD_ Edmunds County	4,367	4,061	-7.0	4	9
46047	SD_ Fall River County	7,453	7,382	-0.9	4	9
46049	SD_ Faulk County	2,640	2,322	-12.0	4	9
46051	SD_ Grant County	7,847	7,227	-7.9	10	4
46053	SD_ Gregory County	4,792	4,233	-11.6	4	9
46055	SD_ Haakon County	2,196	1,854	-15.5	4	9
46057	SD_ Hamlin County	5,540	5,659	2.1	10	4
46059	SD_ Hand County	3,741	3,223	-13.8	4	9
46061	SD_ Hanson County	3,139	3,833	22.1	4	10
46063	SD_ Harding County	1,353	1,178	-12.9	4	9
46065	SD_ Hughes County	16,481	16,921	2.6	10	9
46067	SD_ Hutchinson County	8,075	7,460	-7.6	4	9
46069	SD_ Hyde County	1,671	1,615	-3.3	4	9
46071	SD_ Jackson County	2,930	2,884	-1.5	2	9
46073	SD_ Jerauld County	2,295	2,103	-8.3	4	9
46075	SD_ Jones County	1,193	1,015	-14.9	4	9

fips	county	totpop00	totpop06	chpop	Cat.10_1	Cat.10_2
46077	SD_ Kingsbury County	5,815	5,529	-4.9	10	9
46079	SD_ Lake County	11,276	11,074	-1.7	10	9
46081	SD_ Lawrence County	21,802	22,685	4.0	9	5
46083	SD_ Lincoln County	24,131	35,229	45.9	8	4
46085	SD_ Lyman County	3,895	3,896	0.0	4	9
46087	SD_ McCook County	5,832	5,914	1.4	4	9
46089	SD_ McPherson County	2,904	2,570	-11.5	4	9
46091	SD_ Marshall County	4,576	4,486	-1.9	4	9
46093	SD_ Meade County	24,253	24,536	1.1	8	3
46095	SD_ Mellette County	2,083	2,132	2.3	2	9
46097	SD_ Miner County	2,884	2,504	-13.1	4	9
46099	SD_ Minnehaha County	148,281	162,033	9.2	8	7
46101	SD_ Moody County	6,595	6,684	1.3	10	4
46103	SD_ Pennington County	88,565	93,873	5.9	8	5
46105	SD_ Perkins County	3,363	2,937	-12.6	4	9
46107	SD_ Potter County	2,693	2,274	-15.5	4	9
46109	SD_ Roberts County	10,016	10,050	0.3	4	9
46111	SD_ Sanborn County	2,675	2,482	-7.2	4	9
46113	SD_ Shannon County	12,466	13,872	11.2	8	2
46115	SD_ Spink County	7,454	6,848	-8.1	4	9
46117	SD_ Stanley County	2,772	2,814	1.5	4	9
46119	SD_ Sully County	1,556	1,411	-9.3	4	9
46121	SD_ Todd County	9,050	10,132	11.9	9	4
46123	SD_ Tripp County	6,430	5,974	-7.0	4	9
46125	SD_ Turner County	8,849	8,454	-4.4	10	9
46127	SD_ Union County	12,584	13,593	8.0	9	8
46129	SD_ Walworth County	5,974	5,462	-8.5	4	9
46135	SD_ Yankton County	21,652	21,705	0.2	9	4
46137	SD_ Ziebach County	2,519	2,664	5.7	2	9
47001	TN_ Anderson County	71,330	72,459	1.5	3	10
47003	TN_ Bedford County	37,586	43,092	14.6	6	3
47005	TN_ Benton County	16,537	16,379	-0.9	3	10
47007	TN_ Bledsoe County	12,367	13,034	5.3	9	10
47009	TN_ Blount County	105,823	117,202	10.7	3	10
47011	TN_ Bradley County	87,965	92,761	5.4	3	2
47013	TN_ Campbell County	39,854	40,724	2.1	3	10
47015	TN_ Cannon County	12,826	13,389	4.3	3	2
47017	TN_ Carroll County	29,475	28,934	-1.8	3	2
47019	TN_ Carter County	56,742	59,014	4.0	3	10
47021	TN_ Cheatham County	35,912	38,981	8.5	1	3
47023	TN_ Chester County	15,540	15,971	2.7	9	3
47025	TN_ Claiborne County	29,862	31,284	4.7	3	2
47027	TN_ Clay County	7,976	7,996	0.2	3	2
47029	TN_ Cocke County	33,565	35,145	4.7	3	10
47031	TN_ Coffee County	48,014	51,273	6.7	11	8
47033	TN_ Crockett County	14,532	14,541	0.0	3	2
47035	TN_ Cumberland County	46,802	51,949	11.0	3	10
47037	TN_ Davidson County	569,891	576,361	1.1	8	7
47039	TN_ Decatur County	11,731	11,584	-1.2	3	10
47041	TN_ DeKalb County	17,423	18,348	5.3	3	2
47043	TN_ Dickson County	43,156	46,093	6.8	9	3

fips	county	totpop00	totpop06	chpop	Cat.10_1	Cat.10_2
47045	TN_ Dyer County	37,279	38,008	1.9	3	2
47047	TN_ Fayette County	28,806	35,480	23.1	1	3
47049	TN_ Fentress County	16,625	17,249	3.7	3	10
47051	TN_ Franklin County	39,270	40,998	4.4	9	3
47053	TN_ Gibson County	48,152	48,091	-0.1	3	10
47055	TN_ Giles County	29,447	29,233	-0.7	3	2
47057	TN_ Grainger County	20,659	22,529	9.0	3	2
47059	TN_ Greene County	62,909	65,622	4.3	9	10
47061	TN_ Grundy County	14,332	14,620	2.0	3	2
47063	TN_ Hamblen County	58,128	60,651	4.3	3	10
47065	TN_ Hamilton County	307,896	310,650	0.8	3	7
47067	TN_ Hancock County	6,786	6,722	-0.9	3	2
47069	TN_ Hardeman County	28,105	28,076	-0.1	2	3
47071	TN_ Hardin County	25,578	26,008	1.6	3	2
47073	TN_ Hawkins County	53,563	56,502	5.4	3	2
47075	TN_ Haywood County	19,797	19,506	-1.4	2	3
47077	TN_ Henderson County	25,522	26,581	4.1	9	10
47079	TN_ Henry County	31,115	31,578	1.4	3	10
47081	TN_ Hickman County	22,295	23,752	6.5	3	2
47083	TN_ Houston County	8,088	7,996	-1.1	9	2
47085	TN_ Humphreys County	17,929	18,233	1.7	9	3
47087	TN_ Jackson County	10,984	10,972	-0.1	3	10
47089	TN_ Jefferson County	44,294	48,861	10.3	3	10
47091	TN_ Johnson County	17,499	18,116	3.5	3	10
47093	TN_ Knox County	382,032	407,563	6.6	5	1
47095	TN_ Lake County	7,954	7,455	-6.2	2	3
47097	TN_ Lauderdale County	27,101	26,564	-1.9	2	3
47099	TN_ Lawrence County	39,926	40,951	2.5	3	10
47101	TN_ Lewis County	11,367	11,381	0.1	9	10
47103	TN_ Lincoln County	31,340	32,533	3.8	3	10
47105	TN_ Loudon County	39,086	44,136	12.9	1	3
47107	TN_ McMinn County	49,015	51,609	5.2	3	2
47109	TN_ McNairy County	24,653	25,474	3.3	3	2
47111	TN_ Macon County	20,386	21,801	6.9	9	10
47113	TN_ Madison County	91,837	95,084	3.5	8	5
47115	TN_ Marion County	27,776	27,632	-0.5	9	10
47117	TN_ Marshall County	26,767	28,635	6.9	8	3
47119	TN_ Maury County	69,498	77,693	11.7	8	3
47121	TN_ Meigs County	11,086	11,701	5.5	3	2
47123	TN_ Monroe County	38,961	44,004	12.9	3	10
47125	TN_ Montgomery County	134,768	151,077	12.1	8	7
47127	TN_ Moore County	5,740	6,031	5.0	11	10
47129	TN_ Morgan County	19,757	20,046	1.4	3	2
47131	TN_ Obion County	32,450	31,987	-1.4	3	10
47133	TN_ Overton County	20,118	20,552	2.1	3	10
47135	TN_ Perry County	7,631	7,565	-0.8	5	3
47137	TN_ Pickett County	4,945	4,751	-3.9	3	2
47139	TN_ Polk County	16,050	15,897	-0.9	3	10
47141	TN_ Putnam County	62,315	67,322	8.0	8	3
47143	TN_ Rhea County	28,400	30,000	5.6	9	3
47145	TN_ Roane County	51,910	52,736	1.5	3	10

fips	county	totpop00	totpop06	chpop	Cat.10_1	Cat.10_2
47147	TN_ Robertson County	54,433	61,085	12.2	1	3
47149	TN_ Rutherford County	182,023	226,315	24.3	8	11
47151	TN_ Scott County	21,127	21,866	3.5	9	2
47153	TN_ Sequatchie County	11,370	12,975	14.1	3	10
47155	TN_ Sevier County	71,170	80,943	13.7	8	3
47157	TN_ Shelby County	897,472	908,342	1.2	7	1
47159	TN_ Smith County	17,712	18,697	5.5	9	3
47161	TN_ Stewart County	12,370	12,964	4.8	11	10
47163	TN_ Sullivan County	153,048	152,173	-0.5	9	10
47165	TN_ Sumner County	130,449	147,266	12.8	1	8
47167	TN_ Tipton County	51,271	56,967	11.1	8	3
47169	TN_ Trousdale County	7,259	7,775	7.1	9	10
47171	TN_ Unicoi County	17,667	17,454	-1.2	9	2
47173	TN_ Union County	17,808	19,046	6.9	9	3
47175	TN_ Van Buren County	5,508	5,403	-1.9	9	10
47177	TN_ Warren County	38,276	39,825	4.0	3	8
47179	TN_ Washington County	107,198	113,281	5.6	3	10
47181	TN_ Wayne County	16,842	16,793	-0.2	3	10
47183	TN_ Weakley County	34,895	33,357	-4.4	8	3
47185	TN_ White County	23,102	24,537	6.2	3	10
47187	TN_ Williamson County	126,638	159,010	25.5	8	1
47189	TN_ Wilson County	88,809	102,562	15.4	8	3
48001	TX_ Anderson County	55,109	56,960	3.3	2	11
48003	TX_ Andrews County	13,004	12,653	-2.7	6	9
48005	TX_ Angelina County	80,130	81,848	2.1	3	2
48007	TX_ Aransas County	22,497	25,234	12.1	8	10
48009	TX_ Archer County	8,854	9,093	2.7	4	3
48011	TX_ Armstrong County	2,148	2,235	4.0	3	4
48013	TX_ Atascosa County	38,628	43,824	13.4	6	9
48015	TX_ Austin County	23,590	26,556	12.5	6	10
48017	TX_ Bailey County	6,594	6,738	2.1	6	4
48019	TX_ Bandera County	17,645	20,219	14.5	8	10
48021	TX_ Bastrop County	57,733	71,155	23.2	8	6
48023	TX_ Baylor County	4,093	3,804	-7.0	3	4
48025	TX_ Bee County	32,359	32,811	1.4	6	3
48027	TX_ Bell County	237,974	258,430	8.6	8	11
48029	TX_ Bexar County	1,392,931	1,541,990	10.7	11	7
48031	TX_ Blanco County	8,418	9,274	10.1	1	8
48033	TX_ Borden County	729	629	-13.7	3	4
48035	TX_ Bosque County	17,204	18,172	5.6	4	6
48037	TX_ Bowie County	89,306	91,034	1.9	3	2
48039	TX_ Brazoria County	241,767	284,999	17.8	6	7
48041	TX_ Brazos County	152,415	156,954	2.9	8	5
48043	TX_ Brewster County	8,866	8,982	1.3	6	5
48045	TX_ Briscoe County	1,790	1,611	-10.0	3	4
48047	TX_ Brooks County	7,976	7,632	-4.3	6	9
48049	TX_ Brown County	37,674	39,055	3.6	3	10
48051	TX_ Burleson County	16,470	17,341	5.2	4	2
48053	TX_ Burnet County	34,147	42,988	25.8	8	10
48055	TX_ Caldwell County	32,194	36,818	14.3	6	3
48057	TX_ Calhoun County	20,647	20,668	0.1	6	2

fips	county	totpop00	totpop06	chpop	Cat.10_1	Cat.10_2
48059	TX_ Callahan County	12,905	13,639	5.6	3	10
48061	TX_ Cameron County	335,227	386,451	15.2	6	7
48063	TX_ Camp County	11,549	12,447	7.7	3	2
48065	TX_ Carson County	6,516	6,576	0.9	4	3
48067	TX_ Cass County	30,438	30,087	-1.1	3	10
48069	TX_ Castro County	8,285	7,546	-8.9	6	2
48071	TX_ Chambers County	26,031	28,832	10.7	1	8
48073	TX_ Cherokee County	46,659	48,718	4.4	3	2
48075	TX_ Childress County	7,688	7,699	0.1	3	2
48077	TX_ Clay County	11,006	11,215	1.9	3	2
48079	TX_ Cochran County	3,730	3,243	-13.0	3	6
48081	TX_ Coke County	3,864	3,562	-7.8	3	2
48083	TX_ Coleman County	9,235	8,655	-6.2	3	2
48085	TX_ Collin County	491,675	692,225	40.7	8	1
48087	TX_ Collingsworth County	3,206	2,918	-8.9	3	4
48089	TX_ Colorado County	20,390	20,716	1.6	6	9
48091	TX_ Comal County	78,021	100,372	28.6	8	10
48093	TX_ Comanche County	14,026	13,850	-1.2	3	4
48095	TX_ Concho County	3,966	3,715	-6.3	6	3
48097	TX_ Cooke County	36,363	39,137	7.6	6	3
48099	TX_ Coryell County	74,978	76,023	1.3	3	8
48101	TX_ Cottle County	1,904	1,721	-9.6	3	4
48103	TX_ Crane County	3,996	3,823	-4.3	6	9
48105	TX_ Crockett County	4,099	3,928	-4.1	6	4
48107	TX_ Crosby County	7,072	6,674	-5.6	6	2
48109	TX_ Culberson County	2,975	2,540	-14.6	6	2
48111	TX_ Dallam County	6,222	6,199	-0.3	6	9
48113	TX_ Dallas County	2,218,899	2,317,204	4.4	8	7
48115	TX_ Dawson County	14,985	14,202	-5.2	6	4
48117	TX_ Deaf Smith County	18,561	18,537	-0.1	6	2
48119	TX_ Delta County	5,327	5,471	2.7	3	9
48121	TX_ Denton County	432,976	577,030	33.2	8	1
48123	TX_ DeWitt County	20,013	20,626	3.0	6	3
48125	TX_ Dickens County	2,762	2,619	-5.1	3	6
48127	TX_ Dimmit County	10,248	10,427	1.7	6	9
48129	TX_ Donley County	3,828	3,860	0.8	3	4
48131	TX_ Duval County	13,120	12,529	-4.5	6	9
48133	TX_ Eastland County	18,297	18,443	0.8	3	2
48135	TX_ Ector County	121,123	126,390	4.3	8	6
48137	TX_ Edwards County	2,162	1,971	-8.8	6	9
48139	TX_ Ellis County	111,360	138,157	24.0	8	3
48141	TX_ El Paso County	679,622	730,292	7.4	6	7
48143	TX_ Erath County	33,001	34,196	3.6	8	5
48145	TX_ Falls County	18,576	17,552	-5.5	2	6
48147	TX_ Fannin County	31,242	33,611	7.5	3	8
48149	TX_ Fayette County	21,804	22,563	3.4	6	4
48151	TX_ Fisher County	4,344	4,023	-7.3	3	2
48153	TX_ Floyd County	7,771	7,046	-9.3	6	9
48155	TX_ Foard County	1,622	1,500	-7.5	3	4
48157	TX_ Fort Bend County	354,452	486,505	37.2	8	1
48159	TX_ Franklin County	9,458	10,392	9.8	3	10

fips	county	totpop00	totpop06	chpop	Cat.10_1	Cat.10_2
48161	TX_ Freestone County	17,867	18,806	5.2	4	3
48163	TX_ Frio County	16,252	16,414	1.0	6	2
48165	TX_ Gaines County	14,467	14,927	3.1	3	6
48167	TX_ Galveston County	250,158	282,683	13.0	1	7
48169	TX_ Garza County	4,872	4,869	0.0	6	9
48171	TX_ Gillespie County	20,814	23,474	12.7	6	4
48173	TX_ Glasscock County	1,406	1,298	-7.6	8	6
48175	TX_ Goliad County	6,928	7,145	3.1	6	3
48177	TX_ Gonzales County	18,628	19,806	6.3	6	8
48179	TX_ Gray County	22,744	21,468	-5.6	3	6
48181	TX_ Grayson County	110,595	117,645	6.3	3	9
48183	TX_ Gregg County	111,379	116,360	4.4	8	2
48185	TX_ Grimes County	23,552	25,248	7.2	6	10
48187	TX_ Guadalupe County	89,023	106,515	19.6	8	3
48189	TX_ Hale County	36,602	36,405	-0.5	6	2
48191	TX_ Hall County	3,782	3,683	-2.6	3	6
48193	TX_ Hamilton County	8,229	8,207	-0.2	3	6
48195	TX_ Hansford County	5,369	5,204	-3.0	6	9
48197	TX_ Hardeman County	4,724	4,190	-11.3	3	4
48199	TX_ Hardin County	48,073	51,657	7.4	3	2
48201	TX_ Harris County	3,400,578	3,749,081	10.2	7	1
48203	TX_ Harrison County	62,110	63,771	2.6	3	2
48205	TX_ Hartley County	5,537	5,403	-2.4	3	4
48207	TX_ Haskell County	6,093	5,517	-9.4	3	4
48209	TX_ Hays County	97,589	128,498	31.6	8	11
48211	TX_ Hemphill County	3,351	3,453	3.0	3	9
48213	TX_ Henderson County	73,277	80,906	10.4	1	10
48215	TX_ Hidalgo County	569,463	699,298	22.8	6	7
48217	TX_ Hill County	32,321	35,796	10.7	3	9
48219	TX_ Hockley County	22,716	22,752	0.1	6	2
48221	TX_ Hood County	41,100	49,146	19.5	8	10
48223	TX_ Hopkins County	31,960	33,619	5.1	2	3
48225	TX_ Houston County	23,185	23,051	-0.5	3	4
48227	TX_ Howard County	33,627	32,340	-3.8	8	6
48229	TX_ Hudspeth County	3,344	3,320	-0.7	2	6
48231	TX_ Hunt County	76,596	83,092	8.4	3	8
48233	TX_ Hutchinson County	23,857	22,207	-6.9	3	6
48235	TX_ Irion County	1,771	1,749	-1.2	4	9
48237	TX_ Jack County	8,763	9,072	3.5	3	4
48239	TX_ Jackson County	14,391	14,355	-0.2	6	9
48241	TX_ Jasper County	35,604	35,564	-0.1	3	2
48243	TX_ Jeff Davis County	2,207	2,326	5.3	10	6
48245	TX_ Jefferson County	252,051	246,867	-2.0	2	11
48247	TX_ Jim Hogg County	5,281	5,035	-4.6	6	9
48249	TX_ Jim Wells County	39,326	41,254	4.9	6	9
48251	TX_ Johnson County	126,811	149,780	18.1	8	3
48253	TX_ Jones County	20,785	19,477	-6.2	3	2
48255	TX_ Karnes County	15,446	15,295	-0.9	6	2
48257	TX_ Kaufman County	71,313	92,827	30.1	8	3
48259	TX_ Kendall County	23,743	29,945	26.1	8	6
48261	TX_ Kenedy County	414	416	0.4	6	4

fips	county	totpop00	totpop06	chpop	Cat.10_1	Cat.10_2
48263	TX_ Kent County	859	756	-11.9	3	4
48265	TX_ Kerr County	43,653	47,148	8.0	4	9
48267	TX_ Kimble County	4,468	4,625	3.5	3	6
48269	TX_ King County	356	295	-17.1	3	2
48271	TX_ Kinney County	3,379	3,339	-1.1	6	10
48273	TX_ Kleberg County	31,549	30,429	-3.5	6	5
48275	TX_ Knox County	4,253	3,673	-13.6	3	9
48277	TX_ Lamar County	48,499	49,691	2.4	3	10
48279	TX_ Lamb County	14,709	14,379	-2.2	6	4
48281	TX_ Lampasas County	17,762	19,618	10.4	4	10
48283	TX_ La Salle County	5,866	6,078	3.6	6	9
48285	TX_ Lavaca County	19,210	18,865	-1.8	6	9
48287	TX_ Lee County	15,657	16,529	5.5	6	4
48289	TX_ Leon County	15,335	16,462	7.3	3	6
48291	TX_ Liberty County	70,154	75,415	7.5	3	2
48293	TX_ Limestone County	22,051	22,727	3.0	9	2
48295	TX_ Lipscomb County	3,057	3,085	0.9	6	9
48297	TX_ Live Oak County	12,309	11,620	-5.6	6	9
48299	TX_ Llano County	17,044	18,191	6.7	1	10
48301	TX_ Loving County	67	60	-10.4	6	7
48303	TX_ Lubbock County	242,628	253,193	4.3	8	7
48305	TX_ Lynn County	6,550	6,188	-5.5	6	9
48307	TX_ McCulloch County	8,205	7,992	-2.6	6	4
48309	TX_ McLennan County	213,517	226,871	6.2	8	7
48311	TX_ McMullen County	851	905	6.3	8	6
48313	TX_ Madison County	12,940	13,411	3.6	3	2
48315	TX_ Marion County	10,941	10,885	-0.5	2	10
48317	TX_ Martin County	4,746	4,367	-7.9	6	9
48319	TX_ Mason County	3,738	3,902	4.3	4	9
48321	TX_ Matagorda County	37,957	37,761	-0.5	6	2
48323	TX_ Maverick County	47,297	51,867	9.6	6	2
48325	TX_ Medina County	39,304	43,689	11.1	6	8
48327	TX_ Menard County	2,360	2,161	-8.4	3	6
48329	TX_ Midland County	116,009	122,737	5.8	8	1
48331	TX_ Milam County	24,238	25,240	4.1	6	10
48333	TX_ Mills County	5,151	5,343	3.7	3	10
48335	TX_ Mitchell County	9,698	9,437	-2.6	6	2
48337	TX_ Montague County	19,117	19,827	3.7	3	6
48339	TX_ Montgomery County	293,768	394,838	34.4	1	8
48341	TX_ Moore County	20,121	20,336	1.0	6	8
48343	TX_ Morris County	13,048	12,842	-1.5	3	2
48345	TX_ Motley County	1,426	1,325	-7.0	3	9
48347	TX_ Nacogdoches County	59,203	61,199	3.3	8	2
48349	TX_ Navarro County	45,124	49,294	9.2	6	2
48351	TX_ Newton County	15,072	14,148	-6.1	2	3
48353	TX_ Nolan County	15,802	14,755	-6.6	3	9
48355	TX_ Nueces County	313,645	321,628	2.5	8	7
48357	TX_ Ochiltree County	9,006	9,650	7.1	6	4
48359	TX_ Oldham County	2,185	2,097	-4.0	8	9
48361	TX_ Orange County	84,966	85,419	0.5	3	9
48363	TX_ Palo Pinto County	27,026	27,652	2.3	3	10

fips	county	totpop00	totpop06	chpop	Cat.10_1	Cat.10_2
48365	TX_ Panola County	22,756	22,964	0.9	3	2
48367	TX_ Parker County	88,495	105,279	18.9	8	3
48369	TX_ Parmer County	10,016	9,653	-3.6	6	4
48371	TX_ Pecos County	16,809	15,767	-6.2	6	9
48373	TX_ Polk County	41,133	46,886	13.9	8	10
48375	TX_ Potter County	113,546	121,300	6.8	8	2
48377	TX_ Presidio County	7,304	7,782	6.5	6	2
48379	TX_ Rains County	9,139	11,471	25.5	1	10
48381	TX_ Randall County	104,312	111,438	6.8	8	5
48383	TX_ Reagan County	3,326	2,964	-10.8	3	6
48385	TX_ Real County	3,047	3,053	0.2	3	4
48387	TX_ Red River County	14,314	13,645	-4.6	3	2
48389	TX_ Reeves County	13,137	11,354	-13.5	6	2
48391	TX_ Refugio County	7,828	7,693	-1.7	6	9
48393	TX_ Roberts County	887	840	-5.3	4	9
48395	TX_ Robertson County	16,000	16,413	2.5	2	6
48397	TX_ Rockwall County	43,080	67,229	56.0	8	1
48399	TX_ Runnels County	11,495	10,973	-4.5	6	2
48401	TX_ Rusk County	47,372	48,071	1.4	3	11
48403	TX_ Sabine County	10,469	10,411	-0.5	3	4
48405	TX_ San Augustine County	8,946	8,836	-1.2	2	6
48407	TX_ San Jacinto County	22,246	25,195	13.2	8	6
48409	TX_ San Patricio County	67,138	70,137	4.4	6	11
48411	TX_ San Saba County	6,186	6,061	-2.0	3	6
48413	TX_ Schleicher County	2,935	2,747	-6.4	6	2
48415	TX_ Scurry County	16,361	16,238	-0.7	6	4
48417	TX_ Shackelford County	3,302	3,130	-5.2	3	4
48419	TX_ Shelby County	25,224	26,677	5.7	3	6
48421	TX_ Sherman County	3,186	2,886	-9.4	6	9
48423	TX_ Smith County	174,706	193,908	10.9	1	8
48425	TX_ Somervell County	6,809	7,717	13.3	1	8
48427	TX_ Starr County	53,597	61,892	15.4	2	9
48429	TX_ Stephens County	9,674	9,580	-0.9	3	6
48431	TX_ Sterling County	1,393	1,286	-7.6	6	9
48433	TX_ Stonewall County	1,693	1,338	-20.9	3	4
48435	TX_ Sutton County	4,077	4,277	4.9	6	9
48437	TX_ Swisher County	8,378	7,822	-6.6	3	6
48439	TX_ Tarrant County	1,446,219	1,649,263	14.0	8	7
48441	TX_ Taylor County	126,555	125,226	-1.0	8	5
48443	TX_ Terrell County	1,081	991	-8.3	6	9
48445	TX_ Terry County	12,761	12,295	-3.6	6	9
48447	TX_ Throckmorton County	1,850	1,620	-12.4	3	4
48449	TX_ Titus County	28,118	29,863	6.2	8	6
48451	TX_ Tom Green County	104,010	103,349	-0.6	8	6
48453	TX_ Travis County	812,280	907,917	11.7	8	1
48455	TX_ Trinity County	13,779	14,419	4.6	3	2
48457	TX_ Tyler County	20,871	20,559	-1.4	3	10
48459	TX_ Upshur County	35,291	38,146	8.0	3	10
48461	TX_ Upton County	3,404	2,982	-12.4	6	2
48463	TX_ Uvalde County	25,926	27,064	4.3	6	9
48465	TX_ Val Verde County	44,856	47,958	6.9	6	11

fips	county	totpop00	totpop06	chpop	Cat.10_1	Cat.10_2
48467	TX_ Van Zandt County	48,140	52,925	9.9	3	10
48469	TX_ Victoria County	84,088	85,725	1.9	6	9
48471	TX_ Walker County	61,758	63,706	3.1	8	5
48473	TX_ Waller County	32,663	34,769	6.4	8	6
48475	TX_ Ward County	10,909	10,237	-6.1	6	2
48477	TX_ Washington County	30,373	31,798	4.6	10	9
48479	TX_ Webb County	193,117	230,436	19.3	6	8
48481	TX_ Wharton County	41,188	41,581	0.9	6	9
48483	TX_ Wheeler County	5,284	4,797	-9.2	3	9
48485	TX_ Wichita County	131,664	124,571	-5.3	11	7
48487	TX_ Wilbarger County	14,676	14,031	-4.3	8	5
48489	TX_ Willacy County	20,082	20,544	2.3	6	9
48491	TX_ Williamson County	249,967	349,625	39.8	8	1
48493	TX_ Wilson County	32,408	38,626	19.1	8	6
48495	TX_ Winkler County	7,173	6,563	-8.5	6	2
48497	TX_ Wise County	48,793	57,848	18.5	8	3
48499	TX_ Wood County	36,752	41,581	13.1	1	10
48501	TX_ Yoakum County	7,322	7,473	2.0	6	4
48503	TX_ Young County	17,943	17,835	-0.6	3	4
48505	TX_ Zapata County	12,182	13,637	11.9	6	2
48507	TX_ Zavala County	11,600	11,884	2.4	6	2
49001	UT_ Beaver County	6,005	6,181	2.9	12	6
49003	UT_ Box Elder County	42,745	46,169	8.0	12	8
49005	UT_ Cache County	91,391	97,444	6.6	12	5
49007	UT_ Carbon County	20,422	18,968	-7.1	12	4
49009	UT_ Daggett County	921	959	4.1	12	10
49011	UT_ Davis County	238,994	271,308	13.5	12	1
49013	UT_ Duchesne County	14,371	15,425	7.3	12	8
49015	UT_ Emery County	10,860	10,607	-2.3	12	4
49017	UT_ Garfield County	4,735	4,388	-7.3	12	4
49019	UT_ Grand County	8,485	8,684	2.3	9	10
49021	UT_ Iron County	33,779	39,452	16.7	12	5
49023	UT_ Juab County	8,238	9,214	11.8	12	8
49025	UT_ Kane County	6,046	6,224	2.9	12	10
49027	UT_ Millard County	12,405	12,107	-2.4	12	4
49029	UT_ Morgan County	7,129	7,991	12.0	12	1
49031	UT_ Piute County	1,435	1,347	-6.1	12	4
49033	UT_ Rich County	1,961	2,043	4.1	12	10
49035	UT_ Salt Lake County	898,387	958,537	6.7	8	12
49037	UT_ San Juan County	14,413	14,103	-2.1	8	5
49039	UT_ Sanpete County	22,763	23,983	5.3	12	8
49041	UT_ Sevier County	18,842	19,190	1.8	12	4
49043	UT_ Summit County	29,736	35,743	20.2	8	1
49045	UT_ Tooele County	40,735	52,322	28.4	12	8
49047	UT_ Uintah County	25,224	27,102	7.4	12	3
49049	UT_ Utah County	368,536	466,838	26.6	12	8
49051	UT_ Wasatch County	15,215	19,486	28.0	12	8
49053	UT_ Washington County	90,354	125,589	39.0	8	10
49055	UT_ Wayne County	2,509	2,399	-4.3	12	4
49057	UT_ Weber County	196,533	210,028	6.8	12	8
50001	VT_ Addison County	35,974	37,258	3.5	9	5

fips	county	totpop00	totpop06	chpop	Cat.10_1	Cat.10_2
50003	VT_ Bennington County	36,994	36,916	-0.2	9	5
50005	VT_ Caledonia County	29,702	30,708	3.3	9	4
50007	VT_ Chittenden County	146,571	150,544	2.7	8	5
50009	VT_ Essex County	6,459	6,682	3.4	9	10
50011	VT_ Franklin County	45,417	48,278	6.3	1	9
50013	VT_ Grand Isle County	6,901	7,818	13.2	1	5
50015	VT_ Lamoille County	23,233	24,663	6.1	9	10
50017	VT_ Orange County	28,226	29,489	4.4	4	10
50019	VT_ Orleans County	26,277	28,007	6.5	9	10
50021	VT_ Rutland County	63,400	64,078	1.0	9	5
50023	VT_ Washington County	58,039	59,878	3.1	9	8
50025	VT_ Windham County	44,216	44,044	-0.3	9	5
50027	VT_ Windsor County	57,418	57,913	0.8	9	10
51001	VA_ Accomack County	38,305	39,545	3.2	9	2
51003	VA_ Albemarle County	79,236	92,301	16.4	5	1
51005	VA_ Alleghany County	17,215	20,809	20.8	10	3
51007	VA_ Amelia County	11,400	12,543	10.0	2	3
51009	VA_ Amherst County	31,894	32,233	1.0	9	5
51011	VA_ Appomattox County	13,705	14,006	2.2	3	2
51013	VA_ Arlington County	189,453	199,351	5.2	1	7
51015	VA_ Augusta County	65,615	70,796	7.9	10	3
51017	VA_ Bath County	5,048	4,857	-3.7	3	10
51019	VA_ Bedford County	60,371	66,550	10.2	1	3
51021	VA_ Bland County	6,871	6,961	1.3	9	10
51023	VA_ Botetourt County	30,496	32,139	5.3	1	3
51025	VA_ Brunswick County	18,419	17,780	-3.4	2	3
51027	VA_ Buchanan County	26,978	24,434	-9.4	9	2
51029	VA_ Buckingham County	15,623	16,220	3.8	2	3
51031	VA_ Campbell County	51,078	52,796	3.3	3	2
51033	VA_ Caroline County	22,121	26,945	21.8	1	3
51035	VA_ Carroll County	29,245	29,440	0.6	9	10
51036	VA_ Charles City County	6,926	7,112	2.6	2	3
51037	VA_ Charlotte County	12,472	12,422	-0.4	3	10
51041	VA_ Chesterfield County	259,903	295,490	13.6	8	7
51043	VA_ Clarke County	12,652	14,595	15.3	1	3
51045	VA_ Craig County	5,091	5,153	1.2	9	3
51047	VA_ Culpeper County	34,262	44,660	30.3	1	3
51049	VA_ Cumberland County	9,017	9,521	5.5	2	3
51051	VA_ Dickenson County	16,395	16,349	-0.2	9	4
51053	VA_ Dinwiddie County	24,533	25,673	4.6	11	3
51057	VA_ Essex County	9,989	10,646	6.5	2	3
51059	VA_ Fairfax County	969,749	1,012,302	4.3	1	7
51061	VA_ Fauquier County	55,139	66,799	21.1	8	1
51063	VA_ Floyd County	13,874	14,781	6.5	9	10
51065	VA_ Fluvanna County	20,047	25,441	26.9	8	3
51067	VA_ Franklin County	47,286	50,884	7.6	9	10
51069	VA_ Frederick County	59,209	71,227	20.3	8	3
51071	VA_ Giles County	16,657	17,327	4.0	3	10
51073	VA_ Gloucester County	34,780	38,391	10.3	1	3
51075	VA_ Goochland County	16,863	19,977	18.4	1	3
51077	VA_ Grayson County	17,917	16,243	-9.3	9	4

fips	county	totpop00	totpop06	chpop	Cat.10_1	Cat.10_2
51079	VA_ Greene County	15,244	17,639	15.7	8	3
51081	VA_ Greensville County	11,560	10,912	-5.6	2	3
51083	VA_ Halifax County	37,355	36,094	-3.3	2	9
51085	VA_ Hanover County	86,320	98,745	14.3	8	3
51087	VA_ Henrico County	262,300	286,071	9.0	1	7
51089	VA_ Henry County	57,930	56,136	-3.1	9	2
51091	VA_ Highland County	2,536	2,492	-1.7	4	10
51093	VA_ Isle of Wight County	29,728	34,339	15.5	1	8
51095	VA_ James City County	48,102	59,696	24.1	8	1
51097	VA_ King and Queen County	6,630	6,924	4.4	2	11
51099	VA_ King George County	16,803	21,824	29.8	8	1
51101	VA_ King William County	13,146	15,076	14.6	1	3
51103	VA_ Lancaster County	11,567	11,551	-0.1	4	1
51105	VA_ Lee County	23,589	23,779	0.8	2	4
51107	VA_ Loudoun County	169,599	271,075	59.8	8	1
51109	VA_ Louisa County	25,627	31,202	21.7	1	3
51111	VA_ Lunenburg County	13,146	13,201	0.4	2	11
51113	VA_ Madison County	12,520	13,548	8.2	4	10
51115	VA_ Mathews County	9,207	9,147	-0.6	1	3
51117	VA_ Mecklenburg County	32,380	32,475	0.2	2	10
51119	VA_ Middlesex County	9,932	10,608	6.8	1	10
51121	VA_ Montgomery County	83,629	84,544	1.0	8	5
51125	VA_ Nelson County	14,445	15,231	5.4	9	10
51127	VA_ New Kent County	13,462	16,804	24.8	1	3
51131	VA_ Northampton County	13,093	13,724	4.8	2	9
51133	VA_ Northumberland County	12,259	12,898	5.2	1	10
51135	VA_ Nottoway County	15,725	15,591	-0.8	2	3
51137	VA_ Orange County	25,881	31,481	21.6	1	10
51139	VA_ Page County	23,177	24,038	3.7	10	3
51141	VA_ Patrick County	19,407	19,269	-0.7	3	10
51143	VA_ Pittsylvania County	61,745	61,784	0.0	9	3
51145	VA_ Powhatan County	22,377	27,386	22.3	8	3
51147	VA_ Prince Edward County	19,720	20,730	5.1	8	5
51149	VA_ Prince George County	33,047	36,735	11.1	8	3
51153	VA_ Prince William County	280,813	360,843	28.5	8	1
51155	VA_ Pulaski County	35,127	35,165	0.1	9	3
51157	VA_ Rappahannock County	6,983	7,380	5.6	1	3
51159	VA_ Richmond County	8,809	9,087	3.1	2	3
51161	VA_ Roanoke County	85,778	89,027	3.7	1	5
51163	VA_ Rockbridge County	20,808	21,419	2.9	10	3
51165	VA_ Rockingham County	67,725	72,564	7.1	3	10
51167	VA_ Russell County	30,308	29,049	-4.1	9	2
51169	VA_ Scott County	23,403	22,971	-1.8	9	2
51171	VA_ Shenandoah County	35,075	40,152	14.4	10	3
51173	VA_ Smyth County	33,081	32,550	-1.6	9	10
51175	VA_ Southampton County	17,482	17,761	1.6	2	11
51177	VA_ Spotsylvania County	90,395	120,722	33.5	8	1
51179	VA_ Stafford County	92,446	121,943	31.9	8	11
51181	VA_ Surry County	6,829	7,013	2.6	2	3
51183	VA_ Sussex County	12,504	12,005	-3.9	2	11
51185	VA_ Tazewell County	44,598	44,923	0.7	9	3

fips	county	totpop00	totpop06	chpop	Cat.10_1	Cat.10_2
51187	VA_ Warren County	31,584	36,365	15.1	1	3
51191	VA_ Washington County	51,103	52,404	2.5	9	10
51193	VA_ Westmoreland County	16,718	17,409	4.1	2	10
51195	VA_ Wise County	40,123	42,258	5.3	9	3
51197	VA_ Wythe County	27,599	28,672	3.8	9	10
51199	VA_ York County	56,297	62,529	11.0	2	1
51510	VA_ Alexandria City	128,283	137,307	7.0	1	7
51515	VA_ Bedford City	6,299	6,215	-1.3	9	10
51520	VA_ Bristol City	17,367	17,495	0.7	3	10
51530	VA_ Buena Vista City	6,349	6,479	2.0	3	10
51540	VA_ Charlottesville City	45,049	40,095	-11.0	8	5
51550	VA_ Chesapeake City	199,184	223,610	12.2	3	11
51570	VA_ Colonial Heights City	16,897	17,707	4.7	11	3
51580	VA_ Covington City	6,303	6,109	-3.0	9	10
51590	VA_ Danville City	48,411	45,642	-5.7	2	5
51595	VA_ Emporia City	5,665	5,549	-2.0	2	6
51600	VA_ Fairfax City	21,498	21,961	2.1	1	7
51610	VA_ Falls Church City	10,377	10,923	5.2	1	7
51620	VA_ Franklin City	8,346	8,750	4.8	2	5
51630	VA_ Fredericksburg City	19,279	20,942	8.6	8	5
51640	VA_ Galax City	6,837	6,686	-2.2	3	6
51650	VA_ Hampton City	146,437	145,829	-0.4	11	7
51660	VA_ Harrisonburg City	40,468	40,191	-0.6	8	5
51670	VA_ Hopewell City	22,354	22,832	2.1	2	3
51678	VA_ Lexington City	6,867	6,768	-1.4	8	5
51680	VA_ Lynchburg City	65,269	67,610	3.5	8	5
51683	VA_ Manassas City	35,135	37,588	6.9	8	1
51685	VA_ Manassas Park City	10,290	11,884	15.4	1	3
51690	VA_ Martinsville City	15,416	14,965	-2.9	2	6
51700	VA_ Newport News City	180,150	178,089	-1.1	8	7
51710	VA_ Norfolk City	234,403	226,526	-3.3	11	7
51720	VA_ Norton City	3,904	3,560	-8.8	9	3
51730	VA_ Petersburg City	33,740	32,250	-4.4	2	9
51735	VA_ Poquoson City	11,566	11,848	2.4	1	9
51740	VA_ Portsmouth City	100,565	100,595	0.0	11	7
51750	VA_ Radford City	15,859	14,442	-8.9	5	8
51760	VA_ Richmond City	197,790	193,499	-2.1	2	7
51770	VA_ Roanoke City	94,911	92,541	-2.5	9	5
51775	VA_ Salem City	24,747	24,652	-0.3	1	5
51790	VA_ Staunton City	23,853	23,343	-2.1	9	5
51800	VA_ Suffolk City	63,677	81,540	28.0	1	3
51810	VA_ Virginia Beach City	425,257	438,044	3.0	11	7
51820	VA_ Waynesboro City	19,520	21,556	10.4	3	10
51830	VA_ Williamsburg City	11,998	12,002	0.0	5	8
51840	VA_ Winchester City	23,585	25,404	7.7	8	3
53001	WA_ Adams County	16,428	16,810	2.3	6	9
53003	WA_ Asotin County	20,551	21,322	3.7	9	10
53005	WA_ Benton County	142,475	159,327	11.8	1	8
53007	WA_ Chelan County	66,616	70,820	6.3	6	9
53009	WA_ Clallam County	64,525	70,906	9.8	9	10
53011	WA_ Clark County	345,238	414,898	20.1	8	1

fips	county	totpop00	totpop06	chpop	Cat.10_1	Cat.10_2
53013	WA_ Columbia County	4,064	4,158	2.3	4	10
53015	WA_ Cowlitz County	92,948	98,284	5.7	9	10
53017	WA_ Douglas County	32,603	35,553	9.0	6	9
53019	WA_ Ferry County	7,260	7,602	4.7	2	4
53021	WA_ Franklin County	49,347	67,069	35.9	1	8
53023	WA_ Garfield County	2,397	2,308	-3.7	4	9
53025	WA_ Grant County	74,698	82,133	9.9	6	8
53027	WA_ Grays Harbor County	67,194	71,638	6.6	9	10
53029	WA_ Island County	71,558	80,461	12.4	8	9
53031	WA_ Jefferson County	25,953	29,204	12.5	8	10
53033	WA_ King County	1,737,034	1,809,383	4.1	1	7
53035	WA_ Kitsap County	231,969	241,404	4.0	8	11
53037	WA_ Kittitas County	33,362	37,525	12.4	8	5
53039	WA_ Klickitat County	19,161	19,954	4.1	12	10
53041	WA_ Lewis County	68,600	73,445	7.0	9	10
53043	WA_ Lincoln County	10,184	10,349	1.6	4	10
53045	WA_ Mason County	49,405	55,310	11.9	8	10
53047	WA_ Okanogan County	39,564	40,226	1.6	6	8
53049	WA_ Pacific County	20,984	21,933	4.5	9	4
53051	WA_ Pend Oreille County	11,732	12,876	9.7	9	10
53053	WA_ Pierce County	700,820	758,227	8.1	8	7
53055	WA_ San Juan County	14,077	15,397	9.3	1	10
53057	WA_ Skagit County	102,979	115,210	11.8	8	9
53059	WA_ Skamania County	9,872	10,811	9.5	9	10
53061	WA_ Snohomish County	606,024	664,378	9.6	1	8
53063	WA_ Spokane County	417,939	444,889	6.4	9	7
53065	WA_ Stevens County	40,066	42,524	6.1	9	10
53067	WA_ Thurston County	207,355	232,397	12.0	11	5
53069	WA_ Wahkiakum County	3,824	3,958	3.5	4	10
53071	WA_ Walla Walla County	55,180	57,711	4.5	8	9
53073	WA_ Whatcom County	166,814	186,310	11.6	8	5
53075	WA_ Whitman County	40,740	40,093	-1.5	5	9
53077	WA_ Yakima County	222,581	233,517	4.9	6	12
54001	WV_ Barbour County	15,557	15,764	1.3	9	2
54003	WV_ Berkeley County	75,905	97,404	28.3	8	3
54005	WV_ Boone County	25,535	25,588	0.2	9	10
54007	WV_ Braxton County	14,702	14,855	1.0	9	10
54009	WV_ Brooke County	25,447	24,259	-4.6	5	10
54011	WV_ Cabell County	96,784	93,622	-3.2	9	5
54013	WV_ Calhoun County	7,582	7,405	-2.3	9	2
54015	WV_ Clay County	10,330	10,282	-0.4	9	10
54017	WV_ Doddridge County	7,403	7,505	1.3	9	6
54019	WV_ Fayette County	47,579	46,328	-2.6	9	10
54021	WV_ Gilmer County	7,160	6,932	-3.1	9	5
54023	WV_ Grant County	11,299	11,809	4.5	9	10
54025	WV_ Greenbrier County	34,453	35,021	1.6	9	10
54027	WV_ Hampshire County	20,203	22,426	11.0	9	10
54029	WV_ Hancock County	32,667	31,028	-5.0	9	10
54031	WV_ Hardy County	12,669	13,425	5.9	3	10
54033	WV_ Harrison County	68,652	68,519	-0.1	9	10
54035	WV_ Jackson County	28,000	28,286	1.0	9	10

fips	county	totpop00	totpop06	chpop	Cat.10_1	Cat.10_2
54037	WV_ Jefferson County	42,190	50,453	19.5	1	8
54039	WV_ Kanawha County	200,073	192,382	-3.8	5	2
54041	WV_ Lewis County	16,919	17,263	2.0	9	10
54043	WV_ Lincoln County	22,108	22,438	1.4	9	3
54045	WV_ Logan County	37,710	36,015	-4.4	9	3
54047	WV_ McDowell County	27,329	23,804	-12.9	2	4
54049	WV_ Marion County	56,598	56,686	0.1	9	5
54051	WV_ Marshall County	35,519	33,962	-4.3	9	5
54053	WV_ Mason County	25,957	25,568	-1.5	9	10
54055	WV_ Mercer County	62,980	61,096	-2.9	9	10
54057	WV_ Mineral County	27,078	26,892	-0.6	9	10
54059	WV_ Mingo County	28,253	26,997	-4.4	9	2
54061	WV_ Monongalia County	81,866	84,858	3.6	5	8
54063	WV_ Monroe County	14,583	13,569	-6.9	9	10
54065	WV_ Morgan County	14,943	16,227	8.5	9	10
54067	WV_ Nicholas County	26,562	26,486	-0.2	5	2
54069	WV_ Ohio County	47,427	44,705	-5.7	9	5
54071	WV_ Pendleton County	8,196	7,735	-5.6	9	10
54073	WV_ Pleasants County	7,514	7,307	-2.7	9	4
54075	WV_ Pocahontas County	9,131	8,772	-3.9	10	6
54077	WV_ Preston County	29,334	30,206	2.9	9	10
54079	WV_ Putnam County	51,589	54,957	6.5	1	3
54081	WV_ Raleigh County	79,220	78,878	-0.4	9	10
54083	WV_ Randolph County	28,262	28,666	1.4	9	10
54085	WV_ Ritchie County	10,343	10,575	2.2	5	10
54087	WV_ Roane County	15,446	15,509	0.4	9	10
54089	WV_ Summers County	12,999	13,563	4.3	9	10
54091	WV_ Taylor County	16,089	16,289	1.2	9	10
54093	WV_ Tucker County	7,321	6,823	-6.8	9	10
54095	WV_ Tyler County	9,592	9,291	-3.1	10	4
54097	WV_ Upshur County	23,404	23,579	0.7	9	10
54099	WV_ Wayne County	42,903	41,797	-2.5	9	10
54101	WV_ Webster County	9,719	9,753	0.3	9	4
54103	WV_ Wetzel County	17,693	16,983	-4.0	5	4
54105	WV_ Wirt County	5,873	5,951	1.3	9	10
54107	WV_ Wood County	87,986	86,623	-1.5	9	10
54109	WV_ Wyoming County	25,708	24,394	-5.1	9	4
55001	WI_ Adams County	18,643	21,061	12.9	1	10
55003	WI_ Ashland County	16,866	16,579	-1.7	9	4
55005	WI_ Barron County	44,963	45,966	2.2	10	9
55007	WI_ Bayfield County	15,013	15,182	1.1	9	5
55009	WI_ Brown County	226,778	241,153	6.3	8	5
55011	WI_ Buffalo County	13,804	14,078	1.9	10	4
55013	WI_ Burnett County	15,674	16,660	6.2	9	10
55015	WI_ Calumet County	40,631	44,356	9.1	1	9
55017	WI_ Chippewa County	55,195	61,191	10.8	9	10
55019	WI_ Clark County	33,557	33,982	1.2	10	9
55021	WI_ Columbia County	52,468	55,803	6.3	10	9
55023	WI_ Crawford County	17,243	17,109	-0.7	9	10
55025	WI_ Dane County	426,526	464,105	8.8	5	1
55027	WI_ Dodge County	85,897	88,336	2.8	10	3

fips	county	totpop00	totpop06	chpop	Cat.10_1	Cat.10_2
55029	WI_ Door County	27,961	28,290	1.1	10	9
55031	WI_ Douglas County	43,287	44,446	2.6	9	10
55033	WI_ Dunn County	39,858	42,055	5.5	8	9
55035	WI_ Eau Claire County	93,142	94,223	1.1	8	9
55037	WI_ Florence County	5,088	4,910	-3.5	9	10
55039	WI_ Fond du Lac County	97,296	99,844	2.6	10	9
55041	WI_ Forest County	10,024	9,906	-1.1	9	10
55043	WI_ Grant County	49,597	49,699	0.2	9	5
55045	WI_ Green County	33,647	35,593	5.7	10	9
55047	WI_ Green Lake County	19,105	19,167	0.3	10	9
55049	WI_ Iowa County	22,780	23,665	3.8	9	4
55051	WI_ Iron County	6,861	6,572	-4.2	9	10
55053	WI_ Jackson County	19,100	19,927	4.3	9	10
55055	WI_ Jefferson County	74,021	80,206	8.3	10	9
55057	WI_ Juneau County	24,316	27,374	12.5	9	10
55059	WI_ Kenosha County	149,577	163,011	8.9	9	7
55061	WI_ Kewaunee County	20,187	20,895	3.5	9	3
55063	WI_ La Crosse County	107,120	109,414	2.1	8	5
55065	WI_ Lafayette County	16,137	16,222	0.5	10	9
55067	WI_ Langlade County	20,740	20,641	-0.4	9	6
55069	WI_ Lincoln County	29,641	30,389	2.5	10	9
55071	WI_ Manitowoc County	82,887	81,976	-1.1	9	6
55073	WI_ Marathon County	125,834	129,980	3.2	9	5
55075	WI_ Marinette County	43,384	43,451	0.1	9	10
55077	WI_ Marquette County	15,832	15,448	-2.4	10	6
55078	WI_ Menominee County	4,562	4,565	0.0	2	6
55079	WI_ Milwaukee County	940,164	918,099	-2.3	7	1
55081	WI_ Monroe County	40,899	42,917	4.9	10	9
55083	WI_ Oconto County	35,634	38,045	6.7	10	9
55085	WI_ Oneida County	36,776	36,877	0.2	9	4
55087	WI_ Outagamie County	160,971	172,609	7.2	1	8
55089	WI_ Ozaukee County	82,317	86,577	5.1	1	9
55091	WI_ Pepin County	7,213	7,349	1.8	10	9
55093	WI_ Pierce County	36,804	39,704	7.8	8	9
55095	WI_ Polk County	41,319	44,895	8.6	10	9
55097	WI_ Portage County	67,182	67,541	0.5	8	5
55099	WI_ Price County	15,822	15,134	-4.3	9	10
55101	WI_ Racine County	188,831	197,706	4.7	1	5
55103	WI_ Richland County	17,924	18,472	3.0	9	10
55105	WI_ Rock County	152,307	159,085	4.4	1	8
55107	WI_ Rusk County	15,347	15,166	-1.1	9	10
55109	WI_ St. Croix County	63,155	80,135	26.8	1	8
55111	WI_ Sauk County	55,225	58,330	5.6	10	9
55113	WI_ Sawyer County	16,196	17,128	5.7	9	4
55115	WI_ Shawano County	40,664	41,375	1.7	10	9
55117	WI_ Sheboygan County	112,646	115,148	2.2	10	8
55119	WI_ Taylor County	19,680	19,806	0.6	10	9
55121	WI_ Trempealeau County	27,010	28,056	3.8	10	9
55123	WI_ Vernon County	28,056	29,192	4.0	10	9
55125	WI_ Vilas County	21,033	22,468	6.8	9	10
55127	WI_ Walworth County	93,759	101,488	8.2	6	5

fips	county	totpop00	totpop06	chpop	Cat.10_1	Cat.10_2
55129	WI_ Washburn County	16,036	16,617	3.6	9	10
55131	WI_ Washington County	117,493	127,934	8.8	1	3
55133	WI_ Waukesha County	360,767	381,187	5.6	1	7
55135	WI_ Waupaca County	51,731	52,665	1.8	10	9
55137	WI_ Waushara County	23,154	24,696	6.6	9	10
55139	WI_ Winnebago County	156,763	160,352	2.2	8	1
55141	WI_ Wood County	75,555	75,133	-0.5	10	9
56001	WY_ Albany County	32,014	30,486	-4.7	8	5
56003	WY_ Big Horn County	11,461	11,374	-0.7	12	9
56005	WY_ Campbell County	33,698	37,626	11.6	1	8
56007	WY_ Carbon County	15,639	15,189	-2.8	4	3
56009	WY_ Converse County	12,052	12,994	7.8	4	9
56011	WY_ Crook County	5,887	6,271	6.5	4	10
56013	WY_ Fremont County	35,804	36,826	2.8	4	10
56015	WY_ Goshen County	12,538	12,197	-2.7	4	9
56017	WY_ Hot Springs County	4,882	4,539	-7.0	4	10
56019	WY_ Johnson County	7,075	7,834	10.7	4	10
56021	WY_ Laramie County	81,607	85,382	4.6	8	9
56023	WY_ Lincoln County	14,573	16,282	11.7	12	4
56025	WY_ Natrona County	66,533	70,445	5.8	8	9
56027	WY_ Niobrara County	2,407	2,320	-3.6	4	6
56029	WY_ Park County	25,786	26,920	4.4	4	10
56031	WY_ Platte County	8,807	8,556	-2.8	4	10
56033	WY_ Sheridan County	26,560	27,462	3.4	4	10
56035	WY_ Sublette County	5,920	7,219	21.9	1	10
56037	WY_ Sweetwater County	37,613	38,357	1.9	4	9
56039	WY_ Teton County	18,251	19,157	4.9	8	1
56041	WY_ Uinta County	19,742	19,920	0.9	8	4
56043	WY_ Washakie County	8,289	7,965	-3.9	4	5
56045	WY_ Weston County	6,644	6,627	-0.2	4	9

NOTES

■ ■ ■

1 *The State of Working Immigrants in Colorado,* Colorado Fiscal Policy Institute, March 2004, p. 1.

2 Data from Pew Internet and American Life Center survey, *Home Broadband Adoption 2009,* April 2009. http://www.pewinternet.org/Reports/2009/10-Home-Broadband-Adoption-2009.aspx?r=1.

3 Data from Pew Internet and American Life Center survey, *Twitter and Status Updating, Fall 2009,* October 2009. http://www.pewinternet.org/Reports/2009/17-Twitter-and-Status-Updating-Fall-2009.aspx.

4 EPA Green Power Partnership, Top 20 On-site Generation list. http://www.epa.gov/greenpower/toplists/top20onsite.htm.

5 Elizabeth Svoboda, "America's 50 Greenest Cities," *Popular Science,* February 8, 2008. http://www.popsci.com/environment/article/2008-02/americas-50-greenestcities?page=1.

6 Pew Research Center survey question with answers aggregated over 1992, 1994, 1997, 1999, 2002, 2003, 2007, 2009.

7 Richard R. Nelson, ed. *National Innovation Systems, A Comparative Analysis* (Oxford: Oxford University Press, 1993).

8 President's Hall of Fame Web site. http://www.presidentshalloffame.com/.

9 Pew Monthly Surveys, 2009.

10 Data from Pew Research Center survey, *Not Your Grandfather's Recession—Literally,* March 2009. http://pewresearch.org/pubs/1223/not-your-grandfathers-recession-literally.

11 According to the Kings Ridge Web site. http://www.kings-ridge.org/sub_category_list.asp?category=38&title=About+Kings+Ridge.

12 Data from Zogby International Poll, *53% of Likely Voters Believe Obama's Economic Policies Equal Debt for Future Generations,* August 2009. http://www.zogby.com/NEWS/ReadNews.cfm?ID=1729.

13 Focus on the Family Web site. http://www.focusonthefamily.com/about_us.aspx.

14 *The Manhattan Declaration, A Summary.* http://www.manhattandeclaration.org/.

15 National Association of Evangelicals Immigration Statement. http://www.nae.net/resolutions/347-immigration-2009.

16 James River Assembly Web site. http://jamesriver.org/messages-media-resources/question-and-answer/.

17 Michael Kiefer, Gary Nelson, and J. J. Hensley, "Mesa Mayor Angry over Raid; Sheriff Defends Tactics," *The Arizona Republic*, October 16, 2008. http://www.azcentral.com/community/mesa/articles/2008/10/16/20081016mr-mesaraid.html.

18 Data from the Pew Research Center for the People and the Press values survey, 1987–2009.

19 Census Building Permits Survey, 2001–2008.

20 Ronald J. Hansen, "Report: Illegal Immigrants Cost State $1.4B in Wages," *The Arizona Republic*, January 8, 2008. http://www.azcentral.com/business/articles/0109biz-illlegalscost0110-ON.html.

21 Census Bureau Releases 2008 American Community Survey Data, September 21, 2009. http://www.census.gov/Press-Release/www/releases/archives/american_community_survey_acs/014237.html.

22 Athena D. Merrit, "Pew Poll: 86% Against Nutter's Property Tax Increase Plan," *Philadelphia Business Journal*, April 23, 2009. http://philadelphia.bizjournals.com/philadelphia/stories/2009/04/20/daily43.html.

23 "PSSA RESULTS 2009: TOP 50 SCHOOLS STATEWIDE," interactive chart from *Allentown Morning Call* Web site. http://projects.mcall.com/PSSA-results/top-schools/.

24 "2009 Test Scores," for grade 11 in Pennsylvania, Education.com Web site. http://www.education.com/schoolfi nder/us/pennsylvania/philadelphia/school-of-the-future/test results/.

25 David Cay Johnston, "The Gap Between Rich and Poor Grows in the United States," *The New York Times*, March 29, 2007. http://www.nytimes.com/2007/03/29/business/worldbusiness/29iht-income.4.5075504.html?scp=1&sq=rich%20and%20poor%20gap&st=Search.

26 From Fort Campbell's Web site. www.campbell.army.mil/Pages/Home.aspx.

27 "The Changing Profile of the Army, FY 2008," a report from the Army Office of Demographics, p. 7.

28 Bryan Ross and Jason Allen, "New Blackwater Iraq Scandal: Guns, Silencers and Dog Food," ABC News Web site, November 14, 2008.

29 City of Los Alamos Web site. http://locate.losalamos.com/.

30 Data from the Pew Research Center for the People and the Press survey, *Independents Take Center Stage in the Obama Era*, May 21, 2009. http://people-press.org/report/?pageid=1516.

31 Los Alamos National Laboratory Fact Sheet. http://www.lanl.gov/news/fact_sheets/LANL_overview.html.

32 The Oregon Trail in Idaho Web site. http://www.idahohistory.net/OTcityrocks.html.

33 Kenneth L. Holmes, ed., *The Margaret A. Frink Diary, Covered Wagon Women: 1850 Diaries and Letters from the Western Trails* (Glendale, Calif.: A. H. Clarke Co., 1983).

34 Pew Research Center data from August 2009 filtered through the twelve Patchwork Nation community types.

35   Daniel González, "LDS Members Conflicted on Church's Illegal-Migrant Growth," *The Arizona Republic*, April 2, 2009. http://www.azcentral.com/news/articles/2009/04 /02/20090402ldslatinos0402.html.

36   "*We have been taught by prophets to never blindly obey,*" Mormons for Marriage Web site. http://mormonsformarriage.com/?page_id=14.

37   "12th Article of Faith: Sustaining the Law," Mormon Worker Web site. http:// www.themormonworker.org/articles/issue7/12th-article-of-faith-sustaining-the-law .php.

38   "Devils Lake State Recreation Area," Oregon Parks and Recreation Web site. http:// www.oregonstateparks.org/park_216.php.

39   Lincoln City Web site, Festivals & Events page. http://www.oregoncoast.org/pages/ festivals.php.

40   Lincoln City Web site. http://www.oregoncoast.org.

41   Data from Zogby International Poll, *53% of Likely Voters Believe Obama's Economic Policies Equal Debt for Future Generations*, August 2009. http://www.zogby.com/NEWS/ ReadNews.cfm?ID=1729.

42   Sioux Center Ridge Web site. http://www.siouxcenterridge.com/.

43   Christian Reformed Church Web site, Beliefs and Positions page. http://www.crcna.org/ pages/positions.cfm.

44   Data from Pew Research Center for the People and the Press survey, "Majority Continues to Support Civil Unions, Most Still Oppose Same-Sex Marriage," October 2009. http://people-press.org/report/553/same-sex-marriage.

45   "Putting Meat on the Table: Industrial Farm Animal Production in America," Pew Commission on Industrial Farm Animal Production, pp. 5–6, 17–18.

46   "America's New Post-Recession Employment Arithmetic," *Advance & Rutgers Report* newsletter, September 2009, p. 3.

47   Robert Pollin, "Pollin: Standard of Living Must Be Raised," *Roll Call*, May 18, 2009. http://www.rollcall.com/features/MissionAhead-AmericanWorker-2009_2009/ma_ worker_future/34938-1.html.

48   "A Portrait of Louisiana, Louisiana Human Development Report 2009," American Human Development Project of the Social Science Research Council, September 17, 2009. http://www.measureofamerica.org/louisiana/.

49   Peter Coy, Mara Der Hovanesian, Christopher Palmeri, Amy S. Choi, and Tara Kalwarski, "Where Will Housing Be in 2012," *Business Week*, June 18, 2009. http://www .businessweek.com/magazine/content/09_26/b4137028238311.htm?campaign_ id=rss_innovate.

50   Gary Shilling, "Slow Long-Term Growth and Government's Response," *Insight* newsletter, August 2009.

51   Simon Johnson and James Kwak, "The Home-Buyer Tax Credit: Throwing Good Money After Bad," *The Washington Post*, October 27, 2009. http://www.washington post.com/wp-dyn/content/article/2009/10/27/AR2009102703791.html.

52   Adam Davidson and Alex Blumberg, "Taxpayer Beware: Bank Bailout Will Hurt," *Planet Money Blog*, Feburary 27, 2009. http://www.npr.org/templates/story/story. php? storyId=101224460.

53   Data pooled from three Pew Center for the People and the Press surveys: January 2006, September 2007, and February 2008.

54   Results aggregated from surveys from the Pew Center for the People and the Press on the same question from ten surveys taken from 1987 to 2009. The numbers barely moved in that time.

55   Frank Newport, "Military Veterans of All Ages Tend to Be More Republican," Gallup .com, May 25, 2009. http://www.gallup.com/poll/118684/military-veterans-ages-ten drepublican.aspx.

56   Erick Erickson, "I'm Afraid Sarah Palin Might Be Ruining Herself Unintentionally," *RedState*, January 11, 2010. http://www.redstate.com/erick/2010/01/11/im-afraidsarah-palin-might-be-ruining-herself-unintentionally/.

57   Tea Party Nation Web site. http://www.teapartynation.com/.

58   Benjamin Friedman, "Meltdown: A Case Study," *The Atlantic Monthly*, July/August 2005.

59   Stephen Bates, "*The End of Geography*," *Symposium: Theories and Metaphors of Cyberspace* (Vienna: University of Vienna, 1995). http://pespmc1.vub.ac.be/Cybspasy/SBates .html.

60   Whole Foods Web site. http://www.wholefoodsmarket.com/company/realestate.php.

61   Whole Foods Web site. January 4, 2010.

62   Whole Foods Web site. http://www.wholefoodsmarket.com/company/declaration .php.

63   Data from the 2004 Annenberg Media Consumption Survey.

64   Data from Hollywood.com and the Fridley Theatres.

65   Data from Pew Internet and American Life Survey, Fall 2009.

66   Question from Pew Forum on Religion and Public Life, U.S. Religious Landscape Survey, 2008.

67   Ibid.

68   Ibid.

69   Per *Variety*'s Web site, from Nielsen Media Research. http://www.variety.com/index .asp?layout=chart_pass&charttype=chart_topshowsalltime.

70   Pew Forum on Religion and Public Life, U.S. Religious Landscape Survey, 2008.

71   The list of intellectual debts here is extensive and too numerous to mention, but here is a partial list of previous book-length studies that have informed and inspired the thrust of our work: V. O. Key, Jr., *Southern Politics in State and Nation* (New York: Alfred A. Knopf, 1949); V. O. Key, Jr., *American State Politics: An Introduction* (New York: Alfred A. Knopf, 1956); John H. Fenton, *Midwest Politics* (New York: Holt, Rinehart and Winston, 1966); John A. Agnew, *Place and Politics: The Geographical Mediation of State and Society* (Boston: Allen and Unwin, 1987); Ronald J. Johnston, *A Question of Place: Exploring the Practice of Human Geography* (Oxford: Blackwell Publishers, 1991); James G. Gimpel, Jason E. Schuknecht, Robert Huckfeldt, and John Sprague, *Citizens, Politics and Social Communication: Information and Influence in an Election Campaign* (Boston: Cambridge University Press, 1995); James G. Gimpel and Jason E. Schuknecht, *Patchwork Nation: Sectionalism and Political Change in American Politics* (Ann Arbor: University of Michigan Press, 2003); Bill Bishop, *The Big Sort:*

Why the Clustering of Like-Minded America Is Tearing Us Apart (Boston: Houghton Mifflin, 2008).

72   Bernard R. Berelson, Paul F. Lazarsfeld, and William N. McPhee, *Voting: A Study of Opinion Formation in a Presidential Campaign* (Chicago: University of Chicago Press, 1986), p. 154; Angus Campbell, Phillip E. Converse, Warren E. Miller, and Donald E. Stokes, *The American Voter* (New York: John Wiley and Sons, 1960); Michael S. Lewis-Beck, Helmut Norpoth, William G. Jacoby, and Herbert F. Weisberg, *The American Voter Revisited* (Ann Arbor: University of Michigan Press, 2008).

73   See, for instance: Paul Allen Beck, Russell J. Dalton, Steven Greene, and Robert Huckfeldt, "The Social Calculus of Voting: Interpersonal, Media and Organizational Influences on Presidential Choices," *American Political Science Review* 96, no. 1 (2002): 57–73; Wendy K. Tam Cho, and James G. Gimpel, "Rough Terrain: Spatial Variation in Campaign Contributing and Volunteerism," *American Journal of Political Science* 54, no. 1 (2010): 74–89.

74   Robert Huckfeldt and John Sprague, *Citizens, Politics, and Social Communication: Information and Influence in an Election Campaign* (Boston: Cambridge University Press, 1995); Robert Huckfeldt and John Sprague, "Social Order and Political Chaos: The Structural Setting of Political Information," in John A. Ferejohn and James H. Kuklinski, eds., *Information and Democratic Processes* (Urbana: University of Illinois Press, 1990), pp. 23–58; Robert Huckfeldt, Paul Allen Beck, Russell J. Dalton, Jeffrey Levine, and William Morgan, "Ambiguity, Distorted Messages and Nested Environmental Effects of Political Communication," *Journal of Politics* 60, no. 4 (1998): 996–1030; Paul Allen Beck, Russell J. Dalton, Audrey A. Haynes, and Robert Huckfeldt, "Presidential Campaigning at the Grass Roots;" *Journal of Politics* 59, no. 4 (1997): 1264–1275. On the use of counties to study U.S. electoral history, see: Peter F. Nardulli, "The Concept of a Critical Realignment: Electoral Behavior and Political Change," *American Political Science Review* 89, no. 1 (1995): 10–22. For older but still compelling work drawing upon county data to contexualize political behavior, see Robert H. Putnam, "Political Attitudes and the Local Community," *American Political Science Review* 60, no. 3 (1966): 640–654.

75   William S. Robinson, "Ecological Correlation and the Behavior of Individuals," *American Sociological Review* 15 (1950): 351–357; Gerald H. Kramer, "The Ecological Fallacy Revisited: Aggregate- versus Individual-level Findings on Economics and Elections," *American Political Science Review* 77, no. 1 (1983): 92–111; Christopher H. Achen and W. Phillips Shively, *Cross-Level Inference* (Chicago: University of Chicago Press, 1995); Gary King, *A Solution to the Ecological Inference Problem: Reconstructing Individual Behavior from Aggregate Data* (Princeton, N.J.: Princeton University Press, 1997).

76   David A. Freedman, "Ecological Inference and the Ecological Fallacy," in *International Encyclopedia of the Social & Behavioral Sciences*, vol. 6, N. J. Smelser and P. B. Baltes, eds. (Berkeley, California: Elsevier, 2001), pp. 4027–4030.

77   Glenmary Research Center, "Religious Congregations and Membership, 2000," Cincinnati, Ohio. The Glenmary survey is not without flaws in that congregations volunteer their participation and smaller organizations may not report. Fortunately, for our purposes, the largest church denominations do participate and report accurately on their

membership. More information on the Glenmary survey, and their previous surveys, can be found on their Web site: http://www.glenmary.org/GRC/RCMS_2000/method .htm, accessed March 2010.

78 There are many useful books that explain the methodology and use of factor analysis in social science research. Two that we draw upon here are: Paul Kline, *An Easy Guide to Factor Analysis* (London: Routledge, 1994), and Geoffrey M. Mauyama, *Basics of Structural Equation Modeling* (Thousand Oaks, Calif.: Sage Publications, 1998).

INDEX

■ ■ ■

**Pima County
Public Library**
www.library.pima.gov